One Culture

Science and Literature

A series edited by George Levine

(One Culture)

Essays in Science and Literature

Edited by George Levine
With the assistance of Alan Rauch

The University of Wisconsin Press

Published 1987

The University of Wisconsin Press
114 North Murray Street
Madison, Wisconsin 53715

The University of Wisconsin Press, Ltd.
1 Gower Street
London WC1E 6HA, England

First printing

Printed in the United States of America

For LC CIP information see the colophon

ISBN 0-299-11300-0 cloth; 0-299-11304-3 paper

Contents

Contents

IV. History and Biography

V. Feminist Critiques of Science

Preface

This is the first in a series of volumes on Science and Literature under my editorship. The interaction between science and literature has been a subject of growing concern in criticism; the languages of science have increasingly found their way into literature and into discussions of it. And the traditional assumptions that literary people care nothing about science, scientists care nothing about literature have been belied throughout the twentieth century but particularly in recent years. There remain, however, large gaps of knowledge and of misunderstanding that make fruitful interchange and informed discussion difficult to achieve. And while this series will be aimed primarily at a literary audience, we are hoping not only to be of use as well to historians and philosophers of science and to scientists, but to sustain the standards of discussion of science at a level high enough to ensure the respect if not the agreement of the scientific community.

While the series will not take a "position" in relation to controverted questions and will leave the directions of the arguments to the highly qualified and independent scholars and critics it seeks, it does grow from three assumptions, all of which are explicit in this first volume: first, that science and literature are two alternative but related expressions of a culture's values, assumptions, and intellectual frameworks; second, that understanding science in its relation to culture and literature requires some understanding not only of its own internal processes, but of the pressures upon it exercised by social, political, aesthetic, psychological, and biographical forces; third, that the idea of "influence" of one upon the other must work both ways—it is not only science that influences literature, but literature that influences science. These assumptions, of course, are not uncontroversial, and they impinge on such large issues as the question of "representation" in literature and entail corollaries—about such matters as the "rationality" of science, or the degree to which it actually describes reality—that are at the center of contemporary battles within the philosophy of science. We hope that this series will throw light on these matters.

Preface

Future volumes will approach such questions from many different directions. We expect to publish studies not only of such philosophical and theoretical questions as those suggested above but of historical developments in the mutual relations of science and literature. The series will also include, among other things, analyses of the work of particular scientists and writers, feminist reconsiderations of the status of scientific discourse and its relation to women writers and scientists, and rhetorical studies of the language of professional science. Studies of literature *and* science, moreover, entail contextual cultural studies, and in certain respects the series may sometimes take on the look of an even more ambitious project: no less than a reconsideration of the relations between science and culture as a whole. This first volume is also intended to point in that direction.

The subject is enormous, its importance inescapable. Vague as the enterprise may occasionally seem when viewed in the abstract, its significances are clear when we get down to cases, as the authors of the several essays in this volume do. The range of questions they address intimates the ambitions of the series.

There are a great many people, aside from the authors of the particular essays, involved in the production of this volume. I want to thank them here. The most important is Alan Rauch, whose work on every aspect of the volume, from the most minute detail to its largest conception, has been a condition of its existence at all. Officially, he has been my "assistant" on the project. In fact, he has been my co-editor.

Patricia O'Hara has helped in research and editing through the later stages of the volume, and I am very grateful for her efficiency, intelligence, and warmth of friendship. Peter Givler, now of Ohio State University Press, was the first to discuss this project with me and to help get it off the ground. Rutgers University has provided important resources of space and supplies to allow the editorial work to proceed smoothly. My thanks also to Barbara Hanrahan, of the Press, who is always a pleasure to work with.

Part I

Introduction

GEORGE LEVINE

One Culture:
Science and Literature

"One Culture": the title seems to make a promise that this book will not keep. It obviously echoes Snow's "two cultures," by now a not very helpful cliché, and promises a unity we will not find. Snow's analysis was inadequate in ways that more critics than F. R. Leavis have noted. The simple divergence between those who can gossip about literature and those who can gossip about science is not particularly interesting, nor does it matter very much that "literary" people can't tell us what the second law of thermodynamics is (a surprising number in fact certainly could, as I believe this book will testify). Nor does it matter that—alas!—some scientists haven't read any Shakespeare. These are not the terms of a serious debate.[1]

This book is concerned not to reopen that old debate but to attempt to consider ways in which literature and science might indeed be embraced in the same discourse, ways in which they have been so embraced. I indulge the easy allusion to a well-known cultural war because Snow's formulation, which has caught on, implies a distinction that needs to be denied. Obviously, there are important distinctions between scientific and literary language, and obviously too the intricate specialization of the various sciences closes them to the lay public; but so, too, do the increasingly arcane operations of literary criticism. The distinction is one of degree, not of kind: science is no more exempt from the constraints of nonspecialist culture than literature is; nor has it ever been.

On the whole, this book adopts the position, endorsed by the main directions of contemporary criticism (yet still not unproblematic), that literature and science, whatever else they may be, are modes of discourse, neither of which is privileged except by the conventions of the cultures in which they are embedded. It offers, through a series of

3

various but, I believe, compatible essays, perspectives on the two modes that suggest that they can and should be studied as deriving from common cultural sources.

The "one culture" is *not* a unified science and literature. Indeed, one of the points that most needs elaboration—and that the opening essays of this volume explore—is the *nature* of the differences between literary and scientific language, and the implication of those differences for our sense of the two enterprises. With the transformation of science into "discourse," it has become increasingly difficult to define precisely what science is, as opposed to, say, literature. Both, as Thomas Kuhn has argued, are governed by at least ostensibly rational processes; and the distinction between the two cannot be sustained by "application of the classic dichotomies between, for example, the world of value and the world of fact, the subjective and the objective, or the intuitive and the inductive."[2] The problem, says Kuhn, without attempting to resolve it, is in the way we define the question, for while only subtle analysis causes us to lose the sense of distinction between artist and scientist, the "casual observer has no such difficulties" (p. 41).

Here I take up the position of the casual observer. Many of the essays in this volume will in fact be discussing points of convergence, but they do so in part because of a strong intuitive sense that the discourses and their products are very different. We need not so much worry the issue of whether there are differences between scientist and artist, or critic— of course there are; but it is worth attempting to understand those differences and perhaps discover ways that the enterprises can be seen as mutual. Where the discourses converge, it is important to consider precisely how they do, why they do, whether the convergence is fortuitous, whether it can lead to important illuminations, to something like real dialogue, to genuine "influence." The contributors to this volume, while agreeing that literature and science can fruitfully be studied as parts of the same cultural field, are concerned, that is to say, not so much with arguing the importance of establishing serious relations between science and literature, as with studying the nature of the relations that have always existed, and the usefulness of understanding them.

The test of the usefulness of this volume's various essays into convergence will, necessarily, be in the particularities of the arguments.

4

One Culture

Throwing around comfortably such overwhelmingly complicated words as "science," "literature," "culture" might well indicate a radical failure to appreciate the multiplicity of meanings these words imply. To say that literature and science are products of the same culture is to say little until all three key terms are understood particularly. I have thus far, for instance, been talking about "literature" as though it meant only what we casually describe as "creative" writing. Putting aside the problem, so provocatively exploited by Terry Eagleton in his *Literary Theory*, that we have no adequate definition for "literature,"[3] it probably makes sense to think of science as being on an analogy more with criticism than with "literature." That is, as science attempts to understand nature, so criticism attempts to understand literature. Science and criticism are methods of investigation; nature and literature are the objects.[4] This is a little too easy also, although it points at a distinction that needs considerably more exploration and, I hope, will receive it in later volumes in this series. Certainly, one of the important historical developments in the past century has been the attempt—or, I should say, attempts—to give to criticism some of the authority of science, to see it as a mode of knowledge, incremental, verifiable, systematic. This hasn't worked, nor do I believe it can; and, ironically, it has happened at the same time that history, philosophy, and literary criticism itself have been converging to call into question the rationality, verifiability, and systematic nature of science.[5]

At the outset of these investigations, then, I concede that the questions are too big to evoke more than exploratory answers, localized investigations of aspects of the problems that might help toward larger answers later on. But for me and for the contributors to this volume, the subject of "science and literature" is a major one. It matters because the conjunction of the two sometimes radically separated worlds of discourse helps illuminate each, helps demystify each as they sit apart under cloaks of unmerited authority—objective or subjective. And it forces us to address issues of ultimate importance to the way our culture and our societies are currently shaping themselves.

It is one culture, then, in two senses: first, in that what happens in science matters inevitably to what happens everywhere else, literature included; and second, in that it is possible and fruitful to understand how literature and science are mutually shaped by their participation in

5

the culture at large—in the intellectual, moral, aesthetic, social, economic, and political communities which both generate and take their shape from them.

I

The formula "science and literature," which governs this series, announces, through the "and," a difference; the innocuous copula becomes yet more problematic than the difficult major terms. "And" implies relationship, of course, but (para)tactically refuses to define it. The "and" also intimates the oddity of the relationship: what can the two have to do with each other? It implies, moreover, that in spite of the conventions of literary hostility to science, and of scientific indifference to literature, the relationship matters.

"And" cloaks many different sorts of relationships. If we think of "influence" in this connection, we normally think of science influencing literature, and we have plenty of studies, for example, of the way Shelley used scientific thought, of how Tennyson's *In Memoriam* reflects the geological work of Lyell, or of how the idea of entropy informs literature from Hardy to Pynchon's *Crying of Lot 49*. But the influence works the other way, too, as strong developments in externalist history of science have been demonstrating, and as Gillian Beer has shown with Darwin, as Gerald Holton has shown with Niels Bohr.[6] In a recent essay, Greg Myers describes not only how the rhetoric of science informed the prose of the great Victorian sages, but how the central social, religious, and cultural attitudes of their time informed the scientific thought of John Tyndall and James Clerk Maxwell, among many others.[7] Again, Alfred North Whitehead, describing his experience when he heard that measurement of an eclipse had confirmed Einstein's prediction that rays of light are bent as they pass in the neighborhood of the sun, sees himself and his fellow scientists as like a Greek chorus, "commenting on the decree of destiny as disclosed in the development of a supreme incident." The remorseless inevitability of Greek drama, he says, pervades science, and the Greeks' "magnificent expression . . . deepened the stream of thought" from which grew "the concept of remorseless inevitability which we find in Newtonian theory."[8]

Similarly, as he traces the foundations of science in the West, White-head finds that the development of "Naturalism" in art—the rise of interest in natural objects and in natural occurrences, for their own sakes (p. 16)—was a critical condition for the rise of science. And even the procedures of scholastic philosophy helped contribute to the development of a climate of opinion that encouraged scientific thought. The medieval habit of thinking that "every detailed occurrence can be correlated with its antecedents in a perfectly definite manner, exemplifying general principles," is, of course, closely parallel to the scientist's concern to read each fact into a general order of things (p. 13).

In a way that impressively anticipated recent developments in the history of science, Whitehead, in 1925, against the current of positivist movements to establish the timeless and cultureless authority of scientific knowledge, was already implicating science in the whole matrix of culture—including not only philosophy and literature, but law, art, religion, commerce. While his book has achieved the status of a classic, its implications have still not been fully explored, and the particular philosophy which it ultimately espoused may have helped divert attention from the centrality of its preoccupation with the relations of science to culture. Thus, the "and" can imply yet a third sort of relationship—kinship: science and literature reflect each other because they draw mutually on one culture, from the same sources, and they work out in different languages the same project.[9]

There are, of course, many more questions. Is there some connection between the technical language of professional scientific discourse and the rhetorical and metaphorical manipulations of fiction and poetry? Why is the language of literary criticism these days so full of allusions to science, or at least to discussions of science by historians and philosophers? Are the discontinuities so characteristic of modern literature in any way connected with the discontinuities that contemporary physics, for example, may be discovering in the physical world? Is the science we do find "in" literature—in its themes, its language, its structures—genuinely representative of what is going on in science, or a lay distortion, deliberate or otherwise? Does the difference matter for literature? Does "objective" science in any way learn from nonscientific discourses? Is it reasonable to suggest that science, like literature, is subject to the assumptions, ideologies, prejudices current in the societies from which it grows? If so, how precisely do these manifest themselves? Can the tools of literary analysis, the strategies of literary theory, be usefully employed on scientific discourse? For whose use—the scientists? or the writers? or the critics?

The questions proliferate around the "and." This book obviously leans toward certain kinds of answers—ones that affirm the validity of literary analysis of science, that affirm the crossing of "influences," the blurring of boundaries between discourses; but it does so by addressing discrete problems. The writers of these essays were all independently undertaking projects related to these questions. In the course of their writing they became aware of one another's work and even ventured occasional critiques of it. Clearly, they did not begin working out of a unified vision, but the direction of their work is impressively parallel. All point toward tightening the connections implicit in "and." The margins between literature and science have been blurring, as Michel Serres has suggested, but for a very long time their relations have been closer than most of us are used to thinking.

Literature has been unable to avoid science because science asserts an epistemological authority so powerful that it can determine even how we allow ourselves to imagine the world, or to resist that authority. The authority of objectivity and disinterest, confirmed by the evidence of our senses and by technological developments that touch every part of our lives, demands our respect, answers to values central to our culture certainly since Descartes and Bacon. The long and well-publicized history of hostility to science in the West—particularly on the part of the literary world—reflects the power of the antagonist. Like it or not, we cannot ignore science. It percolates through our imaginations even if we don't know much about it. Our sense of the constitution of matter may be no more up to date than our high school science, our understanding of DNA shadowy, but our vocabularies are thick with the languages of science. Most of what we say has lost its scientific connotations. "Gravity" is no longer Newtonian, "relativity" Einsteinian, or "atomic" Daltonian. DNA gets into all the crossword puzzles. We accept unreflectingly the miracles of science of only a few years ago. Many of us can invoke some technical terms, like "plate tectonics," when we worry about moving to the West Coast.

Science is our new mythology, still close enough to feel like reality

8

rather than a story, yet distant enough to keep us unaware that it is constantly working on our sense of what is possible. It provides the images and language through which we know the material world, and it even shapes (often by indirection) our sense of what it means to be human. What we find credible or kooky depends in large measure on how far we have accepted the (at least ostensible) terms of scientific argument. And it is difficult not to believe that real problems in medicine or manufacture, in space travel or treatment of the common cold, will be solved eventually by careful men (and a few women) in white coats who patiently analyze, observe, experiment, find out. Every particular can be understood within some large general classification, every event is ultimately comprehensible, if we want to bother.

Science, of course, is not the exclusive, or in many cases even the primary, shaper of our imagination of the "real"; but its importance is inescapable, and our understanding of modern narrative and literature in general requires at least some conception of the connections between the assumptions writers make about continuity or discontinuity, causal movement, open-endedness, indeterminacy, what happens next, the ultimate constitution of things (and therefore what questions to ask about them), and the way contemporary science deals with similar problems.

In any case, Frankenstein's monster—perhaps the great popular metaphor of the hostility between science and literature—has been created and, as remake after remake testifies, will not die. He (or it) is implicit in Bacon's pronouncement that "the true and lawful goal of the sciences is none other than this: that human life be endowed with new discoveries and powers."[10]

The engagement of literature with science long preceded Mary Shelley (whose *Frankenstein* is, of course, far more complicated about the relation of science to literature and society than the popular adaptations imply). Since at least the seventeenth century, the peculiar authority of science has made it an intrinsic part of general culture, even when in its specialism it grew beyond the reach of popular understanding. Bacon's essays have become part of the common sense of the West:

One method of delivery alone remains to us; which is simply this: we must lead men to the particulars themselves, and their series and order;

while men on their side must force themselves for awhile to lay their notions by and begin to familiarise themselves with facts. (p. 53)

Ironically, literature itself, a mere construction of language, celebrates Bacon's liberation from words into facts. So Cowley's "Ode to the Royal Society" honors Bacon:

> From words, which are but pictures of the thought
> (Though we our thoughts from them perversely drew),
> To things, the mind's right object, he it brought.

The rejection of inherited authority, the turn to facts, the wariness of the idols that distort knowledge—these are all deeply engrained conventions of Western thought, as is the parallel metaphysical leap away from metaphysics in Descartes's *cogito*. The poet will often agree that things, not words, are the mind's right object, and literature long remained in such a characteristically self-deprecating relation to these conventions. It has not been able to ignore them.

"Science," says Whitehead, "has practically recoloured our mentality so that modes of thought which in former times were exceptions are now broadly spread through the educated world." He is talking here about the slow vast sweep of science through the consciousness of the West from the sixteenth century to the present, and he means in particular the new Baconian preoccupation with "fact": "a vehement and passionate interest in the relation of general principles to irreducible and stubborn facts" (p. 2). That preoccupation, as the Cowley ode makes clear, is an aspect of a deep resistance to traditional authority, to the tyranny of words, and what at any moment the words might deceitfully disguise. The shift is from language to experience: words matter only as they correspond to fact. To draw thoughts from them otherwise is "perverse." It is not, however, only the commitment to "fact" and the ordering principles for fact that distinguishes the impact of science on the cultural consciousness or on literature. The "coloring" Whitehead talks about tinges everything from our conception of matter to our conception of self. We are easy (if hopelessly imprecise) when "atoms" and "ego" color our vocabulary. As G. H. Lewes argued a century ago (but with a happy optimism about where this would take us), "Science is penetrating everywhere."[11]

But relations between humanists and scientists were not always so happy. Science established itself professionally in England in part by rejecting literature—at least those excesses of literature that seemed to the Royal Society to corrupt thought. So the even-tempered Sprat, in his *History of the Royal Society*, notoriously loses his temper when talking about rhetoric:

> And, in few words, I dare say: that of all the Studies of men, nothing may be sooner obtain'd, than this vicious abundance of *Phrase*, this trick of *Metaphor*, this volubility of *Tongue*, which make so great a noise in the World. But I spend words in vain; for the evil is now so inveterate, that it is hard to know whom to *blame*, or where to begin to *reform*. We all value one another so much, upon this beautiful deceit; and labour so long after it, in the years of our education: that we cannot but ever after think kinder of it, than it deserves. And indeed, in most other parts of Learning, I look on it to be a thing almost utterly desperate in its cure: and I think it may be plac'd amongst those *general mischiefs*; such as the *dissention* of Christian Princes, the *want of practice* in Religion, and the like.[12]

Rhetorical excess does not, of course, equal literature: but the insistence on things, the unease with mere ornament or rhetoric, suggest an almost Puritan distrust of literary discourse that seems to make truth claims, for it impedes the severe, disciplined, and patient study of nature requisite for natural philosophy.

Objections to science in literature tend to vary, although I believe they derive from similar reservations. Swift's Laputans are evidence of the total impracticality of scientific knowledge. Leavis' attack on Snow entailed a rejection of the exclusively material orientation of science. The Faust myths, in all their varieties, from Dr. Faustus to Godzilla, imply the dangers of unrestricted pursuit of knowledge. But what all attacks have in common is a deeply uncomfortable sense that science fails to keep touch with the full richness and particularity of human experience. It reduces, abstracts, works impersonally. Its knowledge, whether practical or not, does not address itself to moral or aesthetic issues.

The divergence of scientific and literary discourse remains critically important because of the question of authority. Descartes reached back beyond all inherited cultural assumptions and built knowledge from its base in the perceiving self; and upon that base secular culture ultimately established an authority perhaps even more potent that than of the

11

religious authority it displaced. Western science is constructed on a denial: "The improver of natural knowledge," said T. H. Huxley, the late-Victorian spokesman for the authority of science, "absolutely refuses to acknowledge authority, as such."[13] But Huxley was ready to extend the authority of science to all knowledge and thus—as Bernard Lightman has implied in an essay on "Pope Huxley"[14]—incorporate into science the structure (if not the content) of what it was displacing.

It achieves its authority by standing outside of human interest. Objectivity is a nonhuman condition. And it is not merely a sentimental humanism that has had difficulty with the idea of objectivity. How can we, as Bacon required, "lay our notions by?" The great authority science has achieved derives largely, I believe, from the way it persuades us that its practitioners are disinterested. Such a condition was one of the great aspirations of perhaps the most famous English antagonist to the displacement of humanist by scientific education—Matthew Arnold. Being able to believe by virtue of the sheer power of fact and reason is the ideal condition, and ironically enough it looked as though science, not literature, had attained it. Once achieve disinterest, and objectivity would follow. Reality would come rushing in, unimpeded by the distortions of politics, economics, or any ideology.[15] But much of modern thought has been preoccupied with the impossibility of achieving that disinterest, and only science has, until recently, seemed at all available for exemption.

Thus, we have become used to thinking (or at least feeling) that science tells the truth. On the other hand, much of the history of criticism in the twentieth century has been concerned to ask what it is—since it's certainly not "truth," the province of science—that literature tells.[16] For obvious reasons, then, science felt no corresponding need to attend to literature, and when scientists do so it is rather more for diversion than for illumination. So it is almost with glee that literary critics discover that serious people are wondering in public what it is that science actually tells. And with a sophistication and complexity that too often attempt to emulate science itself, literature is settling for the view that it tells nothing but literature. The great wave of skepticism that, over the course of three centuries, was establishing the scientific method as the only means to truth, and science as its only voice, has been spreading to science itself. Literature, in this regard, has had nothing to lose since even its own practitioners had early developed the Puritan habit of thinking of it as lying or—in better modern dress—myth. Now it turns out that literature is a discourse that simply makes no truth claims. What if it also turned out that all-powerful science, whose clarity and precision and practical results had been demonstrating its epistemological superiority to all other modes of investigation and discourse, was itself only an elaborate myth? What if scientists worked by intuition rather than by the hypothetico-deductive method? What if induction were an ex post facto explanation that rationalized irrational intellectual leaps? What if important scientific discoveries were often made because the scientist *wanted* something to be true rather than because he or she had evidence to prove it true? What if "verification" or, in Popper's terms, the possibility of falsification did not, finally, distinguish the scientific project? What if much important scientific work could never be verified?[17] What if falsification did not finally determine whether a scientific statement were to be accepted?

Philosophers of science, in different ways that have led to some acerbic battles,[18] have been arguing for each of these possibilities. Whatever the details of the battles, Thomas Kuhn's enormously influential theory of scientific revolutions seemed to speak directly to the needs and interests of the literary-critical community and was fairly quickly absorbed into its discourse. "Paradigm," in a Kuhnian sense, or in literary versions of a Kuhnian sense, is part of the critical vocabulary. Despite some grouchy realist dissenters[19] who insist on the possibility of representation and on a correspondence theory of truth, we are in the midst of a pervasive assault on all foundationalist positions, and as one consequence literary people are increasingly taking the risk of contending with scientific texts as if they were literature and are turning with interest to historians of science whose study of their subject is "externalist," rather than "internalist." How much of the history of science can be accounted for in terms of a consistent development of the ideas pertaining directly to the subject? How "rational" are the arguments for, say, natural selection or quantum theory? And how much depends upon social, political, and economic factors—on the pervasive ideology of the scientist's culture? Different as they are, deconstructionist and reader-response theories of literature (combined as they can be with Marxist and Freudian or Lacanian interpretation), Kuhnian theories of the history and philosophy of science, developments in the sociology of science, philosophical hermeneutics—all of these seem to be participating in the same disruption (now we can call it "demystification") of the commonsense notions (often condemned as "positivist") according to which scientific propositions, or indeed any propositions, carry their authority.

Before considering further the consequences of this skepticism, it would be useful briefly to lay out its terms a bit more precisely, if only because literary critics, in their pleasure at the disruption of the concept of traditional objectivity, often play fast and unphilosophically loose with very complex ideas. The contention prevalent in the philosophic community over Kuhn's idea of paradigms occasions embarrassment when one sees how easily the idea of paradigms has been taken over by literary critics. (This volume itself may be occasionally vulnerable to such criticism.) A recent commentator puts it this way:

> It has become fashionable for humanists and social scientists to talk about science as just another "mode of discourse," propelled by its rhetoric and by the social organization of its practitioners, being, ultimately, a nonreferential, constructed reality comparable to the arts. This view belittles science's ability to manipulate nature and asserts that science is defined by its unique authority relation, i.e., by the fact that scientific statements must be certified by the "discourse community" that has assumed the guardianship of science.[20]

Clearly, the rejoicing at our liberation from the authority of science is misguided as long as it fails to confront our commonsense perception of the power of science to manipulate reality (just as, from Kuhn's point of view, it is absurd to identify scientific with artistic activity because of theoretical parallels that do not take into account the commonsense perception of their difference).

Partly for this reason, "scientific realism" remains alive. However theoretically exciting the antifoundationalist position is, most scientists and some philosophers of science are still committed to the notion that scientific statements are "true," or, at least, that science aspires to a true description of the world. "Like the Equal Rights Movement," writes one such philosopher, "scientific realism is a majority position whose advocates are so divided as to appear a minority."[21] The divisions among the realists are, from my point of view, reflections as much of the problems "realism" has in explaining the historical phenomenon of science, as of the epistemological difficulties of the position. Any realist account would itself have to take into account the approximate nature of so much once-confident scientific fact, the unsystematic way in which evidence is gathered and used, the erratic and possibly not progressive movement of science, the unverifiability of the existential reality affirmed by scientific claims, the possibility of the predictive success and theoretical error of any given theory, the fact that much of what science claims is true is not observable, and so on. The sheer common sense that leads one to believe that if a theory is empirically adequate, it must be true, helps sustain realism; and considerable very important work has gone into contemporary defenses of realism. Nevertheless, as Bas van Frassen, perhaps now the most influential of the younger philosophers of science, has put it, "acceptance is not belief":[22] one may, that is to say, accept the empirical adequacy of a scientific theory without believing that the theory describes accurately the physical world. "As far as the enterprise of science is concerned," says van Frassen, "belief in the truth of its theories is supererogatory." In scientific practice, of course, it is likely that most scientists will work with an unselfconscious confidence that they are in the business of describing the real. Philosophers and literary critics, for many reasons, including pleasure in the deflation of scientific authority, are pleased to think that they are not. But in fact, van Frassen's full argument does not at all endorse the kinds of relativistic free-for-alls often engaged in by literary critics as a consequence of liberation from foundationalism. Philosophers of science, if they are to honor their subject, must account for the procedures by which, at least, empirical adequacy is determined.

In any case, what philosophers of science—even scientific realists—have been ready to junk for a long time (and in this, of course, they belong to the same movement that has been dominating critical theory for ten or twenty years) is the convention of naive realism. Mary Hesse lays out the assumptions that underlay traditional conceptions of science:

> There is an external world which can in principle be exhaustively described in scientific language. The scientist, as both observer and language-user, can capture the external facts of the world in propositions that are true if they correspond to the facts and false if they do not.

Science is ideally a linguistic system in which true propositions are in one-to-one relation to facts, including facts that are not directly observed because they involve hidden entities or properties, or past events or far distant events. These hidden events are described in theories, and theories can be inferred from observation, that is, the hidden explanatory mechanism of the world can be discovered from what is open to observation. Man as scientist is regarded as standing apart from the world and able to experiment and theorize about it objectively and dispassionately.[23]

The powerful counterthrusts to these philosophical assumptions range from science fiction films, with their radical distrust of intellectual activity not directly aimed at human improvement, to contemporary philosophy and theory, insisting on disruption, discontinuity, indeterminacy, and the destructive narrowness of Western scientific activity and the epistemologies that underlie it. The counterthrusts have their ideological purposes. In particular, they seem to be designed to bring to wider awareness the nature and power of the quasipositivist assumptions that govern most (at least official) thinking and that authorize the social and economic direction of our culture.

The antirealist argument reverses almost all of the assumptions Hesse describes, and it will probably be most efficient to quote her summary of these, as well:

1. In natural science data are not detachable from theory, for what count as data are determined in the light of some theoretical interpretation, and the facts themselves have to be reconstructed in the light of interpretation.
2. In natural science theories are not models externally compared to nature in a hypothetico-deductive schema, they are the way the facts themselves are seen.
3. In natural science the lawlike relations asserted of experience are internal, because what count as facts are constituted by what the theory says about their interrelations with one another.
4. The language of natural science is irreducibly metaphorical and inexact, and formulizable only at the cost of distortion of the historical dynamics of scientific development and of the imaginative constructions in terms of which nature is interpreted by science.
5. Meanings in natural science are determined by theory; they are understood by theoretical coherence rather than by correspondence with facts. (pp. 172–73)[24]

16

We need not attempt to follow here the various arguments by which Hesse and other philosophers attempt to reauthorize scientific discourse. The hermeneutics of Habermas and Gadamer often figure importantly in such analysis. Hesse will try not to reject the positions just quoted but to show that "the logic of science implied in the account is virtuously rather than viciously circular" (p. 174).

It is obvious, however, how this kind of analysis of scientific statement moves into the literary fold, particularly because of several significant effects. First, the observer no longer stands "apart from the world," dispassionately and objectively commenting upon it. Second, the subjects of science are infused with the consciousness of the perceiver and the constraints of the scientists' culture. Third, science's authority over "fact," so significant in the development of its power, is compromised in the destruction of the correspondence theory of truth: like fiction, like poetry, science, on this account, achieves its status by virtue of its "coherence" rather than its correspondence to external reality. Fourth, science becomes not so much the systematic and cumulative process of discovery as an activity of the creative imagination. And finally, scientific language, with its claims to univocality and precision of correspondence, is understood to be, like literature itself, metaphorical.[25]

The shattering of the myths of disinterestedness and objectivity, or the view that all perception and knowledge are "interested" and historically conditioned, changes the authoritative relations of science to literature. Certainly, in implicitly denying the priority of science over other cultural expressions, it opens (or encourages) the way toward a richer and more complex reading of interchanges between discourses. Nevertheless, critics ought to be proceeding with considerable caution, first because, as Hesse herself and philosophers like van Frassen, Richard Rorty, and Richard Bernstein have been arguing, the rejection of foundationalism entails the subversion only of what they regard as a false tradition of objectivity, not objectivity itself.[26] Antifoundationalism for these thinkers does not endorse an intellectual free-for-all, or make for equivalence between literary and scientific "fictions." Nor does it subvert scientific activity. It historicizes and humanizes it. Second, whatever the philosophical positions now being argued within humanist communities, the historical condition of science's authority within contemporary culture has not radically changed. Frankenstein's monster is still loose, and science continues to exercise its authority in the culture at large. And that suggests that we need within the academy more serious and detailed studies of the relations between science and culture, science and literature.

II

Near the end of *Philosophy and the Mirror of Nature*, Richard Rorty writes:

> The fear of science, of "scientism," of "naturalism," of self-objectivation, of being turned by too much knowledge into a thing rather than a person, is the fear . . . that there will be objectively true or false answers to every question we ask, so that human worth will consist in knowing truths, and human virtue will be merely justified true belief. This is frightening because it cuts off the possibility of something new under the sun, of human life as poetic rather than merely contemplative.
>
> But the dangers to abnormal discourse do not come from science or naturalistic philosophy. They come from the scarcity of food and from the secret police . . . (p. 389)

Rorty's philosophy, by thrusting knowledge into social context, changes philosophy's nature and significance. To consider the relations between science and literature, that shift is crucial, but the change in the theoretical relation of scientific knowledge to ordinary knowledge, of scientific language to ordinary language, is a matter of real import not only for the subject "science and literature" but for the culture at large. Whatever else current theory (or antitheory) has done, it has opened the possibility of a serious critique of science that is not merely sentimental or alarmist. Seeing science not as an absolute authority in the areas of knowledge, but as one (really several) among competing discourses is no longer a particularly daring move, but it remains a healthy one.

One of the growing traditions in history of science, though still somewhat against the grain of more philosophically inclined practitioners, attempts to look more intently and broadly at the full social and political contexts in which particular scientific achievements are made. While addressing itself to the ideological forces that more or less self-consciously shape science, this kind of study is often itself outspokenly ideological. The tradition is, I believe, in harmony with the philosophical developments I have been discussing, but the texture of its work often feels very different. Perhaps the most aggressively outspoken practitioner of this form of history of science is Robert Young, whose essay on biographies of Darwin also appears in this volume. Young makes an unembarrassedly personal case for his method in essay after essay, and willingly places his work within a radical political program for change.

A recent collection of his essays on Darwin[27] manifests this method very clearly. While he has a political program, he believes that to make his case he must demonstrate in great detail how scientific ideas that are normally treated "intrinsically," with reference only to their internal logic and the nature of the evidence available, were in fact developments from ideas very clearly related to the major moral and religious concerns of society. Science, on Young's account, is embedded deeply and inherently in cultural materials, with all their ideological implications. The pressures these exert on scientific thought significantly affect the shape of scientific thinking in spite of their apparent irrelevance to the intrinsic coherence of experiment and theory. Young's particular subject is Darwin and the nineteenth-century concern with the place of the human in nature. "I remain certain," he contends, "that it is not right to separate the Darwinian debate from broader cultural, ideological, political, and economic issues" (p. xiii).[28]

But the real strength of Young's position is that it never remains very long at the level of polemic. He looks, as he says, for the "fine texture" of scientific work and debate in his period, and he traces meticulously the way scientific debate reflects theological debate, the way, for example, Darwin is clearly using the language of Malthus, and the relation between Malthus' language and Paley's (whose whole way of thinking was also deeply influential on Darwin), and their mutual implication in the tradition of natural theology. Young tries to show how much Darwin's work was part of the established way of looking at things, how easily it was assimilable to secular versions of the natural theology that it seemed, at first, to be rejecting. The conclusions are, to be sure, arguable; but the demonstration of Darwin's embedding in broad cultural movements that he seemed not to be addressing in his work is a powerful one.

Once the move has been made to see science as another cultural product, its language opens up for investigation in ways that are of particular interest to students of literature. Perhaps the richest analysis we have of the nature of Darwin's language is in Gillian Beer's *Darwin's Plots*, where Beer attends to the metaphorical profusion of Darwin's text and demonstrates the impossibility of univocal reading and the importance, for Darwin, of the multiple possibilities of meaning. (In her essay in this volume, Beer further pursues the idea of the importance of multivocal language for scientific discourse that would seem to require univocal meaning.) Young, in one of the most interesting essays we have on Darwin (written originally in 1971), pursues Darwin's use of the metaphor of "selection" and considers, in the context of Darwin's quite self-conscious decision to retain the metaphor after fully understanding its difficultires, what the scientific and ideological implications are. To be an externalist critic of the sort Young wants, one needs also to be a literary critic, or at least a rhetorician, to understand the way metaphor works, to locate particular metaphors in a wide range of literature. In other words, Young pursues the objective of his kind of externalist history of science by risking engagement with the full range of intellectual activity of Victorian culture. To read Darwin, he shows, one must know how to read metaphor and how particular metaphors were historically read, and one must be willing to get one's hands dirty in social and cultural history.

There are many others doing Young's sort of work, if usually less polemically. One of the most interesting and effective is Stephen Jay Gould, in his study of psychometrics. Describing his work as "negative science," since it is designed to disprove certain scientific arguments, Gould tries to show how biological determinism, allied to psychometrics, worked for political ends. But, he says,

> I do not intend to contrast evil determinists who stray from the path of scientific objectivity with enlightened antideterminists who approach data with an open mind and therefore see truth. Rather, I criticize the myth that science itself is an objective enterprise, done properly only when scientists can shuck the constraints of their culture and view the world as it really is.[29]

Despite its obvious compatibility with the philosophies of science I have been looking at, Gould's is not a speculative work about a theory of science. It is a study of a particular development within science which can serve as an example strengthening the case against the traditional realist view Mary Hesse outlined above. We can see in Gould's analysis once again that a heightened sensitivity to metaphor is required for an understanding of science itself. He needs to show, for example, that one of the fallacies leading to a biologically determinist position is "reification," in this case the translation of the abstraction "intelligence" into an entity (p. 24). Similarly, Gould shows how the idea of "ranking" belongs to the metaphors of "progress and gradualism" that have had such unfortunate social utility in the West. The battle over "objectivity," and over the question of whether one can learn anything about science by seeing scientific ideas as embedded in culture and its ideologies, loses some of its rarefied abstractness. Gould's analysis has serious extraphilosophical consequences. He confesses that he "was inspired to write this book because biological determinism is rising in popularity again, as it always does in time of political retrenchment" (p. 28).

A very recent example of the kind of history of science Young would seem to be looking for is of major importance in its relations to the philosophical questions raised earlier. Shapin and Schaffer, in *Leviathan and the Air-Pump*, raise their questions about scientific knowledge within a firmly historical context. They reexamine the development of arguments for what is perhaps the source of the whole tradition of experimental science in the West, Boyle's experimental method, which remains canonical. They demonstrate its implication in the polity of Restoration England, and they thus treat experiment, not as the "true way" to scientific knowledge, but as a set of communally accepted conventions, much as "realism" is conventional in Svetlana Alpers' *The Art of Describing*.

"The solution to the problem of knowledge," they claim, "is political; it is predicated upon laying down rules and conventions of relations between men in the intellectual polity" (p. 342). This will not sound particularly stunning to those who have followed the critical wars or learned from Marxist, feminist, and reader response criticism. But Shapin and Schaffer are far from imitative in their analyses, and their demonstration of the social constitution of science, at least at this crucial point in the development of Western science, is likely to gather its own community of readers. At least it ought to.

Thus Young is far from unique in his enterprise, but his work may be the most obvious reflection of the historicizing of ideas that is more abstractly affirmed in the debates among Kuhn, Lakatos, Hesse, Bernstein, the hermeneuticists, van Frassen, and so on. Once one is committed to the view that science is not so clearly separable from the human sciences (a separation on which even Habermas insists) or from other humanist enterprises, history of science begins to blur in with social history. Literature becomes part of the history of science. Science is reflected in literature. And the tools of literary criticism become instruments in the understanding of scientific discourse.

III

Although I have emphasized here elements of the literary critique of science, and, indeed, of scientists' critique of science, another emphasis is possible and necessary, certainly for purposes of this book. Science is a risk-taking enterprise, but, as we have seen, it is also an imaginative one. The relation of literature to science has been one not simply of hostility, rather more of love-hate. Even the myth of Frankenstein includes a fascination with, an attraction to, the enormous possibilities of science that it would be absurd to ignore. We can ignore it only if we take that famous novel as a simple moral parable against intellectual overreaching. Remember that Victor Frankenstein's last words are not "seek happiness in tranquility, and avoid ambition," but "yet another may succeed."[30]

Nineteenth-century English literature is by no means a continuous litany of romantic complaints against science. Ruskin himself—that campaigner against modern science, Darwinism, and the fruits of technology—wanted to be president of the Geological Society. His hostility to science and particularly to John Tyndall had to do with his very peculiar reading of the ways science reduces the human to the merely material and is responsible for the disruptions of his favored landscapes. Ruskin's is the romantic response, which always included, as with Shelley, deep respect for the scientific enterprise and even scientific ambition. Much of his later work was an attempt to make a better science, or at least better natural history. He was fighting the professionalization of science, the way its language was splitting off from the language available to the common reader, and he proposed a new system of naming birds and flowers, incorporating into our scientific understanding the way human culture had perceived these things. For Ruskin, true science included the history of human experience with natural phenomena; but he longed for true science. Or again, George Eliot takes science as a kind of model for moral and intellectual growth, and the notorious failure of her scientist-doctor Lydgate is a failure to live up to science, not a failure of science itself. Even Dickens, whose attitudes toward science we might think are summed up in his satire in *Hard Times*, was favorably disposed to science, filled the pages of his weekly journals with popularizations of scientific thought, celebrated the scientific spirit in Daniel Doyce of *Little Dorrit*. Perhaps more important, we can find throughout nineteenth-century literature frequent reflections of scientific thought, even in the very texture of narrative. One need only consider the splendid analyses of Gillian Beer in her study of Darwin to recognize how complexly enmeshed in the general understanding Darwin's theories were and in how many and how far-reaching ways those theories were manifested (and resisted) in literature.

The attack on science that we have witnessed from so many quarters was, of course, partly a consequence of science's power, and of the special status it seemed to claim within the world of philosophy. The main target has been an imperialist positivism which claimed that in the scientific method, as it defined that method, we have our only way to truth, and at its most extreme dismissed all others forms of statement as "nonsense," since they could not be verified according to "scientific method." Positivism, which in the nineteenth century was in part a reaction to the claim by "authority" to the status of objective truth—a claim unsupported by any but verbal evidence—ultimately incorporated the structure of the displaced authority into itself. I would argue, however, that by questioning authority as it did and insisting on the necessity for constant skepticism about authority claims, it made its own authority vulnerable. Most of the more powerful attacks on positivism in fact assimilate its antimetaphysical stance and incorporate its critique of metaphysics as a disguise for interest. "Objectivity" itself was seen as such a disguise. But positivism is not the form in which the truth claims of science are now most seriously affirmed, and recent developments in science and scientific theory have made them even more attractive and important to the arts and literature than they were in the promising days of the third quarter of the nineteenth century when it seemed to many very intelligent people that science was, at last, going to transform the world into a new and better place.

John Tyndall wanted to claim that science was among the greatest achievements of the human imagination (he used the term "imagination").[31] In his famous Belfast Address he claimed science's kinship with literature:

> It has been said by its opponents that science divorces itself from literature; but the statement, like so many others, arises from lack of knowledge. A glance at the less technical writing of its leaders—of its Helmholtz, its Huxley, and its Du Bois Reymond—would show what breadth of literary culture they command. Where among modern writers can you find their superiors in clearness and vigour of literary style? Science desires not isolation, but freely combines with every effort towards the bettering of man's estate. (2: 198–99)

We can still, I believe, agree with Tyndall that science is a great imaginative achievement, although our terms may not mean what he intended; and we can, if we read those writers he named, agree that they wrote brilliantly. We cannot, to be sure, accept his intellectual imperialism, but it is certainly worth bringing to bear on his writing the literary sophistication of modern criticism. Surely we can allow him that participation in the general culture that he wanted for science.

That great Victorian moment has itself been subjected to radical critiques. Victorian scientific naturalism has been "exposed" both as an incoherent philosophy and as an attempt as much to establish science as a respectable profession as to bring the gospel of the new truth to fellow scientists and the society as a whole.[32] But that exposure neither diminishes the importance of the scientific work (and its popularization) for literature, nor entails any reduction of respect for the scientific enterprise.

This volume, that is to say, is not in the business of debunking. It takes seriously the view that science is one of the great achievements of the human mind, that it matters powerfully to us, for better or worse, in the way we live, the way we think, and the way we imagine. There is no literature more important. And even if we accept now the view that it is merely one of many competing discourses, that it is no more grounded in a foundation of reality that gives special authority to its language than the language of literature, we need neverthless to consider the nature of that discourse in great detail, to understand the ways in which the "and" genuinely connects science and literature, genuinely marks difference.

George Steiner has argued that "a view of post-classic civilization must, increasingly, imply a vision of the sciences,"[33] and he talks of science as though it were the greatest of literatures:

> At seminal levels of metaphor, of myth, of laughter, where the arts and the worn scaffolding of philosophic systems fail us, science is active. Touch on even its more abstruse regions and a deep elegance, a quickness and merriment of the spirit come through. . . . That "poetry of facts" and realization of the miraculous delicacies of perception in contemporary science, already informs literature at those nerve points where it is both disciplined and under the stress of the future. It is no accident that Musil was trained as an engineer, that Ernst Junger and Nabokov should be serious entomologists, that Broch and Canetti are writers schooled in the exact and mathematical sciences. . . . (pp. 98–99)

And so on. There is something perhaps a little show-offy in Steiner's celebration of the great imaginative achievements of science and of the centrality of science to the imagination of modern artists. Yet there is no denying either the centrality of science to contemporary literature, or the literary power of the great modern scientific discoveries. What matters for this volume is that these discoveries make their claims in the same way as great literature does, that to get to the heart of the culture one can travel the road of science, the road of literature, or—better—both.

IV

This volume, then, assumes that science is embedded in culture. It accepts the analysis that empirical statements can never produce determinate meaning, for "there are in principle always an indefinite number of theories that fit the observed facts more or less adequately" (Hesse, p. viii). Beyond that, it accepts the impossibility of disinterest in any investigation and recognizes that developments in science are closely related to developments in the culture at large. Thus it builds on the assumption that science does not make "universal" statements, that its discourse is as historical as that of literature (and the assumption, of course, is that literature too is historical, not universal). It proceeds then by accepting the demystification of science that has been so much the object of antipositivist philosophy in the twentieth century, and therefore the view that the history of science entails as well a sociology of science. Science is socially constituted; knowledge is culturally constituted.

In a sense this is all very old news. Yet the exploration of the implications of this widely shared view is in a relatively primitive state. When scientific texts become texts, wrenched from the correspondence theory of truth and denied universality, they become subject to the sorts of analyses Gould, and Young, and Beer practice. In this volume, the essays move back and forth, from scientific to literary texts, examining them in their complex relationships, assuming those relationships, working from the assumptions we have just outlined. As a collection, they make what I believe to be an important contribution to the understanding of what it means in practice to accept these views, the consequence for the study of literature and the consequence for the study of science.

In Part II, the essays attempt to deal with aspects of the language that constitute the different discourses of science and literature. In an essay which offers a speculative overview of the relations between scientific and literary language, Gillian Beer identifies a critical difference in the attitude toward univocality, and locates, too, in both discourses an ultimate need for multivalence if either is to break from the constraints of language itself into something new. James Paradis, working more historically, attempts to trace the history of the divergence of the two discourses, the increasing specialization of scientific language. Yet both opening essays assume a common base, which Beer locates in a historical past, Paradis in the nature of language itself. I have included Peter Dale's essay on G. H. Lewes in this section because it presents a fascinating example of the way the two discourses, apparently at odds, seem to reconverge in the career of this Victorian polymath. Lewes provides an example of how even the most extreme polarities—positivism on the one hand, modernist symbolism on the other—can be shown to work into each other. The divergence, to be sure, is there: but the possibility of connection in minds of exceptional brillance is there also.

In Part III, four essays explore differently, but with a unanimity of general view that I could not have anticipated, ways in which literature and science can be seen in conjunction fruitfully. All of them assume the cultural embedding we have been talking about, and all of them are enabled by that assumption. N. Katherine Hayles in fact offers a theory of such conjunction, using the metaphor of the unified field theory as a method, and juxtaposes to remarkable effect Barthes's criticism with Shannon's information theory. Donald Benson talks about the conjunction as "illustration," avoiding (as do all the essayists here) the idea of influence, but showing how the theory of ether illuminates Pater's work and that of the impressionists. Richard Pearce considers in several of its artistic manifestations the culture's interest in symmetry and disruption. And David Bell not only explores the problem of "chance," but suggests that Balzac's handling of it representatively in a short novel actually anticipates later scientific uses.

In the final two sections, there are two different kinds of critique of the scientific enterprise. Part IV examines the question without direct recourse to theory. It examines some biographical and historical consequences of the convergence of scientific and social discourse. The essays are not concerned with literary analysis, yet demonstrate vividly ways in which science and literature are combined in the texture of individual lives, how the ideologies of science help define at any given moment what constitutes imagination, what lies beyond the margins of social acceptability. Robert Young discusses the genre of biography, through the example of Darwin, to suggest once again how the history of science entails a thickening of the subject beyond the rational coherence of scientific argument. Biography, Young suggests, is an aspect of scientific theory that should not be ignored. So here again literaure becomes a part of science. Roy Porter examines the curious connections between the idea of madness and its actuality in the eighteenth century; and James Moore offers a fascinating case study of a now neglected Victorian woman poet, whose life and thought manifest an extraordinary crossing of the scientific and the poetic and the culture's "scientific" assumptions about the nature of woman.

Part V offers two readings of novels by women which demonstrate the centrality to those texts of the scientific literature of the time. But both

Anne Mellor with *Frankenstein* and Sally Shuttleworth with *Villette* attempt to disentangle various of the scientific elements and demonstrate how the novels mount strong criticisms of a scientific enterprise that implies in its very constitution male domination. The essays, then, provide us with further evidence of the ideological implications of science, the literary involvement with science and preoccupation with its ideologies.

Notes

1. For two very different responses to Snow's Rede Lecture on the two cultures, see *Two Cultures: The Significance of C. P. Snow* by F. R. Leavis (New York: Pantheon, 1963), which includes an essay, "Sir Charles Snow's Rede Lecture," by Michael Yudkin. Yudkin makes a telling case for the irrelevance of Snow's formulation and for the impossibility of training nonscientists in science in the same way that one can expose scientists to great literature.

2. Thomas Kuhn, "Comment on the Relations of Science and Art," *The Essential Tension: Selected Studies in Scientific Tradition and Change* (Chicago: University of Chicago Press, 1977), p. 340.

3. See Terry Eagleton, *Literary Theory: An Introduction* (Oxford: Basil Blackwell, 1983). "We have still not discovered the secret, then, of why Lamb, Macauley and Mill are literature but not, generally speaking, Bentham, Marx and Darwin" (p. 10). Eagleton denies that literature is an "objective" category, and links its status to "assumptions by which certain social groups exercise and maintain power over others" (p. 16). The battle over the definition of literature is millennia long, and I don't propose to enter it here, except insofar as I want to suggest that the questioning of the boundaries of literature healthily breaks down the artificial barriers that constructed the two cultures in the first place and reminds us that any construction of human language can be usefully submitted to critical interrogation.

4. For an interesting discussion of this point, see Alexander Nehamas, "Convergence and Methodology in Science and Criticism," *New Literary History* 17 (Autumn 1985): 81–87.

5. Hayden White has recently made forcefully a point that has been crucial in the way literature has attempted to define itself against or to turn itself into science in the twentieth century: "The problem has to do with the fragmenting of humanistic studies into discrete disciplines which must feign to aspire to the status of sciences without any hope of achieving the kind of procedures developed in the physical sciences for the resolution of conflicting interpretations of the specified objects of study. The result of this circumstance is that, in order to enable research in any field of humanistic studies, investigators must presuppose that at least one other field of study or discipline is effectively secured, that

is to say, is effectively free of the kind of epistemological and methodological disputes that agitate their own area of inquiry." "Historical Pluralism," *Critical Inquiry* 12 (Spring 1986): 484.

6. See Gillian Beer, *Darwin's Plots: Evolutionary Narrative in Darwin, George Eliot, and Nineteenth-Century Fiction* (London: Routledge Kegan Paul, 1983), and Gerald Holton, *The Thematic Origins of Scientific Thought: Kepler to Einstein* (Cambridge, Mass.: Harvard University Press, 1973).

7. Greg Myers, "Nineteenth-Century Popularizations of Thermodynamics and the Rhetoric of Social Prophecy," *Victorian Studies* 29 (Autumn 1985): 35–66.

8. A. N. Whitehead, *Science and the Modern World* (New York: New American Library, 1948), p. 11.

9. For Michel Serres, the model of one culture leading to diverse discourses is too simple. Science is a kind of myth, has no priority over other kinds, exists variously at different intersections with other discourses. Serres is also brilliant in his discussion of the way in which the dialectical ideal, initiated by Plato, as a way to exclude "noise" or any interference in the transference of meaning from speaker to listener, is actually a way "to supppose a third man and to seek to exclude him." The mathematical ideal excludes any empirical interruption; so, we may infer, modern science, seeming to aspire to the ideal of generalization discussed by Whitehead, above, seeks to exclude the third man, the lay public. In the nineteenth century, despite a commitment to empirical investigation, science did indeed aspire to that kind of authoritative—one might almost say authoritarian—exclusion of nonspecialists, who might interrupt the flow of meaning and implicitly challenge the authority of scientific discourse. Serres' whole enterprise is such a challenge, as he talks about the way the dialectician and mathematician close their eyes and cover their ears "to the song and the beauty of the sirens." See *Hermes: Literature, Science, Philosophy*, ed. Josué V. Harari and David F. Bell (Baltimore: Johns Hopkins University Press, 1982). The editors' introduction lays out lucidly the central elements of Serres' thought. Note, for example, the following: "Science is the totality of the world's legends. The world is the space of their inscription. To read and to journey are one and the same act" (p. xxi). And "The domains of myth, science, and literature oscillate frantically back and forth into one another, so that the idea of ever distinguishing between them becomes more and more chimerical" (p. xxix).

10. Francis Bacon, *The New Organon*, vol. 4 of *The Works of Francis Bacon*, ed. James Spedding, Robert Leslie Ellis, Douglas Devon Heath (London: Longman, 1860), p. 79.

11. G. H. Lewes, *Problems of Life and Mind*, 2 vols. (London: Trubner, 1874), 1: 1.

12. Thomas Sprat, *History of the Royal Society*, ed. Jackson Cope and Harold Whitmore Jones (St. Louis: Washington University Studies), pp. 112–13.

13. T. H. Huxley, "On the Advisableness of Improving Natural Knowledge," *Methods and Results* (London, 1893), p. 40.

14. Bernard Lightman, "Pope Huxley and the Church Agnostic: The Religion of Science," *Historical Papers* (1983), pp. 150–63. Lightman points out that "by

severely limiting knowledge the agnostics inadvertently created problems for themselves in their attempt to justify the validity of scientific principles. Some of these principles were in fact closely connected to the belief in a natural order which was the basis of the agnostic religion." This belief Huxley—self-contradictorily, to be sure, and inconsistently with his Cartesianism—was to call a "postulate," not, "strictly speaking, demonstrable" (p. 162).

15. For an interesting discussion of this idea in Arnold and in Hazlitt and earlier romantic thought, see David Bromwich, "The Genealogy of Disinterestedness," *Raritan Review* 1 (1982): 62–92.

16. Scientific, or quasi-scientific, models have been offered frequently. Obviously, I. A. Richards, bearing a rich but essentially positivistic notion of language and communication, tried to define literature in terms that would keep it from conflict with science. Leavis' program was, in part, to affirm an Arnoldian, deliberately antiscientific notion of literary truth, and required literature to offer moral wisdom. Northrop Frye has tried to order literature scientifically, discriminating criticism from mere reading by arguing that it is concerned with an order of language. The key text here is *Anatomy of Criticism* (Princeton: Princeton University Press, 1957).

17. See Steven Shapin and Simon Schaffer, *Leviathan and the Air-Pump: Hobbes, Boyle, and the Experimental Life* (Princeton: Princeton University Press, 1985). This remarkable detailed study of Boyle's experiment against the background of Restoration society is too complicated in its analysis and in the questions it raises to be summarized here. But the social constitution of science, at least at this crucial point in the development of Western science, is impressively demonstrated. The authors conclude: "As we come to recognize the conventional and artifactual status of our forms of knowing, we put ourselves in a position to realize that it is ourselves and not reality that is responsible for what we know" (p. 344).

18. For an interesting collection of essays by many of the major contenders in the battles—Kuhn, Popper, Lakatos, Feyerabend, for example—see *Criticism and the Growth of Knowledge*, ed. Imre Lakatos and Alan Musgrave (Cambridge: Cambridge University Press, 1970). The essays all deal with Kuhn's conception of normal and revolutionary science, most of them more or less negatively. Yet most of them subscribe to the view that the naive realism of traditional empiricism cannot hold. Witness, for example, Lakatos: "the direction of science is determined primarily by human creative imagination and not by the universe of facts which surrounds us" (p. 187).

19. It is not at all fair to call all contemporary philosophical "realists" merely grouchy. There are, indeed, some extremely interesting and important philosophers of science who are attempting to work out ways to recuperate the real. Mary Hesse's work, alluded to elsewhere in this essay, attempts, as she says, "to steer a course between the extremes of metaphysical realism and relativism" (p. xiv) and goes outside of science, even to theology, to resist the powerful assault on realism and empiricism. The work of Roy Bhaskar builds on current debate in a very different way, and argues for a concept of the real that he

believes is the only way to account for the fact that scientific thought actually succeeds. Using many of the techniques of contemporary philosophy with strong relativist implications, Bhaskar is moving in an original way to break the hermeneutic circle with which most critics and many philosophers are now living so comfortably. See Roy Bhaskar, *A Realist Theory of Science* (Sussex: Harvester Press, 1978).

20. John Neubauer, "Models for the History of Science and Literature," in Harry R. Garvin, ed., *Science and Literature* (Lewisburg, Pa.: Bucknell University Press, 1983), p. 32.

21. Jarrett Leplin, ed., *Scientific Realism* (Berkeley: University of California Press, 1984), p. 1.

22. Bas C. van Frassen, "Empiricism in the Philosophy of Science," in Paul M. Churchland and Clifford A. Hooker, ed., *Images of Science* (Chicago: University of Chicago Press, 1985), p. 247. Van Frassen's theory of "Constructive Empiricism" is antirealist, but attempts to account for the success of science by, among other things, demonstrating the irrelevance of truth claims to scientific argument, whose acceptance does not require belief.

23. Mary Hesse, *Revolutions and Reconstructions in the Philosophy of Science* (Bloomington: Indiana University Press, 1980), p. vii.

24. It is interesting that Hesse describes these positions in an essay called "In Defence of Objectivity." Like many philosophers, she is concerned to avoid the easy relativism that is often assumed to follow, and adopts, as many others do, aspects of the hermeneutic tradition, and particularly the work of Habermas, for her purposes.

25. It is important to note that Ernan McMullin not only recognizes the metaphorical nature of science but as a scientific realist finds no difficulty in assimilating that view to realism: "The language of theoretical explanation is of a quite special sort. It is open-ended and ever capable of further development. It is metaphoric in the sense in which the poetry of the symbolists is metaphoric, not because it uses explicit analogy or because it is imprecise, but because it has resources of suggestion that are the most immediate testimony of its ontological worth." *Scientific Realism*, p. 36.

26. The obvious text for Rorty is *Philosophy and the Mirror of Nature* (Princeton: Princeton University Press, 1979). An inadequate summary of what Rorty does with the idea of objectivity might be suggested by this quotation: "To be behaviorist in epistemology . . . is to look at the normal scientific discourse of our day bifocally, both as patterns adopted for various historical reasons and as the achievement of objective truth, when 'objective truth' is no more and no less than the best idea we currently have about how to explain what is going on." Rorty's relaxation into historicizing knowledge has the curious possible effect of simply reinforcing the current structure of authority, allowing only for a great deal of conversation about it. Richard Bernstein's *Beyond Objectivism and Relativism* (Philadelphia: University of Pennsylvania Press, 1983) provides an exceptionally lucid analysis of developments in philosophy and philosophy of science that put foundationalism to question. Bernstein, using hermeneutics, tries to

show that the anxiety produced by the fear of the loss of any "foundation" for knowledge derives form a Cartesian antithesis, and that one can move beyond that anxiety, and the antithesis itself, through the construction and recognition of "dialogical communities."

27. Robert M. Young, *Darwin's Metaphor: Nature's Place in Victorian Culture* (Cambridge: Cambridge University Press, 1985).

28. Part of the interest of Young's work is that he tries to place himself within a cultural and ideological framework, and much of this book is devoted to explaining both how he developed his interest in the particular areas he discusses and how the profession he worked in regarded those interests and his method then—and now. This is a very personal reading of his battles with the intellectual establishment, but it remains interesting both as narrative and as exemplification of a rounded, socially contextual view of history of ideas.

29. Stephen Jay Gould, *Mismeasure of Man* (New York: W. W. Norton, 1981), p. 21.

30. Mary Shelley, *Frankenstein: or, The Modern Prometheus*, ed. M. K. Joseph (New York: Oxford University Press, 1971), p. 218.

31. See John Tyndall, "On the Scientific Uses of the Imagination," *Fragments of Science*, 2 vols. (New York: Appleton, 1899).

32. See the work of Frank Turner, *Between Science and Religion: The Reaction to Scientific Naturalism in Late Victorian England* (New Haven: Yale University Press, 1974); "Public Science in Britain, 1880–1919," *Isis* 71 (1980): 589–608; "The Victorian Conflict between Science and Religion: A Professional Dimension," *Isis* 69 (1978): 356–76. For a splendid discussion of the mixture of professional and scientific motives in a scientific debate between Huxley and Richard Owen, see Adrian Desmond, *Archetypes and Ancestors: Palaeontology in Victorian London, 1850–1875* (Chicago: University of Chicago Press, 1982). This book strikes me as very much the kind of work Young has been asking for in his own essays.

33. George Steiner, *In Bluebeard's Castle: Some Notes towards the Redefinition of Culture* (London: Faber and Faber, 1971), p. 98.

Part II

*Diverging and Converging
Languages*

G I L L I A N   B E E R

Problems of Description in the Language of Discovery

Discovery is a matter not only of reaching new conclusions but of redescribing what is known and taken for granted. Scientific inquiry constantly revives questions which are answered both in science and literature at changing levels of description. Description must find ways out of the circle of current presumptions if it is to create knowledge or fresh insight. Yet all description draws, often unknowingly, upon shared cultural assumptions which underwrite its neutral and authoritative status and conceal the embedded designs upon which describing depends. How can the language of scientists and of poets (in the broadest sense) resist such designs and disturb teleological patterns which may otherwise lock their project into the circle of the foreknown? How much do the discursive strategies of scientists and poets have in common? Are we able to pinpoint stable distinctions between scientific communication and poetic communication in relation to the problem of describing? These are questions I shall consider by means of example in this essay.

Much recent work on "science and literature" has emphasized—as several essays in this collection valuably do—those features which the two enterprises have in common, particularly in their relation to language. In the chapter which follows, James Paradis locates historically a point of divergence, when professional scientific discourse breaks off from the more general language for describing experience. We can note and reaffirm that the discourses begin together, and continue to draw

This essay is revised and much extended from an earlier article published in the *Times Literary Supplement*, special History of Science number, November 1984. I am grateful to the editor of the *T.L.S.* for permission to reprint the material from that article.

on common cultural sources. But without at all dissenting from that insistence on setting close together categories of knowledge that have been misleadingly polarized, I want in this essay to analyze differences as much as similarities between the discourse of scientists and poets. The status of description in the two discourses allows us to focus the question of difference: I shall suggest that professional scientific writing has to rely on tacit agreements with a projected readership to a degree that literature evades, and that the shifting of linguistic levels has notably different functions in literary and in scientific communication.

Though kinds of evidence and levels of description may change, some questions have a way of remaining intact to be answered creatively again:

> the ideas of time and space—or how we came by those ideas—or of what stuff they were made—or whether they were born with us—or we picked them up afterwards as we went along—or—whether we did it in frocks—or not till we had got into breeches—with a thousand other enquiries and disputes about INFINITY, PRESCIENCE, LIBERTY, NECESSITY, and so forth, upon whose desperate and unconquerable theories so many fine heads have been turned and cracked.[1]

The great physicist James Clerk Maxwell put it another way in his paper "Molecules" given to the British Association for the Advancement of Science in 1873. His problem is how to describe the new concept, "molecule," since "no one has ever seen or handled a single molecule" and molecular science is "one of those branches of study which deals with things imperceptible by our senses, and which cannot be subjected to direct experiment." He does it by framing his study of this "smallest possible portion of a particular substance" at first with the largest unanswered questions:

> The mind of man has perplexed itself with many hard questions. Is space infinite, and if so in what sense? Is the material world infinite in extent, and are all places within that extent equally full of matter? Do atoms exist, or is matter infinitely divisible?
>
> The discussion of questions of this kind has been going on ever since men began to reason, and to each of us, as soon as we obtain the use of our faculties, the same old questions arise as fresh as ever. They form as essential a part of the science of the nineteenth century of our era, as of that of the fifth century before it.[2]

He ends his analysis by discovering a complete rhetorical congruity between the characteristics of molecules and the desired characteristics of the moral and physical universe in which he has faith. Molecules, he declares, are unchanging, "the foundation stones of the material universe remain unbroken and unworn":

> They continue this day as they were created, perfect in number and measure and weight, and from the ineffaceable characters impressed on them we may learn that those aspirations after accuracy in measurement, truth in statement, and justice in action, which we reckon among our noblest attributes as men, are ours because they are essential constituents of the image of Him Who in the beginning created, not only the heaven and the earth, but the materials of which heaven and earth consist. (p. 86)

The questions Maxwell raised at the outset are allayed rather than answered. The description of a novel concept has here been permitted by its familiarization; but the activity of that description, as Maxwell himself acknowledges, is not so much "scientific" in the Baconian sense ("subjected to direct experiment") as it is speculative and persuasive. It persuades by calling upon the argument from design. Molecules, it proves, are God's characters (as so often in Victorian science, the senses of "characteristics" and "inscribed codes" combine). They are understandable as having complete congruity with a foreknown order: they vouch for, and are vouched for by, that order. The circle of description is complete. The discovery of such fortunate congruity gives pleasure, and still persuasively does so even to those of us who do not share the beliefs relied upon by Maxwell. The pleasure here depends upon individual moral assurance and communal reassurance, but that is by no means always the case in the activities of poets or of scientists.

Wordsworth's insistence in the 1802 Preface to the *Lyrical Ballads* on the inseparable association of knowledge and pleasure takes us straight to a profound conjunction in the work of scientist and creative writer. "We have no knowledge, that is, no general principles drawn from the contemplation of particular facts, but what has been built up by pleasure, and exists in us by pleasure alone. . . . The knowledge both of the Poet and the Man of Science is pleasure." The passage points also to a central paradox in their achievements. "However painful may be the objects with which the Anatomist's knowledge is connected, he feels that his knowledge is pleasure," just as the poet studying the "infinite complexity of pain and pleasure" experiences "an overbalance of enjoyment."[3] The "happy ending" of successful theorizing, satisfactory experiment, achieved work of art, creates pleasure. And so—at least since the Middle Ages—does the process, or story, of discovery. Such pleasure has no inherent accord, as Wordsworth points out, with the processes observed or the outcome of the narrative.

Enigma and its resolution have an allure which has colored the popular image of the scientist in literature itself, where he frequently figures (as Augustine Brannigan also has noted) as the transgressor.

> Science directed its attention to a quasi-physical "nature" or underlying order of things which had a characteristic intrigue associated with it. And because of the mystery associated with nature, the procedure of its becoming known came to exhibit a dramatic social significance. Consequently we find a curious feature in accounts of scientific discoveries; they are recurrently characterised as being bizarre achievements made by eccentric personalities under curious circumstances, often having horrible consequences.[4]

The scientist in narrative, moreover, can figure the narrative's own intense desire to break the bounds of encoded story and discover meaning not hitherto admitted to consciousness. Faust and Dr. Frankenstein flout the stories permitted in their cultures. The scientist is perceived as system breaker as much as system maker. His role as demystifier is less celebrated than his role as magic individual—and indeed the power of the creative thinker to outgo the evidence and to generalize convincingly from not-yet-adequate data is a powerful fact of scientific history. So Einstein writes of Niels Bohr's achievement with an emphasis upon "miracle" and "unique instinct," and in his final metaphor from music reminds us of the powers of Thomas Mann's Doctor Faustus:

> That this insecure and contradictory foundation was sufficient to enable a man of Bohr's unique instinct and tact to discover the major laws of the spectral lines and of the electron-shells of the atoms together with their significance for chemistry appeared to me like a miracle—and appears to me as a miracle even today. This is the highest form of musicality in the sphere of thought.[5]

38

Problems of Description in the Language of Discovery

Wordsworth's distinction between scientist and poet insists on "uniqueness" and on the resulting solitariness in the scientist—quite in contrast with the teamwork we now habitually associate with scientific activity. It is worth reminding ourselves that Wordsworth's term "the Man of Science" itself marks a new isolating of "scientific" from other intellectual and creative activity. What we now call "science" was still called philosophy earlier in the eighteenth century, while in the Middle Ages the seven sciences or arts were the Trivium (Grammar, Logic, Rhetoric) and the Quadrivium (Arithmetic, Music, Geometry, and Astronomy). It is not until 1840 that Whewell remarks, "We need very much a name to describe a cultivator of science in general. I should incline to call him a Scientist."[6] That "name to describe a cultivator of science" begins to privilege as well as demarcate a particular method of coming to know and allows summary description of an enclosed professional group. Wordsworth's emphasis on the separation of the scientific thinker from the rest of humankind has continued to be a source of unease—an unease which finds its focus in the nature of scientific language.

Claude Bernard, in his great methodological work *Introduction à l'étude de la médècine experiméntale* (1865), distinguishes between art and science in contrary terms: "l'art, c'est moi; la science, c'est nous." He insists on the communality of the scientist's enterprise as well as of his material. He expresses this sense of a shared culture by means of images of the household, and at the same time suggests the "irregularity" of the scientist's pathways to knowledge which disturb the sociogeography of the house. "La science de la vie . . . c'est un salon superbe tout resplendissant de lumière, dans lequel on ne peut parvenir qu'en passant par une longue et affreuse cuisine."[7] The only route to the brilliantly lit drawing room of truth, in this surreal household (which is our household), is through a long and bloody kitchen: the kitchen of animal experiments.

Scientists, including Einstein, have continued to claim the authority of "we," but that first person plural contains a shifting population. Does it represent the physical conditions of life experienced by all animate beings? Does it represent humanity in general? Does it refer to the subcommunity of scientific workers, or, more exactly, to the specific discourses agreed among them to convey technical information? Each

of these questions may be answered in the affirmative, but rarely all at
the same time.

Owning and Observing

In "The Daemon of the World" Shelley projects a possible future, in
which man gives up his separation from other forms of life and thereby
discovers the fullest powers of mind:

> All things are void of terror: man has lost
> His desolating privilege, and stands
> An equal amidst equals: happiness
> And science dawn though late upon the earth.[8]

What Shelley calls man's "desolating privilege"—the desire to set
ourselves apart from all other phenomena of the material world, to
claim special status, and to exercise control through knowledge—has
been a matter of wry commentary in many forms of writing, as in these
lines from Donne's "An Anatomy of the World":

> For of Meridians, and Parallels
> Man hath weav'd out a net, and this net throwne
> Upon the Heavens, and now they are his owne.[9]

That claim to "own," to possession, is more openly mocked by
Darwin in the notebooks of the 1830s: "Mayo (Philosophy of Living)
quotes Whewell as profound because he says length of days adapted to
duration of sleep in man!! whole universe so adapted!!! and not man to
Planets—instance of arrogance!!!" The human desire to know about the
universe and so subjectively to make it "his own" readily merges into
the claim of human centrality to the universe. Darwin caustically analyzes the further implications of such claims to dominance; writing of
man's insistence on special status and denial of kinship with other
animals, he observes: "Has not the white man, who has debased his
nature and violated every such instinctive feeling by making slave of his
fellow Black, often wished to consider him as another animal.—it is the
way of mankind."[10] The separation of the observer too readily becomes
the separation of the oppressor.

The paradox for both scientific and literary writer is that writing is itself the inscription of human distinctiveness. No other animals write, and the events of the physical world are language-free. Human language is necessary for our apprehension and description of events beyond the human. Yet at the same time language is anthropocentric, persistently drawing the human back to the center of meaning. It thus both exaggerates the power of the human and blurs the limits of our perception of what lies beyond. But it has also, through scientific knowledge, greatly extended our control over the nonhuman.

Language is therefore both a limiting condition on knowledge and a liberating discipline which makes possible the formulation of knowledge. Thus, we are told that John Tyndall had an extraordinarily developed mental awareness of relations in space, which helped to advance his work on radiation. That talent was trained by the language of Milton's epic of cosmic and syntactic spaces, *Paradise Lost*.

> English grammar was the most important discipline of my boyhood. The piercing through the involved and inverted sentences of *Paradise Lost*, the linking of the verb to its often distant nominative, of the relative to its transitive verb, of the preposition to the noun or pronoun which it governed, the study of variations in mood or tense, the transpositions often necessary to bring out the true grammatical structure of a sentence, all this was to my young mind a discipline of the highest value, and a source of unflagging delight.[11]

What Tyndall valued was the intensification of linguistic organization in a great writer, the pace of whose work plays off the syntax of the reading eye moving from line to line, against the energetic demands of meter, and against the act of rationalization implicit in the completed syntactical ordering of each sentence and verse paragraph. This complex multiple ordering in Milton's writing often includes a delay and accumulation so extreme that it rouses the reader's *attention* both to his own activity of syntactic speculation and to the writer's spatial organization of sense.

Certain conditions of language bear particularly hard on the scientific writer whose domain of inquiry, unlike that of literature, is not primarily or necessarily the human. Language is anthropocentric; it is also historically and culturally determined; it is never neutral; and it is multivocal. It potentiates diversity of meaning. At the same time, not all potential significations are active. One of the most remarkable powers of the human mind—less often commented on that its power to prolifer-ate senses—is its power to exclude, or suppress, feasible meanings. The terms of agreement between writer and implied reader can for the time being select and exclude significations. Thus "races" and "wild aborig-inal stock" may be taken to refer solely to cabbages in a sentence like this, from *The Origin of Species*: "It seems to me not improbable, that if we could succeed in naturalising, or were to cultivate, during many generations, the several races, for instance, of the cabbage, in very poor soil (in which case, however, some effect would have to be attributed to the direct action of the poor soil), that they would to a large extent, or even wholly, revert to the wild aboriginal stock."[12] However, as I have argued in *Darwin's Plots*, such an agreement is neither permanent nor inclusive: signification may be controlled and focused within a like-minded group (particularly any professional group), but the excluded or leftover meanings of words remain potential.[13] They can be brought to the surface and put to use by those outside the accord or professional "contract," as well as by those future readers for whom new historical sequences have intervened. Senses shift to and fro from periphery to center, both in history and in the action of the particular reader. They are not fixed at particular points on the spectrum. Furthermore, any radical new theory will itself have the effect of disturbing the "taken for granted" elements in the language it employs.

The attempt to control and curtail the power of language within scientific activity can be seen in this century in two contrary modes. One is that of linguistic positivism; the other is the recent fashion for high-ly impressionistic terms, such as "charm" and "quark." If we turn to the work of early positivists such as Ernst Mach and then Leonard Bloomfield, we find an insistence on the univocal and the unireferen-tial, as in Mach's *The Analysis of Sensations and the Relation of the Physical to the Psychical* (1914) and Bloomfield's *Linguistic Aspects of Science* (1939). Mach, in fact, reached the position that because mathematics is a linguistic system which cannot be directly referred to observable en-tities or events, it must be cleansed from scientific theory. For example, he held that concepts such as "plus," "sum," or "differential" were meaningless because without empirical referent. Paradoxically, his views would have returned scientists to the situation of nineteenth-century workers such as Darwin who had very little mathematical training or mastery. Darwin compensated for this lack by a combination of stupendously accretive observation crosshatched with a powerful multivalent discourse. But Darwin also saw that all observation is theory-laden and therefore subject to interpretative sentences: "No facts without theory," he wrote. The naive positivistic equivalence between object and event, or utterance, presupposes a single necessary theoretical outcome. This problem has led to the contrary mode of impressionistic or whimsical naming which is fashionable in high theory today: words such as "charm," "quark," or "black hole" deliberately evade severe equivalence in order to allow space for correction and enhancement without the need constantly to replace and to move on from terms. One Nobel Prize winner informed me that his research group had deliberately favored terms such as "beads" and "bumps" while working on their project because any prematurely analytical terms might have hampered the speculative multiplicity of their work, or else resulted in their having to abandon and replace their terminology at embarrassingly frequent intervals. Language is a heuristic tool but it may best function at the frontiers of scientific knowledge by adopting a mode which sounds strangely belletristic. Severe one-to-one equivalence may prove to be paradoxically less exact as a working tool than the larger term during the period of theory formation.

We can, moreover, see how difficult it is for even workers like Bloomfield, with his praise of parsimony of signification, to avoid the mythic or affective in their discourse. Because he repudiates metaphor and multivalency, he cannot bring it under control as a necessary element in discourse. He remarks:

> The use of language in science is specialized and peculiar. In a brief speech the scientist manages to say things which in ordinary language would require a vast amount of talk. His hearers respond with great accuracy and uniformity. The range and exactitude of scientific prediction exceed any cleverness of everyday life: the scientist's use of language is strangely effective and powerful. Along with systematic observation, it is this peculiar use of language which distinguishes science from non-scientific behaviour.[14]

The curtness and severity at first described (and implicitly praised) is then (without any signaled shift) extended into something romantically potent by using the intensive "strangely" with "effective" and adding "powerful" as a larger parallel term for "effective." As a result of these shifts, when the word "peculiar" recurs in the next sentence its sense has expanded from that of "specific" to include that of "mysterious." The discourse is already beginning to undermine the positivism of the proferred argument. Bloomfield's attack on connotative language has recourse to unremarked, emotive metaphor which takes its power from the kind of language he represents himself as repudiating: "It is our task to discover which of our terms are undefined or partially defined or draggled with fringes of connotation, and to catch our hypotheses and exhibit them by clear statements, instead of letting them haunt us in the dark." The rapid succession and confluence of metaphors there—draggled fringes, hunter/collector, catching and exhibiting, the haunting night thoughts, hardly dispel the shamanistic linguistic world he seeks to escape. It is no wonder that he feels the need for "a redefinition of speech-forms" and asserts that "even number words like 'seven' and 'thirteen' have to be stripped of superstitious connotation" (p. 47).

To Bloomfield, the differences between languages "are merely part of the communicative dross." His own unaware linguistic practice reveals how even the most parsimonious thought process must depend for its stabilization on such "dross." The attempt to exclude it may (to pursue his own metaphor) result simply in an unstable and overmalleable ore, not a controlled discourse. Just as Max Müller, in the Victorian period, believed metaphor to be "a disease of language" and then transformed it into a mythic adversary, so Bloomfield and other positivist thinkers seeking to minimize language find themselves helplessly a party to such adversarial mythologizing. Historically, what such work makes clear is that the attempt to control levels of statement and description must depend more upon the agreement of a close professional community than upon rigorous linguistic exclusion. Not what is said, but the agreement as to constraints on its reception, will stabilize scientific discourse. Such stabilization will be temporary, and unagreed elements may later prove powerful.

Levels of Description

Steven Rose, Leon Kamin, and R. C. Lewontin give a helpful account of an important difficulty encountered within highly technical "descriptive" language: how to move levels openly and without implying that what holds good at one level of relations can be applied without scruple to another.

> Conventional scientific languages are quite successful when they are confined to descriptions and theories entirely within levels. It is relatively easy to describe the properties of atoms in the language of physics, of molecules in the language of chemistry, of cells in the language of biology. What is not so easy is to provide the translation rules for moving from one language to another. This is because as one moves up a level the properties of each larger whole are given not merely by the units of which it is composed but of the organising relations between them. . . . these organising relationships mean that properties of matter relevant at one level are just inapplicable at other levels. Genes cannot be selfish or angry or spiteful or homosexual, as these are attributes of wholes much more complex than genes: human organisms.[15]

The "quite successful" one-level language that Rose et al. here specify might be encountered in any number of *Nature*: a concentrated technical address to like-minded and similarly prepared readers, emphasizing specification of meaning and offering few means of entry to nonspecialists. The enclosing within a community is a necessary condition for assuring stable signification. The unreliable "amateur" reader is kept out and thereby, it is hoped, the range of other potential significations with which he or she may endow the scientist's parsimonious discourse. But, as Rose indicates, as soon as scientific writers move across levels of language and reference, the apparent autonomy and neutrality of description are shaken. One might add that the shared assumptions of the group begin to be visible. Indeed, the language he characterizes is very unlike that which we meet in Harvey or Lyell or Darwin or Clerk Maxwell.

Rose emphasizes that "the language to be used at any time is contingent on the purposes of the description; the muscle physiologist is interested in a different aspect of the question of the frog-muscle twitch from the ecologist or evolutionary biologist or biochemist; their difference of purpose should define the language of description used" (p. 282). Yet he also insists on the need for complementary description just as Waddington and Toulmin have done. Stephen Gould has gone farther and insisted, not only on the need for multilevel description, but on such description as endemic to any understanding of interactions

45

between levels of organization.[16] He sees this interaction across levels as essential to the evolutionary process. Gould's argument raises the question of how to describe such interaction without making the "individual" the normative unit of description, which would misleadingly reproduce in the theory assumptions embedded in the language available for description and at odds with his emphasis on free interaction without privileged levels. Rose is here, properly, emphasizing the need for scientists to clarify their purposes and to regulate their language in such a way that they make no hubristic or deterministic claims drawn from unanalyzed anthropomorphism. His account relies upon accord between writer and reader, what Toulmin in "The Construal of Reality" calls the "polis" of the scientific community.[17]

Description depends upon such accord since what is considered necessary to be described is culturally determined, as well as to some extent genre-determined. The stories of the culture, or "themata," as Gerald Holton calls them,[18] go largely *undescribed*: symmetry (see, for example, Richard Pearce's essay in the present volume), simplicity, development, hierarchy, chance (see David Bell's essay), provide models, ideals, and implied narratives in science as much as literature. If symmetry is the ideal of scientific elegance, it is likely to be extensively observed and studied; if simplicity is anticipated it will be found. But from time to time, such sequestered stories move out from beneath description into debate, as has recently been the case with work such as that of T. F. H. Allen and Thomas B. Starr on hierarchy.[19]

The apparent neutrality of description is the source of much of its authority; it is openly informative, but it is also more covertly predictive. Description stands *in place of* assertion and prediction and, as Thomas Kuhn remarks in *The Structure of Scientific Revolutions*, "there are important contexts in which the narrative and the descriptive are inextricably mixed."[20] Even more important, description works at an agreed *upper* level of specification, and ignores (and is often ignorant of) shared and unmarked assumptions. When we describe the taken-for-granted we change its status: "an old yellow car *on wheels*"; the last phrase is either redundant or crucial. This observation does not, of course, apply only to scientific discourse; it is powerful throughout literary language. Beckett gains many of his most disturbing effects by detailed recounting of reflex actions of the body usually left undescribed.

Empson's poem, "Doctrinal Point," observes precisely the false triumph of teleology in description. Describing becomes a form of designing and is used to infer design as inherent to the universe. Using metaphors from natural growth and development, the project of both scientist and poet becomes self-fulfilling. How can we distinguish design from description? How prevent "the Assumption of the description," since description creates its own transcendental level? Through the multiplying senses of *assumption* he shows this transformation at work.

The god approached dissolves into the air.

Magnolias, for instance, when in bud,
Are right in doing anything they can think of;
Free by predestination in the blood,
Saved by their own sap, shed for themselves,
Their texture can impose their architecture;
Their sapient matter is always already informed.

Whether they burgeon, massed wax flames, or flare
Plump spaced-out saints, in their gross prime, at prayer,
Or leave the sooted branches bare
To sag at tip from a sole blossom there
They know no act that will not make them fair.

Professor Eddington with the same insolence
Called all physics one tautology;
If you describe things with the right tensors
All law becomes the fact that they can be described with them;
This is the Assumption of the description.
The duality of choice becomes the singularity of existence;
The effort of virtue the unconsciousness of foreknowledge.[21]

"The Assumption" of the description raises into essence what began as account—and it presumingly, or "assumingly," uses its own "assumptions" as a means to authority without bringing them into question: so Empson suggests, in the caustic second verse of a poem which opens in sumptuous enjoyment of the aptness of the magnolia to its own performance, the perfect accord of possibility and purpose, form and information, sap and sapience.

Eddington had commented on the tendency of the mind to recover its own anticipated patterns from the universe, what Empson calls "tautology": "The mind has by its selective power filled the processes of Nature into a frame of law of a pattern largely of its own choosing; and in the discovery of this system of law the mind may be regarded as regaining from Nature that which the mind has put into nature."[22] Or, as Einstein suggests, "All concepts, even those which are closest to experience, are from the point of view of logic freely chosen conventions, just as is the case with the concept of causality."[23] Toulmin has recently emphasized that the loss of the detached spectator "out there" has been a characteristic movement in recent scientific thinking.[24]

This loss, while it may remove some of the dangers of "owning," further complicates and destabilizes the concept of description. If the observer is always necessarily a part of what he or she observes, no authoritative distance can be sustained. ("How describe the world seen without a self?" asks Virginia Woolf.) Etymologically, as Toulmin also observes, the word "theory" recalls the idea of the observer or symbolic representative since the *theoros* was the delegate sent by the city sage to consult the oracle. The loss of spectator status makes also for a loss of theoretical "space"; it leads to "implication" or folding in.

Darwin's sturdy sense of a thronging physical world only partly within the domain of human reason is further tempered in Einstein's essay on Clerk Maxwell in the collection perhaps riddlingly entitled *The World as I See It*: "The belief in an external world independent of the perceiving subject is the basis of natural science. Since, however, sense perception only gives information of this external world or of 'physical reality' indirectly, we can only grasp the latter by speculative means. It follows from this that our notions of physical reality can never be final."[25]

Umberto Eco, among others, has entered an important *caveat* on the question of "ingenuous transposition" from one field to another:

> Epistemological thinkers connected with quantum methodology have rightly warned against an ingenuous transposition of physical categories into the fields of ethics and psychology (for example, the identification of indeterminacy with moral freedom). . . . Hence it would not be justified to understand my formulation as analogy between the structures of the

work of art and the supposed structures of the world. Indeterminacy, complementarity, noncausality are not *modes of being* in the physical world, but *systems for describing it* in a convenient way.[26]

Scientists seek to delimit the application of their terms and respect the exigencies of their topic. But at the same time it is essential to recognize that any such containment of meaning will be local and temporary. It may allow a satisfactory completion of a phase of discussion and demonstration, but it cannot be held enclosed once it is read by other readers or in a different context of discussion. And this is not a matter of careless or ignorant reading by those outside the technical argument (though it may sometimes also be that); it is that the insurgency of signification, the perception of fresh relations, is inherent to all language—though most particularly to that intensified form of discourse which we call "literary language."

Literary language moves, often openly, and with great flexibility from level to level, achieving much of its intensity by means of allusion and connotation across levels. Such language opens out connections which technical discourses exclude from notice and, Rose suggests, at their most honest must abjure considering. The free and multiple movement across levels in literary language is its characteristic resource for discovery. As Waddington emphasized in *The Nature of Life*, for any adequate appraisal of complexity many kinds of description are needed.[27] An example of such unfolding, reconnecting, and enwebbing is to be found in the opening of Adrienne Rich's poem "Waking in the Dark":

> The thing that arrests me is
> how we are composed of molecules
>
> (he showed me the figure in the paving stones)
>
> arranged without our knowledge and consent
>
> > like the wirephoto composed
> > of millions of dots
>
> > in which the man from Bangladesh
> > walks starving
> > > on the front page
> > > knowing nothing about it
>
> which is his presence for the world[28]

The human body as "molecules," and the "millions of dots" which compose the newspaper photograph of the starving man, are both seen as part of an order which denies "our knowledge and consent." The shift from molecules to information suggests a congruity between them which does not need to be voiced. What *is* voiced is the sense of exposure and helplessness that the poet feels both in her arranged body and in her unwilled act of voyeurism, looking at the man starving "on the front page, knowing nothing about it." The human body is exposed, not only to a watcher out there, but in its predetermined composition irrelevant to will or individuality. She is "arrested"—imprisoned as well as startled. In the poem there lurks also a recognition that the starving man knows nothing of either the poem or its language, that print, as much as those other "millions of dots" of the wirephoto, cannot connect with the man's starvation. Knowledge is not solution; the power to perceive connections may itself be a trap which has no issue.

Construing and Predicting

The enterprises of scientist and of writer both act out the paradox that narrative implies teleology even when its argument denies it. The acknowledgment of the foreknown in the imprinting of writing; the process of discovery which has now become disclosure; the fact that the book ends (even when the argument of the ending is peremptory and unresolved): all this makes for an organization in which the future is already disposed, and is thus apparently under the control of the writer's description at least, if not of his free choosing. Narrative implies successful prediction. Greimas, indeed, argues that each semantic unit, each word, carries a potential narrative. So the "fisherman" implies all the possibilities of his employment:

> Le pêcheur porte en lui, évidemment, toutes les possibilités de son faire, tout ce que l'on peut s'attendre de lui en fait de comportement; sa mise en isotopie discursive en fait un rôle thématique utilisable par le récit.[29]

But he mitigates the apparent determinism of a single fixed narrative program by emphasizing that it is not until the last page of the narrative that "le personnage de roman . . . déploie sa figure complète . . . grâce à la mémorisation opérée par le lecteur."

Problems of Description in the Language of Discovery

The attempt to break out of a prediction-dominated narrative was one of the most important features of the French New Novel (Pinget's *Passacaille*, for example), and the attempt was strongly connected to a distrust of the anthropomorphism of language, particularly in the work of Robbe-Grillet.

In another work which allures the reader with a promise of a system, enigmatically disappointed, or enigmatically delayed, *The Crying of Lot 49*, Thomas Pynchon examines the problems of the observer, within the system or outside of it, and of the self-referential nature of any cyclic system. The heroine here is named deterministically but multiply. She is Oedipa Maas (Maze, Mass, Ma's). Instead of the traditional male scientist exploring a female "Nature," we are shown a woman exploring an information system dominated by male scientists, psychoanalysts, playwrights, and writers. The "maze" she enters turns out to be a closed system in which not only the topics but the materials of the writing are part of a sinister chain, economic, political, scientific, literary. Cigarette filters, and the ink with which the writer writes, the printer prints, are products of the bones of drowned and murdered men. Here, information theory, religious language, and entropy are overtly linked. (In a later essay N. Katherine Hayles will discuss the relationship between information theory and entropy that Pynchon exploits.) Clerk Maxwell becomes a kind of fairy godfather within the work; his concept of a "demon" which outplays the entropic system provides a counternotion of design (though one whose vagrancy is very different from the benign accord in the Maxwell essay quoted earlier.)

> "Entropy is a figure of speech, then," sighed Nefastis, "a metaphor. It connects the world of thermodynamics to the world of information flow. The Machine uses both. The Demon makes the metaphor not only verbally graceful, but also objectively true."
> "But what," she felt like some kind of heretic, "if the Demon exists only because the two equations look alike? Because of the metaphor?"
> Nefastis smiled; impenetrable, calm, a believer. "He existed for Clerk Maxwell long before the days of the metaphor."[30]

Coincidence proves—or seems—to be coded warning: "What, tonight, was chance?" Free invention, it appears, is no longer possible for scientist or writer:

51

How can you blame them for being maybe a little bitter? Look what's happening to them. In school they got brainwashed, like all of us, into believing the myth of the American Inventor—Morse and his telegraph, Bell and his telephone, Edison and his light bulb, Tom Swift and his this or that. Only one man per invention. Then when they grew up they found they had to sign all their rights to a monster like Yoyodyne; got stuck on some "project" or "task force" or "team" and started being ground into anonymity. Nobody wanted them to invent—only perform their little role in a design ritual, already set down for them in some procedures handbook. (pp. 63–64)

And yet at the book's conclusion there remains just the possibility of what Eddington calls "anti-chance," the cheater or demon in the system. Joseph Bertrand, the great mathematician, remarked that "Chance has neither consciousness nor memory": the specific powers of human intelligence are exactly those of consciousness and memory. The problem, common to scientists, poets, and other people, which Pynchon here disturbs is how to represent chance without knitting it into a language whose conditions inevitably imply teleology. The reader's eagerness to discover system is employed by Pynchon so that we zealously uncover multiple systems which will not accord: this systematic or asystematic dance becomes itself the narrative figuring of narrative's problem. The nature of discovery may be predetermined by the conditions for its description. The refusal to describe, as well as overdescription (as in the jammed plotting of the Jacobean tragedy), draws our attention to the designs implicit in construal and the predictions implicit in recounting.

Exchanges between Poets and Scientists

Scientific ideas and writing are often of most value within literature precisely where the risks of translation are great. We should not look for stable one-to-one correspondences between scientific exposition and literary creation. Works of art press on the uncontrolled implications of science, while new scientific ideas, theories, and products make it possible to articulate what has earlier been taken for granted (and therefore was not available to be recounted, so embedded was it in assumptions beneath the level of description). Sometimes the level of allusion vanishes again as scientific theories change.

Problems of Description in the Language of Discovery

New scientific and technical knowledge allows the poet to contemplate with fresh intensity intransigent questions which grip language in all generations. For example, the intervention of a new scientific meaning for a word poignantly marks the shifting of levels in Donne's "A Nocturnall upon S. Lucies Day. Being the Shortest Day" (first published in 1633). Subsequent changes in the signification of the word cluster "nocturnal" and "nocturne," as well as the disappearance of the object referred to, have disguised Donne's substantive meaning here. The most common form is and always has been adjectival, "of or pertaining to the night," as the *Oxford English Dictionary* puts it. So we speak of a "nocturnal animal." As a substantive the O.E.D. lists first, as obsolete and rare, the sense "a night-piece" and instances *only* the title of Donne's poem for this sense. The next, more substantial, listing, beginning in the seventeenth century (1627), is an "astronomical instrument adapted for taking observations by which to ascertain the hour of the night."

The poem is an act of mourning which takes place on the shortest day of the year (13 December, old style), that day when there would be most need to keep time's bearings in the dark. Lucy was the saint associated with light. The "nocturnall" was, when Donne wrote, a very recently invented instrument.

The poem opens:

> Tis the yeares midnight, and it is the dayes,
> *Lucies*, who scarce seaven houres herself unmaskes
> The Sunne is spent, and now his flasks
> Send forth light squibs, no constant rayes;
> The Worlds whole sap is sunke.

The poet mourns the death of a woman. The poem itself becomes the poet's "nocturnall," an instrument for telling the time, keeping his bearings as he moves through the darkness of grief.

> I am re-begot
> Of absence, darknesse, death; things which are not.

He is, yet, "Of the first nothing, the Elixer grown."

> But I am by her death, (which word wrongs her)
> Of the first nothing, the Elixer grown;

53

Were I a man, that I were one,
I needs must know; I should preferre,
If I were any beast,
Some ends, some means; Yea plants, yea stones detest
And love; All, all some properties invest;
If I an ordinary nothing were,
As shadow, a light, and body must be here.

Shadow implies light, but he is beyond all such renewal. Donne intensifies the expectation of the return of light and the coming of dawn by combining in his night-piece the new instrument, "the nocturnall," and an allusion backward to the old monastic form of service, matins, which took place at 3:00 A.M., long before dawn, and consisted of three "nocturns," each of which brought the hour nearer to the light. But within this poem day never returns, "nor will my Sunne renew." It ends:

Since shee enjoyes her long nights festivall,
Let mee prepare toward her, and let me call
This houre her Vigill, and her Eve, since this
Both the yeares, and the dayes deep midnight is.

(pp. 44–45)

The "nocturnall" becomes the poem's only measure. Since Donne's time, works like Chopin's "Nocturnes" and Whistler's "Nocturnes" have reinforced for the modern reader the idea of a dreamy impressionistic composition not at all in key with Donne's poem. Donne is never obscure or vague, though sometimes difficult when we do not know enough. Here, as elsewhere, he intensifies emotion by the tension between senses within a word and by bringing current scientific material into close relation with older world pictures.

Distrust of the simultaneity of reading levels distinguishes scientific discourse from the ideals of other forms of creative writing. The shifting of levels, which in scientific discourse may blur exact description, yet brings to our attention the excluded or taken-for-granted elements in the social language of theory. When they are writing outside the tight circle of fellow professionals, the best scientific communicators excel by using the possibilities of current literature. It is a commonplace that Freud used the techniques of Victorian narrative to structure his recounting (and perhaps they structured his understanding) of his case

54

histories, "The Wolf-Man" being the most discussed example. We can certainly measure the extent of that reliance on current literary reference if we set Freud's narratives against the postmodernist narrative form of D. W. Winnicott's case history, *The Piggle*.[31] But an equally remarkable congruity, at the level this time of style rather than of form, can be found in other fields than those of psychoanalysis, fields less obviously centered upon the human subject.

Take the passage below. Are we reading Virginia Woolf? Here not only the lucid description of hesitation, the combination of hyperbole and matter-of-fact statement, may lead us to believe that we are reading Woolf: there is also the matter of sentence length and of the paced gaps between the sentences. If we know her work well we are likely immediately to think across to the discourse of Rhoda in *The Waves*, standing always on the threshold, seeking the permanent; "Putting my foot to the ground I step gingerly and press my hand against the hard door of a Spanish inn":[32]

> I am standing on the threshold about to enter a room. It is a complicated business. In the first place I must shove against an atmosphere pressing with a force of fourteen pounds on every square inch of my body. I must make sure of landing on a plank travelling at twenty miles a second round the sun—a fraction of a second too early or too late, the plank would be miles away. I must do this whilst hanging from a round planet headed outward into space, and with a wind of aether blowing at no one knows how many miles a second through every interstice of my body. The plank has no solidity of substance. To step on it is like stepping on a swarm of flies. Shall I not slip through? No, if I make the venture one of the flies hits me and gives a boost up again; I fall again and am knocked upwards by another fly and so on. I may hope that the net result will be that I remain about steady; but if unfortunately I should slip through the floor or be boosted too violently up to the ceiling, the occurrence would be, not a violation of the laws of Nature, but a rare coincidence. (Eddington, p. 342)

Eddington's *The Nature of the Physical World*, from which this passage is taken, was written in 1927, giving him slightly the priority over *The Waves*. Virginia Woolf read Eddington, certainly. Did Eddington read Woolf? Very probably, although I know of no direct evidence. The congruity, however, has more than one significance: it demonstrates that ways of viewing the world are not constructed separately by scientists and poets; they share the moment's discourse. This particular instance, moreover, makes clear that we would be mistaken to read Virginia Woolf as an isolated sensibility, edged with madness, unaware of the movements of thought, the reshaping of the physical world, in her time. Her "waves" are also those of light, of time, of Einstein and Eddington:

> The progress of a wave is not progress of any material mass of water, but of a form which travels over the surface as the water heaves up and down. . . . These forms have a certain degree of permanence amid the shifting particles of water. Anything permanent tends to become dignified with the attribute of substantiality. . . . Ultimately it is this innate hunger for permanence in our minds which directs the course of development of hydrodynamics, and likewise directs the world-building out of the sixteen measures of structure. (Eddington, p. 242)

Virginia Woolf's achievement, like that of hydrodynamics, comes from the attempt to describe anew that hunger.

The "hunger for permanence" Eddington sees as another deluding constituent of the human imagination which leads us to discover in the universe the patterns that our minds have put there. The utmost resourcefulness and probity of language are needed, both by scientists and poets, to outwit the tendency of description to stabilize a foreknown world and to curtail discovery. Notwithstanding the requirement for precise expression of procedures and results, it becomes clear that—in the phase of experiment and again in the phase of communication—scientists need to have recourse to the linguistic dexterity, and sometimes even the instability of reference, with which literary language recognizes multiple simultaneous levels of event and meaning.

Notes

1. Laurence Sterne, *The Life and Opinions of Tristram Shandy, Gent.*, ed. G. Saintsbury (London, 1912), p. 136.

2. James Clerk Maxwell, "Molecules," *Nature* 8 (1873): 441. Collected in Noel G. Coley and Vance M. D. Hall, eds., *Darwin to Einstein: Primary Sources on Science and Belief* (London, 1980), p. 86.

3. William Wordsworth, *Lyrical Ballads* (1798–1805), ed. George Sampson (London, 1940), pp. 24–25.

Problems of Description in the Language of Discovery

4. Augustine Brannigan, *The Social Basis of Scientific Discoveries* (Cambridge, 1981), pp. 2–3.

5. Albert Einstein, "Autobiographical Notes," in P. A. Schilpp, ed., *Albert Einstein: Philosopher-Scientist*, Vol. 1, (London, 1970), pp. 45–47.

6. William Whewell, *The Philosophy of the Inductive Sciences* (London, 1840), 1: 113.

7. Claude Bernard, *Introduction à l'étude de la médècine expérimentale* (1865), ed. F. Dagognet (Paris, 1966), pp. 39–40.

8. Percy Bysshe Shelley, *The Complete Poetical Works*, ed. T. Hutchinson (Oxford, 1934), p. 10.

9. John Donne, *The Poems of John Donne*, ed. Herbert Grierson (Oxford, 1912), 1: 239.

10. Howard E. Gruber and Paul H. Barrett, *Darwin on Man: A Psychological Study of Scientific Creativity together with Darwin's Early Unpublished Notebooks* (London, 1971), pp. 455, 450.

11. John Tyndall, *Fragments of Science for Unscientific People* (London, 1868), 2: 92.

12. Charles Darwin, *The Origin of Species*, ed. John Burrow (Harmondsworth, 1968), p. 77.

13. Gillian Beer, *Darwin's Plots: Evolutionary Narrative in Darwin, George Eliot, and Nineteenth Century Fiction* (London, 1983).

14. Leonard Bloomfield, *Linguistic Aspects of Science, International Encyclopedia of Unified Science*, no. 4 (Chicago, 1939), pp. 1, 4.

15. Steven Rose, Leon Kamin, and R. C. Lewontin, *Not in Our Genes* (Harmondsworth, 1984), p. 278.

16. Stephen Jay Gould, "Darwinism and the Expansion of Evolutionary Theory," *Science* 216 (1982): 380–87.

17. Stephen Toulmin, "The Construal of Reality," in W. J. T. Mitchell, ed., *The Politics of Interpretation* (Chicago, 1982), pp. 99–117.

18. Gerald Holton, *The Thematic Origins of Scientific Thought* (Cambridge, Mass., 1973).

19. T. F. H. Allen and Thomas B. Starr, *Hierarchy: Perspectives for Ecological Complexity* (Chicago, 1982).

20. Thomas Kuhn, *The Structure of Scientific Revolutions*, 2d ed. (Chicago, 1970).

21. William Empson, *Collected Poems* (London, 1955), pp. 39–40. Empson's poem is collected in a useful anthology, *Poems of Science*, edited by John Heath-Stubbs and Phillips Salman, which in its chronological arrangement shows the changing common themes of science and literature, from Copernican cosmology to relativity theory.

22. Arthur Eddington, *The Nature of the Physical World* (Cambridge, 1928), p. 224.

23. Einstein, in Schilpp, ed., *Albert Einstein*, p. 13.

24. Stephen Toulmin, *The Return to Cosmology: Postmodern Science and the Theology of Nature* (Berkeley, 1982).

25. Albert Einstein, *The World as I See It* (London, 1935), p. 60.

26. Umberto Eco, *The Role of the Reader* (Bloomington, Ind., 1979), p. 66.

27. C. H. Waddington, *The Nature of Life* (London, 1961).

28. Adrienne Rich, *Poems, Selected and New, 1950–1974* (New York, 1975), p. 18.

29. Algirdas Julien Greimas, "Les actants, les acteurs et les figures," in Claude Chabrol, ed., *Sémiotique narrative et textuelle* (Paris: Larousse, 1973), p. 174.

30. Thomas Pynchon, *The Crying of Lot 49* (Harmondsworth, 1967), pp. 77–78.

31. D. W. Winicott, *The Piggle* (London, 1977).

32. Virginia Woolf, *The Waves* (New York, 1959), p. 319.

JAMES PARADIS

Montaigne, Boyle, and the Essay of Experience

Experience has not yet learned her letters.
—Bacon, *Novum Organum*

The scientific aspiration toward univocality, compromised by the need for an almost literary flexibility and dexterity of language, can be traced through the history of the essay form in which science sought a language of experience. Ironically, the literary form through which Michel de Montaigne sought to embody the self—the Cartesian center of experience—became also the form from which the self was expelled, and in which experience was depersonalized. Thus it was made available to a community of scientific specialists. Where Gillian Beer has suggested the necessity for science to speak with literary instabilities, this essay emphasizes the way in which "experience" split apart in literary and scientific texts; and it suggests that the literary form that came to embody scientific discourse helped shape the substance of science itself. —G.L.

Robert Boyle's "experimental essay," the literary instrument of scientific experimentalism, was an innovation of considerable importance in the history of letters. Attempting to free himself from literary tradition, in order to negotiate a new relationship between text and human experience, Boyle consciously modeled his essay after the French familiar essay.[1] Moving outside art and tradition in quest of a better fit between experience and text had been a prominent theme of Michel de Montaigne, who sought with his new *essai* to legitimize his own unprecedented subject matter, the self. In order to insulate his innovation from criticism, Montaigne claimed in his famous preface that his narcissistic efforts were but trifles: "Thus, reader, I am myself the matter of my book; you would be unreasonable to spend your leisure on so frivolous and vain a subject." Yet, even as he was calling attention to his own frivolity, Montaigne was challenging the accumulated wisdom newly

59

revealed in the humanistic literary revival and claiming for his own literary product powers no less than consubstantiality with his person.[2]

The attempt to authenticate versions of experience in literary trials, or *essais*, was an innovation most attractive to British scientific "trialists" like Robert Boyle, for reasons I wish to explore in this essay. In the familiar essay, as conceived and exploited by Montaigne, we find the self-conscious mind sifting through and reconstructing ordinary experience. Admitting its own low "domestic" subject matter, its tentativeness, and its narcissism, this prose form claims a private community for its audience. Its abbreviated structure reflects both a perspectivist world view, empirical in spirit and observational in method, and a skeptical despair of achieving any unified cosmological view. The kind of discursive informalism and ordinary subject matter epitomized by the French familiar essay had immense philosophical appeal for growing scientific interests in seventeenth-century England, which, Bacon had cautioned, would not succeed without a profound literary reform.

In his "Pröemial Essay, . . . with Some Considerations Touching Experimental Essays in General" (1661), a remarkable piece of literary strategy, Boyle seized upon the French essay as a form that would actively promote the experimentalist ideal of a demonstrative, atomistic discourse consistent with communal standards of verifiable knowledge. For Boyle, as for Montaigne, *essay* referred both to the literary form and to the speculative or experimental action itself. Hence, the literary strategies of Montaigne and Boyle were uniquely constitutive of their literary ends, for the text was held by both to summon forth the thing itself. For Montaigne, text became self, in an act of mimetic self-reconstitution; for Boyle, text became experimental action, in an act of material dramatization. In this parallelism, however, also lay a decisive literary divergence. For, in adapting the essay to the goals of the experimentalist, Boyle shifted its focus from the internal, psychological world of Montaigne's uniquely personal speculations to the external, physical world of replicable material process. In so doing, he transformed the self, a unique expressive intelligence in Montaigne's essay, into a passive instrument of observation, reporting on self-demonstrated material truths. Boyle's experimental essay thus became the literary expression, par excellence, of the motto of the Royal Society, *Nullius in Verba* (On the word of no man)—a literary nullification of the self, in virtue of its objectification in the text. This epistemological convention has long been a mainstay of two-literatures dualisms.

In its insistent perspectivism, the essay resolved the world into fragments of discourse. As experiential trial, pass, run, it became both literary instrument and emblem of the philosophical abandonment of a cosmological truth of final ends. Textual informality asserted an epistemology that responded to a naturalistic world of illusion, inconsistency, and incompleteness, as explored, for example, in Montaigne's influential Pyrrhonist essay "The Apology for Raymond Sebond." The same admission of human limits was converted to method in the philosophical skepticism of Descartes's *Discourse on Method*, just as it motivated that Baconian project, framed in the *Novum Organum*, of the redemption of nature. Literary strategy attempted to subordinate mind to the data of experience, in a literature of perspectives, where particulate, informal texts sought new equivalencies with concrete experience. This effort to make text assume the contours of experience seems to have been driven by the idea that we can, through the literary reconstruction of the world, attain a new image of the world beyond the phenomenological reach of the individual mind. In what follows, I explore some of the factors that, between the appearance of Montaigne's *Essais* (1580) and Henry Oldenburg's *Philosophical Transactions* (1665), helped to create this new literary concept of experience-as-text. I examine ways in which this elaborating power of the experiential text became an indispensable part of seventeenth-century experimentalist strategy, deflecting, in the process, the literature of science from traditional literary forms.

Montaigne's Perspectivism

The intellectual crisis of sixteenth-century France, precipitated by forces as diverse as the religious wars, the humanist revival of knowledge, and the spread of print technology, found expression in Montaigne's revival of the Greek skepticism of Sextus Empiricus.[3] In "The Apology for Raymond Sebond," Montaigne's doubts about the sufficiency of human knowledge rested on naturalistic rather than religious grounds. He questioned the ability of the human sensory apparatus to construct a world of facts, upon which the reason might support itself. Montaigne's skepticism conceived a literary reticence and indefiniteness that greatly contrasted with the robust a priori thinking of the Academy and the Church. "I put forward formless and unresolved notions," he observed in Book I, nodding with respectful irony to the *absolute* authority of the Church, "as do those who publish doubtful questions to debate in the schools, not to establish the truth but to seek it."[4] Essays were but notions in search of truth and were humbly written in counterpoint to the certainties of the Church. But Montaigne's humility, maintained throughout the *Essais*, contrasted markedly with his claim that his prose had the power to create an authentic, realistic self.[5]

Montaigne's ambition as a literary strategist is immediately apparent in the 1580 Preface to the *Essais*, where he initiates a strain of metadiscourse that throughout the work interprets for his readers the methods and intentions of his essays. He contrasts his work not just to a priori thought and dogma, but also to art itself. This distinction between art and reality, between artistic self-aggrandizement and domestic indifference, is pursued throughout the work and becomes the basis of his famous claim to consubstantiality with his book.

> If I had written to seek the world's favor, I should have bedecked myself better, and should present myself in a studied posture. I want to be seen here in my simple, natural, ordinary fashion, without straining or artifice; for it is myself that I portray. My defects will here be read to the life, and also my natural form, as far as respect for the public has allowed. . . .
>
> Thus, reader, I am myself the matter of my book; you would be unreasonable to spend your leisure on so frivolous and vain a subject. (*Complete Works of Montaigne*, p. 2)

In thus rejecting artifice and dedicating himself to "naked form," Montaigne articulates a theory of realism that equates truth with ordinary, unmediated fact. Not only does he deny his own artistic intention, but he claims for the low style, given to domestic detail, a superior ability to create an authentic image of life itself. His commitment to reconstructing facts deemphasizes such internalist or stylistic priorities as rhetorical balance, fullness, or logical consistency. Praise of his style becomes the slighting of his substance (*CWM*, p. 185). Rejecting the "studied posture," indeed, all conscious artifice, Montaigne claims the recreation of his real self in virtue of his radical subordination of text to experience. In dissolving the conventions of artifice, Montaigne in a stroke asserts the primacy of subject matter and his claim to mimesis.[6]

The subordination of the text to its subject matter is negotiated by the perspectivism inherent in essay brevity and formlessness. These characteristics of informality enable the essay to assume the contours of experience as perceived imperfectly by the senses. Self-contradiction and tentativeness are inevitable. The mind, unable to find firm ground, is destined to exercise itself in trials.

> My history needs to be adapted to the moment. I may presently change, not only by chance, but also by intention. This is a record of various and changeable occurrences, and of irresolute and, when it so befalls, contradictory ideas: whether I am different myself, or whether I take hold of my subjects in different circumstances and aspects. So, all in all, I may indeed contradict myself now and then; but truth, as Demades said, I do not contradict. If my mind could gain a firm footing, I would not make essays, I would make decisions; but it is always in apprenticeship and on trial. (*CWM*, p. 611)

This effort to reflect the flux of things precludes the sustained unfolding of a unified reality. In the world of human experience, unity and certitude are illusory.

Montaigne's vision of things in motion is fully congruous with the dynamism of an emerging scientific world view. In language worthy, as Basil Willey has noted,[7] of an eighteenth-century naturalist, Montaigne observes: "The world is but a perennial movement. All things in it are in constant motion—the earth, the rocks of the Caucasus, the pyramids of Egypt—both with the common motion and with their own. Stability itself is nothing but a more languid motion" (*CWM,*.p. 611). Essay form negotiates this reality by dissolving mind-forged unities into a loose confederation of conflicting concepts and objects. We witness this broken world by subordinating ourselves to the detail and impermanence of Montaigne's experience, as rendered in the atomized text of his perspectivism. Essay informality provides a means to loosen the grand unities of philosophy, art, and mental state.

The philosophical basis of Montaigne's perspectivism resides in the formidable limitations of human reason and sensory apparatus explored in "The Apology for Raymond Sebond." The human senses,

63

more gross than those of the beasts, distort experience itself and, so, the framework of the human understanding. So subjective is sensation that it intermingles reality with personal conditions—"The jaded man assigns the insipidity to the wine; the healthy man, the savor; the thirsty man, the relish" (*CWM*, p. 453). The mixing of fact and personal circumstance supports at once Montaigne's claim to consubstantiality with his text, and his challenge to human knowledge.

> Now, since our condition accommodates things to itself and transforms them according to itself, we no longer know what things are in truth; for nothing comes to us except falsified and altered by our senses. When the compass, the square, and the ruler are off, all the proportions drawn from them, all the buildings erected by their measure, are also necessarily imperfect and defective. The uncertainty of our senses makes everything they produce uncertain . . . (*CWM*, p. 453)

This attack on the integrity of sense experience underscores the limitations of the reason, the manipulator of sensory data, but it also delivers to the mechanisms of instruments the crucial role of simplifying the demands made on sense perception. Instrumentation, emblem of human impotence, is installed at the foundation of Montaigne's own motto *Que sçay-je?* which is "inscribed over a pair of scales" (*CWM*, p. 393).

Much as Montaigne challenges the possibility of knowledge, he also rejects the total skepticism of the Pyrrhonists, who "use their arguments and their reason only to ruin the apparent facts of experience; . . . they demonstrate that we do not move, that we do not speak, that there is no weight or heat . . ." (*CWM*, p. 430; see also p. 817). Reason may be the "two-handled pot, that can be grasped by the left or the right," but it can be disciplined. "In study, as in everything else," Montaigne argues, "[the mind's] steps must be counted and regulated for it; the limits of the chase must be artificially determined for it" (*CWM*, p. 419). Self-scrutiny locates the flawed being and inaugurates the relativistic climb through fact to a limited knowledge of experience.

This skepticism drives Montaigne toward a physicalism of materialist proportions, lodged in the concreteness of experience. Like his physician-progenitor, Sextus Empiricus, Montaigne views experience as antidote to dogma: "I had rather follow facts than reason." Thus, Montaigne's themes return to the fundamental experiental act, self-observation. Within these "fricassees" of domestic, prosaic selfhood, we find the driving spirit of specialist detail: "No man ever treated a subject he knew and understood better than I do the subject I have undertaken . . . no man ever penetrated more deeply into his material or plucked its limbs and consequences cleaner, or reached more accurately and fully the goal he had set for his work" (*CWM*, p. 612). This exploration of the concreteness and particularity of the self, Erich Auerbach once noted, proceeds by "tests upon one's self" so rigorous and concrete that they constitute "a strictly experimental method."[8] Such experiential departures are later formalized by Descartes in the assertion that knowledge must begin with a close scrutiny of the self. For Montaigne, this self-consciousness sustains itself in a series of textual perspectives devoted to the act of his own becoming.

In "Of Experience," the last essay of Book III, Montaigne traces man's confusion partly to the artificiality of language itself. The formal discourse of the Academy provides a striking contrast to Montaigne's own informal language; yet the ordered world of the academician's categories is ultimately isolated from life itself.

> Our disputes are purely verbal. I ask what is "nature," "pleasure," "circle," "substitution." The question is one of words, and is answered in the same way. "A stone is a body." But if you pressed on: "And what is a body?"—"Substance."—"And what is substance?" and so on, you would finally drive the respondent to the end of his lexicon. We exchange one word for another word, often more unknown. (*CWM*, p. 819)

These constructs of the mind are inflated verbal artifacts with little basis in experience. The philosophers who refer men to "the rules of Nature" are suspect, for they deliver to men "the face of nature painted in too high a color" (*CWM*, p. 822). For Montaigne, experience, the pathway to self-knowledge, finds its most authentic expression in the empirical knowledge associated with medicine: "Experience is really on its own dunghill in the subject of medicine, where reason yields it the whole field" (*CWM*, p. 826). Not only is empiric an episodic, utilitarian form of knowledge, but its insights are gleaned through interaction of the body with a world of objects and events. If the individual that Montaigne creates for his audience is weak and confused, he is also recognizable. Indeed, so compromising is this self-image that we can not doubt that Montaigne has located generic man.

In medical knowledge, the perspective is established by an episode and its circumstances, which may or may not recur. Bodily experience gives rise to medical practice, whose generalizations seek a balanced relationship between physical experience and human reason. Because one's physical condition is impressed in concrete sensory terms on one's own physical being, it is difficult to dispute. The patient is less vulnerable than the rest of us to the real physical risk of careless hypothesizing and dogmatizing. In medicine, the experience of the body is absolute, the body becoming its own instrument, a physical framework that delimits the material phenomenon. If Montaigne's skepticism achieved severe, sometimes acataleptic proportions, his narcissistic cult of the self also used the process of human self-scrutiny as the basis for making new claims about the powers of text to reconstitute the subject matter of experience.[9] In Montaigne's self-conscious exploration of a deeper, more complex self, we find a vigorous empiricism—an accumulation of fact under protest that the apparatus transacting the scrutiny is flawed.

The Literature of Prosthesis

Montaigne's sustained program of self-examination evoked the limits and possibilities of the senses and reason in detail fully reinforced by the epistemological drift of seventeenth-century natural philosophy. We see this drift in a different dimension in Francis Bacon's *Novum Organum*, whose fundamentalist Doctrine of the Idols was inspired by a Puritan vision of innate human frailty that quite matched the Pyrrhonism of Montaigne's own mimetic quest.[10] Montaigne, however, had acquiesced in man's limited ability to erect an extensive positive knowledge. Bacon transformed that acquiescence into a principle of purification, the origin of the radicalism Joseph Agassi has held to be Bacon's central idea: presume nothing, collect all the available evidence, and let the facts lead you to the formation of generalizations.[11] This principle applied both to systems of knowledge and to each particular instance, making the experiment, as phenomenological *trial*, the symbol of knowledge in the new organon.

That Bacon associated intellectual revolution with his years as the young attaché to the British embassy in Paris (1576–79) is seen in his setting of the anti-Aristotelian orations *Cogitata et Visa* (1607–9) and *Redargutio Philosophiarum* (1608) in Paris. Preludes to the *Novum Organum*, these works displayed the fundamentalist fervor of Bacon's Puritan upbringing: works (and texts) are instruments of truth and revolution. "It is by the witness of works rather than by logic or even observation," he wrote, "that truth is revealed and established."[12] Because that witness is to be negotiated in texts, Bacon's radicalism demands a textual revolution by means of which knowledge, as based on the relationships of material to mental phenomena, could be liberated from the traditionalism of academic education and exposed to the criticism of adepts. Pushing beyond the quiet revolution of Montaigne, Bacon envisioned a public knowledge of works, whose ultimate object was the society of transformations projected in *The New Atlantis*.[13]

Bacon's radicalism, like Montaigne's skepticism, was conceived in part as a literary reform. The witnessing of nature was to be carried out by transforming it into text and, thus, opening it to public inquiry or exegesis. In his "Aphorisms on the Composition of the Primary History," Bacon holds that the composer should faithfully relate more subtle experiments, so that "men may be free to judge for themselves whether the information obtained from that experiment be trustworthy or fallacious. . . ."[14]

> This book of nature is conceived as a metaphor of scripture itself: If in any statement there be anything doubtful or questionable, I would by no means have it suppressed or passed in silence, but plainly and perspicuously set down by way of note or admonition. For I want this primary history to be compiled with a most religious care, as if every particular were stated upon oath, seeing that it is the book of God's works and (so far as the majesty of heavenly may be compared with the humbleness of earthly things) a kind of second Scripture. (*Works of Francis Bacon*, 8:368–69)

Bacon's metaphorical linking of the scientific text to Scripture reveals the purifying function of his new organon. Like Scripture, natural history witnesses the works of God. But if natural history is the second Scripture, it must, without the assistance of divine intervention, locate and purge human imperfections. For the human element, insofar as it mingles itself with this text, compromises it. Scriptural truth descends through the divinely inspired scribe; primary or natural history must ascend to its perfection by degrees through self-correcting human works.

Bacon's attack on scholastic and Aristotelian science took a skeptical view of sense perception and reason nearly identical to that of Montaigne (Willey, pp. 40–42, 93). But where Montaigne exploited human limitations to construct a realism of the self, Bacon argued the need to compensate for the senses by artificially extending their reach and simplifying their labors. Thus we are introduced to the idea of prosthetic correction. Experiment and text are props to the infirm body we find in Montaigne's "Of Experience." By such means, we may construct a physical nature in text that no individual could deliver.

> For the sense by itself is a thing infirm and erring; neither can instruments for enlarging or sharpening the senses do much; but all truer kind of interpretation of nature is effected by instances and experiments fit and apposite; wherein the sense decides touching the experiment only, and the experiment touching the point in nature and the thing itself. (WFB, 8:83)

This subordination of the sensory apparatus to experiment lowers the status of the sensorium, casting doubt on the immediate disclosures of sense experience. Man is sick. Bacon summons "helps for the sense—substitutes to supply its failures, rectification to correct its errors" (WFB, 21:267). Experiment compensates for human infirmity by supporting the sensory apparatus. "I do not take away authority from the senses," Bacon argues, "but supply them with helps; I do not slight the understanding, but govern it" (WFB, 8:158). Instrument and experiment thus become material extensions of mind, and a framework of mechanics now helps to define the field upon which the senses and understanding may legitimately operate.

For Bacon, literary strategy is an essential part of this program to retrieve a true image of nature. He argues: "I am building in the human understanding a true model of the world, such as it is in fact, not such as a man's own reason would have it to be; a thing which cannot be done without a very diligent dissection and anatomy of the world" (WFB, 8:113). By converting nature to text through the witness of experiments, the natural philosopher accumulates a primary history that can be interpreted and improved. Textual exegesis offers to the adept the opportunity to manipulate facts in the so-called method of experience, wherein "experience duly ordered and digested" is drawn out into axioms, which lead to new experiments, "even as it was not without order and method that the divine work operated on the created mass" (*WFB*, 8:115).

These literary manipulations demand our "submitting [the] mind to things" and seeking in the literary product the shape of the thing itself (*WFB*, 8:145). Such a priority has a fragmenting, disintegrating thrust— against ornamental metaphor, against humanistic synthesis, against philology:

> First, then, away with antiquities, and citations, or testimonies of authors, and also with disputes and controversies and differing opinions— everything, in short, which is philological. . . . And for all that concerns ornaments of speech, similitude, treasury of eloquence, and such like emptinesses, let it be utterly dismissed. Also let all those things which are admitted be themselves set down briefly and concisely, so that they may be nothing less than words. For no man who is collecting and storing up materials for ship building or the like, thinks of arranging them elegantly, as in a shop, and displaying them so as to please the eye; all his care is that they be sound and good, and that they be arranged so as to take up as little room as possible in the warehouse. (*WFB*, 8:359)

Notwithstanding his own stylistic exuberance, Bacon advocates purging natural philosophy and its language of human idiosyncrasy and personal signatures. Style assumes functional aspirations.[15] Bacon's metaphor, the warehouse, reflects the stylistic object of the new literary enterprise to purge self from text, and the structural object to dismantle the received systems and store what remains in a literature of elements and parts. Literary product thus becomes a means to unidentified future ends and no end in itself. This deferment fundamentally alters our relationship with text by presenting us with a fragment of discourse whose ultimate purpose remains, as yet, undisclosed.

Bacon thus takes a perspectivist's view of literary function as the experiential dismantling of received systems. He prefers the approach of Democritus, who, abjuring final causes in his pursuit of natural knowledge, "did not suppose a mind or reason in the frame of things" (*WFB*, 6:224). Bacon's concept of essay form, however, derived little from Montaigne's, which Bacon did not consider an innovation.[16] Few essayists differ more from one another: where Montaigne is tentative, concerned with process, stylistically familiar, Bacon is didactic, reasoned, and pregnantly sententious.[17] For natural philosophy, he advocates the use of a combined literary strategy of concentrated aphorisms alternating with extended primary (natural) histories. Where aphorisms, "representing only portions and fragments of knowledge, [and] invit[ing] others to contribute," break up systems of knowledge, experimental histories collect the fragments together to "take in the image of the world as it is in fact" (*WFB*, 8:361; 9:125). This alternation between fragmented knowledge and historical synthesis was to become one of the primary rhythms of natural philosophical discourse.

Montaigne seeks the mimetic reconstitution of the self by incorporating his very personality, including imperfections, into the text; Bacon demands the isolation of the self from the text, because the individual who mingles self with observation distorts the image of the world (*WFB*, 8:77). Bacon seeks a parity between text and a clarified experience in a verisimilitude fully as ambitious as Montaigne's mimesis. For Bacon, the human senses are supported and circumscribed in the interests of this experiential clarity with experimental correctives that isolate the self from the physical world.[18] Montaigne's acquiescence turns to celebration as he extracts an essential truth from the human condition: man cannot separate his mind from his body, his sensual operations from his environment. For Montaigne, to be human is to perceive the world in a manner unique to the individual; identity is contoured with one's own distortions and irregularities. The Baconian suppression of self in the pursuit of natural knowledge seeks something quite different: to understand the properties of matter in the terms of motion.[19]

Natural knowledge becomes in Bacon's view a communal product. We see the implications of Bacon's literary reforms in the institutionalized knowledge production of Solomon's House in the *New Atlantis*. Institutional structure supports a self-conscious methodology for collecting and generating knowledge in the same spirit that the exegetical, interpretive community of the religious society "operates" on received text. The seekers of Solomon's House are engaged in a program of literary production, in which some thirty-three individuals collect texts from abroad, produce experiments, and recombine these into new texts. This literary enterprise had few precedents, save for the great collaborative effort of fifty-four Jacobean scholars and translators at

Hampton Court that, beginning in 1604, produced the King James Bible in 1611. The communal effort envisioned by Bacon is likewise driven by a desire to realize the truths of God. But this second Scripture is purified knowledge, rid of its sensory misapprehension as the result of the disciplined trials and consensus of the communal whole.

The "Experimental Essay"

That the natural world, a world in flux, could not be circumscribed by human senses was a theme by no means unique to Bacon. Renaissance natural philosophy consistently undermined the unity of appearance and reality by demonstrating the relativity of sense experience. What more profound ambiguity could be imagined than a Copernican earth that, contrary to all immediate sensory impressions, *moved*. Montaigne cited Copernicus against Aristotle as an instance of cosmological relativity, observing, moreover, that "Copernicus has grounded this doctrine so well that he uses it very systematically for all astronomical deductions" (*CWM*, p. 429). "What letters-patent," he asked, "have [Aristotle's principles], what special privilege, that the course of our invention stops at them?" Within the next generation, Kepler had published *De Stella Nova* (1606) on the appearance of a new star in the supposedly "immutable" region of the fixed stars, and Galileo, in his widely disseminated *Sidereus Nuncius* (1610), had disclosed a mass of stars, an irregularly shaped lunar landscape, and four moons of Jupiter, existing beyond the reach of the naked senses.[20] These challenges to the closed cosmology of classical thought raised doubts about the integrity of unaided sense experience and demanded a means of disentangling the perceiver's intuitions from the circumstances of the thing perceived.[21]

In Galileo's *Dialogue Concerning the Two Chief World Systems* (1632) and his *Dialogues Concerning Two New Sciences* (1638), material illustration—beams, weights, ropes, hooks, and the like—supplies the occasional simplified sensory analogue to geometrical generalizations of physical phenomena.[22] Although not vigorously experimentalist, Galileo's work was based on material phenomena which could be characterized at a simplified sensory level by mechanical motion and measurement and at a theoretical level by geometrical, often highly Platonic, idealizations removed from the immediate realm of the senses.[23] The material trend in demonstration was pushed toward a new experimentalism by Robert Boyle, who between the ages of twelve and seventeen (1639–44) had studied in Europe, acquired a native fluency in French, and become a convert to Galileo's thought. Boyle had been in Florence studying "the new paradoxes of the great star-gazer" during the winter of Galileo's death, 1641–42.[24] Established in English circles of experimental philosophy a decade later, Boyle sought literary reforms that went beyond those advocated by Bacon: new forms of philosophical argument that would diminish the role of abstract argumentation, forms based on the demonstrative experience.

Boyle argued, in his "Pröemial Essay . . . Touching Experimental Essays in General," that "experimental essays," modeled on the French familiar essay, could unify the literary trial of the essay form with the material trial of experimental operation. In this new model of discourse, literary form would encode sense experience in such a way that the experience could be reconverted from text to its original physical terms. Text was thus to assume an unprecedented claim to material verisimilitude as a new instrument of Baconian reform.[25]

Noting the "usefulness of writing books of essays, in comparison to that of writing systematically" (*Works of Robert Boyle*, 1:302), Boyle advocated essay economy for precisely the reason that Descartes argued that truth was to be discovered by degrees.[26] Essay perspectivism imposed discipline on potential system builders, who like Aristotle

> have found themselves, by the nature of their undertaking, and the laws of method, engaged to write of several other things than those, wherein they had made themselves proficients; and thereby have been reduced, either idly to repeat what has been already. . . . written by others on the same subject; or else, to say anything on them rather than nothing, lest they should appear not to have said something to every part of the theme. (*WRB*, 1:300)

The literary pursuit of complete, balanced systems, Boyle observed, drives the process of fanciful abstraction, thus corrupting the development and transmission of knowledge. The obligations of writing the grand text so overwhelm the "few peculiar notions or discoveries of [one's] own," that a finding "which would have made an excellent and substantial essay, passes for a dull and empty book" (*WRB*, 1:301).

In adapting the French familiar essay, Boyle promotes the same spirit of perspectivism that, as we have seen, was central to Montaigne's theory of the essay. Although he does not mention Montaigne by name, Boyle, a student of contemporary French culture, would have been on intimate terms with Montaigne's essays.[27] For Boyle, the literary product in natural philosophy is vastly unequal to the immensity of physical phenomena. The experimental essay can be but a *trial*, a particle of truth. In his "The History of Fluidity and Firmness," a three-part comparative study of the physical states of liquids and solids from the prospect of the corpuscular theory, Boyle "invite[s] abler pens to contribute their observations towards the compleating of what he is sensible he has but begun; . . . because he may hereafter if God permit, do something of that kind himself" (*WRB*, 1:377; see also *DM*, p. 128). This Baconian admission of incompleteness leaves experimentalist discourse in transit between the known and the unknown. The literary product ceases to be a stable, enduring entity, because it is written with the understanding that it will be superseded. Literary production becomes, as Bacon and Descartes had advocated, a collective effort motivated by the notion of intellectual frontiers (*DM*, p. 120). Essay form thus instantiates the pervasive atomism of Boyle's progressivist epistemology.

In spite of a legendary prolixity, celebrated by Swift in "A Meditation upon a Broomstick," Boyle's corpus of more than forty scientific and religious volumes and thirty-six papers in the *Philosophical Transactions* was among the most prestigious and widely-recognized sources of British experimentalism and physico-theology.[28] The scientific works were all essay compilations that Boyle variously labeled *histories, meditations, tracts, dialogues, reflections, memoirs, considerations, notes, accounts, discourses, experiments, observations, paradoxes, letters,* and *essays.* Boyle's essay format varied considerably with subject matter and intent. The early *Sceptical Chymist* (1661) takes a dialogue form, rambling from topic to topic in a manner reminiscent of Montaigne's loose essay structure and Galileo's *Dialogo.* Set in the garden of Carneades, an experimentalist, Boyle's discourse invokes material exemplification to illustrate the many inconsistencies between, on the one hand, peripatetic and Paracelsian systems of elements and principles and, on the other, simple demonstrable sense phenomena.[29] The discourses in the *Sceptical Chymist* are not true dialogues, but rather critical essays by

73

authors who hold different views concerning a given phenomenon, such as burning. We thus see the workings of the multifaceted human reason that Montaigne had in "The Apology" called the "two-handled pot, that can be grasped by the left or the right." Each dialogue voice has its perspective that, in the cycle of short essays, contributes to the communal construction of a subject matter. This same exercising of theoretical debates in extended essay-dialogues, exploited three years later by Dryden in the brilliantly executed *Essay of Dramatic Poesy*, introduces modern critical method into text. Hence, in a literature of contraries, theory contends with theory, practice with practice, in forms of civil discourse that manifest the ideal of rational decision making.[30] Essay trialist spirit animates a progressive discourse.

We see the disintegrative power of Boyle's skepticism formidably applied to the material world in *The Sceptical Chymist*, which is made up of three extended dialogues and five essay appendices. Carneades, with occasional references to "Mr. Boyle," attacks peripatetic theories of the four elements, as well as more recent Paracelsian doctrines of the three principles—salt, sulphur, and mercury—by juxtaposing them with the controlled experiences of experiment. He asserts, for example, that fire cannot be the "universal resolver of bodies," because treatments of wood by different intensities of fire can be shown to produce different products. Burning can be shown to resolve soap not into its source substances but into entirely new ones. The object of this treatise is to promote a corpuscular or particulate theory of material quality by establishing the primacy of number over essence, of quantity over quality (*WRB*. 1:115–16).[31] Referring to hundreds of demonstrable examples, Carneades pummels theories of essence by showing how sensory experience, disciplined by the terms of controlled experiment, reveals the vast, fanciful, and inconsistent texture of a classical chemistry of essences.

In its purer form, Boyle's scientific essay is found in such compilations as the famous *New Experiments, Physico-Mechanical, Touching the Spring of Air* (1661); *Experiments and Considerations Touching Colours* (1664); and his *Certain Hydrostatical Paradoxes* (1666). In these works, the essay assumes a more formal, idealized, and austere structure. Boyle frequently refers to these essays as "paradoxes," by which he usually means a sensory phenomenon with two interpretations. In most instances, the competing explanations behind the paradoxes are based on conflicting theories of essence and mechanics. The object of the essay then becomes to dismantle the paradox with the assistance of experimental action and the reasoned weighing of its resultant controlled sensory data.

Each of the two first experiments of Boyle's *Hydrostatical Paradoxes* is reported in a sequence that begins with propositions or hypotheses; is followed by discussions of theoretical implications; and is concluded with experiment. Stripped of all but a narrow range of detail, these essays are severely regulated to the testimonial support of their propositions. They are not inductivist in the pure Baconian sense of unbiased observation; rather they test stated hypotheses. The first essay, "paradox," proposes "That in water, and other fluids, the lower parts are pressed by the upper" (*WRB*, 1:750). After discussing the physical arrangements of apparatus, Boyle proceeds to demonstrate his proposition with a simple apparatus consisting of a long open glass tube filled with oil, which the experimenter immerses in a jar of water. The oil level in the tube sinks to a position of equilibrium with the water partway down the tube, allowing Boyle to establish its pressure "aequilibrium" along an "imaginary" line drawn where the oil column rests on the water. Boyle's essay is written entirely in reference to an illustration of the physical apparatus, and verbally manipulates the image through well over two-thirds of the text. Paradox I is followed unceremoniously by Paradox II, which proposes its reverse: "That a lighter liquor may gravitate or weigh upon a heavier." Boyle notes that many adepts reject this proposition on the visual evidence "that a lighter liquor (or other body) being environed with a heavier, will not fall down, but emerge to the top: whence they conclude, that, it is not to be concluded as a heavy, but as a light body" (*WRB*, 1:754). He rejects this explanation as a theory of heavy and light essences and argues that heaviness and lightness of liquids are relative, not absolute, qualities. All liquids have "absolute gravity" or weight. He again proceeds to the experimental demonstration of his argument by verbally manipulating a visual figure to show that certain operations on the physical apparatus will cause the lighter liquid to exert pressure on the heavier liquid.

Boyle's privileging of physical process in these and hundreds of similar essays radically materializes experience. Called by Boyle "examining by experience," the experimental essay is a rigidly controlled idealization of narrative in which experience is transformed into procedural protocol, individual opinion is sequestered from physical facts, and a formal logical flow is imposed upon the text. By such means, the idiosyncratic, personalized self is made thoroughly incidental and thus removed from the text.[32] Experimental demonstration, carried out in the text, makes human experience portable and measurable, freeing it from its spatial and temporal dependency in a manner quite different from the mathematical rarefactions of Descartes and Galileo.[33] Such is the ideal, although, as Boyle notes in the preface to his *New Experiments and Observations Touching Cold* (1665), some of his experiments have not been completed, for lack of resources or conditions (*WRB*, 2:471–73). The experimental apparatus of the *Hydrostatical Paradoxes* is accurately illustrated for us, so that we may recreate and manipulate it to achieve the very physical effects described in the text. This curious literary manufacture of phenomenological experience is the object of Boyle's experimental essay.

In his preface to *Hydrostatical Paradoxes*, Boyle distinguishes his experiential approach from the mathematical and geometrical methods of demonstration associated with Cartesian and Galilean idealization (*WRB*, 2:740–42). He criticizes Blaise Pascal for introducing, in his *Hydrostatics*, experimental substantiation that unrealistically requires an individual to sit under twenty feet of water, holding an immense glass tube that no contemporary craftsman could possibly construct.[34] Boyle's experimentalism is thus a theory of realism, in which the phenomenological incident that replicates in experiment counteracts the essential abstractness of text. This variation of Montaigne's theories of the consubstantiality of text and its subject matter is achieved by Boyle in the manipulating of object equivalents, summoned forth in the text. In his experiments, Boyle creates an "active" knowledge of praxis that certifies his own reason-driven universe of predictable physical actions.

There is a relentless driving out of quality from things in Boyle's scientific discourse.[35] In his mechanistic *The Origin of Forms and Qualities According to the Corpuscular Philosophy* (1666), Boyle argues that all essences ultimately can be traced to configurations of particles (*WRB*, 3:1ff.). Qualities and fluxes of sense experience should be converted wherever possible, he argues, to terms of matter and motion. This drive to diminish the authority of descriptive language by denying the status of fact to the sense-determined qualities—color, sound, touch, smell—threatens, although it does not achieve, the destruction of sensuous essences pursued in much figurative language. Boyle's programmatic diminishment of the subtleties of descriptive language sets limits upon the textual manipulation of material objects and introduces a new restrictive attitude to language.

The experiential repetition achieved in experiment seeks to remove accident and personality from the argument of the text. Citing Harvey's anatomical work, Boyle demonstrates how repetition overcomes accident by relating his own experience of cutting a nerve in several places (*WRB*, 1:343–44). After each cut, a drop of red blood emerges, demonstrating that the blood is an integral part of the nerve. Such repetition relegates the senses to the role of discriminating *iteration*, rather than of elaborating new descriptive matrices. The senses are held to the mechanical terms of the discourse established by the apparatus and its relation to its subject. The sensorium is thus called upon to make crude generic distinctions, rigidly conditioned by terms of action that can be iterated in the broad community of observers. Human sensory apparatus becomes an instrument of verification, with a subordinate, intermediary role of properly linking the physical domain of experiment with the conceptual arena of the reason (*WRB*, 1:342).

Knowledge, for Boyle, becomes independent of individuals to the extent that it is encoded as replicable action in text. Boyle's essay becomes an iterative literary mechanism designed to create and sequester facts, so as to liberate the discourse and reader from the tyranny of the author. As Boyle notes in the "Pröemial Essay," essays "competently stocked with experiments" provide the reader leverage against the author:

> For let his opinions be never so false, his experiments being true, I am not obliged to believe the former, and am left at liberty to benefit myself by the latter; and though he have erroneously superstructed upon his experiments, yet the foundation being solid, a more wary builder may be very much furthered by it in the erection of more judicious and consistent fabrics. (*WRB*, 1:304)

We now contemplate a literature in which experience and reason have no necessary or integral connection with an individual. Text becomes an instrument that distances its subject from its author, an atomizing literary force that fragments the apparent continuity of experience, so as to make those elements available to new uses. The nucleus of the text is the experimental matter, which is surrounded by a more contingent level of authorial "superstruction."

We thus arrive at a literature whose perspectives are not resynthesized by the intensely personal "I" or self, as in the case of Montaigne's essay. Boyle's experimental essay has a core of experimental fact that, by convention, is at a remove from the idiosyncratic self. As a removed witness, Boyle as "I" renders the physical truth in terms of motion. The prolific first person is not a self-actuation, seeking like Montaigne to discover his own human character, but is managerial—a disembodied voice that seeks to codify physical elements and to sequester them.

> I must declare to you, Pyrophilus, that as I desire not my opinions should have more weight with you, than the proofs brought to countenance them will give them; so you must not expect, that I should think myself obliged to adhere to them any longer, than those considerations, that first made me embrace them, shall seem of greater moment, than any that I can meet with in opposition to them. (*WRB*, 1:311)

Boyle's "I" is not the unifying consciousness imposing continuity on events. It is more the self-conscious intellect, devoted to establishing a parcel of physical truth that will accumulate with like truths and so contribute beyond its own physical limits to higher levels of generalized truth. Boyle seeks to dissociate potential expressive forces and narcissism we find in the works of Montaigne from the factual core of his experimental essay. His "I" is an extension of the material world, creating perspectivism by stripping away all but physical circumstance that is continuous with experiment. Such an "I" is a particle of consciousness, awash in a world of physical objects and motion. Boyle's world is unmediated by human sensibility and does not exist in a continuum with the accidents and desires of personality. It is the world discovered in Newtonian physics.

Underlying Boyle's concept of an atomistic knowledge in experimental essays is the assumption that nature is uniform. The idea that facts can be discovered, sorted, and recombined to contribute to the Baconian model of the world subverts the profound literary instinct to achieve unity and closure with each utterance. Thus the discourse is radically disintegrative, thriving on the faith that particulate truth can eventually be resynthesized in the Baconian image of the world in a mosaic pattern that would reveal an order no individual could hope to envision alone. Such uniformitarian faith prevents the inability to secure closure at the experiential level from suggesting nihilism. This explains the extraordinary force and persistence of Boyle's abstract physico-theology. Against an atomistic world of fearful incompleteness, one that drove his illustrious French contemporary, Pascal, into a mystical retreat, Boyle projects an abstract, corpuscular theory on the hypothesis "that the world being but, as it were, a great piece of clock-work, the naturalist, as such, is but a mechanician" (*WRB*, 6:724–25).[36] God, author of "the automaton," exists in a separate ideal world, projected in an extravagant figurative language that is not accountable to experimental discipline. Mechanism replaces immutability as the principle of perpetuity, installing a new teleology at the center of experimental inquiry.[37]

The Essay Temporalized

Boyle's experimental essay not only formalized an atomistic world view, but also promoted the social ideal of knowledge that had been nurtured in the experimental science clubs, including the Royal Society, which was chartered by Charles II in 1662. The standards of demonstration expected by members of the Society, as expressed in its famous motto *Nullius in Verba*, called for the severance of argument from personal authority.[38] Such rhetorical neutrality or impersonality was advocated, although not necessarily secured, by the establishment of open public discussion at meetings, in which reported observations and actual experiments might be examined by a community, which afterward could seek consensus on their meaning. One of the rhetorical objects of Boyle's *Sceptical Chymist*, as a volume, is to record the interactive discourse of such a community. In other volumes such as the *Hydrostatical Paradoxes*, the formally structured experimental essay assumes a social object of providing a detailed transcription of actions witnessed in a communal setting. Whether or not each action has in reality been witnessed, the structure of the text itself is intended to dramatize the action in question with sufficient operational accuracy to assure a public iteration, even though, as Boyle admits to his nephew, experimental replication may be discouragingly difficult.[39] Boyle's experimental essay, in its ideal form, has the ultimate social object of promoting its own reenactment.

Although the literary transmission of physical observations and actions that could be witnessed by others had long furnished a private means among virtuosi of securing one's claim and priority,[40] the chartering of the Royal Society created a formal social network in which the dynamic of claims and corroboration could operate. The intimate science club, now an institution, became a theater of public inquiry and claims in which correspondents, whether in England or abroad, could seek recognition of their accounts. The community of adepts imagined in the compact literary worlds of Bacon, Galileo, and Boyle was in reality a growing interpretive community bound together by a mounting literary traffic of society journal books and correspondence.

The responsibility of regulating this traffic of oral and verbal proceedings fell to the Society's first Acting Secretary, Henry Oldenburg. An intimate of Boyle, who had secured him his position as Acting Secretary, Oldenburg was also Boyle's editor and factotum, assisting in the publication of both his *Experiments and Considerations Touching Colours* and his *New Experiments and Observations Touching Cold*. Oldenburg had helped to shape, under the eye of England's most renowned experimentalist, new forms of discourse prepared for a community of individuals with increasingly specialized interests.[41] His secretarial duties to the Society further expanded his role as literary agent-general, which he described in 1668 as follows:

> He attends constantly the Meetings both of the Society and the Councill; noteth the Observables, said and done there; digesteth them in private; takes care to have them entered in the Journal- and Register-books; reads over and corrects all entrys; sollicites the performances of taskes recommended and undertaken; writes all letters abroad and answers the returns made to them, entertaining a correspondence with at least 50 persons; employes a great deal of time, and takes much pain in inquiring after and satisfying forrain demands about philosophicall matters, disperteth farr and near store of directions and inquiries for the Society's purpose, and sees them well recommended etc.[42]

Oldenburg served as the link between diverse, sometimes highly specialized, scientific observers and experimenters. His literary products were both the journal books, into which went the descriptions of meetings and experiments, and an immense correspondence that he built up and maintained with a circle of acquaintances, intelligencers, and adepts.

Correspondence, as a literary phenomenon, was intimately associated with essay tradition. Montaigne thought of his *essai* as a letter without a specific addressee (*CWM*, pp. 185–86). Bacon had associated the essay with Seneca's epistles to Lucilius, which he called "dispersed meditations."[43] Boyle's essay compilations were frequently initiated as letters to acquaintances, as in the case of his *A Continuation of New Experiments, Physico-Mechanical* (1666), which began with an epistolary address to the Rt. Honorable the Lord Clifford and Dungarvan, after which it promptly turned to "Experiment I" (*WRB* 3:175ff.). The letter, which flourished alongside the gazette and quarto pamphlet, had been praised by Bacon in *The Advancement of Learning* as one of the most effective literary vehicles for "passages of action" and for "affairs" (*WFB*, 6:201).[44] By virtue of their "interactiveness," letters constituted the most vigorous, immediate, and flexible means by which scientific virtuosi exchanged views, conducted controversies, and sought corroboration of their observations and findings. Samuel Hartlib, whom Boyle had known intimately, had indulged his internationalist interests in a vast correspondence, which constituted his "Office of Address," by which he promoted the grand Pansophic scheme of educational reform.[45] It was as a letter to Hartlib that John Milton had written his essay "Of Education" in 1644.

Oldenburg's own far-ranging program of correspondence, however, went well beyond the informal bureaucracy of Hartlib's "Office." For Oldenburg transformed his activities as correspondent into a formal literary dynamic of journal making. In March of 1665, he brought out the first number of the *Philosophical Transactions*, two months after the appearance of its French rival, the *Journal des Sçavans*.[46] It was conceived as a monthly; volume 1 (1665–66) consisted of twenty-two numbers in 407 pages, or about twenty pages per number, with anywhere from two to fifteen articles. These short pieces were based on correspondence from the early 1660s on practical topics such as German mining and English agriculture, as well as on theoretical topics with the virtuosi, learned men such as Huygens, Hevelius, and Leeuwenhoek, not to mention Hooke and Boyle. Oldenberg's correspondents, who frequently asked that their letters be read at Society meetings, already considered the Acting Secretary's letter network to be a system of quasi-official claims to observational and experimental precedents.[47] As Oldenburg stripped these letters of their personal digressions, further translated or paraphrased them, and, finally, published them as short "parcels" of text in the *Transactions*, they became similar in many respects to the essays of Montaigne—letters without specific addressees. Although Oldenburg made it clear that the contents of his new journal did not represent the views of the Royal Society, the conformity of the *Transactions* with Society policy in matters of knowledge production effectively married the institution and the literary skepticism of Montaigne's *essai*.

Periodical journal publication introduced a new interactive dynamic to literary production. The first number of the *Philosophical Transactions*, of which 1,200 copies were printed, contained ten short pieces that were largely summaries of letters from Oldenburg's recent correspondence.[48] The first item summarized a letter from the Italian astronomer Giuseppe Campani, describing recent improvements he had made in a tool used to grind large optical glasses for telescopes. In addition, Campani confirmed Christian Huygens' observations, some six years earlier, concerning Saturn's rings. Campani also related a plan to determine whether Jupiter turned on its axis, by searching for possible movement of notable features of its surface. Campani's one-page "article" was followed by Oldenburg's note that Robert Hooke,

> with an excellent twelve-foot Telescope, observed, some days before, he than spoke of it, (*videl.* on the ninth of *May*, 1664, about 9 of the clock at night) a small Spot in the biggest of the 3 obscurer *Belts* of *Jupiter*, and that, observing it from time to time, he found, that within 2 hours after, the said spot had moved from East to West, about half the length of the Diameter of *Jupiter*. (*PT*, 1:3)

Hooke's account confirmed Campani's hunch that Jupiter might rotate, and Hooke, ever concerned about securing credit for his own precedents, had included enough detail to fix the conditions and results of his observation.

In the mere placement of these two initial pieces, Oldenburg, quite gratuitously it seems, changes the temporal scope and function of the essay in natural philosophy. For, using the particulate structure of the multi-articled periodical, he juxtaposes parcels of text taken from the correspondence of two individuals to create a public display of dialogue, corroboration, and antecedence. In the iterative structure inherent in periodical form, accounts of separate, detailed observations and experiments invite comparison over time. By dating his observation, Hooke exploits the heightened consciousness of time inherent in dialogue structure to make a public claim of intellectual precedence over his counterpart, Campani. The accurate dating of accounts, a policy of the Royal Society that Oldenburg had discussed at length with Boyle, is institutionalized in the periodical structure itself, thus fixing in memorable irony the collaborative yet fundamentally competitive nature of the scientific literary enterprise.[49]

The observations of Campani and Hooke in the first number are followed by Oldenburg's five-page summary of a "printed paper" or pamphlet, *Ephemerides*, by Adrien Auzout, the French astronomer, predicting a comet's path on the basis of a series of observations. Auzout hypothesizes: contrary to popular opinion that their motion was irregular, comets moved predictably, according to laws. Auzout, Oldenburg announces, invites English astronomers to check his predictions and calculations and either to "confirm the *Hypothesis* . . . or to undeceive him" (*PT*, 1:4). And he lists Auzout's detailed observations, "that the intelligent and curious in England may compare their observations therewith," in order to verify or improve upon the hypothesis. The next issue of the *Transactions* begins with Cassini's confirmation of Auzout's hypothesis of comet motion, followed by another letter from an unnamed Italian observer elaborating the comet's path (*PT*, 1:17–20).

Periodical publication thus created a unique occasional world of textual redundancy and corroboration, but the essay-fragments, called "Parcels" by Oldenburg, intensified the atomist approach to knowledge to the point of incoherence. To counteract this centrifugal tendency, Oldenburg riddled issues of the *Transactions* with marginal references to other related essays, added innovative indexes, and encouraged authorial interactions. Mariotte responded to Pecquet concerning the locus of the organ of sight with a series of detailed critiques of Pecquet's experiments (*PT*, 3:668–71, 5:1023–42). Huygens supported

Hooke's theory of the parallax, promising observational assistance (*PT*, 9:90). Linus called for clarification of the experimental procedure that led Newton to his essay on the theory of colors (*PT* 6:3075–87; 9:217–19; 10:499–504). These reflexive literary mechanisms were all meant to counteract the radical tendency of subject matter in the *Philosophical Transactions* to spin outward in an irretrievable fragmentation, each detailed observation, book summary, or reported experiment isolated from a constituent subject matter. In the works of Montaigne, Bacon, and Boyle, essay clusters had been the products of a single conscious-ness, unified by a single mental habit. Clustering in the *Transactions*, however, authentically reconstructed the views of many minds. If serial publication intensified the sense of tentativeness that had inspired Montaigne's and Boyle's own experiments with essay form, it also offered a new compensation in its very repetitiveness, which implied that its particulate accounts would eventually accumulate and help to redeem a still incomplete and thus imperfect subject matter.

The essays of the *Philosophical Transactions* become texts at second remove by virtue of Oldenburg's editorial interventions. Oldenburg controls the inclusions, as well as the topics of the essays, which he has himself often edited, summarized, or "Englished." By so intervening, he creates a textual middle ground, a literary shell, in which he self-consciously manipulates the context in which each entry has been accepted as text. This literary shell effectively distances the text and its original letter-author from the reader: "There came lately from Paris a relation concerning . . ." (*PT*, 1:2); "The ingenious Mr. Hook did, some months since, intimate . . ." (*PT*, 1:3); "There is in Press, a new Treatise, entitled . . ." (*PT*, 1:8). Letter salutations, digressions, and endings, which individualize and direct the discourse, are neutralized by Olden-burg's supervening consciousness. His interventions weaken the au-thority of the original authorial voice and help to establish each text as a unit of discourse on a par with its companions, whether it be Cassini's theory of comet motion, Boyle's recipe for preparing Helmontian lauda-num, or Newton's theory of colors. Individual essays, thus stripped of their own diverse local circumstances, are isolated by the voice of the editor. This textual middle ground or periodical shell becomes a media-tive domain that serves the same self-reflexive, contextualizing function that Montaigne's extensive metadiscourse had served in the *Essais*.

Conclusion

Although the development of scientific periodical literature was far from complete with the publication of Oldenburg's *Philosophical Transactions*, the distinctive textual atomism and skepticism of experimental science had been well established as a periodic, public form by the third year of its publication. It has been noted, with justification I think, that the modern version of the refereed periodical article as a disciplinary phenomenon was not to emerge for some time after Oldenburg had established his journal. Gale Christianson and Charles Bazerman have both traced the prototype of the experimental paper to Newton's famous letter on the theory of colors, published in the eightieth issue (1672) of the *Philosophical Transactions* (*PT*, 6:3075–87).[50] And the periodical journal as a rigorous, refereed instrument of scientific innovation was not to develop for at least another century. On the other hand, the developments I have traced in this study reveal a fundamental textual revolution in the making that was so integral a part of the experimentalist strategy that we are likely to take it for granted. Moreover, we are likely to think of literary form as an epiphenomenon rather than a constitutive force in experimental science. And that, as I have tried to illustrate, would be a serious oversight.

Boyle was both a conscious inventor of the form he called the "experimental essay" and its first extensive exploiter. We can hardly doubt that Newton took many of his literary cues from Boyle, whose work he had studied and mastered. On the other hand, Oldenburg, with few intentions other than to generate financial support for himself and to save labor, effectively temporalized essay form, by giving it a stable, periodical shell in which to evolve. This highly self-conscious literary structure, which was almost inevitable, it seems to me, once science was institutionalized, also furnished a self-adjusting mechanism that has since become the hallmark of progressive knowledge. The same interactive periodical mechanism with its inherent skepticism has become central to the establishment of the modern professional discipline and the notion that knowledge has its perpetual frontiers and, thus, limits.[51]

Finally, Montaigne's essay was a literary innovation that thrived on its own self-conscious informality. Its reflexive quality succeeded in creating a relationship between text and human experience that supported its author's claims to mimesis. Montaigne's perspectivism was authentically individualist in that every view or trial was phenomenologically unique. In the modified perspectivism of Boyle and his counterparts, that assumption gives way, by virtue of a shared perspective in the phenomenological experience of experiment, to a stylized elimination of personality.

Notes

1. John Ziman in his *Reliable Knowledge: An Exploration of the Grounds for Belief in Science* (Cambridge: Cambridge University Press, 1978), gives one of the best general accounts of the epistemological basis of scientific discourse; this should be compared with Michael Polanyi's classical study, *Personal Knowledge: Towards a Post-Critical Philosophy* (Chicago: University of Chicago Press, 1958). Stephen Shapin's article "Pump and Circumstance: Robert Boyle's Literary Technology," *Social Studies of Science* 14 (1984): 481–517, provides an excellent study of Boyle's literary stratagems for manufacturing scientific facts. Charles Bazerman has kindly shared with me his working paper "Evolution of the Genre of the Experimental Article" (Baruch College, N.Y., n.d.), pp. 1–14. Historical background on the origins of the essay is given in Wilbert L. Macdonald's *The Beginnings of the English Essay*, University of Toronto Studies, no. 3 (Toronto: University of Toronto Library, 1914); and in Elbert N. S. Thompson's *The Seventeenth-Century English Essay, University of Iowa Humanistic Studies*, vol. 3, no. 3 (Iowa City: University of Iowa, 1926).

2. On Montaigne's literary duplicity, see Barbara Bowen's *The Age of Bluff: Paradox and Ambiguity in Rabelais and Montaigne* (Urbana: University of Illinois Press, 1972), esp. pp. 105–10, 127; Erich Auerbach's classic, *Mimesis: The Representation of Reality in Western Literature*, trans. Willard Trask (Princeton: Princeton University Press, 1953), chap. 12, examines Montaigne's mimetic program.

3. Montaigne's skepticism is set into historical perspective in Richard Popkin's *The History of Scepticism from Erasmus to Descartes* (Berkeley: University of California Press, 1979); see also P. M. Rattansi, "The Social Interpretation of Science in the Seventeenth Century," in Peter Mathias, ed., *Science and Society, 1600–1900* (Cambridge: Cambridge University Press, 1972), pp. 1–33; see also Elizabeth Eisenstein, *The Printing Press as an Agent of Change*, 2 vols. (Cambridge: Cambridge University Press, 1979), 1:84, 230.

4. *The Complete Works of Montaigne*, trans. Donald Frame (Stanford: Stanford University Press, 1957), p. 229.

5. Popkin, *History of Scepticism from Erasmus to Descartes*, p. 540.

6. Auerbach, *Mimesis*, pp. 294–95.

7. Basil Willey, *The Seventeenth-Century Background* (New York: Doubleday, 1953), pp. 40–41.

8. Auerbach, *Mimesis*, p. 292. Auerbach argues, somewhat inconsistently, I think, that Montaigne uses an experimental method, yet rejects all forms of specialization.

9. Barry Lydgate, "Mortgaging One's Work to the World: Publication and the Structure of Montaigne's *Essais*," *PMLA* 96 (1981): 220–21.

10. Robert K. Merton, *Science, Technology, and Society in Seventeenth-Century England* (New York: Howard Fertig, 1970), pp. 112–113. See also Dorothy Stimson, "Puritanism and the New Philosophy in Seventeenth-Century England," *Bulletin of the Institute of the History of Medicine* 3 (1935): 321–34. Several commentators have noted the resonance of Montaigne's and Bacon's thought. See Morris Croll, "Attic Prose: Lipsius, Montaigne, Bacon," in *Schelling Anniversary Papers: By His Former Students* (New York: Century, 1923), pp. 143–46; cf. Brian Vickers, *Francis Bacon and Renaissance Prose Style* (Cambridge: Cambridge University Press, 1968), p. 107. The French mathematician Marin Mersenné, in his *La vérité des sciences* (1625), associated Bacon with the Pyrrhonist attack on sense knowledge—see Popkin, *History of Scepticism from Erasmus to Descartes*, p. 84.

11. Joseph Agassi, *Science and Society: Studies in the Sociology of Science* (Boston: D. Reidel, 1981), p. 357; see also Margery Purver, *The Royal Society: Concept and Creation* (Cambridge: MIT Press, 1967), pp. 34–37.

12. Quoted by Benjamin Farrington, *Francis Bacon: Philosopher of Industrial Science* (New York: Schuman, 1949), p. 68.

13. See Charles Webster, *The Great Instauration: Science, Medicine, and Reform, 1626–1660* (New York: Holmes and Meir, 1976), p. 342.

14. Francis Bacon, *Novum Organum, The Works of Francis Bacon*, trans. James Spedding, Robert Ellis, and Douglas Heath, 15 vols. (Cambridge, Mass.: Riverside Press, 1863), 8:368.

15. Robert Adolph, *The Rise of the Modern Prose Style* (Cambridge: MIT Press, 1958), pp. 58–77. See also Brian Vickers, "The Royal Society and English Prose Style: A Reassessment," in Brian Vickers and Nancy Struever, *Rhetoric and the Pursuit of Truth: Language Change in the Seventeenth and Eighteenth Centuries* (Los Angeles: Clark Memorial Library of the University of California, Los Angeles, 1985), pp. 11–14. Vickers demolishes, with considerable zest, Richard Jones's well-known claim that Bacon was at war with language in general. See Richard Foster Jones, "Science and Language in England of the Mid-Seventeenth Century," in Jones et al., *The Seventeenth Century: Studies in the History of English Thought and Literature from Bacon to Pope* (Stanford, Cal.: Stanford University Press, 1951), pp. 143 ff. See also James Paradis, "Bacon, Linnaeus, and Lavoisier: Early Language Reform in the Sciences," in Paul Anderson et al., eds., *New Essays in Technical and Scientific Communication* (Farmingdale, N.Y.: Baywood, 1983), pp. 200–24.

16. In the unpublished dedication of the second (1612) edition of his *Essays* to Henry, Prince of Wales, Bacon noted, "The word [essay] is late, but the thing is ancient"; see James Spedding, *The Letters and Life of Francis Bacon*, 7 vols. (London: Longman, Green, 1861–74), 4:340. See also Jerome Zeitlin, "The Development of Bacon's Essays, with Special Reference to the Question of Mon-

taigne's Influence upon Them," *Journal of English and Germanic Philology* 28 (1928):496–519; and William F. Bryan and Ronald S. Crane, "Introduction," *The English Familiar Essay* (Boston: Ginn, 1916), pp. xvi–xix.

17. See Vickers, *Francis Bacon and Renaissance Prose Style*, pp. 32–34. See also Ronald S. Crane, "The Relation of Bacon's Essays to His Program for the *Advancement of Learning*," in *Schelling Anniversary Papers*, pp. 87–105.

18. The stylistic effects of this dissociative effort are examined in L. C. Knights's "Bacon and the Seventeenth-Century Dissociation of Sensibility," *Explorations: Essays in Criticism, Mainly on the Literature of the Seventeenth Century* (London: Chatto and Windus, 1946), pp. 92–111. If Knights's case for Bacon's "mathematical plainness" (p. 97) and "Positivism" (p. 100) overlooks the dense imagery and stylistic complexity of most of Bacon's prose, it does capture the spirit of Bacon's antirhetorical program for a scientific language of restricted sensory content. Bacon's views were echoed by Locke in the *Essay concerning Human Understanding*: "If we would speak of things as they are, we must allow that all art of Rhetorick, besides order and clearness, all the artificial and figurative application of words eloquence hath invented, are for nothing else but to insinuate wrong ideas, move the Passions, and thereby mislead the Judgement, and so indeed are perfect cheats" (quoted in Thompson, *Seventeenth-Century English Essay*, p. 135). See also Marjorie Nicolson, *The Breaking of the Circle: Studies in the Effect of the "New Science" on Seventeenth-Century Poetry*, rev. ed. (New York: Columbia University Press, 1960), pp. 5–9. Nicolson argues that figurative language becomes increasingly self-conscious among many seventeenth-century poets, as metaphor is replaced by analogy. Maurice Mandlebaum, citing Boyle's and Newton's corpuscular theories of matter and light as instances, argues that figurative language necessarily persists in the language of the sciences, because by a logical process he calls *transdictive inference* it extends data beyond the domain of sense experience. *Philosophy, Science, and Sense Perception: Historical and Critical Studies* (Baltimore: Johns Hopkins University Press, 1964), pp. 62–66, 107.

19. Marie Boas Hall, in *Robert Boyle on Natural Philosophy: An Essay, with Selections from His Writings* (Bloomington: Indiana University Press, 1966), p. 62, discusses Bacon's efforts to drive qualities out of language in his distinctions of form in the *Novum Organum*.

20. Stillman Drake, *Galileo at Work: His Scientific Biography* (Chicago: University of Chicago Press, 1978), p. 184.

21. Nicolson, *Breaking of the Circle*, pp. 123–30. The question arises of whether the true effort here is to *conceal* the derivation of fact, as Medawar and Shapin argue, or to *disentangle* self from the accounting of fact, as I am arguing. If the net rhetorical effect in either case would be nearly identical, the moral implications would not. See Shapin, "Pump and Circumstance," pp. 509–11; Peter Medawar, "Is the Scientific Paper Fraudulent? Yes, It Misrepresents Scientific Thought," *Saturday Review* 47 (1964): 42–43. See also Charles Coffin, *John Donne and the New Philosophy* (New York: Columbia University Press, 1937), p. 25.

22. Drake, *Gallileo at Work*, pp. 86–87. See also William R. Shea, *Galileo's*

Intellectual Revolution: Middle Period, 1610–1632 (New York: Science History Publications, 1972), p. 39.

23. See, for example, Alexandre Koyré, *Galileo Studies*, trans. John Mepham (Atlantic Highlands, N.J.: Humanities Press, 1978), pp. 206–7; Shea, *Galileo's Intellectual Revolution*, p. 39; and Drake, *Galileo at Work*, pp. 86–89.

24. Robert Boyle, *The Works of the Honorable Robert Boyle*, ed. Thomas Birch, 3d ed., 6 vols. (1772; facsimile rpt. Hildesheim: George Olms, 1965), 1:xxiv. On Galileo's influence on Boyle, see Hall, *Robert Boyle on Natural Philosophy*, pp. 61–62.

25. See also Ziman, *Reliable Knowledge*, pp. 42–50; and Shapin, "Pump and Circumstance," pp. 490–93.

26. René Descartes, *Discourse on the Method of Rightly Conducting the Reason and Seeking for Truth in the Sciences*, in *The Philosophical Works of Descartes*, trans. Elizabeth S. Haldane and G. R. T. Ross, 2 vols. (Cambridge, Eng.: Cambridge University Press, 1911–12; rpt. 1931), 1:119, 126–27.

27. Boyle had thoroughly assimilated contemporary French culture during his continental study tour of 1639–44; in Italy, religious feeling against the English led him to use his fluent French to pass as a Frenchman. See Louis T. More, *The Life and Works of the Honourable Robert Boyle* (New York: Oxford University Press, 1944), pp. 44–45.

28. Thomas Birch, in his Introduction, *WRB*, 1:1xxii, rebukes Swift for this levity.

29. Boyle's literary strategy of evoking dialogue to sustain a challenge to traditional views was similar to Galileo's strategy in the *Dialogo*, which was very likely Boyle's literary model. The right to public discussion, typified by the give-and-take of dialogue, was clearly a central cultural concern at this time among intellectuals in England and abroad. Milton in *Areopagitica* (1644) and Boyle both viewed Galileo's troubles with the Inquisition as a matter of freedom of expression.

30. See also Descartes, *DM*, pp. 128–29. In "A Defense of *An Essay of Dramatic Poesy*," Dryden denies that he is dictating laws for dramatic poesie, as Robert Howard charges. Dryden cites the term *essay* as proof of his skepticism. His literary methodology, he notes further, is after Socrates, Plato, and "the modest inquisitions of the Royal Society": "a dialogue, sustain'd by persons of several opinions, all of them left doubtful, to be determined by the Readers in general." *The Works of John Dryden*, ed. John Loftis (Berkeley: University of California Press, 1966), 9:15. See also George Watson, "Dryden and the Scientific Image," *Notes and Records of the Royal Society of London* 18 (1963): 25–35.

31. See Mary Hesse, *Forces and Fields: The Concept of Action at a Distance in the History of Physics* (Totowa, N.J.: Littlefield Adams, 1965), pp. 98–125.

32. In Ziman's terms, the observer of the experimental event is interchangeable with any other observer (*Reliable Knowledge*, pp. 42–43). Medawar, concerned about the Whiggishness of scientific reportage, argues that the "distortion" of narrative "falsifies" the process of fact making ("Is the Scientific Paper Fraudulent?" p. 42). For a review of recent scholarship on the scientific text as

social artifact, see Charles Bazerman, "Scientific Writing as a Social Act: A Review of the Literature of the Sociology of Science," in *New Essays in Technical and Scientific Communication*, pp. 156–84.

33. Koyré, *Galileo Studies*, pp. 206–7.

34. Blaise Pascal, *Treatises on the Equilibrium of Liquids and on the Weight of the Mass of the Air, Scientific Treatises*, trans. Richard Scofield (Chicago: University of Chicago Press, 1952), 33:391, 399. See also A. W. S. Baird, "Pascal's Idea of Nature," *Isis* 61 (1970): 297–320.

35. Hall, *Robert Boyle on Natural Philosophy*, pp. 61–63.

36. J. E. McGuire, "Boyle's Conception of Nature," *Journal of the History of Ideas* 33 (1972): 523–42; Laurens Laudan, "The Clock Metaphor and Probabilism: The Impact of Descartes on English Methodological Thought, 1650–65," *Annals of Science* 22 (1966): 81–86, 91.

37. The sociopolitical objects of Boyle's and Newton's physico-theology are examined in chapter 1 of Margaret Jacob's *The Newtonians and the English Revolution, 1689–1720* (Ithaca, N.Y.: Cornell University Press, 1976), pp. 22–71.

38. See Martha Ornstein, *The Role of Scientific Societies in the Seventeenth Century*, 3rd ed. (Chicago: University of Chicago Press, 1938), p. 198; See also Purver, *Royal Society*, pp. 128–42. The motto of the society is from Horace's *Epistles*, 1.1:14, "Nullius addictus jurare in verba magistri" (I am not bound over to swear as any master dictates).

39. See Boyle's "Two Essays concerning the Unsuccessfulness of Experiments," *WRB*, 1:318 ff.; Robert K. Merton and Harriet Zuckerman, "Patterns of Evaluation in Science: Institutionalization, Structure, and Functions of a Referee System," *Minerva* 9 (1971): 63–102; Shapin, "Pump and Circumstance," p. 511.

40. Arthur Koestler illustrates the importance of independent printed corroboration in his account of Kepler's dilemma after he had publicly endorsed, in an open letter, Galileo's claims in *Sidereus Nuncius* concerning the moons of Jupiter. Kepler was pressed for evidence by his associates and put in a very awkward position because he did not have a telescope the quality of Galileo's to confirm the observation. See *The Sleepwalkers: A History of Man's Changing Vision of the Universe* (New York: Grosset and Dunlap, 1963), pp. 370–78.

41. Samuel Pepys, for example, noted in his diary (28 April 1667): "Mightily pleased with my reading Boyle's book of Colours today; only, troubled that some part of it, endeed the greatest part, I am not able to understand for want of study." Quoted in Marjorie Nicolson, *Pepys's Diary and the New Science* (Charlottesville: University Press of Virginia, 1965), p. 32. For a study of specialization, see Margaret Denny's "The Early Program of the Royal Society and John Evelyn," *Modern Language Quarterly* 1 (1940): 481–97.

42. Marie Boas Hall, "Henry Oldenburg and the Art of Scientific Communication," *British Journal for the History of Science* 2 (1964–65): 289. Oldenburg, educated in Bremen, took his master of theology degree in 1639 and entered Oxford in 1656, while tutoring Robert Boyle's nephew, Richard Jones, the "Pyrophilus" of *Certain Physiological Essays*. See also Dorothy Stimson, "Hartlib, Haak, and Oldenburg: Intelligencers," *Isis* 31 (1940): 317–22; and James Paradis, "The

Royal Society, Henry Oldenburg, and Some Origins of the Modern Technical Paper," *Proceedings, 28th International Conference of Technical Communication* (1982), pp. E82–86.

43. Spedding, *Letters and Life of Francis Bacon*, 4:340. See also Macdonald, *Beginnings of the English Essay*, pp. 87–94.

44. For a survey of the periodical journal and its antecedent forms, see David Kronick, *A History of Scientific Periodicals: The Origins and Development of the Scientific and Technical Press, 1665–1790*, 2d ed. (Metuchen, N.J.: Scarecrow Press, 1976), pp. 53–76; see also Harcourt Brown, *Scientific Organizations in Seventeenth-Century France, 1620–1680* (New York: Russell and Russell, 1934), pp. 186–87.

45. Purver, *Royal Society*, pp. 200–205; G. H. Turnbull, "Samuel Hartlib's Influence on the Early History of the Royal Society," *Notes and Records of the Royal Society of London* 10 (1953): 110.

46. Oldenburg wrote Boyle (24 November 1664) that the French were planning a "Journall of all what passeth in Europe in matter of knowledge both philosophicall and politicall: in order to which they will print." He was referring to the *Journal des Sçavans*, the prototype of the periodical journal, first published on 5 January 1665 by Denis de Sallo, a counselor to the French Parliament. See Ornstein, *Role of Scientific Societies in the Seventeenth Century*, pp. 190–203. See also Walter Graham, *English Literary Periodicals* (New York: Octagon Books, 1966), pp. 22–26.

47. Henry Oldenburg, *The Correspondence of Henry Oldenburg*, ed. A. Rupert Hall and Marie Boas Hall, 11 vols. (Madison: University of Wisconsin Press, 1965–77), 2:xx.

48. Henry Oldenburg, ed., *Philosophical Transactions* 1 (1665–66) (New York: Johnson Reprint Corporation, 1963), pp. 1–16.

49. In November 1664, Oldenburg wrote to Boyle, acknowledging the importance of dating correspondence: "The Society [is] very carefull of registering as well the person and time of any new matter imparted to them as the matter itself; whereby, the honour of the invention will be inviolably preserved to all posterity" (Oldenburg, *Correspondence*, 3:319).

50. See, for example, Gale Christianson, *In the Presence of the Creator: Isaac Newton and His Times* (New York: Free Press, 1984), p. 156; Bazerman, "Evolution of the Genre of the Experimental Article," p. 12.

51. Nicholas Rescher, *The Limits of Science* (Berkeley: University of California Press, 1984), p. 172.

PETER ALLAN DALE

George Lewes' Scientific Aesthetic: Restructuring the Ideology of the Symbol

> I believed . . . that I had caught nature in the lawful work of
> bringing forth living structures as the model for all artifice.
> —Goethe

"Since art and science move in entirely different planes, they cannot contradict or thwart one another."[1] The words happen to be Ernst Cassirer's, but they may stand apart from any particular author as an epitome of one of our most persistent modern beliefs about the relation, or rather nonrelation, between art and science. This belief has been a mainstay of both neo-Kantian (broadly speaking, New Critical) and phenomenological defenses of art in an increasingly technological age. In our more recent critical discourse the resistance to science's efforts to bring all human endeavor within its own methodological realm has become less compromising and more encompassing. Not only is current literary theory unlikely to allow science its separate plane (a point to which we must return), it jealously watches its own discourse, and that of the neighboring humanities, for signs of unconscious scientism. Indeed, the epithet "positivist" is now far more likely to be aimed at the work of fellow critics than at what the scientists are doing. Thus Jonathan Culler warns us against the "positivist claim" that criticism can attain a "true reading," an absolute interpretation of a text,[2] and J. Hillis Miller regrets that " 'happy positivism' " by which we are "lulled into the promise of a rational ordering of literary study."[3]

The object of the present study is twofold. On the one hand, it is simply historical. I examine the phenomenon of literary positivism in the period, roughly the middle third of the past century, when it seemed to offer a new and exciting departure in criticism, when the notion of establishing a genuinely scientific or objective approach to art was as intellectually attractive as, say, our current notion of an absolutely decentered and radically anti-objective criticism. But of course postmodernism has taught us nothing if not the naiveté of supposing one's studies of the past to be "simply historical," so I acknowledge at the outset that another purpose of the essay is revisionist. By resurrecting the dispute literary positivism had with the Romantic aesthetic that preceded it and by showing how this dispute crucially redefined contemporary concepts of imagination and symbolization, I hope to make a fair case for its intellectual respectability. My object is not to initiate a neopositivist movement in literary theory. One could scarcely imagine a more quixotic gesture. Rather, I seek, in some degree, to deliver what I take to be a very important theoretical movement from the marginalization, not to mention caricaturization, it has suffered at the hands of its modernist and postmodernist detractors.

We need, to begin with, a short and reasonably neutral definition of the phenomenon. By "positivism" I mean the belief that science or scientific method is the only reliable route to knowledge, not only of the natural world but also—and here we see its revolutionary import—of the cultural one.[4] As a philosophy in the hands, say, of Auguste Comte, John Stuart Mill, or Herbert Spencer it claimed nothing less than the regeneration of society. What concerns me here is one small part of that regenerative program, the effort to "scientize" the theory of art. In particular I am considering the work of George Henry Lewes (1817–79), whom we in literature know primarily as the companion of George Eliot and who, unfortunately, exists too much in the shadow of that great artist. In fact, Lewes was probably the Victorians' foremost philosopher of science after Mill, and one of their two or three most important psychologists. He was also a very talented and prolific literary critic, who needs to take second place to no one, including George Eliot, in the seriousness with which he engaged the problem of the relation between science and art. Still more particularly, I shall be looking at Lewes' concept of the literary symbol, an especially telling aspect of nineteenth- and early-twentieth-century efforts to define the meaning and function of art. What I hope to show is how Lewes' positivist aesthetic first disengages itself from the Romantic "ideology of the symbol" and then gradually reclaims the meaning of symbolic representation in a way that profoundly affects his concept not simply of artistic practice but of scientific method and social order as well. The result, as we shall see, is clearly anticipatory of Cassirer's philosophy of symbolic form and distantly (but interestingly) of our own "deconstructive turn."[5]

I

The expression, "ideology of the symbol," comes to me from Paul de Man's late article "Sign and Symbol in Hegel's Aesthetics." De Man is arguing that Hegel enshrines the Romantic doctrine of the beautiful as the symbolic and that "whether we know it or not" we are "most of us ["us" being literary critics] Hegelians and quite orthodox ones at that."[6] What de Man means by this, as I read him, is that we are most of us still essentially New Critics, Romantics manqués, if you like, who value literature because it is a sensuous, concrete representation of an inwardness, a consciousness that is, in some sense, deemed to be universal and, at the same time, beyond or behind language. De Man, of course, is rejecting this Romantic-cum-New Critical ideology of the symbol in favor of a Derridean grammatology, according to which language is not a symbol that refers to some ontological form of being other than itself, but a sign that has its meaning only as part of a larger linguistic system of differences. "Contrary to the metaphysical, dialectical, 'Hegelian' interpretation" of linguistic signs as deferring to an absent presence, writes Derrida, the only possible principle of signification lies in the differential relation of any given sign to the other terms of its language system: "Essentially and lawfully, every concept is inscribed in a chain or in a system within which it refers to the other, to other concepts, by means of the systematic play of differences."[7]

I shall come back to de Man's case against the ideology of the symbol. For the moment I want only to make the point that Lewes' positivist aesthetic, no less than de Man's deconstructionist one, begins with an attack on the Romantic ideology of the symbol although, of course, with a quite different philosophical end in view. For the positivist, no less than the deconstructionist, Romanticism is a metaphysical *ideology* (Lewes actually uses the word) whose cultural products—political, ethical, or, as in the present case, aesthetic—must be exposed as at once unrealistic and repressive. De Man would no doubt argue that the positivist's realism and the positivist's liberalism are themselves only expressions of another kind of metaphysics, but this need not concern us just yet.

Let me now briefly indicate Hegel's concept of the artistic symbol in the hope (following de Man) that it may be allowed fairly to represent not just an aspect of the Romantic aesthetic but its essence:

> [Art displays] the highest [reality] sensuously, bringing it thereby nearer to the senses, to feeling, and to nature's mode of appearance. What is [symbolically] displayed is the depth of a suprasensuous world which thought pierces and sets up as . . . a *beyond* . . .

> The external appearance [of art] has no immediate value for us [except as a representation of something else]; we assume behind it something inward, a meaning whereby the external appearance is endowed with the spirit. It is to this soul that the external points.

Through the faculty of imagination, the artist transforms "what exists in nature" into a symbol of the "something inward":

> Our imaginative mentality has in itself the character of universality, and what it produces acquires . . . thereby the stamp of universality in contrast to the individual thing in nature.[8]

To illustrate this doctrine in Romantic artistic practice is, of course, not difficult. I shall offer an example from Wordsworth (whom A. C. Bradley long ago connected with Hegel) in a moment.

Lewes' first substantive essay in criticism was, in fact, a review article on Hegel's *Aesthetics* (1842; so far as I know, he was the first to introduce this great Romantic text to England).[9] At the time he wrote the review, he was in the process of making a philosophical transition from his own youthful Romanticism (inspired mainly by Shelley) to positivism under the guidance first of Mill and subsequently of Comte. Three years later, with the publication of his famous *Biographical History of Philosophy*, it is clear that the transition is complete. "One Method must preside [over philosophy]," he writes at the close of that book. "Auguste Comte was the first to point out the fact. . . . When the positive method is universally accepted . . . then shall we again have unity of thought."[10] By the time he comes to the 1871 edition of the *History* (it went through four editions in his lifetime), he has a still sharper conception of the essential plot of nineteenth-century thought. Hegel, he writes, imagined that he had begun an epoch in philosophy. In fact, he merely closed out the latest epoch of metaphysics initiated by Fichte's misguided correction of Kant. Hegel, as well as the "incompetence" of metaphysics in general, has now been displaced by Comte's philosophy of science, which genuinely marks a new and, as far as Lewes is concerned, the ultimate epoch in philosophy.[11]

Lewes' application of the positivist philosophy to criticism is of a piece with his larger historical and epistemological argument. He evidently sees himself as doing in the sphere of aesthetics what Comte had done in general philosophy: overturning an "incompetent" mode of enquiry. Not surprisingly, Coleridge comes in for the brunt of Lewes' attack on the "abuses of English criticism."[12]

> Unless we are greatly deceived this [metaphysical] philosophy of art is a vain and misplaced employment of ingenuity. . . . To understand Nature, we must observe her manifestations, and trace out the laws of coexistence and succession of phenomena. And in the same way, to understand Art, we must patiently examine the works of art; and from a large observation of successful efforts deduce a general conclusion respecting the laws upon which success depends.[13]

Hegel's *Aesthetics* receives gentler treatment, but only because, at the time of writing about it, Lewes had not fully gone over to positivism. Yet even in this early, transitional phase of his thinking, he takes care to demystify Hegel's concept of mind, transforming the phenomenology of spirit into a psychological theory. What Hegel teaches us, finally, is that "the real way to set about [the] examination [of art] must be the investigation of those laws of the mind from whence it proceeds; . . . thus it becomes . . . a branch of psychology. . . . [Y]ou have only to translate [his] principle into your own formula, and the thing becomes intelligible" ("Hegel's Aesthetics," pp. 43–44). In later, more informed treatments of Hegel, Lewes is less cavalier about the possibility of reconciling the German's "laws of mind" to a scientific philosophy. But one notes that what he is doing here is symptomatic of the reformation in aesthetics he is attempting to accomplish: metaphysical entities must be "translated" to psychological ones before we can hope to talk responsibly about art.

The attack on the Romantic metaphysic of art, when turned to questions of the *form* of art, becomes an attack on the idea that the essence of beauty is the symbolic. Preoccupation with the "symbolic in Art," Lewes writes in his book on Goethe (1855), reached its height in the Romantic school's desire to create "a new Religion, or at any rate, a new Mythology." But "the poet who makes symbolism the substance and purpose of his work has mistaken his vocation," symbolism "being in its very nature *arbitrary*—the indication of a meaning not directly expressed, but arbitrarily thrust *under* expression." Incidents "however wonderful, adventures however perilous, are almost as naught when compared with the deep and lasting interest excited by anything like a *correct representation of life*" (my emphasis).[14]

What is motivating Lewes here is the belief—we would now call it a realist or objectivist fallacy—that it is possible somehow to represent things as they are without the intervention of symbolic representation which distorts them into the shapes or forms we "arbitrarily" wish them to have. As Comte had said, "Le but le plus difficile et le plus important de notre existence intellectuelle consiste à transformer le cerveau humain en un miroir exact de l'ordre extérieur."[15] In effect, Lewes is collapsing the well-known Romantic distinction between the symbol as true representation of reality ("consubstantial" with it, as Coleridge insists) and the allegory as arbitrary or conventional and, hence, false representation. The Romantic symbol, for Lewes, is always only an allegory, the "thrusting under [concrete] expression" of beliefs about the world that have no scientific standing, that do not "mirror the external order." So, for example, Wordsworth's claim that a particular Alpine setting at a particular moment became for him the "type and symbol of Eternity," "the character of the great Apocalypse" (*The Prelude* [1850], 6.624 ff.) is simply an illusion, perpetrated by the poet's metaphysical-cum-theological belief that imagination is actually a divine power flowing through him, shaping nature by means of his art to what it really means, "stamping" it, as Hegel says, with "universality." In fact, what Wordsworth calls symbolic is simply semiological. The Romantic poet, far from suffering from a "sad incompetence of speech," displays an excess of competence at connecting his speech with the ungrounded system of language (essentially scriptural language) that signifies divine presence.

Lewes' nineteenth-century positivism has not yet taken the "linguistic turn" of the Vienna circle, but it is clear from his discussion of Hegel that he considers the heart of the German's, and of Romanticism's, problem to be the merely verbal (symbolic) creation of nonexistent universals, "pseudo-concepts," as Carnap will later label them.[16]

> In his *Logic* [Hegel] makes it a special merit of the German language that more than all other modern languages it permits of ambiguity, many of its words containing not only different but directly opposed meanings "so that a speculative spirit in the language is not to be overlooked." . . .
>
> He is fond of revealing philosophic principles involved in ordinary terms [*aufheben* is Lewes', as it will later be Derrida's, principal example], and his derivations are often as ingenious as they are etymologically incorrect. (*History of Philosophy*, 2: 628–29.)

The Romantic symbol thus emptied of its metaphysical content is discarded in favor of the "correct representation of life," one that does not begin with what Lewes calls Hegel's "arbitrary suppression of concretes" (p. 638).

At this point, I have pressed the similarity between the positivist aesthetic and deconstructionism about as far as it will go. Lewes' notion that it is possible to have signs (aesthetic or otherwise) that represent some reality in the world obviously marks the parting of the ways. We now need to look at what exactly Lewes expects a realistic, nonsymbolic art to represent.

II

Passing over the many essays Lewes wrote in the 1840s and 1850s applying his positivist criteria to the discussion of particular works of art, I will note only that these essays make a case for essentially two things, that the novel is the genre most appropriate to the new scientific age and, what is closely related, that art must strive, above all, for *psychological* realism. (We may in passing distinguish Lewes' position from the positivist aesthetics of Hippolyte Taine and Emile Zola, both of whom show a characteristically French tendency to privilege the social rather than the psychological as the real.)

What Lewes means by the psychologically real, as we see from his essays on contemporary novels and poetry, is the deep elemental or instinctual nature of man. Balzac, for example, is admired for portraying the "secret springs" that determine action and, at the same time, criticized for allowing the intellect too large a role as cause of action. The French novelist's characters "calculate" too much; he overrates the "power of intelligence."[17] Again, Dickens is not a psychological realist because he does not understand how deeply rooted human motivation is, how inaccessible to conscious control. What Lewes is after in the literary presentation of human psychology is, in short, that which is furthest removed from the possibility of "intellectual conversion," the possibility, that is, of being controlled or transmuted by the reason.[18]

We may attribute Lewes' interest in the psychology of subrational motivation to his reading of Comte and the work of contemporary psychologists either directly influenced by Comte or working independently on positivist principles. One of the impulses behind Comte's work, as Marcuse has observed, was a desire to end the metaphysicians' and, in particular, Hegel's subordination of reality to "transcendental reason."[19] The foundations of human action, Comte insists, lie in biological or instinctual causes. As Lewes says, the *Politique positive* leads us to a "new cerebral theory"; Comte's reduction of psychology to biology has made a "philosophical revolution" and given the science of mind its proper basis.[20] The history of the rise of the "new cerebral theory" and its implications for nineteenth-century concepts of human behavior has been told elsewhere.[21] It is enough to note here that Lewes, as scientist, participated in that history to an extent beyond any of his British contemporaries, an extent still not properly recognized. He drew heavily upon the work of all the major continental figures, not only the pioneers—Gall, Cabanis, and Comte—but the later German animal and human physiologists, from Johannes Mueller to Fechner, Lotze, Helmholtz, and Wundt. The most important consequence of his study was to convince him that by far the greater and more influential part of human behavior is determined by unconscious (in his physiological and not, of course, Freud's psychoanalytical sense) motivation. This is the resounding conclusion of his first original scientific work, *The Physiology of Common Life* (1859–60), in which the study of animal physiology merges with that of human psychology. What we learn from exploring the continuum between animal and human physiology is that consciousness, pace Descartes and his many followers, forms but a small item in the total of human psychical processes.[22]

We need to bear in mind that Lewes' location of psychological reality in unconscious volition, while it may partake of a revolution in the theory of mind, does not represent a revolution in ethics in the way, for example, Freud's concern with similar issues does. Unconscious volition, as Lewes understands it, is not without its Aristotelian *eidos*. The instincts have their form, and this form closely approximates certain moral presuppositions. Balzac, for example, is criticized for displaying instincts that go beyond the "natural" limit. Adultery is within that limit, but incestuous feelings are not ("Balzac," pp. 269–73). Later, following Comte, Lewes will argue that there is in human nature a fundamental structure that makes for disinterested love or altruism, as opposed to self-interest or egoism.[23] The latter instinct, one notes, was the mainstay of the contemporary associationist or utilitarian school, against whose claims to being a scientific theory of mind Lewes and the Comteans were in conscious reaction.

Applying his psychological concepts to art, Lewes comes up in the 1850s with what he considers a properly scientific theory of artistic form. The form of art must mirror or reflect the essential structure of human feeling. The only "legitimate style of idealization," he writes in his 1858 essay "Realism in Art," lies in representing the inner emotional structure of the human subject. His principal example of this, Raphael's "Madonna di San Sisto," is also a favorite of George Eliot's and figures importantly in her own realist efforts to express a "legitimate idealization." In Raphael's painting, says Lewes, we see "at once the intensest realism of presentation, with the highest idealism of conception." The Christ child expresses an "undefinable something" which we feel is a "perfect truth" of human nature: "we feel that humanity in its highest conceivable form is before us." The virgin mother's expression is also in the "highest sense ideal" precisely because "it is also in the highest sense real." This artistic "conception," as Lewes insists, is not grounded in any theological or metaphysical principle, but is the product of a "sympathetic," a purely psychological, projection of the artist's self into the unapparent emotional center of another human being. What is "ideal" is the sentiment felt by the artist in the actual human subjects and then "thrown into" the images on the canvas.[24] We note as well that in this particular image the emotional structure represented as ideal is a conspicuously altruistic one. Later, in *The Principles of Success in Literature* (1865), Lewes gives fuller theoretical attention to this issue of the ideal-cum-formal in art. There he objects to what he calls "the rage for 'realism.'" Realism is "healthy in as far as it insists on truth," but "unhealthy in as far as it confounds truth with . . . predominance of unessential details." A "rational philosophy" of art understands that the "natural means *truth of a kind*," or, to use what has become for him an absolutely central concept, the truth of "type."[25]

Obviously, the more Lewes' notion of a legitimate idealization or truth of type seems to coincide with values that have their roots in the Judeo-Christian ethical tradition, the more we feel that, for all his positivist protestations, metaphysical presuppositions have seeped into his concept of realism. To understand what makes him so confident that this, in fact, has not taken place, that the forms of feeling or instinct which he seeks in art actually exist in human nature, we need to return to his work in scientific psychology.

Like many other contemporary researchers in the field, Lewes had come to believe one could find hard biological evidence of the reality of the psychological-cum-moral types that were the objects of the artist's vision. This is very much the sort of confidence we find in a modern biologist like Melvin Konner who, on seeing a photograph of the pyramidal brain cells, believes he has seen the essence of mind: "somehow it is structure—that most ancient of biological subjects—seen and drawn or photographed through the microscope—that most classic of tools— that persuades at last."[26] Lewes, of course, had no means of photographing, let alone seeing, the brain cells that determine thought. Yet by the close of the 1850s he was no less convinced than Konner that human consciousness is the result of typical neurological structures that are potentially observable.

Here Lewes' inspiration comes initially from Goethe, the one artist of the Romantic era whom he admires, the poet whose work in science taught him the necessity of an "objective" approach to art.[27] The German poet's greatest contribution to science was in formulating the principles of morphology, the "soul" of biological study, as Darwin says.[28] He was the first to express in definite terms the idea of the unity of plan or structure within all organic nature. His object, as he writes in the *Erster Entwurf einer allgemeinen Einleitung in die vergleichende Anatomie* (1795), is "to arrive at an anatomical *type* [anatomischer Typus], a general picture in which the forms of all animals are contained in potentia, and by means of which we can describe each animal in an invariable order" (my emphasis).[29]

There is no need to review here the story of Goethe's search for the fundamental organic type, the *Urbild*, from which all animal life has evolved. It is a commonplace at once of Goethe studies and the history of biology.[30] What we do need to note is that Lewes effectively made Goethe's theory the basis of all his work in physiology and psychology. "It is impossible," he writes in the *Life of Goethe*, "to be even superficially acquainted with biological speculations and not to recognise the immense importance of [the theory of the] Type" (p. 351). By the time he comes five years later to the climactic chapter in *The Physiology of Common Life*, the chapter on the definition of life, he believes modern science has found that type in the cell, "the true biological atom," the structural unit from which all life derives (*Physiology*, 2: 357).[31] Is it any wonder that when George Eliot comes at last to give us a representative scientist in the figure of Tertius Lydgate, that scientist should be devoting his life work to the search for the "primitive tissue"? For Lewes, no less than Lydgate, the existence of a universal organic type at the source of all life argues the likelihood of a universal and scientifically demonstrable form of human consciousness.

Again we note that the form of consciousness Lewes, as well as George Eliot, wants most to demonstrate is that of an innate structural propensity for disinterested love:

> As the Aggressive Instinct springs from the Nutritive, so the Sexual Instinct springs from the Reproductive. It is the first of the sympathetic tendencies, the germ of Altruism. Love, which is the social motor, has this origin. (*Problems*, 1st ser., 1:176)[32]

There is, of course, an important connection here with the Romantic aesthetic Lewes is seeking to displace, for no less than the Romantics he wants to affirm a vision of nature and mind united in an encompassing economy of love, to demonstrate, as Wordsworth has it, that "to love as prime and chief" we owe "all lasting [human] grandeur" (*The Prelude* [1850], 14.168–69). The difference is that Lewes seeks to ground that vision in the science of biology and not, like Wordsworth et al., in the phenomenology of spirit or imagination.

102

III

We come at this point to the classical disjunction in the positivist theory of mind, the disjunction that, in effect, generates the late-century neo-Kantian reaction to positivism, of which Cassirer, with whom we began, is a distinguished product. This reaction, in turn, leads to a revitalization of the concept of the symbol and a reassertion of its centrality in the aesthetic process. Mid-nineteenth-century "naturalistic theories of art," writes Cassirer, set out to refute "romantic conceptions of a transcendental" idea at the heart of the aesthetic. But

> they missed the principal point since they failed to recognize the symbolic character of art. . . . Art is, indeed, symbolism, but the symbolism of art must be understood in an immanent, not a transcendental sense. (*Essay*, p. 157)

What I now want to show is how Lewes, following out the logic of his own positivist theory of mind, or rather the breakdown of that logic, and influenced by one of Cassirer's own mentors, anticipates by a generation this critical modernist move toward a new, "immanent" understanding of the symbol.

The problem Lewes faces is that of moving from organic structures, which he can verify using ordinary scientific procedures, to psychological or mental ones, which he cannot verify by those procedures. Comte's assertion, for example, that the brain's physiological structure contains the germ of altruism is, as Lewes comes to understand, sheer speculation; it cannot be scientifically substantiated according to the principles of Comte's own method. Yet one contemporary psychologist seemed to Lewes to have approached a solution to this problem of moving from organic to mental forms. This was Hermann von Helmholtz, a man whom, in his later writing, he placed with Bacon, Newton, and Comte on his shortlist of the greatest thinkers of the modern world (*Problems*, 1st ser., 1:175),[33] the clear implication being that Helmholtz had become for him Comte's successor in science's effort to define the nature of mind.

A student of Kant and at the same time fully devoted to the natural sciences, Helmholtz made a critical contribution to the positivist theory of mind. In a word, he naturalized Kant's transcendental aesthetic, reducing the a priori forms of that aesthetic to physiological structures through the laboratory analysis of perception.

> Perceptions of external objects being . . . of the nature of ideas, and ideas themselves being invariably activities of our psychic energy, perceptions also can only be the result of psychic energy. Accordingly, . . . the theory of perceptions belongs properly in the domain of psychology. . . . [We] have to determine, scientifically as far as possible, what special properties of the physical stimulus and of the physiological stimulation are responsible for the formation of this or that particular idea as to the nature of the external objects perceived. . . . Thus, our main purpose will be simply to investigate the material of sensation whereby we are enabled to form ideas.[34]

As Cassirer has observed, with Helmholtz we have "a new and unique bond . . . forged between empirical science and philosophy."[35] For Lewes, Helmholtz's research seems to have come as a revelation, making for him the crucial connection between organic structure and thought.

We see clear evidence of Helmholtz's impact on Lewes in the latter's first theoretical treatise on psychology attached as "Prolegomena" to the 1867 edition of his *History of Philosophy*, the point presumably being to present his reader with the latest advance in that scientific psychology which the *History* announces as the goal of philosophy. The "sensationalist" (that is, the associationist or utilitarian) theory of mind must now, says Lewes, give way to an entirely new conception.

> The Sensational School [postulates an] unscientific conception of the mind as a *tabula rasa* upon which Things inscribe their characters—a mirror passively reflecting the images of objects. This presupposes that Consciousness is absolved from the universal law of action and reaction, presupposes that the Organism has no movement of its own. . . . The *a priori* [metaphysical] School commits the opposite mistake of conceiving Consciousness as a pure spontaneity, undetermined by the conditions of the Organism and its environment; a spontaneity . . . derived from a supra-mundane, supra-vital source.
>
> We cannot take a step unless we admit that Consciousness is an active reagent. . . . Nor is this all. Biology teaches that the Sensitive Organism inherits certain [mental] aptitudes. . . . Forms of Thought . . . are evolved, just like the Forms of other vital processes. (*History of Philosophy*, 1: xcv–xcvi)

George Lewes' Scientific Aesthetic

In his criticism of Hegel at the close of the *History of Philosophy*, Lewes had focused on the German's metaphysical transmutation of the logical into the real. "How does the Logical become the Real, how are the Forms of Thought shown to be at the same time the Forms of Things?" Hegel, says Lewes, resolves this Kantian dilemma from the wrong direction by making the forms of thought prior to and productive of the forms of things (2: 635). Using Helmholtz, with an admixture of Darwin, Lewes, as we see, believes he has established the proper relation of mental to external form: the forms of things are prior to and productive of the forms of thought, the latter being an evolution from the former.

This is a promising approach to anchoring mental structure in reality, to achieving Comte's goal, noticed earlier, of assimilating the shape of human thought to "l'ordre extérieur." If it can be made to work, one may (to return to our central concern) dispense with symbols, at least in the sense in which Lewes objected to them. Taking what Lewes himself comes to regard as the most fundamental institution of human thought, the structure of language, we see that by extending the spirit of Helmholtz's inquiry, one might, theoretically, reduce that structure to "un miroir exact" of the world in which there need be no symbolic, no merely "arbitrary," overdetermination of what "never was on sea or land." Indeed, this was to become the project of the Vienna positivists in our own century. But for Lewes, I may as well say at once, this move does not succeed. He is all right as long as, like Helmholtz, he is concerned only with forms of thought as sensuous *apperceptions* of the real. But when he tries to move from apperception to the forms of thought that really matter to him, both as psychologist and as critic, that is, *moral* forms, he still has no way of making the transition from organic structure to consciousness. Here his scientific realism collapses into a quasi-Kantian assertion of the subjective universality of moral law. In short, he founders on G. E. Moore's "naturalistic fallacy," the fallacy of seeking to identify *ought* with *is*.[36] And, one must add, his original project of a scientific aesthetic, insofar as it cannot transcend the association of artistic form with moral order (as Helmholtz, for example, does), necessarily founders on the same rock. How, then, does Lewes extricate himself from this difficulty? The answer, as I have suggested, lies in a reconsideration of the nature of symbolization, a reconsideration to which he is led by a side of Helmholtz's thought we have not yet adequately developed.

IV

There is a substantial Kantian residue in Helmholtz of which, as we have seen, Lewes is well aware: "we cannot take a step unless we admit that consciousness is an active reagent." One of the things that the study of Helmholtz—and the extensive rereading of Kant occasioned by that study[37]—does for Lewes is awaken in him a full recognition of the radically *constitutive* function of mind. On this issue he ponders increasingly in the late work, becoming more and more preoccupied with scientific epistemology and, specifically, with the formation and function of hypothesis in scientific discovery. This turn of thought we first see, significantly, in *The Principles of Success in Literature* (1865), his last serious dissertation on art and, at the same time, the beginning for him of a new way of perceiving the intersection between the aesthetic and scientific planes. Lewes, as we shall see, is a central nineteenth-century instance of Gillian Beer's argument in her essay that there is a profound conjunction in the work of scientist and creative writer.

The first principle of success in art is the one we have already noticed, the principle of vision. This, again, is a power of "insight" into the unapparent, typical structure of things. In my earlier discussion of this concept I was concerned to show how Lewes used it to develop the point that what the artist imitates is not empirical reality but its inner form. Now I want to turn to a different implication of the principle, one that reflects the new direction in which Helmholtz and Kant are taking him. As we examine what he says about aesthetic vision, we soon see that it is a faculty not only for detecting what is potentially there in nature but also for "inferring" or "constructing" what is "apparently" not there. From the most fundamental level of perception to the highest expression of reason and imagination, Lewes says, the mind in some sense constructs the order of nature, and this is equally true whether that mind belongs to artist or scientist: "both poet and [scientific] philosopher draw their power from the energy of their mental vision—an energy which disengages the mind from the somnolence of habit and from the pressure of obtrusive sensation" (*Principles*, p. 18). Here Lewes is almost certainly following Helmholtz, who identifies the essential process of scientific discovery as an "aesthetic" rather than "logical" induction. The scientist's hypothetical conclusions rest, finally, says the German, "on a certain psychological instinct [for order] not on conscious reasoning."[38] Helmholtz, in fact, is initiating a significant shift in the concept of scientific method. By the 1870s, observes a recent historian of scientific method, "mechanistic materialism" with its reliance on inductivism was, "in the German scientific community," "gradually [giving] way to a neo-Kantian philosophy of science developed initially by Helmholtz."[39]

Lewes, who closely followed "the German scientific community," obviously had not missed the point. A decade after *Principles*, in the first volume of his uncompleted organon of scientific philosophy, *Problems of Life and Mind*, Lewes produced a far more extensive and sophisticated account of what amounts to the aesthetic "principle of vision," only now he talks of it exclusively as a principle of scientific discovery. "Science is fertile not because it is a tank but because it is a spring. The grandest discoveries . . . have not only outstripped the slow march of Observation, but have revealed by the telescope of Imagination what the microscope of Observation could never have seen" (*Problems*, 1st ser., 1: 315). We need only be careful—and here the positivist bent of mind reasserts itself—to make sure we distinguish between the artistic and the scientific process. The scientist, having made his imaginative construct, must then *verify* it against observation, the "logic of feeling," as Lewes calls it. "Flights of imagination" are "legitimate tentatives of scientific Research" only if "they submit to the one indispensable condition . . . of ultimate verification" (p. 317).

But what principle of verification does Lewes have in mind for art? Returning to *Principles*, we find under the heading of the "principle of sincerity" that the successful literary artist is one who writes only about what he has directly experienced and genuinely believes.

It is always understood as an expression of condemnation when anything in Literature or Art is said to be done for effect. . . . It is desirable to clear up this moral ambiguity, as I may call it, and to show that the real method of securing the legitimate effect is not to aim at it, but to aim at truth, relying on that for securing effect. . . . Nothing but what is true, or is held to be true, can succeed. (p. 42)

Good intentions notwithstanding, Lewes, far from clearing up an ambiguity, is creating one. Truth in the present formula ceases to be one. It is both "what is" and "what is held to be." The former is presumably the scientist's concern, the latter, what Lewes elsewhere calls "subjective truth," the artist's. If we sincerely believe something to be true, then it is, in some sense, so. In precisely what sense? In the sense that one's sincere conviction creates conviction in others; "belief creates belief," says Lewes (*Principles*, p. 45). This represents a significant departure from what he was arguing throughout the essays of the 1840s and 1850s. Now "falsity" in art is not necessarily failure to conform to things as they are, but failure to conform to things *as we hold them to be*. By this new criterion, to be false in art is to be self-consciously rhetorical, to aim at an effect rather than sincerely to express what one believes to be true.

The difficulty with this distinction is apparent. Whether the artist intends to deceive or genuinely believes what he says is immaterial to the question of whether his interpretation of life is true. As Yeats says, "The rhetorician would deceive his neighbours, / The sentimentalist himself" ("Ego Dominus Tuus," lines 46–47), or, put another way, the sincere believer in mere "sentiment" is but marginally less deceptive than the rhetorician who sets out to deceive. The former is honest only by virtue of lying to himself. In more consistent, less transitional phases of his thinking, Lewes is aware enough of the problem. Discussing "the place of sentiment in philosophy" in *Problems*, he asks what we are to say about the role of "Sentiment or Emotion" in the construction of our beliefs. We have "Moral Instincts and Aesthetic Instincts which determine conduct and magnify existence," but we have absolutely no more ground for believing in their truth than our "conviction" that their effects are beneficial, and we cannot identify conviction with verification. Our moral beliefs can "in a last resort . . . only be justified by asserting the facts are so" (1st ser., 1: 456–57). The principle of sincerity, which begins as a strategy for grounding artistic vision in reality, ends by leading Lewes to a bifurcation of truth into that which can be properly verified by scientific method and that which can be verified only by subjective assent. The second kind of truth, associated at first with the relatively innocuous category of aesthetic expression, eventually works its way into the far more critical category of ethical belief. At this point Lewes seems to say, in anticipation of William James, that "the desire for a certain kind of truth . . . brings about that special truth's existence,"[40] and insofar as he is saying this, he has placed himself at a considerable distance from the positivist faith that one can construct a new morality and hence a new social order by scientific means alone. Once in this position he is ready for a revaluation of the nature of symbolic discourse.

This is precisely what begins to happen at the close of *Principles*. The third and final principle of art, the "principle of beauty," Lewes effectively identifies with style and, more specifically, *symbolic* expression. The artist's vision and his sincerity are useless unless he can express what he sees and believes in "accurate" symbols.

> It is not enough that a man has clearness of Vision, and reliance on Sincerity, he must also have the art of Expression. . . . The power of seizing unapparent relations of things is not always conjoined with the power of *selecting the fittest verbal symbols by which they can be made apparent to others.* (p. 55, my emphasis)

What we notice immediately in this reinstatement of symbols as crucial to the artistic process is not simply the reversal of Lewes' previous position, but the fact that the symbolization he is talking about is still very much an arbitrary expression into which preconceived concepts are *thrust*. There is no pretense of an organic or "consubstantial" relation between symbolic medium and that to which it refers. The symbols Lewes is talking about are clearly not Romantic ones. They require no verification beyond that of their *effectiveness* in conveying the artist's beliefs. Effectiveness becomes, as it were, a substitute for presence or, in Lewes' terms, for verification. This new willingness to countenance symbolic expression in art is, as I have suggested, a direct consequence of the bifurcation of truth we have just noticed. Once introduce a notion of subjective truth as the basis of art's reality, and the idea of art as the direct nonsymbolic representation of "what is" gives way to that of art as a system of communication aimed at causing the audience to "hold as true" what the artist believes "is." In short, the symbol becomes a means of embodying and imparting an order that cannot be scientifically demonstrated to exist in nature.

The concept of symbolization developed here at the close of *Principles*, like his "principle of vision," returns in *Problems of Life and Mind* as a crucial element in Lewes' theory of scientific discovery. In the last volume of *Problems*, he turns to what he calls "the Sphere of Intellect and the Logic of Signs." The logic of signs he also calls the "logic of symbols," and the hesitation between the two terms "sign" and "symbol" no doubt reflects the tension between his conventional positivism and his growing awareness of the pragmatic force of symbolic expression.

The logic of symbols, he writes, is essentially the representation of concepts. It involves the "mental constructions" or "abstract general signs" of what we receive through the logic of feeling or remember through the logic of images. It is a "notation," in "artificial marks" or "verbal symbols," of a "class," which it "signifies and condenses." It is also "conventional," the "result of social influence." In the last analysis, the logic of symbols is what makes us human: "the power of thinking by means of symbols . . . demarcates man from animals" (*Problems*, 3d ser., pp. 485–96).

As we pursue this discussion, we find some striking developments beyond Lewes' earlier treatment of symbolization in *Principles*. First, symbolization is no longer a process peculiar to artistic production, but an essential component of scientific reasoning. Using the symbolic logic of algebra as a metaphor for scientific thought in general, he speaks of how with algebraic notation the mind enters a "new sphere," where "letters are symbols of any values we please," and "although the values are changeable, yet once assigned, they must remain fixed throughout the operations." The process of scientific discovery is just such an algebraic tentative:

> Although it is impossible to frame an image of Infinity, we can, and do, form the idea, and reason on it with precision. Nay the paradox is demonstrable that the chief part of our scientific knowledge, so accurate and so important in its direction of our conduct, consists of ideas which cannot be formed into corresponding images and sensations. (pp. 469–71)

The freedom from referentialilty that characterized the symbol as an artistic notation in *Principles* now is carried over for use in a scientific process that had hitherto decisively excluded it. One may go further: Lewes seems at this point actually to be replacing the principle of vision as the primary means of scientific discovery with that of symbolization.

The objective of both principles, identifying the typical, lawlike structures within the real, is the same, but the shift from the metaphor of vision to that of symbol is crucial. When Lewes speaks of the scientist's *vision* of a type, he implies its real existence. When he speaks of the scientist's *symbolic construction* of the type, he implies its fundamental fictivity.

In his final chapter, "The Potency of Symbols," Lewes turns briefly to what we may call the sociology of the symbol. So "mighty is the power of names" that it is "capable of determining action" even among "highly-cultivated people."

> Ideas are verbal symbols. The power such ideas have over feelings and actions is incalculable. . . . It is Language which records and generalises experience and opens a vista of experiences about to be. [The logic of symbols] underlies all our planning, connects our actions with the lives of those who are to succeed us, and moulds our conception of the world. . . . The invention of a new symbol is a step in the advancement of civilization. (pp. 494–95)

We might almost be reading Cassirer. Indeed, for all practical purposes we are, for Lewes—by way of Helmholtz and, again, within the positivist tradition that Cassirer deplores—has arrived at the same "immanent" concept of the symbol which forms the ground of Cassirer's own philosophy. Like Cassirer, he understands the symbol not as the embodiment of a transcendent, metaphysical presence, but as simply a tentative ordering of experience. Like Cassirer, he has come to see the artist's construction of symbolic form as a universal humanistic gesture that informs all cultural production.

What I have been describing is how one well-read and very sophisticated literary theorist arrived at this demystified concept of the symbol well before Cassirer and the advent of literary modernism, and arrived at it from within a tradition that modernism believes to be inherently inimical to art. Partly Lewes makes this movement of mind under the influence of a scientific thinker who felt, even as he radically modified, the force of Kant's thought. But it is important to emphasize that influence is not the only issue here. Helmholtz, after all, has little to tell Lewes about the nature of symbolism. Lewes' thought develops as it does ultimately, I believe, because of his acute understanding, unusual in so accomplished a scientific philosopher, of the way aesthetic and, in particular, literary discourse functions. More precisely, the difficulty he has in bringing aesthetic phenomena within the scope of scientific method, as he originally conceived it, effectively compels him to examine the function of that in art which is least commensurable with the scientific ideal, namely, its radical fictivity. The more he examines this fictivity, the more he realizes that he is working with a form of symbolic discourse whose object is not to picture existent realities but to affect certain attitudes and beliefs in the beholder. This mature understanding of fictivity and its symbolic conveyance comes eventually to "contaminate" his concept of scientific method in the ways we have just seen. Having begun with the conventionally positivist notion of scientizing art, he ends by, in effect, aestheticizing science, and, in the process, redefining the positivist enterprise at its methodological core.

De Man and deconstructionists in general would not consider that the Lewes I have described—any more than the neo-Kantians they are, in effect, displacing as arbiters of contemporary literary theory—has finally liberated himself from the ideology of the symbol. They would argue that Lewes, having begun by "deconstructing" a Romantic ideology of the symbol in favor of a positivist "metaphysic" of organic presence, has, after all, ended by reconstructing the ideology of the symbol in its new Kantian or "immanent" form. The symbol thus redefined no longer refers to a transcendent spiritual presence, but it is still a centered structure, whose origin is the creative human intelligence and whose object, however distant, is still correspondence to the structure of the world.

Yet do we not see in Lewes' final move toward the aestheticization of the sacred category of science itself a gesture that looks toward our distinctly postmodernist concerns? The ultimate effect of the Derridean assault on the ideology of the symbol has been, as Geoffrey Hartman has suggested, the "foregrounding of the artistic as the philosophical, or the birth of philosophy out of the spirit of art."[41] It would be impertinent of me to cast Lewes in the role of protodeconstructionist. He is still firmly in the positivist camp. Yet in his late discovery of the spirit of art *in* science, if not at its origin, he has embarked on a path which, if pursued, might well lead to such "deconstructive" approaches to this heartland of rationality and objectivity as those offered in our own time by Paul Feyerabend, Thomas Kuhn, W. V. Quine, and others. The principal controversy among modern philosophers of sciences, as Richard Rorty has said, is "about whether science, as the discovery of what is really out there in the world, differs in its patterns of argumentation from discourses for which the notion of 'correspondence to reality' seems less apposite (e.g., . . . literary criticism)."[42] Lewes at his most aesthetic would never abandon science to the "conceptual relativism" that Rorty is alluding to. Yet, at the same time, he could not help probing that persistent discontinuity between world and word, or, as he called it, "life and mind," which has issued in our "postempiricist" skepticism over whether science, any more than art, can ever deliver on its promise to bring the two realms together, to make mind the mirror of life.

Notes

1. Ernst Cassirer, *An Essay on Man: An Introduction to a Philosophy of Human Culture* (New Haven: Yale University Press, 1944), p. 170.

2. Jonathan Culler, *On Deconstruction: Theory and Criticism after Structuralism* (Ithaca: Cornell University Press, 1982), p. 178.

3. Cited by Culler, *On Deconstruction*, p. 23.

4. There are any number of definitions of positivism. The most comprehensive is that developed by Leszek Kolakowski in his historical survey *The Alienation of Reason: A History of Positivist Thought*, trans. N. Guterman (Garden City: Doubleday, 1968). See especially chapter 1. Like Kolakowski I do not restrict "positivism" to its Victorian connotation of the philosophy developed by Comte.

5. The phrase I borrow from Christopher Norris' *The Deconstructive Turn: Essays in the Rhetoric of Philosophy* (London and New York: Methuen, 1983), which does much to show us how pervasive a move deconstruction is in modern thought.

6. Paul de Man, "Sign and Symbol in Hegel's Aesthetics," *Critical Inquiry* 8 (1982): 763. For a more general discussion of Romantic metaphysics as ideology, see Jerome J. McGann's *The Romantic Ideology: A Critical Investigation* (Chicago: University of Chicago Press, 1983).

7. Jacques Derrida, *Margins of Philosophy*, trans. Alan Bass (Chicago: University of Chicago Press, 1982), pp. 20, 11.

8. G. W. F. Hegel, *Aesthetics: Lectures on Fine Arts*, trans. T. M. Knox (Oxford: Clarendon Press, 1975), 1: 7–8, 19, 164.

9. George Lewes, "Hegel's Aesthetics," *British and Foreign Review* 13 (1842): 1–49.

10. G. H. Lewes, *A Biographical History of Philosophy* (London: Routledge and Sons, 1846), p. 650.

11. G. H. Lewes, *The History of Philosophy from Thales to Comte* (London: Longmans, Green, 1871), 2: 689–98.

12. From the title of one of Lewes' earliest critical essays, "The Errors and Abuses of English Criticism," *Westminster Review* 38 (1842): 466–86. Here he first refers to the "truly deplorable condition" of contemporary English criticism. As becomes clear in subsequent essays, Lewes considers the "romantic spirit" responsible for this situation and, in particular, Coleridge's importation (and, as Lewes was perhaps the first to note publicly, plagiarism) of German sources. See especially, "August William Schlegel," *Foreign Quarterly Review* 32 (1843): 160–81; "Shakespeare and His Editors," *Westminster Review* 43 (1845): 40–77.

13. G. H. Lewes, "Shakespeare's Critics: English and Foreign," *Edinburgh Review* 90 (1849). This is, one notes, an early statement of an aesthetic project which Lewes will at last accomplish some twenty-five years later in *The Principles of Success in Literature* (see Section 4 below).

14. G. H. Lewes, *The Life of Goethe*, 3d ed. (London; Smith Elder, 1875), pp. 408–10, 447–48.

15. Auguste Comte, *Système de politique positive, ou traité de sociologie instituant la religion de l'humanité* (Paris: Mathias, 1851–54), 2: 382. Cited by Lewes in *Problems of Life and Mind* (London: Trubner, 1874–79), 1st ser., 1: 195.

16. Rudolf Carnap, "The Elimination of Metaphysics through Logical Analysis of Language," in A. J. Ayer, ed., *Logical Positivism* (New York, 1959), pp. 60–61.

17. G. H. Lewes, "Balzac and George Sand," *Foreign Quarterly Review* 33 (1844): 269, 284–85.

18. G. H. Lewes, "Julia von Krudener, as Coquette and Mystic," *Westminster Review* 57 (1852): 162–64. George Eliot, one notes, follows Lewes closely in the priority she gives to subrational motivation; see my " 'Brother Jacob': Fables and the Physiology of Common Life," *Philological Quarterly* 59 (1985): 17–35.

19. Herbert Marcuse, *Reason and Revolution: Hegel and the Rise of Social Theory* (Atlantic Highlands, N.J.: Humanities Press, 1983), pp. 323–30.

20. G. H. Lewes, *Comte's Philosophy of the Sciences: Being an Exposition of the Principles of the "Cours de Philosophie Positive" of Auguste Comte* (London: George Bell, 1875), section 21, "Psychology: A New Cerebral Theory." Lewes' primary source in Comte is the *Politique positive*, vol. 1, "Introduction fondamentale," chap. 3.

21. Notably by Frederick Gregory, *Scientific Materialism in Nineteenth-Century Germany* (Dordrecht: Reidel, 1977); John T. Mertz, *A History of European Thought in the Nineteenth Century* (Edinburgh: Blackwood, 1928), Vol. 2; and Robert M. Young, *Mind, Brain, and Adaptation in the Nineteenth Century: Cerebral Localization and Its Biological Context from Gall to Ferrier* (Oxford: Clarendon, 1970).

22. G. H. Lewes, *The Physiology of Common Life* (Edinburgh: Blackwood, 1859–60); see especially chap. 8.

23. Beginning with *Comte's Philosophy of the Sciences*, pp. 217–24. See also note 32 below.

24. G. H. Lewes, "Realism in Art: Recent German Fiction," *Westminster Review* 70 (1858): 493–95.

25. G. H. Lewes, *The Principles of Success in Literature* (Westmead: Gregg International Publishers, 1969), pp. 40–41; these essays were first published in the *Fortnightly Review*, May–November 1865. Lewes' preoccupation with "types" and their ontological status begins with his close study of Goethe in the early 1850s. See, e.g., "Goethe as a Man of Science," *Westminster Review* 52 (1852): 497, and the further development of the thought in that essay in the later *Life of Goethe*, especially book 5, chapter 9, "The Poet as a Man of Science."

26. Melvin Konner, *The Tangled Wing: Biological Constraints on the Human Spirit* (New York: Harper Colophon Books, 1983), p. 61.

27. Goethe, of course, is himself reacting against the excesses of contemporary Romanticism. Lewes' scientific aesthetic shares with Matthew Arnold's neoclassicist one a view of Goethe as the poet for the modern, post-Romantic era.

28. Cited by Ernst Mayr, *The Growth of Biological Thought: Diversity, Evolution, and Inheritance* (Cambridge, Mass.: Harvard University Press, 1982), p. 455.

29. J. W. Goethe, *Werke*, ed. E. Beutler (Zurich: Artemis, 1952), 17: 233. The translation is E. S. Russell's from *Form and Function: A Contribution to the History of Animal Morphology* (Chicago: University of Chicago Press, 1982), p. 46.

30. See Mayr's and Russell's discussions of Goethe in the works cited above. For more detailed treatments see Heinrich Henel, "Type and Proto-Phenomenon in Goethe's Science," *PMLA* 71 (1956): 652–68, and H. B. Nisbet, "Herder, Goethe, and the Natural 'Type,'" *Publications of the English Goethe Society* 37 (1966–67): 82–119.

31. The fullest development of Lewes' concept of the type of "germinal matter" and the relation of that type to evolution (not discussed in *Physiology*) is in *The Physiological Basis of Mind* (London: Trubner, 1877; this is the Second Series of *Problems of Life and Mind*), "Problem I: The Nature of Life," pp. 3–136.

32. The enterprise Lewes is engaged upon represents an important strain of Victorian efforts to discover a biological basis for, essentially, Christian ethics. See Ashley Montague, *Darwin: Competition and Cooperation* (New York: Henry Schuman, 1952) for a brief (and impressionistic) survey of the movement.

33. The earliest mention I find of Helmholtz in Lewes' work is in the 1855 *Life of Goethe* (p. 141) where he quotes him on Goethe's scientific method. Given Lewes' growing interest in physiology in the late 1850s, it is likely he would have looked into Helmholtz's best-known work, *Handbuch der physiologischen Optik*, which began coming out in 1856. In any case, he admired Helmholtz's work enough to make a special effort to visit him on his German trip of 1868 (Journal 12 [Beinecke Library], 10 January 1868) and was reading him regularly in 1869 while working on what was to become *Problems* ("Diaries" [Beinecke Library], January–February 1869).

34. Hermann von Helmholtz, *Treatise on Physiological Optics*, trans. from third German ed. by J. P. C. Southall (New York: Dover Publications, 1962), 3: 1.

35. Ernst Cassirer, *The Problem of Knowledge: Philosophy, Science, and History since Hegel*, trans. W. H. Woglom and C. W. Hendel (New Haven: Yale University Press, 1950), p. 4.

36. G. E. Moore, *Principia Ethica* (Cambridge, Eng.: Cambridge University Press, 1903), chap. 2. See also W. D. Hudson, *Modern Moral Philosophy* (Garden City: Doubleday, 1970), chap. 3, part 1, "Moore and the Rejection of Ethical Naturalism."

37. Both the Prolegomena to the 1867 edition of *History of Philosophy* and the chapter on Kant evidence a much more comprehensive grasp of Kant and his commentators than one finds in the 1857 edition.

38. Hermann von Helmholtz, "The Relation of the Natural Sciences to Science in General" (1862), trans. H. W. Eve, *Selected Writings of Hermann von Helmholtz*, ed. Russell Kahl (Middletown, Conn.: Wesleyan University Press, 1971), pp. 131–32. Helmholtz, in turn, is inspired, as Lewes well knows, by Goethe's "aesthetic" approach to scientific method; see "The Scientific Researches of Goethe" (1853), trans. H. W. Eve, *ibid.*, pp. 64–69, and Lewes' comments on Helmholtz on Goethe in *Life of Goethe* (1875), p. 351.

39. Frederick Suppe, introduction, in Suppe, ed., *The Structure of Scientific Theories* (Urbana: University of Illinois Press, 1974), pp. 8–9.

40. William James, *The Will to Believe and Other Essays in Popular Philosophy* (New York: Longmans Green, 1897), p. 24.

41. Geoffrey Hartman, *Saving the Text: Literature/Derrida/Philosophy* (Baltimore: Johns Hopkins University Press, 1981), p. 72.

42. Richard Rorty, *Philosophy and the Mirror of Nature* (Princeton: Princeton University Press, 1979), p. 332. The postempiricist movement in science against positivist presuppositions about the nature of truth is discussed in detail by Frederick Suppe, Introduction to *Structure of Scientific Theories*, pp. 119–90. I refer to this movement as "deconstructionist" only with the qualification indicated by the quotation marks. The movement, in fact, preceded and developed independently of the rise of Derrida and continental deconstructionism.

Part III

Crossing the Barriers:
Mutual Influences

N. KATHERINE HAYLES

Information or Noise?
Economy of Explanation in
Barthes's *S/Z* and
Shannon's Information Theory

Traditionally, studies in literature and science have assumed that scientific concepts have "influenced" writers, and that their task is to elucidate these influences for other readers who may be less knowledgeable about science. A recent review essay, for example, suggests that works in this field should be evaluated according to whether the critic has shown "that the author's consciousness as a writer is affected by contact with ideas from science."[1] In my view, this methodology is seriously misleading if taken as a model of how culture is formed and transmitted. Because it assumes that "influence" flows from science to literature, it necessarily implies that science occupies a privileged position within the culture instead of being itself part of the culture.

One of the objectives of this volume is to demonstrate the inadequacy of this model. The pressures of language toward teleology, design, and anthropocentrism, discussed by Gillian Beer, suggest the community of source and expression between science and literature. Donald Benson's essay, to take another example, posits, as he puts it, "an integrated culture in which science and art are complementary enterprises, both of them significantly shaped by and at the same time giving shape to common cultural fictions and assumptions." Similarly, David Bell, drawing on the work of Michel Serres, will be concerned with the very

This essay was written under a grant from the Woodrow Wilson International Center for Scholars, in Washington, D.C., for whose generosity and assistance I am grateful. The statements and views expressed herein are those of the author and not necessarily those of the Wilson Center.

vaguely defined frontiers "between the discursive regions belonging variously to science and to other cultural manifestations." Of course, each analysis of the inadequacy of the "influence" model has different ends, explores different aspects of the confluence of discourses.

But surely one must say that *both* literature and science are cultural products, at once expressing and helping to form the cultural matrix from which they emerge. Rather than assume a horizontal model, where "influence" travels from science to literature, I envision a vertical model, with both science and literature emerging from underlying forces at work within the culture generally. To understand their isomorphism, especially in instances where direct influence is unlikely, is to begin to understand the parameters shaping the culture as a whole.

In this essay, the implications of cultural isomorphism for the study of literature and science are explored through what I shall call the "information perspective." Although technical definitions of information can be complex, the essence of the information perspective is simplicity itself. It consists of considering information as a more fundamental entity in the world than either matter or energy.[2] "Information" in this sense does not mean only UPI news releases or computer printouts, although these contribute to our sense that we live in an "information age." It also denotes a rigorously defined quantity that can be measured with scientific instruments and expressed by mathematical equations.

When Claude Shannon, an engineer working for Bell Laboratories, gave information its definitive quantitative expression in two seminal papers published in 1948, his equation for information turned out to be essentially identical to Boltzmann's statistical equation for entropy.[3] Traditionally, entropy in Boltzmann's formula had been interpreted as a measure of the randomness or disorder present in a system; yet we think of information as intrinsically ordered. It seemed counterintuitive, then, to say that information is the *same* as entropy. During the next decade there were debates in the technical literature on whether information should have the same sign as entropy (Shannon's convention), or whether it should have the opposite sign (the convention used by Leon Brillouin). By about 1960, the debate was decided: the Shannon convention was adopted, and "information" and "entropy" were used as interchangeable terms by most information theorists.[4] (See, for a "literary" use of this convention, Gillian Beer's discussion of Pynchon's *The Crying of Lot 49*.)

In retrospect, the argument over information's sign was anything but trivial, for within the next decade it would lead to a radical reevaluation of the relation not only between information and entropy but, more fundamentally, between order and chaos. In the research that was to emerge through considering physical systems as transmitters of information rather than as matter/energy systems, chaos is no longer simply the opposite of order. Rather, it is the precursor to order, an infinitely rich information source from which all potential order and form come. This view has redirected the attention of scientists to how prevalent chaos is in natural systems. It has also raised fundamental questions about human comprehension of a universe rich in disorder. If chaos is information too complex to comprehend, then perhaps the limiting factor for composing a workable number system, for example, is the human mind rather than the inherent rationality of numbers.[5] Some scientists, in a dramatic departure from scientific tradition, have responded to this and similar speculations by privileging chaos over order.[6] Although I will not have space here to indicate the nature of the research results that lead to this view, their scope and generality are indicated by the fact that this perspective appears in various ways in irreversible thermodynamics, nonlinear dynamics, algorithmic complexity theory, information theory, and meteorology.

In literary theory during the parallel period, a similar reevaluation of the relation between order and chaos occurred with deconstruction. Shannon's first move in defining information was to separate message from meaning; similarly, the first move in deconstruction was to separate sign from signification. Conceiving of language as a system of signs, Ferdinand de Saussure argued that each sign is composed of a signifier and signified.[7] But since the signified is a *concept* and not an external referent, it can be viewed as another signifier in turn. Thus language becomes an endless chain of signifiers whose meanings are necessarily indeterminate, since they can be specified only in terms of other signifiers. In Jacques Derrida's hands, this indeterminacy is linked to the absence of an originary Logos. Because origin is always an illusion or pretense, Derrida argues, indeterminacy is "always already" present.[8] Deconstructive reading reveals this intrinsic indeterminacy, transforming the apparently closed and bounded verbal structure of a book into a text possessing an infinite amount of information. As in the "science of chaos," this methodology is accompanied by a change in values: chaos is privileged over order, increasing information over closure.

The comparison of deconstruction with the "science of chaos" is instructive, because the sources that theorists in the two disciplines identify as formative influences on their work have nothing in common with each other. Derrida, for example, works in the philosophic tradition of Nietzsche, Hegel, and Heidegger; Mitchell Feigenbaum, the physicist who formulated universality theory and used it to demonstrate that chaotic systems possess a deep structure, was intrigued with how deterministic equations become unstable through iteration.[9] Did Derrida read Mitchell Feigenbaum? Did Feigenbaum read Derrida? I have been able to find no evidence for direct influence between the two, and I doubt that it exists. Yet both Derrida and Feigenbaum talk about iteration, about "folds" that when "unfolded" demonstrate radical indeterminacy, and about the infinite information to which such indeterminacy gives rise. In the absence of influence, what can account for this isomorphism?

Two different strategies of explanation are possible. One is to look for some cataclysmic, culturally shared experience, and argue that from this common experience emerged a deeply shared perspective that manifests itself through conceptual isomorphism between different fields.[10] The second is to take the approach developed by Henri Lefebvre, and look for common factors in the "banality" of everyday life.[11] In the case of the information perspective, both explanations have evidence to support them.

The cataclysmic event that made the concept of information seem real was World War II. The cracking of the Enigma code by Alan Turing was crucial to Allied strategy in the last phases of the war; Turing's breakthrough was dramatic evidence that information could be as important to the war effort as weapons or troops. Turing was also responsible for proving certain theorems about information that greatly advanced the nascent art of computer technology. A similar connection exists in the work of Norbert Wiener. Although Wiener's contribution to the war effort doubtless loomed larger in his mind than in anyone else's, it was nevertheless his attempt to construct a guidance system for anti-aircraft weapons that directed the attention of theorists to the concept of information as a way to deal with intrinsically uncertain situations. Wiener, like Turing, was quick to see applications to postwar technology, and promoted them in his book on cybernetics published a few years after the war.[12] Further evidence for the catalyzing effect of the war is Donald MacKay's account of his discovery of two different kinds of information. "Towards the end of the Second World War in the Admiralty's radar establishment," MacKay writes, "I found myself trying to follow the behavior of electrical impulses over extremely short intervals. . . ."[13] MacKay, an important early researcher in the field, recalls that the idea of information was very much "in the air" during and immediately following the war. In his view, the pervasiveness and urgency of that atmosphere were directly related to the war effort. Additional indications of the importance of World War II are the dates of the first dramatic breakthroughs in information theory. Shannon's two seminal papers were published in 1948, Wiener's book on cybernetics the same year, Brillouin's analysis of information and entropy in 1951.[14]

The war left its stamp on information theory in other ways as well. Information as it came to be formalized within theory not only was a function of uncertainty; it also *generated* uncertainty. Information can be quantified only when it is separated from meaning; once quantified, it can be used as the basis for information technology. The result is a technology that can transmit information in increasing amounts and with increasing accuracy, but at the expense of having nothing to say about what information means. Especially intensive during wartime, the anxiety of trying to interpret uncertain information has become an important part of postwar society. Consider, for example, the extensive information available on the arms race. What this information *means*, however, is always problematic, since the same data can be interpreted in many different ways; and the uncertainty rises exponentially as data increase.

In a thousand everyday encounters, then, postwar culture experiences information as at once proliferating, problematic, and crucial. The mutually interactive forces within the culture that worked to make information an important concept also invested it with certain widely shared connotations. In turn, these connotations received formal and theoretical expression in critical and scientific theory through models that regard chaos as a form of information and information as inherently chaotic. Conceptual isomorphism between deconstruction and the "science of chaos" is thus best understood not as a case of "influence," but as expressions of forces active within the cultural matrix. Deconstruction and information theory then feed back into the culture to help create a cultural climate that sees the separation of sign from signification, message from meaning, as an important part of the postmodern condition.

Of course, deconstruction and information theory are not the only models that manifest this isomorphism. Theories in other disciplines are also isomorphic with them and with each other, so that if one looks selectively at the right areas, one may be led to the impression of a "world view" at work within the culture as a whole. Here, however, we must be cautious, for the development of any view, including the information perspective, will not be uniform across the culture. For example, the theory of nonlinear dynamics has undergone a dramatic transformation since it adopted an information perspective, while agriculture, although it has been changed to a small extent by information technology, has been virtually unaffected theoretically. We must therefore distinguish between affected and unaffected disciplines, consider rifts and discontinuities as well as convergences. Nor is discontinuous development the only objection to a "world view" approach. Also important are different discursive practices within disciplines that can cause conceptually isomorphic theories to take on very different, even opposed, tonalities and values. The rest of this essay is devoted to exploring how different disciplinary economies within deconstruction and information theory cause them to arrive at different conclusions, even though the theories themselves are conceptually similar.

For the scientific side I will use Claude Shannon and Warren Weaver's *The Mathematical Theory of Communication*, which includes Shannon's 1948 papers and an essay by Weaver, originally published in *Scientific American*, interpreting the significance of Shannon's theory for a general scientific audience.[15] This text has considerable historical importance; it is the form in which Shannon's work reached the widest audience, and remains the single most frequently cited work in information theory. For my purposes, Weaver's essay is as important as Shannon's papers, for it extends Shannon's conclusions beyond practical considerations to questions of meaning and value.

For the literary side, I will use Roland Barthes's *S/Z*.[16] Barthes has the advantage of being easily accessible, and has perhaps been read even more widely than Derrida, especially among audiences who are not themselves deconstructionists. More important, in *S/Z* Barthes explicitly contrasts his methodology to information theory, and so has passages that directly parallel Shannon's theory of information. An additional bonus is that David Bell's essay elsewhere in this volume deals with Balzac's interest in chance, and *S/Z* is about Balzac's story *Sarrasine*. I hope that my essay will connect with Bell's remarks to suggest implicitly how a nineteenth-century interest in chance is transmuted into a twentieth-century emphasis on chaos in Barthes's re-presentation of Balzac.

Difference(s) in Information Theory and Deconstruction

When Shannon published his 1948 papers, communication theorists were amazed by the elegance and power of his theorems. Simple in form, the theorems applied to media as diverse as an old-fashioned telegram and Leonard Bernstein conducting the Boston Pops on TV. Warren Weaver attributes the power and economy of the theorems to the way Shannon analyzes the communication situation. Declaring at the outset that he is concerned only with the "engineering aspects" of communication, not its semantic content, Shannon represented his

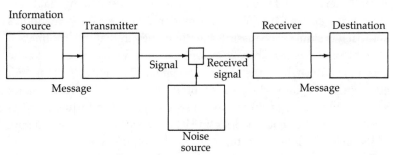

Schematic diagram of a general communication system (Shannon and Weaver, *The Mathematical Theory of Communication*, p. 5)

analysis in a diagram that divides the communication process into a sender, an encoder that prepares the message for transmission, a channel (which can be more or less "noisy") to transmit the message, a decoder, and a receiver.

Shannon's diagram of the communication system makes clear that there is no such thing as the direct transfer of a thought from one mind to another. Every thought, whether spoken, written, or transmitted by electronic pulses, is mediated through signals, which are in turn subject to the codes used to prepare the message for transmission through the channel. Because message transmission is considered entirely independently of what the message means, the theory is able to distinguish unequivocally between signals and noise. For Shannon there is no ambiguity about what it means for a message to be "correct"; it means that if the message before it is *encoded* is compared with the message after it is *decoded*, the two will be identical. The theory thus recognizes complexity in its admission that all messages are mediated, but finds a way to control that complexity by separating the concept of information from meaning.

To see how an analogous perspective developed within deconstruction, consider its treatment of message versus meaning. Deconstruction is rooted in semiotics, particularly in the Saussurean distinction between the signifier and signified. Saussure, in proposing that the proper study for linguistics was *la langue* rather than *la parole*, was led to the proposition that relations within *la langue* could not be specified absolutely, but existed only as a series of differences. In deconstruction this relational analysis is made more extreme as difference becomes "differance," a delayed, deferred relation in which the distinctions that allow meaning to emerge are themselves rendered problematic.[17] Shannon's approach is similar to Saussure's methodology in that the information content of a message can be calculated only with reference to the ensemble from which the message elements are drawn, that is, not absolutely but through a series of differences.[18] The resemblance emerges because meaning is no longer considered an intrinsic part of the message. Thus both theories find it necessary to define the structure of the message internally, through a series of differences.

Despite the similarities, there is an important difference between deconstruction and information theory. Shannon's theorems are directed toward controlling the proliferation of noise. They prove that it is possible to reduce noise to an arbitrarily small amount by proper coding.[19] By contrast, deconstruction assumes it is desirable to increase message "noise" as much as possible, for example through split writing, dense syntax, elusive wordplay, and elliptical style. Perhaps we have here, on a small scale, the kind of divergence between scientific and literary discourse discussed earlier by James Paradis. Certainly the attempt to suppress "noise" is a characteristic of scientific discourse, as Beer points out.

Intent on releasing as much signification as possible, deconstruction regards "correctness" as an illusion perpetrated by a logocentric philosophy to control texts, language, and power structures within society. Thus Shannon's theory appears essentially conservative, whereas the deconstructive approach styles itself as radical. But this difference disappears when the economic infrastructures of the two disciplines are taken into account. From this perspective both economies appear equally conservative, serving to perpetuate rather than challenge the disciplinary economies in which they are embedded.

Two Economies of Explanation: The Few and the Many

The radical stance that differentiates deconstruction from information theory is apparent in Barthes's text. Declaring that he is not interested in what *Sarrasine* means, Barthes asserts that he will consider only the codes that make meaning possible. Distinguishing five codes at work within his "tutor text," Barthes identifies them with so many "voices" speaking *Sarrasine* and refuses to arrange them hierarchically in search of a total meaning. Moreover, even within one code there are often disparate connotations at work, as if two voices were speaking at once over the same channel. These "equivocations," as Barthes calls them, are to be encouraged:

> In relation to an ideally pure message (as in mathematics), the division of reception constitutes a "noise," it makes communication obscure, fallacious, hazardous: uncertain. Yet this noise, this uncertainty are emitted by the discourse with a view toward communication: they are given to the reader so that he may feed on them: what the reader reads is a countercommunication. (p. 145)

Thus Barthes concludes that "literatures are in fact arts of noise," declaring that this "defect in communication" is "what the reader consumes."

The equivocation in Barthes's own text comes into focus with the word "consumes." With his assertion that literature is noise, Barthes situates his project in opposition to the information theory from which he takes his terms. "Consumes" is a pivotal word because it recalls the capitalistic context of Shannon's career. Working at Bell Labs, Shannon was necessarily concerned with commercial applications of his theory. He accordingly devoted considerable attention to how to get a message through correctly. Any deviation from the intended message Shannon called "equivocation," attributable to noise in the channel. One of his most important theorems demonstrates that it is possible to reduce the equivocation to zero if the code is chosen correctly. What AT&T would like to eliminate, throw away as useless information, Barthes offers up for consumption, claiming that it is precisely *what has been added* to the original message that nourishes the reader. If Barthes shares with information theory its terminology and conceptual perspective, he strenuously rejects the commercial orientation that makes correctness an important value.

The different economic systems within which Shannon and Barthes work are reinforced by different *conceptual* economies. Warren Weaver remarks that Shannon's theory of information is powerful because of its economy of explanation (pp. 114–15). Implicit in the comment is the assumption that the best theory is that which can explain the most diverse phenomena with the fewest principles. The tendency in science is to simplify, to reduce the many to the few—millions of chemicals to some hundred elements, for example, then a hundred elements to three atomic particles. When this basic atomic triad proliferates into hundreds of subatomic particles with the advent of high-energy physics, the scientific community is disturbed; economy has been violated. An intensive search is undertaken for a grand unified field theory. When it is found, it reduces the unruly many to the few again, the four forces that govern the organization of matter.[20]

The economy of explanation that obtains in science has not won the same consensus in literary theory. Although there have been critical methodologies that have styled themselves "scientific" in this sense—

archetypal criticism and structuralism, for example—they are the exception rather than the rule. Deconstruction, which makes every text, even seemingly simple ones, infinitely complex, is more in the mainstream of literary studies. Deconstruction takes to the extreme a deeply shared belief within the discipline that explanations which reduce the many to the few are reductive rather than powerful. Instead, literary criticism favors convoluted explanations that expand the few to the many. The phenomenon can, I believe, be understood in terms of the economic infrastructure of the discipline.

Before deconstruction, critical theory was confined to an accepted corpus of literary texts for its subject material. This body of texts has remained essentially constant for decades, except for the influx provided by living writers; meanwhile the academic literary establishment increased enormously. Even taking the influx of new texts into account, the domain of critical theory has been extremely restricted compared with the scientific domain, where increasingly powerful instrumentation continually opens new areas for research. It has therefore operated according to an economy of scarcity—too many critics, too few texts.

The advantage of deconstruction, from an economic viewpoint, is that it overcomes this scarcity by showing how each text can be an infinite number of texts. Moreover, deconstruction not only corrects scarcity, but actually converts it to excess by proclaiming that theory's proper subject is not only literature but theory itself. By this stroke deconstruction converts a closed system operating according to a scarcity economy into an open system based on autocatalysis. The more theory that is written, the more texts there are for theory to write about, because the theory itself *produces* the texts that the next generation of theory will consume. As Ilya Prigogine has shown in his Nobel prize-winning work on irreversible thermodynamics, physical systems that are autocatalyzing can, under certain conditions, spontaneously reorganize themselves at a high level of complexity.[21] Theorists, unlike molecules, are conscious of the systemic organization they help to build; but the analogy is useful because it suggests that increased complexity arises not merely because of an individual, idiosyncratic decision by a given theorist, but because the systemic economy demands it. Thus the increasing numbers of theoretical texts in literary criticism, as well as their tendency to organize themselves in increasingly complex ways, can be understood as a necessary result of the discipline's systemic economy. Derrida and Barthes may be accidents of history, but deconstruction is not. It appeared because it was a logical response to an already existing economy.

What happens when conceptually isomorphic theories are embedded within different disciplinary economies? In response to pressure from the systemic economies, they take on diametrically opposed values. Thus, Shannon and Barthes differ in their evaluations of what it means for a message to be *economical*. For Shannon, communication is essentially an engineering problem. He considers that progress has been made if he can reduce every imaginable kind of signal to a few limit cases that can be described through an even fewer number of equations. His approach is reinforced both by the scientific community that gives him recognition, and the commercial information conglomerate that gives him a paycheck. For AT&T, room in the channel translates directly into more expense for the company. So Shannon seeks not just any economical explanation; he looks for the one that will allow language itself to be more compressed. Accordingly, he not only gives information theory its modern formulation, but also does pioneering work on how to eliminate the redundancy of language through proper coding.[22] His credo is compatible with the disciplinary and institutional economies within which he works: reduce and simplify, shorten and compress.

Barthes's approach is the exact opposite. He takes a short story by Balzac of about 13,000 words and turns it into a 75,000-word analysis. Moreover, he implies that there is no valid way to compress his interpretation into a shorter theoretical formulation. The five codes he uses are defined in an appendix, for example, suggesting that in their compressed form the codes are peripheral to his enterprise, not its concentrated essence. His rejection of the scientific and commercial economy embodied in Shannon's work is conscious and deliberate. In Barthes's view, any such "economic" view of information is a will to power over the text that suppresses its richly cacophonous voices. His ideological decision to opt for an economy of excess is not, of course, unconnected to his own economic situation. He writes as a critic within the literary establishment, where fame, money, and power come from generating new words from old texts. The more texts are "opened" to accommodate his words and others, the more the community in which he works will reward him.

Put side by side, then, Shannon's papers and Barthes's analysis demonstrate how similar concepts emerge with radically different values when they are embedded within different disciplinary economies. The pivotal term that assumes different values for Shannon and Barthes is, appropriately enough, equivocation. For Barthes the equivocation, attributable to noise in the channel, is a "countercommunication" that he claims is more "delectable" for the reader than the official message. In view of Barthes's equivocal use of equivocation, it is worthwhile to look more closely at what Shannon means by the term. Equivocation is also important for Shannon, but, as we shall see, it has a connotation in his theory very different from that in Barthes's analysis.

The Equivocal Values of Equivocation

Shannon considers the informational content of a message to be defined by the probability distribution of its elements.[23] If we calculate the information contained in the message, "Hello," for example, it is a sum dependent on how probable it is that each of the constituent letters will appear. The more probable the letter, the less information it carries. For example *e*, the most common letter in an English text, can often be omitted without rendering a word "unintelligibl." The element containing the most information will be that least likely to occur. Thus it is possible for a message contaminated with noise to contain more mathematical information than if it were correct, assuming the contaminating elements are unlikely to occur. This "extra" information, unintended by the person who sent the message, Shannon calls the equivocation.

We can understand the concept of "extra" information in a commonsense way by supposing I send a telegram that begins, "To Helen with love." Somewhere, however, an error occurs, and when Helen is handed the message, she reads, "To hell with love." This may be a surprising message for her to receive; it may, in fact, contain more information than the correct message. The added information responsible for this surprise is the equivocation. To Shannon, information and equivocation are not simply opposites. Rather, both are functions of the probabilities of their elements, and are calculated in essentially the same way.

131

What distinguishes them, Shannon suggests, is *usefulness*. While both are forms of information, the equivocation is not useful information.

The different values Barthes and Shannon assign to this term can now be brought into clearer focus. Shannon supposes that it is the purpose of communication to be useful, and seeks ways to define mathematically what "useful" means. Barthes, however, appropriates the language of capitalism only to subvert it, as when he suggests that the product most worth consuming is what AT&T wants to throw away. When Barthes advocates rereading as the primary value, he makes this difference in values explicit:

> Rereading, an operation contrary to the commercial and ideological habits of our society, which would have us "throw away" the story once it has been consumed (or "devoured"), so that we can then move on to another story, buy another book, and which is tolerated only in marginal categories of readers (children, old people, and professors), rereading is here suggested at the outset, for it alone saves the text from repetition (those who fail to reread are obliged to read the same story everwhere) . . . rereading is no longer consumption, but play. (p. 16)

The emphasis on play is thus Barthes's answer to Shannon's emphasis on use. It appears that literature's traditionally dual purpose—to instruct and delight—has been divided and parceled out. When it is useful, it is information and belongs to Ma Bell and her associates; when it is a form of play, it is equivocation and belongs to professors, children, and other marginal groups.

Except, of course, that the situation cannot be this simple. I would like now to show that Shannon's perspective is less identified with consumption and control than Barthes thinks, and that Barthes's is more identified with coercive control than he thinks.

A New Value for Entropy

Shannon's view of entropy was very different from the way thermodynamics interpreted it. The great British thermodynamicist, Lord Kelvin, for example, saw the entropic increase of the universe as a "dissipation," a squandering of heat that implied the universe could not be successfully "subjected to the will of an animated creature."[24]

Shannon turned this view on its head when he saw in entropy, not a threat to imperialistic control, but a liberating potential that allowed new combinations to come into being. In Shannon's view, it is precisely because not everything is certain, because uncertainty exists, that we can create new information. Shannon credited Norbert Wiener's work on cybernetics with suggesting this view to him, and in Wiener the shift toward a reevaluation of control is clear. Wiener defines cybernetics as the "science of maintaining control," but unlike Kelvin he is not concerned that "animate creatures" be in control of a universe that seems stubbornly, perversely, to resist them. Rather, cybernetics attempts to show how informational systems can control *themselves* through feedback loops with their environments.[25] With this shift in perspective, chance is seen not as the enemy of human organization but as its partner. Thus, although Shannon is undeniably interested in maintaining control over the communication process, what "control" means has undergone a crucial shift in connotation. Entropy becomes identified with unforeseen possibilities that allow organisms to evolve, new information to come into being, coercive control to be evaded. (The idea that chance, contrary to much nineteenth- and even twentieth-century opinion, can be understood as a creative force, a necessary condition for creativity, would seem to be a peculiarly modernist literary theory. But it marks a major confluence between literary and scientific views, as Beer shows in her discussion of predictability, and, in particular, as David Bell argues in his essay. The kind of reliance on chance Bell detects in Balzac actually seems to anticipate modern scientific theories of the sort I have been attributing to Shannon. But we can see the importance of chance in the stochastic models of Darwin and in many of the developments of modern physics, as well.)

In positing his disseminative reading in opposition to information theory, Barthes remains oblivious to this shift. I do not know if he takes his information terms directly from information theorists or from popularizations, but if he had read Shannon and Weaver, he would have seen that much of what he situates in opposition to the "science of control" is in fact anticipated by Weaver. In the closing portion of his essay, Weaver tries to imagine how Shannon's results might be extended beyond how messages are transmitted to how they convey "*desired* meanings" (emphasis added), and how these meanings affect behavior. As Weaver leaves behind the terminology of use for the language of desire, his perspective undergoes a significant shift. He suggests that into Shannon's diagram one might insert a box for "semantic noise," responsible for "perturbations or distortions of meaning which are not intended by the source but which inescapably affect the destination" (p. 116). This sounds conventional enough; but he then goes on to say that "it is also possible to think of an adjustment of original message so that the sum of message meaning plus semantic noise is equal to the desired total message meaning for the destination" (p. 116).

Thus the "desired meaning" goes from being what the sender intended, to whatever comes out at the end after semantic noise has been included. With this shift Weaver comes very close to Barthes's position. Barthes's text is designed to increase the "semantic noise" as much as possible, both in the interpretations it brings to bear on Balzac and in the extensive commentary it physically inserts between Balzac's message units. Since Weaver suggests that a "desired meaning" could result from *adding* semantic noise, his formulation is in sympathy with Barthes's assertion that *S/Z*'s extremely "noisy" version of Balzac increases desire and, presumably, pleasure.

In light of this similarity, why does Barthes see only an opposition? Because the economy of his theory requires it. He appropriates concepts and terminology from information theory to posit it as a putative center of control and communication, and then situates himself (and implicitly the reader) on the margin, removed from—and disdainful of—the "controlling" center. He further suggests that what emanates from the center is not the real message; more interesting, more "nourishing," more "delectable" is the noise that he as commentator provides. Seen in this way, Barthes's misunderstanding of Shannon's position is fundamentally equivocal, for it repudiates the control over communication that it imputes to information theory, at the same time that it seeks to gain control over the "delectable" noise that it offers for consumption. Repudiation of control in one context is thus inseparable from the strategy of gaining control in another.

This interpretation of Barthes's equivocal relationship with information theory is the more compelling because it is manifest not only in the way Barthes "manhandles" Balzac's text but also in what he sees in it. Barthes writes as if the codes he distinguishes are preexistent in the culture, in the text, or in both together. But this, as Shannon could tell him, is not true. Codes are a matter of choice: they may be chosen well or ill, but they are always chosen, not inherent in the message itself. The code that carries the most interpretive weight in Barthes's reading is what he calls the "Hermeneutic Code," the "Voice of Truth."[26] This code traces Sarrasine's simultaneous pursuit and evasion of the truth that Barthes situates at the center of Balzac's tale: that Zambinella, the singer with whom Sarrasine has fallen violently in love, is not a woman but a castrated man. To see how Barthes's choice of code becomes in effect an economic interpretation, it will be helpful to trace the convoluted exchanges that comprise Balzac's story.[27]

Sarrasine: Castrated Hero or Narcissistic Artist?

The first exchange occurs when Sarrasine, a talented but willful youth, is adopted by a famous sculptor as his protégé. Sarrasine gives up his rebellious life for the sculptor's tutelage and guidance; the sculptor exchanges his instruction for strict discipline over Sarrasine, implicitly including celibacy. The contract ends when Sarrasine travels to Italy and falls passionately in love with "La Zambinella," a famous castrato who performs dressed as a woman. Taking Zambinella at face value, Sarrasine is consumed by passion and exchanges his dedication to art for love of the singer. La Zambinella, egged on by her friends, encourages Sarrasine's mistake, but at the same time gives him enigmatic hints that she would like to exchange a lover for a friend. Frustrated by her apparent coyness, Sarrasine compensates by creating a statue of her. At a party Sarrasine learns the truth about La Zambinella—that she is not a woman at all, but a castrato—but refuses to believe it and kidnaps her, whereupon he is confronted by her own admission that "she" is not a woman. He vows to exchange his passion for his life, but before he commits suicide attempts to destroy the statue he has sculpted of the singer. At that moment assassins sent by the Cardinal, La Zambinella's lover, break in and kill Sarrasine. The statue survives and becomes the inspiration for a portrait of Adonis, where it is again transformed into a male. The story thus consists of a series of parallel exchanges: art into life and life into art, male into female and female into male.

This central narrative is made more complex by its frame. The narra-

tor tells the story at a ball held at the house of the fabulously wealthy
Lantry family, descendents of La Zambinella who have concealed their
link with this scandalous figure, now an old man who makes a brief,
enigmatic appearance at the ball before the family whisks him away.
The narrator, who has escorted the Marquise to the ball, tantalizes her
with the hint that the old man and painting of Adonis are connected by a
secret. He agrees to reveal it to her if she will allow him to come to her
apartment for the evening. In the frame as in the tale, the economies of
sex and art are linked—a story for sex, sex for a story. But when the
narrator tells his tale, the Marquise is disgusted by it, breaks the implied
contract, and sends the narrator away.

Barthes's decoding of the story suggests that all the exchanges proceed according to an economy of castration. In his reading, every
character, male and female, is located in relation to the phallus: whether
they want one, pretend to have one, or want to take one away from
someone else. Moreover, castration is presented as being highly contagious, so that by the end of the story virtually every character is presented as having caught it, even those who never had a penis to begin
with.[28] Barthes thus reads the story as a superstructure erected on the
economic base of the phallus.

There is, however, a very different way to read Balzac's text, implicit in Barbara Johnson's critique of Barthes. She points out that
Barthes *supplies* the word "castration"; Balzac's text never uses it.
"Castration is what the story must, but cannot, say," Johnson comments. "But what Barthes does in his reading is to label those textual
blanks 'taboo on the word castrato.' He fills in the textual blanks with a
name. He erects castration into *the* meaning of the text, its ultimate
signified."[29]

In contrast to Barthes's economic interpretation, Johnson's reading
puts not castration, but narcissism, at the center of Balzac's story. In her
view, Sarrasine's transgression consists not in coming into contact with
the highly contagious disease of castration, but in preferring an essentially male fantasy of what a women is—a man without a penis—to the
radical otherness of woman herself. Johnson's reading makes clear that
Barthes's coding of Balzac's text is not merely a neutral decoding of
what is already there, but a strategy to gain control of the text's meaning. Disclaiming any desire to control the text, to silence or neglect any

of its multivalent voices, Barthes nevertheless centers it on a void for which he then supplies the name. Moreover, his claim that it is *what has been added* that most satisfies desire, that is most delectable for consumption, itself resembles the narcissistic fixation that he ignores in Sarrasine. Deleting from Sarrasine's actions the egotism of which he too is guilty, Barthes gets the pleasure of a narcissistic correspondence between his strategy and Sarrasine's character, while at the same time interpreting both so as to conceal this common feature.

In its generalized version, the essence of this strategy is to claim that the center, though it appears to be full, is really empty, and to substitute for this void the author's own "marginal" communications. Barthes cagily begs the question of why he chooses *Sarrasine* as his "tutor text," but *Sarrasine* is ideal for his purposes despite its "readerliness," for it has an absent center in the missing phallus. Because this center is *already empty*, Barthes's strategy of filling it as he desires can be hidden from notice. Instead, it appears as if this dynamic were called forth solely by the nature of the text, originating in preexisting textual codes rather than in Barthes's problematic "decoding."

Barthes's view of the women in Balzac's text confirms that, despite his protestations of marginality, he identifies with the phallus as a historically oppressive center of control. When the women in Balzac's story refuse sexual encounters, Barthes reads their refusal as a retreat into false idealism (not a view he takes when males refuse sex). When La Zambinella pleads with Sarrasine to be her friend, for example, Barthes ironically comments that she "sublimates the condition of castration (or of exclusion) beneath a noble and plaintive theme: that of the Misunderstood Woman" (p. 16). There is justification for this view, because La Zambinella is in fact a castrato and cannot allow Sarrasine to be intimate enough with her to find it out. But when the Marquise, to whom the narrator tells the story of Sarrasine as a seductive ploy, reacts to it with disgust and also refuses sex, Barthes sees this as another false retreat. That the Marquise might refuse sex because she is sickened by Sarrasine's voracious narcissism, and because she suspects that the narrator wants to possess her only as a narcissistic reflection of himself, is not a prospect Barthes entertains. According to Barthes, the Marquise refuses because she too has become castrated. Coding this section "Alibi of castration," Barthes asserts that the Misunderstood Woman, a replete figure, an ennobled role, an image fraught with imaginary meanings . . . profitably substitutes for the horrid emptiness of the castrato, who is the one about whom there is nothing to say (who can say nothing about himself: who cannot *imagine* himself). (p. 214)

If we think of this comment in light of Barthes's own text, the failure of signification, the lapse of language, most aptly applies not to La Zambinella, about whom Barthes says a great deal, but to the Marquise—the real and not the pretend woman. Because he fails to recognize Sarrasine's narcissism, Barthes can see nothing in the Marquise's refusal but an alibi, nothing in her femaleness but another castrated male. The Marquise's last words are prophetically revealing in light of Barthes's interpretation: "At least no one shall have known me. I am proud of that!" Finding "there is nothing to say" about Woman, phallocentric discourse puts in her place the castrated male, the only version of Woman it *can* imagine.

Is Deconstruction Radical?

Like the equivocation between margin and center that characterizes Barthes's relation to Woman, his relation to information theory also relies on an illusory repudiation of control. In the same way that he posits his own discourse on the margin, then uses it to fill an absent center, so Barthes attributes to information a centrality, and to his own "noise" a marginality, that implies he does not share in the economy of information theory. But marginality is a stance that can be maintained only when the center is occupied. When the center is empty—or *has been emptied* by discourse on the margin—the constituting difference ceases to operate. Add to this the fact that Barthes's "economy of excess" reinforces the power base of theory within the discipline, and it becomes an open question whether Barthes's text is in any meaningful sense more radical than Shannon's.[30]

One question raised by these economic issues is whether deconstruction is in fact what it styles itself, a radical movement that aims to destabilize established power structures as well as texts. In at least two significant senses, it is not. Because it transforms an economy of scarcity into an economy of excess, it reinforces rather than challenges the academic literary establishment. By providing more and more material to occupy theorists, this theory perpetuates the *activity* of theorizing, though theory itself may proceed in a different direction. Moreover, to the extent that deconstructive discourse serves to distinguish "in" critics from "out," it reinforces the existence of a power structure within the academy, though it may change who occupies the powerful positions. As Michael Ryan has shown in his study of deconstruction and Marxism, a philosophy of verbal dissemination does not necessarily translate into a dissemination of power.[31]

A larger question is the extent to which the economies of information theory and deconstruction are representative of scientific and literary discourses in general. Gillian Beer points out in this volume that description, though it poses as a neutral and thus authoritative mode of discourse, has embedded within it latent significances that scientific discourse tries to control by restricting the presumed community of readers, and which literary discourse tries to liberate by moving between different descriptive levels. These two strategies are strikingly apparent in Shannon's and Barthes's discursive practices. Shannon, writing for an audience of technicians, tries to control the dissemination of meaning within his text by staying resolutely on the engineering level. Barthes, intent on releasing as much signification as possible, moves freely between the "lexias" of Balzac's story, his successive encoding and decoding of these lexias, and "divagations" on a general theory of reading. The irony is that neither Barthes nor Shannon escapes the problem Beer identifies: "the tendency of description to stabilize a foreknown world." The two worlds are different, and operate according to different economies. Nevertheless, they are alike in that their discursive practices so shape isomorphic concepts that they take on values foretold by the theories and language through which they are expressed.

Notes

1. Lance Schachterle, "A Review Essay: Contemporary Literature and Science," *Modern Language Studies* (forthcoming, 1987).

2. A more extended definition of the information perspective is given in my book-in-progress, *Cosmic Chaos: The Information Perspective in Modern Literature and Science*, from which the material for this article was drawn.

3. Claude E. Shannon, "A Mathematical Theory of Information," *Bell System Technical Journal* 27 (July and October 1948): 379–423, 623–56.

4. See for example John Arthur Wilson, "Entropy, Not Negentropy," *Nature* 219 (August 1968): 535–36.

5. This proposition is advanced by Joseph Ford, "How Random is a Coin Toss," *Physics Today* (April 1983): 40–47, especially 46–47.

6. Examples include Ilya Prigogine in Prigogine and Isabelle Stengers, *Order out of Chaos: Man's New Dialogue with Nature* (New York: Bantam, 1984), and Robert Shaw, "Strange Attractors, Chaotic Behavior, and Information Flow," *Zeitschrift für Naturforschung* 36a (January 1981): 80–112, especially 108.

7. For a detailed consideration of this progression, see Jonathan Culler, *Ferdinand de Saussure* (New York: Penguin, 1977), and *The Pursuit of Signs: Semiotics, Literature, Deconstruction* (Ithaca: Cornell University Press, 1981).

8. Jacques Derrida, *Of Grammatology* (1967), trans. Gayatri C. Spivak (Baltimore: Johns Hopkins University Press, 1976).

9. Mitchell J. Feigenbaum, "Universal Behavior in Nonlinear Systems," *Los Alamos Science* 1 (Summer 1980): 4–27, especially 4–5.

10. I am endebted to Steven Ungar for suggestions about these explanations.

11. Henri Lefebvre, *Everyday Life in the Modern World*, trans. Sacha Rabinovitch (New Brunswick, N.J.: Transaction Books, 1984).

12. Norbert Wiener, *Cybernetics: Or Control and Communication in the Animal and the Machine* (Cambridge, Mass.: MIT Press, 1948).

13. Donald MacKay, *Information, Mechanism and Meaning* (Cambridge, Mass.: MIT Press, 1969), p. 1.

14. Leon Brillouin, "Maxwell's Demon Cannot Operate: Information and Entropy I," *Journal of Applied Physics* 22 (March 1951): 334–51.

15. Claude E. Shannon and Warren Weaver, *The Mathematical Theory of Communication* (Urbana: University of Illinois Press, 1949).

16. Roland Barthes, *S/Z* (1976), trans. Richard Miller (New York: Hill and Wang, 1974).

17. Jacques Derrida develops the concept in "La Différance," *Bulletin de la société française de philosophie* 62 (July–September 1968): 73–101.

18. For an explanation of how difference enters into Shannon's theory, see Normal Abramson, *Information Theory and Coding* (New York: McGraw-Hill, 1963), pp. 1–44.

19. See especially Theorem 9, Shannon and Weaver, *Mathematical Theory of Communication*, p. 28.

20. An overview of grand unified field theory (GUT) can be found in Paul Davies, *Superforce: The Search for a Grand Unified Theory of Nature* (New York: Simon and Schuster, 1984).

21. G. Nicolis and I. Prigogine, *Self-Organization in Nonequilibrium Conditions:*

Information or Noise?

From Dissipative Structures to Order through Fluctuations (New York: Jon Wiley and Sons, 1977).

22. Claude E. Shannon, "Prediction and Entropy of Printed English," *Bell System Technical Journal* 30 (1951): 50–64. The passion for economical expression seems to have been a personal as well as professional aesthetic for Shannon. Colleagues recall him as a brilliant theorist who could not bear to relinquish his ideas for publication until they were expressed in the most elegant and economical form imaginable. In an anecdote recounted by Jeremy Campbell in *Grammatical Man* (New York: Simon and Schuster, 1982), Edward Moore recalls that Shannon "would let a piece of work sit for five years, thinking it needed to be improved, wondering if he had made the right choice of variable in this or that equation. Then, while he was still contemplating improvements, someone else would come out with a similar result that was correct, but so lacking in formal elegance that Shannon would have been ashamed to have done such a shoddy job" (p. 21).

23. The general equation for information, assuming the simplest case of n independent symbols, is $H = -\Sigma_{i=1}^{n} p_i (\log p_i)$, where the summation sign $\Sigma_{i=1}^{n}$ indicates $p_1 (\log p_1)$, $p_2 (\log p_2) \ldots p_n (\log p_n)$ are to be added together. For a fuller explanation of more complicated cases, see Weaver in Shannon and Weaver, *Mathematical Theory of Communication*, p. 105.

24. Sir William Thompson (Lord Kelvin), "On a Universal Tendency in Nature to the Dissipation of Mechanical Energy," *Mathematical and Physical Papers* (Cambridge: Cambridge University Press, 1882), 1: 514.

25. Norbert Wiener, *Cybernetics*. Weaver comments on Wiener's influence on Shannon (Shannon and Weaver, *Mathematical Theory of Communication*, p. 95n).

26. Barthes provides a summary of the codes on pp. 261–63.

27. Barthes includes the story in an appendix, pp. 221–54. It is also reproduced as fragments in his "lexias."

28. "Penis" is used advisedly. I do not accept Lacan's assertion that the phallus is a symbolic construction that has nothing to do with the penis, because such a claim is imbued with the very phallicism I am concerned to explore.

29. Barbara Johnson, "BartheS/BalZac," *The Critical Difference: Essays in the Contemporary Rhetoric of Reading* (Baltimore: John Hopkins University Press), pp. 3–12, especially p. 11.

30. I do not mean to imply by this, however, that Barthes is more phallocentric than information theory. Consider, for example, how Weaver ends his essay. He makes a revealing analogy between Shannon's theory and "a very proper and discreet girl accepting your telegrams. She pays no attention to the meaning, whether it be sad, joyous, or embarrassing. But she must be prepared to deal with all that comes to her desk." Like Barthes, Weaver appears to identify Shannon's theory, and implicitly his own discourse, with the marginality of the office "girl." But then he continues, "Language must be designed (or developed) with a view to the totality of things that *man* may wish to say; but not being able to accomplish everything, it too should do as well as possible, as often

as possible" (*Mathematical Theory of Communication*, pp. 116–17). The implication is that language, like the harassed office girl, is a tool to be used in the service of male discourse. If information theory is no worse than Barthes in the control it exercises over discourse, it is not necessarily better.

31. Michael Ryan, *Marxism and Deconstruction: A Critical Articulation* (Baltimore: Johns Hopkins University Press, 1982).

DONALD R. BENSON

"Catching Light": Physics and Art in Walter Pater's Cultural Context

A notable feature of history of science scholarship over the past three decades or so has been a growing recognition of the fictional and cultural dimensions of scientific knowledge and its grounding assumptions. This recognition has in effect begun a process of reintegrating science into our conception of post-Renaissance culture at large, and thus of refashioning that conception in fundamental ways. This reintegration has particular implications for students of literature and art, who have for so long tended to regard science as an alien, if in important respects privileged, mode of understanding experience, threatening or at best indifferent to, but in any case somehow separate from, the common culture. To posit an integrated culture in which science and art are complementary enterprises, both of them significantly shaped by and at the same time giving shape to common cultural fictions and assumptions, is to unsettle some of our given notions about art and about interpretation, as well as about science itself. Some of the consequences of this revised sense of the place of science in culture are elaborated in key essays in this volume: Gillian Beer helps define the way, starting from similar positions, science and literature diverge in their attempts to narrow or exploit the multivalence of language; Katherine Hayles, taking a similar direction, locates the divergence not in the nature of the discourses but in their "economic" contexts. I want here to suggest how this revision of our sense of the relation of science to general culture opens new possibilities of interpretation. Not only are we brought to relocate artists and writers in this integrated culture, and in the process to begin reinterpreting their work, we also find scientific texts opened to us as cultural expressions, available to the sort of close reading we have generally reserved for literary texts.

Nineteenth-century culture has left us a formidable test case for this

143

kind of reintegration and reinterpretation. That culture comprehended, in high classical physics, the supposed epitome of pure, autonomous science, and, in the impressionist theory and practice of Walter Pater, the supposed epitome of pure, autonomous art. Perhaps it is appropriate to begin with Pater's own consideration of an at least remotely similar culture, with his statement of the theory of culture which underlies his account of the Renaissance. At least in appearance, he says, "the various forms of intellectual activity which together make up the culture of an age" are disparate and unconnected, their practitioners isolated into separate groups incurious about one another. But at a deeper level, "as products of the same generation they partake indeed of a common character, and unconsciously illustrate each other." And in the most fortunate ages—specifically the Renaissance—this commonality becomes manifest:

> The thoughts of men draw nearer together than is their wont, and the many interests of the intellectual world combine in one complete type of general culture. . . . Artists and philosophers . . . do not live in isolation, but breathe a common air, and catch light and heat from each other's thoughts.[1]

Without claiming for Pater's age the cultural coherence he found in the Renaissance, I am going to argue that what are usually taken to be the most disparate intellectual activities of its culture, art and science, do "unconsciously illustrate each other," that their practitioners do "breathe a common air, and catch light and heat from each other's thoughts," and that just this interplay is fundamental to Pater's own thought and imagining, and thus to our interpretation of his writing. Indeed the very metaphors of Pater's description here—a common air, a radiation of intellectual light and heat—may suggest a language of unconscious mutual illustration between an ether physics of radiant energies and an atmospheric art of light vibrations and diffused consciousness. These are, in any case, major modes of science and art that illustrate each other in Pater's cultural context and in his writing.[2]

Pater's term "illustrate" is an accurate one. The interplay is not so much the direct conceptual transfer (usually from science to art) described in cultural histories of the period as it is illustration—lighting up—achieved in both fields by the elaboration of foundational constructs or metaphors or fictions. These are the "illuminating metaphors for organizing reality, whatever their origins in particular disciplines," that Hayden White has found early-nineteenth-century artists and scientists sharing. White grounds this sharing in "the common constructivist character" of the two fields,[3] Peter Dale (elsewhere in this volume), in their "fundamental ficitivity," and Gillian Beer (also in this volume), in the inherent "insurgency of signification" in their languages. Two related sets of these fictions, as I shall call them, are basic to the interplay of science and art in which Pater was involved. Both are fictions of continuity, discovered or posited out of the profound crisis of discontinuities that beset the whole of later-nineteenth-century culture: discontinuities in the orders of space and matter, of causation, of consciousness and spirit. These are the fictions of force and energy and of ether and atmosphere.[4]

I

Force initially, and subsequently energy, were the most powerful fictions of causal continuity and coherence in mid-nineteenth-century physical science. Vague notions of interchangeability or identity among the various forces associated with heat, chemical processes, and electrical phenomena, which "tantalized the imagination" of many early-nineteenth-century physicists,[5] gave way to formal assertion of the correlation of all physical forces and establishment of a rigorous law of conservation of heat energy by W. R. Grove, James Prescott Joule, and others about mid-century, and finally to James Clerk Maxwell's integration of electric, magnetic and light energy later in the century. Significant as this remarkable series of elaborations was to the conceptual development of the period's science, what interests us about it here is its basis in a cultural fiction.[6]

The ways in which force qualifies as a nineteenth-century cultural fiction are suggested in a recent study by Ronald E. Martin. Most basic, perhaps, was the peculiarly intimate association of the concept, extending back over its long history, with immediate kinesthetic experience. This association supported its expression, even in physics, "in figurative, analogical [as well as] definitional, and . . . mathematical terms," and also fostered claims for its ontological reality. Thus the crucial elaboration of the concept in the law of conservation of force came as an "intuitive insight, based on metaphysical and linguistic usage," and proves, on examination, to have been "a semantic redundancy," a recasting of the basic scientific assumption of the proportionality of cause and effect.[7] As Martin shows, awareness of these fictional aspects of the force concept varied widely among nineteenth-century physicists: from Hermann von Helmholtz, who took force as a real entity and cause, to Joule, who supported his widest generalizations of the concept with religious assumptions about universality and order, to Grove, who recognized "the powerful pull of existing patterns of thought on the formation of scientific theory" (p. 22), to Ernst Mach, who argued that the laws of force are only "hypothetical constructs . . . concerning relations," not "absolute truths about real substances and causal necessities" (p. 29).

Grove's classic account of the correlation of physical forces illustrates very well the ontological ambiguity which attended the force fiction; skeptical as he is of realist assumptions, he is nevertheless reluctant to admit constructivist claims. Grove would like to avoid "hypotheses of subtle or occult entities."[8] He therefore distrusts his own key terms for their metaphysical suggestions and is constantly at pains to reduce them to a positive content. "Correlation," with its hint of conscious interaction, he would reduce to "co-relation" if the former usage were not so well established (p. v). "Force" he reduces to an "affection . . . of matter" (p. 4), and he asserts that these affections "are, and will ultimately be resolved into modes of motion" (p. 16). "Causes" he reduces to "facts and relations" (p. 10). But, as Beer has suggested in another context, the figural nature of language is inescapable. Neither the occult entities nor the ambiguities will be suppressed. Grove can maintain, with respect to the motion it is said to produce, that force is simply a convenient term for generalizing observed (and real) motion, but with respect to the physical effects ascribed to it, he finds it difficult "not to recognize a reality in force" (p. 19). In the end he concludes that conventional symbols, including language, are necessary to the acquisition as well as to the transmission of knowledge, that ultimately matter and motion and perhaps force, whatever their reality status, are fundamental categories of our conception of phenomena beyond which we cannot go. Grove's summary derivation of correlation epitomizes the way in which the force fiction, in its ambiguity, serves to resolve or at least give tolerable expression to this dilemma, and thus permits scientific speculation to proceed. On the ontological side skepticism prevails—or faith: We simply cannot conceive of a truly originating, thus an essential, force; always "our evidence of force is the matter it acts upon" (p. 266). We can only believe that essential "causation is the will . . . of God" (p. 271). But on the epistemological side we have to accept the fiction and work out its implications: *because* our only evidence of force is the matter it acts upon, force and matter must be "correlates, in the strictest sense of the word; the conception of the existence of the one involves the conception and existence of the other" (p. 266). At this point, however, Grove becomes uneasy about "metaphysics" and stops short.

By no means were all Grove's contemporaries so constrained. So strong was "the anthropomorphic, holistic impulse" with respect to force, says Martin, "that every use of the concept tended to echo other uses of it and set resonating a great metaphysical diapason which would take even a cautious, methodical, and well-respected scientist into rhapsody over the force-interconnectedness of things" (p. 5). No one rhapodized more enthusiastically than Herbert Spencer, whose synthesis finally has him "asserting or implying that everything which could conceivably be designated as force, is force" (p. 38). Force for Spencer is "the ultimate of ultimates," which generates everything else in the universe and thus gives it coherence and continuity. Even the primary Newtonian categories—space, time, matter, and motion—however compelling their apparent reality, are abstracted from something "deeper down than these," namely, "the primordial experiences of Force."[9] An important corollary of this fundamental reality of force is its persistence, a "truth transcending demonstration," an assertion of "an Unconditioned Reality, without beginning or end," the founding fiction of science that serves it in stead of God (pp. 199–200).

From these basic fictions, for which he claims reality even as he admits they are not demonstrable, Spencer derives the standard physical elements—matter, energy, ether, and motion—in a framework of causal and spatial continuity. Distinguishing matter from space by "its opposition to our efforts" (a distinction that illustrates the fiction's persistent anthropomorphism), he conceptualizes it "by joining in thought extension and resistance" to establish a definition of matter as a primary mode of force—"the space-occupying kind of force" (pp. 194–95). The other primary mode, the one which constitutes effort, which causes or can cause change in matter, is energy. And, given the association of force with "occupied extension" and the evidence of its operation across what appears to be a void (action at a distance), he concludes that we must "fill the apparent vacuity with a species of matter—an ethereal medium" (p. 229). Finally Spencer interprets the universally rhythmic, oscillatory character of motion as a "primordial" expression of the persistence of force (only in an infinite void could a body move without such action and reaction) (p. 273).

Spencer fully realizes the great diapason of forces when he extends the fiction to organic life, to social experience, to consciousness itself. The force relations established at the simpler physical level, he insists, hold too at the vital and social levels and prevail with respect to "all super-organic products—Language, Science, Art, and Literature" (p. 536). Otherwise this coherent universe of force collapses into discontinuities, not only between material and conscious realms, but within' the conscious realm itself: Either the law of conservation of forces must apply to human feelings and "mental energies," or "our successive states of consciousness are self-created," which means that "nothing must become something and something must become nothing" (p. 227).

The other important set of fictions which concerns us here are the various ethers which came to complement if not to replace force as the dominant fictions of continuity in a major segment of later-nineteenth-century culture. Like force, ether is marked by the variety and ambiguity of the constitutions, functions, and ontological statuses ascribed to it, even in scientific contexts, as the following description indicates: Some ethers

> have been supposed material, others immaterial; some fluid, others solid; some continuous, others particulate; some conforming to various laws of mechanics, others not. Some, moreover, have been interpreted literally, as truly existing *in rerum natura*; others agnostically, as possible representations of real physical processes; yet others strictly as fictions useful in the correlating of sensible phenomena.[10]

"Catching Light"

What all nineteenth-century ethers do have in common is a capacity to mediate between material and immaterial—whether the immaterial be spatial void, human consciousness, or supernatural spirit. Thus all are characterized by an absolute tenuity; a perfect elasticity or fluidity; and the capacity to transmit or store or even originate a range of forces and energies such as I have described earlier. Ether, in short, is the perfect fiction of continuity, with respect to matter and space, to causation, and, ultimately, to conscious and spiritual experience.

Throughout the latter half of the nineteenth century, it was the ether fiction which enabled physics to cope with pressing anomalies concerning radiant energy, the basic constitution of matter, and the measurement of motion, anomalies reflecting a general crisis over the nature of space which would eventually lead to relativity and quantum physics. The fiction saved spatial and causal continuity by permitting the description of radiant energy as wave motions in a continuous medium and of basic matter as sets of vibrations in or concentrations of the same medium, and it saved absolute motion by providing a fixed matrix for its measurement. Again, as was the case with the force fiction, these remarkable achievements were possible in spite of—or perhaps because of—the lack of agreement among scientists about the ontological status of ether. One extreme is represented by Lord Kelvin, who took the existence of a luminiferous ether as "a fact that cannot be questioned," the other by Lord Salisbury, who remarked that "the main, if not the only function of the word ether has been to furnish a nominative case of the verb 'to undulate.'" More tolerant of the fiction's ambiguity were G. G. Stokes, who considered ether a "mysterious medium" which nevertheless "does really exist"; John Tyndall, who ascribed ether waves to the scientific imagination but believed the grounds for a "universal ether" to be firmer than those for gravity; and J. H. Poynting, who recognized ether as a fiction of continuity but could "suppose that it is a necessity of thought" about the constitution of nature.[11]

Conveniently, we can turn to the most important physicist of the period for a summary expression of this ambiguity. James Clerk Maxwell, who has been credited with working ether "right into the bone and texture of classical physics" in his electromagnetic field theory,[12] shortly before his death prepared the "Ether" entry for the ninth edition of the *Encyclopaedia Britannica* (1879). At the outset of this essay Maxwell indicates his awareness of the fictional character of some ethers, at least, in his ironic reference to their invention and multiplication since the seventeenth century, "till all space had been filled three or four times over with aethers"—with "extensive and mischievous" effects for science. His irony quickly dissolves, however, when he turns to the formidable task of defining the veritable ether, that "material substance of a more subtle kind than visible bodies, supposed to exist in those parts of space which are apparently empty." His insistently positivist derivation of ether begins with a careful account of the relevant experimental evidence—the interference phenomenon of light—from which he infers that light is not a substance but process in a substance. He then expresses the distance-time-amplitude relationship in this phenomenon mathematically and, finally, gives names to the functions, and to the medium, involved:

> Whatever the nature of the process, if it is capable of being expressed by an equation of this form, the process going on at a fixed point is called a *vibration*. . . . The configuration at a given instant is called a *wave*. . . . When we contemplate the different parts of the medium as going through the same process in succession, we use the word undulatory to denote this character of the process without in any way restricting its physical nature. . . . Having determined the geometric character of the process, . . . we may use the term aether to denote this medium, whatever it may be.

This keenly defensive sensitivity to the fictional potential of his subject persists in Maxwell's development of it. He can say with assurance what this medium is not: gross matter, specifically air. He can without embarrassment name its calculable physical properties—elasticity, tenacity, density, energy capacity—and calculate them. He can describe how and where it functions: it contains and transmits radiant energies and it "interpenetrates all transparent bodies and probably opaque bodies too." But in his anxiety to avoid at this crucial point in his definition a metaphorical smuggling in of unwarranted, uncalculated properties, he is loath to name the medium and its functions.

Yet we know that Maxwell was not, even in principle, satisfied with positive phenomenal fact or mathematical abstraction. He required a model, a fiction. His attempt to find mathematical expression for Faraday's electromagnetic lines of force, which was to lead to his own field theory, required that "the mind at every step . . . lay hold of a clear physical conception, without being committed to any theory founded on the physical science from which that conception is borrowed."[13] And, in what C. C. Gillispie terms "a return from the algebraic or analytic to the palpable and the geometric imagination,"[14] Maxwell ingeniously modeled the electromagnetic forces as infinitesimal tubes of flowing liquid filling local space, and applied to them the mathematics of hydrodynamics. His aim was "to present the mathematical ideas to the mind in an embodied form, . . . not as mere symbols, which neither convey the same idea, nor readily adapt themselves to the phenomena to be explained."[15] In the latter part of the *Britannica* essay, in fact, where he turns to the largest and most speculative questions about ether, Maxwell shows himself decidedly willing to name and model. Is ether fixed in space, and thus a possible reference for the measurement of absolute motion? We must ask, Maxwell responds, "whether, when . . . dense bodies are in motion through the great ocean of aether, they carry along with them the aether they contain, or whether the aether passes through them as the water of the sea passes through the meshes of a net when it is towed along by a boat." Is there really an ether? Maxwell makes an ontological commitment of a sort: "Whatever difficulties we may have in forming a consistent idea of the constitution of the aether, there can be no doubt that the interplanetary and interstellar spaces are not empty, but are occupied by a material substance or body." And what are the ultimate capacities of ether? Here, perhaps ironically again, Maxwell makes an important admission:

> Whether this vast homogeneous expanse of isotropic matter is fitted not only to be a medium of physical interaction between distant bodies, and to fulfill other physical functions of which, perhaps, we have as yet no conception, but also, as the authors of the *Unseen Universe* seem to suggest, to constitute the material organism of beings exercising functions of life and mind as high or higher than ours are at present, is a question far transcending the limits of physical speculation.

The limits of the ether fiction, that is to say, are not defined by the limits of scientific knowledge—and indeed the fiction was just then stretching the limits of that knowledge in remarkable ways.

What the authors of *The Unseen Universe*, Balfour Stewart and P. G. Tait, had suggested, and indeed tried to frame *within* the limits of physical speculation, was the existence of "an unseen [ethereal] universe . . . full of life and intelligence," a "spiritual universe and not a dead one," which might very well support life after death.[16] Though this work may have been the most specifically apologetical expression of the ether fiction produced by late-nineteenth-century scientists, it was hardly eccentric. Oliver Lodge, William Crookes, and Ernst Haeckel, for example, constructed ethereal accounts of what was commonly taken as spiritual experience. Stewart and Tait, in the process of their spiritual argument, also resolved the period's most disturbing problem of energetics, that of entropy. Or perhaps more accurately, they extended the basic law of conservation of energy into the realm of the unseen and thereby transformed the ultimate material catastrophe of entropy into the ultimate spiritual promise of life beyond death. Not the visible universe, they claim, but the visible *and* invisible universe constitute the true system of energy, and the conservation law applies to the whole.[17] Thus the available energy of the visible universe, instead of simply dissipating, "will ultimately be appropriated by the ether, and we may . . . imagine that as a separate existence itself the visible universe will ultimately disappear" (p. 157). At that point the invisible universe will have become a great energy reservoir, and we can "well imagine that after death, when the soul is free to exercise its functions, it may be replete with energy" and thus maintain "a continuous intelligent existence" (p. 200). It has been noted that in its details Stewart and Tait's argument posits a scale of ethers, wherein the subtler, higher energy ethers beget successively less subtle ones and finally, at the bottom of the scale, matter—or looked at the other way around, a scale that "rose towards God and tended to become identical with his attributes of omnipresence, omnipotence (having infinite energy), and existence for all time." This was, in fact, a scale that had entered nineteenth-century science along with the ether fiction itself, in the original speculations of Thomas Young about light waves.[18]

II

Such were the capacities of the force and ether fictions to "illuminate" later-nineteenth-century physical thought, and indeed some of its shadowy metaphysical perimeters. Assuming these were truly cultural fictions, as much a part of the "common air" of the age as its deep anxieties about physical, psychological, and spiritual discontinuities, we will not be surprised to find them serving a major strain of aesthetic and humanistic thought as well. But whereas in physical thought they were invoked to accommodate a material order to various immaterial ones, in aesthetic and humanistic thought the opposite is true. In both cases there was constructed on these fictions an integral order, energetic—in some sense vital—and spatially continuous. Such an order informed the initiating modernist movement to which Pater would contribute so significantly, impressionism.

The early impressionist painters, as is well known, sought to render the color effects of light in a manner faithful to visual experience. Less well known is their intention to render light itself as a substance; or the medium of that light, in and through which perception occurs; or the vibration and flow of the medium. These painters and their critics return again and again to this intention. An early reviewer claims to "feel the light and the heat vibrate and palpitate," to experience "an intoxication of light" before impressionist canvases, to see rendered there "the vibration of air inundated with light" or "the soft ambiance of a grey day."[19] A later reviewer remarks that "they enveloped their subjects with light and air," that "sunlight was at last captured on their canvases."[20] Monet himself says he seeks an "envelopment, the same light spread over everywhere," and an acquaintance describes Monet's aim to paint "not the object isolated . . . but the object enveloped in sunlight and atmosphere."[21]Whistler is praised as an artist who "has painted the air."[22] Cézanne is criticized for paintings where "there are absences of atmosphere, of the fluidity through which the planes must be separated," and praised for those where "he erects, within a limpid atmosphere, his dear hill of Sainte-Victoire" or "where the landscape is crushed beneath an atmosphere of heat" or where "lights glide mysteriously into *transparently solid* penumbras."[23] For Cézanne himself light is "the envelope" of the object and the painter's primary interest.[24] And a commentator claims that for Rodin "the participation of the atmosphere in the composition" was most important, for he found that "the surrounding air seemed to give more life . . . to the embraced surfaces" of his sculptures.[25]

153

This medium, this atmosphere which so preoccupied the impressionists and their immediate successors seems to have been, as I implied
earlier, a version of the ether fiction, similar in form and function: a
tenuous and elastic medium of vibration and flow, essential to the true
and lively rendering of visual experience and, as we shall see shortly,
capable of expressing a wide range of physical and spiritual forces or
energies and a universal continuity among material and immaterial
orders. In fact, though the speed of light and its transverse-wave
character led to a common scientific distinction between ether as a
medium which could transmit light, and atmosphere, no less an ether
physicist than Lord Kelvin apparently believed as late as the 1860s that
the ether was simply "a continuation of our own atmosphere."[26] About
the same time another physicist, John Tyndall, was describing the ether
as "a second, finer atmosphere" which exists "within our atmosphere"
and unites not only the atoms of that atmosphere "but star with star;
and the light of all suns, and of all stars, is in reality a kind of music,
propagated through this interstellar air."[27] Later he would indirectly
relate the atmosphere to the "aerial perspective" of artistic rendering, as
well as to the extended ether: "It is not the interposition of haze *as an
opaque body* that renders the [distant] mountains indistinct, but . . . the
light of the haze which dims and bewilders the eye. . . . The haze is a
piece of more or less perfect sky; it is produced in the same manner, and
is subject to the same laws, as the firmament itself. We live *in* the sky,
not *under* it."[28]

The ontological implications of the impressionist program were
formulated as atmospheric versions, we may then say, of the ether
fiction. Charles Baudelaire, the prophet of the movement, describes
nature as the impressionists would later paint it—as that atmosphere of
molecular and luminiferous motion that constitutes color. Baudelaire
imagines "an expanse of nature . . . where all things, variously coloured
in accordance with their molecular structure, suffer continual alteration
through the transposition of shadow and light; where the workings of
latent heat allow no rest, but everything is in a state of perpetual
vibration which causes lines to tremble and fulfills the law of eternal and
universal movement. . . . The vaporous atmosphere of the season . . .
bathes, softens, or engulfs the contours."[29] Whether Baudelaire would
want to claim a spiritual dimension here—he says elsewhere that "the

marvelous envelops and drenches us as the atmosphere"—this vibrating physical atmosphere constitutes exactly the dynamic and continuous medium the impressionist program required.[30] Later, when the program was fully developed, Jules Laforgue would reaffirm this ontology and explicitly incorporate consciousness into it. It has been the great task of impressionism, he claims, to liberate the "natural eye" from the three controlling "illusions" of traditional painting, line, perspective, and conventional light, to replace these with "luminous vibration" so the eye might once again see "reality in the living atmosphere of forms, decomposed, refracted, reflected, [see] light as bathing everything." But even during the few moments of the *plein air* sketch "everything within the insubstantial network of the rich atmosphere with the constantly undulating life of its invisible reflecting or refracting corpuscles—has undergone infinite changes, has, in a word, "lived," as has the consciousness of the painter. It has been the genius of the impressionist painters, by a kind of participation in this atmosphere, to connect living consciousness and living nature, "subject and object . . . irretrievably in motion, inapprehensible and unapprehending," in those "flashes of identity" which are the most authentic realizations of continuity we can hope for.[31]

III

No artist or theorist of impressionism, however, exploited the capacity of atmosphere and force fictions to sustain continuity more fully or more subtly than Walter Pater. Sharing with so many of his contemporaries that "immense spiritual dread of space" which Wilhelm Worringer would find at the root of late-nineteenth-century sensibility, Pater looks back nostalgically at the bounded, material, "painted toy" cosmos of Pico della Mirandola, a "map" held "in the hands of the creative *Logos*," and laments, "how different from this childish dream is our own conception of nature, with its unlimited space . . .; how different the strange new awe, or superstition, with which it fills our minds" (*Ren.*, p. 32). Yet the Logos speaks even into this indifferent and dividing void, now in the language of atmospheres and forces.[32] Pater's formulation of these fictions not only integrates physical reality and consciousness into the diffused, continuous spatial order required by impressionist art, it informs the whole with the pervasive spiritual energy to be proclaimed by symbolist literature. To begin, Pater resolves both consciousness and the world outside into flowing force-atmospheres. Physical life, in the well-known formulation of the Conclusion to *The Renaissance*, is a perpetual motion of "elementary forces," the "concurrence, renewed from moment to moment, of forces parting sooner or later on their ways" (*Ren.*, pp. 186–87). Submerged in this atmosphere of restless force-currents are our inner worlds, whose motions are exactly those of the outer one: "whirlpool," "drift," "weaving and unweaving," the flow of impressions, the pulsing of sentient experience (*Ren.*, pp. 187–88). Consciousness, then, and identity itself are fluid. What is real for us is the impression, the "tremulous wisp constantly re-forming itself on the stream," the moment carrying a sense of past moments. The continuum of these, their movement, is "that continual vanishing away, that strange, perpetual, weaving and unweaving of ourselves" (*Ren.*, p. 188).

Aesthetic experience for Pater is to be realized in the exact discrimination of the outer flow of forces, of its significant nodes in "strange dyes, strange colours, and curious odours" and in the "passionate attitude[s] in those about us" (*Ren.*, p. 189). Consciousness must manipulate itself so as to "be present always at the focus where the greatest number of vital forces unite in their purest energy" (*Ren.*, p. 188).[33] Positioned thus in the outer atmosphere of forces it can challenge time itself, expanding the interval which life allots by "getting as many pulsations as possible" into it (*Ren.*, p. 190), though always aware of the inevitable, "tragic dividing of [the] forces on their ways" (*Ren.*, p. 189).

Under the shaping power of the artist, works of art for Pater become themselves "receptacles" and in their turn sources of "powers or forces" (*Ren.*, pp. xviii–xix). It is the genius of the artistic imagination, as Pater explains in "Winckelmann," to "generat[e] . . . around itself an atmosphere with a novel power of refraction, selecting, transforming, recombining the images it transmits," or to "define, in a chill and empty atmosphere, the focus where rays, in themselves pale and impotent, unite and begin to burn . . ." (*Ren.*, pp. 170–71).[34] Leonardo is the preeminent instance of an aesthetic consciousness finding and imaging the significant foci of atmospheric energy. Unlike Prosper Mérimée, whose characters Pater would describe as "painfully distinct in outline," standing in "hard, perfectly transparent day," in purely "empty space," and thus lacking "soul" (*Ren.*, pp. 15, 37), Leonardo saw the world in a medium, "as in faint light" or through "falling rain" or "deep water" (*Ren.*, p. 87). Certain of his figures are like "delicate instruments" through which we become "aware of the subtler forces of nature," of "those finer conditions wherein material things rise to that subtlety of operation which constitutes them spiritual. . . . Nervous, electric, faint always with some inexplicable faintness, [they] seem to be subject to exceptional conditions, to feel powers at work in the common air unfelt by others, to become, as it were, the receptacle of them, and pass them on to us in a chain of secret influences" (*Ren.*, p. 91).[35] This energetic atmosphere, as Pater describes it in a painting of Leonardo's contemporary Giorgione, is a sort of "liquid air, with which the whole picture seems instinct, filling the eyes and lips, the very garments, of its sacred personages, with some wind-searched brightness and energy" (*Ren.*, p. 114). Thus atmosphere constitutes that region of the ontological spectrum where matter, or perhaps physical energy, is subtilized into spirit, or spiritual energy; it is ambient, continuous in space; it is, at least to a keen sensibility, perceptible.[36] Thus it is vital to an art—and to a spirituality—preoccupied with discontinuity, an art which aims to connect, to resolve in particular the isolation of consciousness from the world around it.

Pater drew the ultimate spiritual implications of his energetic-atmospheric ontology in *Marius the Epicurean*, an account of life itself as a search for the foci where the vital forces unite in their purest energy. Marius, like his even more patently autobiographical prototype, Florian Deleal, moves across the matter-spirit boundary, in a fluid world which confounds the very distinction. Florian had reconstructed in memory "that half-spiritualised house" of childhood where he could watch "inward and outward being woven through and through each other into one inextricable texture—half, tint and trace and accident of homely colour and form, from the wood and the bricks; half, mere soul-stuff, floated thither from who knows how far."[37] Marius learns that it is only our static imaging of the "fluid impressions" which are our immediate experience of the world that leads us to "regard as a thing stark and dead what is in reality full of animation, of vigor, of the fire of life—that eternal process of nature"; he learns that true being is "a perpetual energy, from the restless stream."³⁸ Though he is skeptical of the notion that this energy is the expression of some divine intelligence, Marius nonetheless seeks harmony with the "soul of motion in things" by cultivating his sensitivity to the flow of impressions, and he is rewarded with an epiphany.

In "Winckelmann" Pater had defined "necessity" in energetic-atmospheric terms, as "a magic web woven through and through us, like that magnetic system of which modern science speaks, penetrating us with a network, subtler than our subtlest nerves, yet bearing in it the central forces of the world." It is the function of modern art, he had argued, to represent our enmeshment in such a way as to "give the spirit at least an equivalent for the sense of freedom" that is lost to the present age, to represent it as tragic (*Ren.*, p. 185). Pater's account of Marius' epiphany may be taken as a spiritual transformation of this tragic pattern, a working out of the ultimate spiritual implications of the underlying fictions. Marius realizes that his body, so wholly his own, is nonetheless "determined by a far-reaching system of material forces external to it, a thousand combining currents from earth and sky," and that the perfection of its capacities depends on "its passive surrender . . . to the motions of the great stream of physical energy" outside it (*Marius*, 2: 67–68). But he also understands his "intellectual frame" as a "series of impulses, a single process, in an intellectual or spiritual system external to it, diffused through all time and place—that great stream of spiritual energy" of which his thoughts are "imperfect pulsations" and "the material fabric of things . . . but an element" (*Marius* 2: 69–70). In this atmosphere of physical-spiritual energy he becomes aware of a "divine companion," a creator without whose constant "inspiration and concurrency he could not breathe or see, instrumenting his bodily senses, rounding, supporting his imperfect thoughts" (*Marius*, 2: 70).³⁹ Though Marius never again finds so exact a focus of spiritual energies, he devotes the rest of his short life to a search for whatever traces of them he may find "among so-called actual things" (*Marius*, 2: 72), and he does recognize a concentration of these in the infant Christian community he becomes attached to briefly, a community which understood that "the world of sense . . . set forth the veritable unction and royalty of a certain priesthood and kingship of the soul within" and thus enabled "a delightful sense of freedom" (*Marius*,

2: 116). Whatever its authenticity, this sense of freedom, unlike that envisioned in "Winckelmann," is spiritually rather than aesthetically grounded.

Pater's formulation of the fictions, then, posits a physical and ultimately spiritual energy expressing itself through a subtle medium in space, part of which is an inner space of consciousness. Ceaselessly concentrating and dispersing itself in currents and pulses, this energy generates physical phenomena, conscious experience, and, in a mysterious way, human identity and a sense of freedom, and thus it resolves the most unsettling of all discontinuities, the apparent isolation of consciousness and the spatial-material order from any spiritual source. It is, in short, an assertion of continuity and meaning, however tenuous, in the whole of experience. As Arthur Symons would put the matter with respect to the achievement of symbolist literature in general, "mystery is no longer feared, as the great mystery in whose midst we are islanded was feared by those to whom that unknown sea was only a great void," because that literature has revealed the forces which fill space and give it life, established "the links which hold the world together," affirmed "an eternal, minute, intricate, almost invisible life, which runs through the whole universe."[40]

The intellectual and imaginative experience of the later nineteenth century, certainly as this is expressed in late classical physics and impressionist art and theory, was marked by bewildering refinements, dislocations, and discontinuities, manifested in immediate perception and formal observation, in conscious and self-conscious reflection, in imaginative projection. The consequence was a cultural reconstruction of that experience, of the inner and outer worlds it presupposed, shaped as we have seen in both physics and art by fictions that both accommodated and resolved the refinements, dislocations, and discontinuities. Basic to this undertaking was a medium that could embody, literally, motion and energy of every character, a medium that could resolve space, energy, and spirit into matter, and matter into space, energy, and spirit. Pater in his discipline contributed to this reconstruction, and was supported by it, as did and was Maxwell in his. The two and their respective copractitioners did "breathe a common air, and catch light and heat from each other's thoughts," particularly as these were mediated in the force and ether fictions they shared.

Notes

1. Preface to *The Renaissance: Studies in Art and Poetry*, ed. Donald L. Hill (Berkeley: University of California Press, 1980), pp. xxiii–xxiv.

2. There has been some recognition of science as an element in Pater's culture. Fifty years ago Helen Hawthorne Young addressed Pater's comment that the immediate business of literature might be the "liberal naturalisation of the ideas of science," which she took to mean the ideas of scientific materialism, but she concluded that his true course was "escape from . . . 'Copernican revolutions' in physical theory, into the mental world of our elders." *The Writings of Walter Pater: A Reflection of British Philosophical Opinion from 1860 to 1890* (1933; rpt. New York: Haskell House, 1965), p. 130. Later Anthony Ward argued that the assimilation of "scientific discovery, and more importantly, scientific methods of thought, into literary theory" was a major concern of Pater's. For Ward the discoveries and methods in question were primarily those of Darwin and Goethe, framed within a controlling Hegelianism. *Walter Pater: The Idea in Nature* (London: MacGibbon and Kee, 1966), p. 30. Recently Billie Andrew Inman has pursued certain ideas expressed in the Conclusion of *The Renaissance* back into Pater's reading in contemporaneous biology and chemistry. "The Intellectual Context of Walter Pater's 'Conclusion,'" in Philip Dodd, ed., *Walter Pater: An Imaginative Sense of Fact* (London: Frank Cass, 1981), pp. 12–30.

3. Hayden White, *Tropics of Discourse: Essays in Cultural Criticism* (Baltimore: Johns Hopkins University Press, 1978), pp. 42, 28. Similar foundations for scientific knowledge are posited by many historians of science, e.g., Ludwick Fleck's "creative fictions," Norwood Hanson's "conceptual Gestalts," Thomas Kuhn's "paradigms."

4. I have discussed this crisis, and the view of science and cultural fictions just mentioned, more fully in "Facts and Fictions in Scientific Discourse: The Case of Ether," *Georgia Review* 38 (1984): 825–37.

5. C. C. Gillispie, *The Edge of Objectivity: An Essay in the History of Scientific Ideas* (Princeton: Princeton University Press, 1960), p. 370.

6. The distinction between force and energy and the increasing dominance of the latter concept were of course basic to this development, as the abstract, at-distance forces appropriate to a mechanics of gross bodies and molecules in absolute space gave way to the subtle and inherent energies required by a physics of radiating heat, light, and electromagnetism in a medium. However, the distinction was not rigorously maintained outside science (or always within science for that matter), and it will not be possible to maintain it consistently in this discussion. See Yehuda Elkana, *The Discovery of the Conservation of Energy* (London: Hutchinson, 1974), chap. 1, for a discussion of the confusion between the two terms in later-nineteenth-century physics, a confusion which he argues was "a necessary prerequisite for the final clarification of the concepts" (p. 9).

7. Ronald E. Martin, *American Literature and the Universe of Force* (Durham: Duke University Press, 1981), pp. 5, 7, 8.

8. W. R. Grove, *The Correlation of Physical Forces*, 5th ed. (London: Longmans, Green, 1867), p. 269.

9. Herbert Spencer, *First Principles* (New York: DeWitt Revolving Fund, 1958), pp. 174–76.

10. G. N. Cantor and M. J. S. Hodge, Introduction to *Conceptions of the Ether: Studies in the History of Ether Theories* (Cambridge: Cambridge University Press, 1981), p. 2. Though this description summarizes modern conceptions (1700s–1900s), all its elements were still current in nineteenth-century thought. The essays in this book cover a wide range of ether speculation and application during the modern period.

11. Kelvin and Stokes are cited by David Wilson in his unpublished paper "The Aerial Aether: Kelvin and Stokes on Aether, Matter, and Method." Salisbury is quoted by Cantor and Hodge, *Conceptions of the Ether*, p. 33. Tyndall discusses ether in "Radiation" and "On Radiant Heat" *Fragments of Science*, Vol. 1 (London: Longmans, 1879), Poynting in the President's Address to Section A, *Report of the Sixty-ninth Meeting of the British Association for the Advancement of Science* (London: John Murray, 1900).

12. Gillispie, *Edge of Objectivity*, p. 490.

13. Quoted in ibid., p. 460.

14. Ibid., p. 462.

15. Quoted in ibid., p. 464. According to Daniel Seigel, Maxwell at this time took ether itself to be "a material system" which could only be described in terms of an "imaginary model." *Conceptions of the Ether*, p. 259.

16. Balfour Stewart and P. G. Tait, *The Unseen Universe, or Physical Speculations on a Future State*, 6th ed., (London: Macmillan, 1889), pp. 5–6. Albert Einstein would claim that by the very "invention" of ether in nineteenth-century physics "space itself had been brought to life" (*New York Times*, 3 February 1929).

17. P. M. Heimann, "*The Unseen Universe*: Physics and the Philosophy of Nature in Victorian Britain," *British Journal for the History of Science* 6 (1972): 73–79, sees this as the mark of Stewart and Tait's originality. Their view lies between Newton's that the universe is God's artifact and the materialists' that the universe is absolutely self-contained.

18. G. N. Cantor, "The Theological Significance of Ethers,"*Conceptions of the Ether*, pp. 140–41.

19. Linda Nochlin, ed., *Impressionism and Post-Impressionism, 1874–1904* (Englewood Cliffs, N.J.: Prentice-Hall, 1966), pp. 5, 7. This and subsequently cited passages were translated by Nochlin.

20. Nochlin, *Impressionism and Post-Impressionism*, p. 108.

21. Ibid., pp. 34, 35.

22. Elizabeth G. Holt, ed., *From the Classicists to the Impressionists* (Garden City, N.Y.: Doubleday, 1966), p. 397.

23. Nochlin, *Impressionism and Post-Impressionism*. pp. 106, 101.

24. Ibid., p. 95.

25. Ibid., p. 76.

26. Wilson, "Aerial Aether," quotes Kelvin's statement of 1854 and shows that Kelvin maintained this view well into the 1860s.

27. John Tyndall, *Heat: A Mode of Motion* (New York: Appleton, 1869), p. 416.

28. Tyndall, *Fragments of Science*, 2:270.

29. Holt, *From the Classicists to the Impressionists*, pp. 176–77. Passage translated by Jonathan Mayne.

30. Eric Warner and Graham Hough, eds., *Strangeness and Beauty* (Cambridge: Cambridge University Press, 1983), 1: 182. Passage translated by P. E. Charvet.

Roger Shattuck argues that in this description Baudelaire "carries the principle of vibration to its extreme limit and places it also at the seat of consciousness," that he "used vibration to express a dynamic combination of materialism and transcendence, in nature and in man." "Vibratory organism: *crise de prose*," in Marcel Tetel, ed., *Symbolism and Modern Literature* (Durham, N.C.: Duke University Press, 1978), p. 202.

31. Nochlin, *Impressionism and Post-Impressionism*, pp. 15–18. Passage translated by William Jay Smith.

32. J. Hillis Miller writes that for Pater "the *Logos* is a ubiquitous and multiple force, energy, *energeia*," which speaks only out of a dialectic between its subjective and material modes. Neither "subjectivity" nor "material energy is the *Logos*. . . . Meaning is in neither of the two forces separately, nor in their sum. It arises in the space between them." "Walter Pater: A Partial Portrait," *Daedalus* 105 (1976): 104, 106. Miller accurately locates the epistemological crux for Pater at the border of the material and the immaterial, but he does not recognize the even more basic ontological crux at the same place. I will argue that for Pater the fundamental energy is spiritual not material and that the ether fiction—as opposed to pure "subjectivity"—enabled him to integrate the subjective, the material, and the spiritual.

33. Pater does not systematically distinguish force and energy. Insofar as he does distinguish them, he tends to construe force as abstract and mechanical, energy as immediate and vital: "Modern science explains the changes of the natural world by the hypothesis of certain unconscious forces; and the sum of these forces, in their combined action, constitutes the scientific conception of nature." But alongside this "more mechanical conception" is "an older and more spiritual, Platonic" one, grounded not in controlled observation of phenomena but in our feeling of "the genial processes of nature actually at work," of "some spirit of life, akin to that which makes its energies felt within ourselves." *Greek Studies* (London: Macmillan, 1911), p. 96. The reference, then, to "*vital forces*" uniting "in their purest energy" would indicate identification rather than distinction. It also suggests another basic feature of Pater's conception, that energy is more fundamental than force. Thus I take energy as the primary term for my conclusions about Pater.

34. Inman ("Intellectual Context of Walter Pater's 'Conclusion,'" p. 23) cites Tyndall's *Fortnightly Review* essay on radiant heat (15 February 1866) as a possible source for this and the related notion in the Conclusion of a focus where

"Catching Light"

"vital forces unite in their purest energy." Tyndall maintains that the air at the focus of a collection of filtered light rays remains cold despite the presence of enough potential energy "to set London on fire" because the actual transmitting medium, ether, remains separate from the air. Though I believe such notions were widely seated in Pater's culture, I agree with Young (*Writings of Walter Pater*, p. 8) that intellectual journals such as the *Fortnightly* were for Pater their primary forum. During approximately the time that Pater was publishing in the *Fortnightly*, Spencer, T. H. Huxley, John Herschel, C. K. Akin, W. K. Clifford, and G. H. Lewes joined Tyndall in writing there about such topics as force, basic matter, radiant energy, and the relation between matter and spirit.

35. Pater's attribution of the particular figures he cites here to Leonardo is inaccurate, but this does not affect his general argument.

36. Pater argues that the distinction of matter and spirit is a false one, deriving from scholastic abstraction, whereas "in our actual concrete experience, the . . . phenomena which the words *matter* and *spirit* do but roughly distinguish, play inextricably into each other." "Dante Gabriel Rossetti," *Appreciations with an Essay on Style* (London: Macmillan, 1895), p. 221.

37. Walter Pater, "The Child in the House," *Miscellaneous Studies* (London: Macmillan, 1924), p. 173.

38. Walter Pater, *Marius the Epicurean: His Sensations and Ideas*, 2 vols. (London: Macmillan, 1929), 1: 129.

39. Lee McKay Johnson formulates Marius' epiphany in terms of the impressionist-symbolist expanded moment, wherein "time is arrested and replaced with spatial organization." Pater achieves this, says Johnson, by means of a system of correspondences between a spiritual vocabulary and his "physical view of life." Out of a profound introspection Marius becomes aware of a double that had always been present in him, and he connects this double with "a sort of corresponding divine companion on the other side of the veil, . . . a living and companiable [sic] spirit at work in all things." *The Metaphor of Painting* (Ann Arbor: UMI Press, 1980), pp. 196, 204–5.

40. Arthur Symons, *The Symbolist Movement in Literature* (London: Heinemann, 1899), pp. 10, 146.

RICHARD PEARCE

Symmetry/Disruption: A Paradox in Modern Science and Literature

In 1865 Friedrich August Kekulé dreamed of a serpent swallowing its own tail. He had already established the foundation of organic chemistry by demonstrating that carbon atoms were capable of linking with themselves. Now he showed that they could be closed into a ring (actually a symmetrical hexagon), and when the benzene ring was synthesized, a new world of synthetics was born. The frightening symmetry between life and synthetics becomes an obsession for Thomas Pynchon, for whom, in *Gravity's Rainbow*, Kekulé's apocryphal dream becomes a major theme.

In another guise Kekulé's synthetic ring turns up at the root of life itself. James Watson "felt slightly queasy" at lunch that winter day in 1953 when Francis Crick "winged into the Eagle to tell everyone within hearing distance that we had found the secret of life."[1] The structure of DNA, they postulated, was a double helix, a figure resembling a symmetrical, spiral staircase or ladder. Thus DNA, the genetic material responsible not only for an organism's development but for passing its characteristics on to its descendants, works like Kekulé's serpent, by a symmetrical transformation that preserves its basic structure.

While there may be no single discovery in physics that displays the importance of symmetry so graphically as those in chemistry and biology, major breakthroughs have been governed by the same kind of recognition of the significance of symmetry. As Heinz Pagels explains, symmetry has come to play an increasingly important role in physics. Elementary particles are elementary because they are not composed of simpler parts: they have no structure. But they do have symmetries. A sphere or an ellipsoid suspended in space would look spherical or ellipsoidal as we walked around it and would continue to be spherical or ellipsoidal if it were shrunk or stretched. That is, it would retain its symmetrical properties. And, Pagels points out, Eugene Wigner used just these properties to classify particles that seem increasingly mysterious.

Indeed the history of modern physics may be described as the search for what Pagels calls "perfect symmetry." Clerk Maxwell sought the equations that would identify the symmetries of the magnetic and electrical fields. Einstein sought the symmetrical invariants of electromagnetism and gravity that would unify their fields. More recently Sheldon Glashow, Steven Weinberg, and Abdus Salem were awarded a Nobel Prize for their work toward the unification of electromagnetism and the weak force. Scientists are now seeking to unify the weak and strong forces in a "grand unified-field theory." Some are even trying to describe a field that would unify all forces in what are called "supersymmetry" theories.[2]

There is a long tradition of literary hostility toward science; indeed modernism is rooted in a reaction to the scientific world view. Yet, as Gillian Beer shows elsewhere in this volume, they often share a historical moment's discourse. One example of this sharing is an impulse toward symmetry.

In his major study of the subject, Hermann Weyl points out that symmetry has two meanings. The first is well proportioned, well balanced, the integration of parts into a whole. It goes back to the Greek *syn* + *metron*, "with measure," and relates to the harmony of music as well as the balance of the golden mean. The second, which has come to dominate science, is a strictly geometrical balance. It is bilateral, or mirror, symmetry—like that of the right and left hands when placed side by side.[3]

But symmetry is not just a static form; it is also a mathematical operation, or process, a kind of motion. When a symmetrical figure turns, it remains unchanged as a whole, with only its parts undergoing permutation. And geometer H. S. M. Coxeter defines symmetry as "the transformation of something into itself."[4] He emphasizes the invariance reflected in the symbol of a serpent swallowing its own tail, and—with the original structure preserved—being reborn.

But invariance, harmony, and balance are certainly not the characteristics of modern consciousness. Indeed, the acceptance of disruption, discontinuity, dislocation, or just those characteristics that destroy balance and symmetry, marked the beginning of modern science and literature. Max Planck worked on the problem of black body radiation for many years, trying to find a mathematical model that would explain how something like a piece of charcoal turns from red to white as the fire gets hotter, or how it moves continuously through all the colors of the spectrum. Though he fought against it, in 1900 he had to conclude that light moved not in a continuous stream but in bursts, discontinuous packets, quanta—or that physical reality was discontinuous. Discontinuity and uncertainty became the basis of quantum mechanics, the science of elementary particles.

James Joyce also began by trying to press a traditional model of explanation to its limit. Explanation—the causal pattern in realistic fiction that explains characters and events—requires a picture of the world where everything can be accounted for, where there are no discontinuities. And Joyce wanted "to give a picture of Dublin so complete that if the city one day suddenly disappeared from the earth it could be reconstructed out of my book."[5] Moreover, he wanted to establish the continuity between Leopold Bloom as he walked through Dublin on 16 June 1904 and Ulysses as he traveled in classical times.[6] But he ended by establishing the disruptions and discontinuities in "real" space, time, thought, and language.

The impulse toward symmetry in modern science and literature may have begun as an attempt to discover a basic invariance in a world becoming increasingly various. But it was at once conservative and radical. It may have been based on a desire to find permanent structures: the more sharply Yeats, Eliot, Joyce, Woolf, and Faulkner reflected the threats to continuity and permanence, the more importance they gave to the symmetries of what were considered archetypal or mythic scaffolding. But the symmetries of modern literature like the symmetries in modern physics did not become scaffolds, or, like their classical counterparts, invariant *structures* that balanced and enclosed reality. They generated invariant *processes* open to contradiction and the unexpected.

First, however, let me show how science and literature share a discourse based on symmetry, and how the language of science can open new perspectives on literature. I will focus on fiction and drama, rather than poetry, where logical disruption and symmetrical patterning are more readily expected. We will look at the symmetries in four major modern works marked by their dislocations, and where our expectations of continuity are continually undermined: James Joyce's *Ulysses* (1922), Samuel Beckett's *Molloy* (1951), John Barth's "Night-Sea Journey" (1969), and Beckett's *Waiting for Godot* (1952). These three writers are key figures in the three generations between high modernism and what is distinguished as postmodernism. I think it is important to question this distinction, though, or explain it as reflecting the needs of critics and even writers themselves to maintain control of a literature that threatened our assumptions about meaning, knowing, and language.

Symmetry in the Literature of Disruption

Of course I will describe only the most obvious symmetries in Joyce's enormously complex work, but I won't apologize for this, for the obvious symmetries—in the story line, the major mythic parallel, and the novel's structure—are notoriously an aspect of the Joycean literary revolution. The story of this eight-hundred-page novel is simple, or I should say the two symmetrical stories are. At eight o'clock in the morning of 16 June 1904 Stephen Dedalus wakes up. He leaves the tower where he has been living with a group of friends, resigns his job at a school in Dalkey, and wanders through Dublin for the rest of the day and night. He meets a fatherly man named Leopold Bloom in the maternity ward of a hospital, who follows him to the brothel, settles his account with the madam, saves him from the wrath of two policemen, and takes him home. He has a long conversation with Bloom in the backyard, where "the heaventree of stars hung with humid nightblue fruit" and they urinate in the penumbra formed by the light from Molly's window.[7]

Leopold Bloom wakes up at the same time as Stephen. He too leaves home to wander through Dublin, while Molly has an affair with Blazes Boylan—and his recurring thoughts about Molly are symmetrical with Stephen's guilty thoughts about his dead mother. Indeed, both are wearing black that day, Stephen for his mother, Bloom for Paddy Dignam, whose funeral he attends. Just as Stephen needs someone to replace his irresponsible father, Bloom needs someone to replace the infant son who died ten years earlier. He meets Stephen, assumes a fatherly role, takes him home, and, although he fails in his attempt to bring him into the family, the meeting seems to result in a feeling of reconciliation as he joins Molly in bed. In fact, after kissing "the plump mellow yellow smellow melons of her rump" (p. 734), he transforms himself into a son by gathering into the fetal position.

Joyce took great pains to capture everything that happened in Dublin on 16 June 1904. Indeed, affirming the realist assumption of the symmetry between life and language,[8] he recorded in great detail what Stephen and Bloom did during almost every moment of their wanderings. But the story also takes us back to the time of Homer, for it mirrors the story line of the *Odyssey*. Both begin with a son in search of his father, shift to the longer story of the wandering father, and end with the reunion of the father and son as well as husband and wife. In fact Joyce mirrored not only the story but even the structure of Homer's *Odyssey*—beginning with a short "Telemachia" and ending with a short "Nostos." That is, he accentuated the symmetry of a plot that begins with a departure and ends with a return, and of a circle where the protagonist is transformed into a new self.

There are mirror symmetries, then, between the two stories within the novel, between the story of the novel and the story of Homer's *Odyssey*, and in the very structure of the novel. But what are we to make of them? Is Bloom a diminutive reflection of Ulysses or a reversal of the classical hero—the symmetry designed to satirize modern heroism? Does the reflection add a dimension to Joyce's "allaroundman"—stimulating us to transvalue the values of heroism? Is there really a reunion of father and son? Is there a reunion of husband and wife? For over half a century critics have been arguing about whether the patterns in *Ulysses* are finally positive or negative—whether they show the inadequacy of modern men and women, the futility of their relations, and the failure of modern institutions; or celebrate the possibilities of love and human striving in a world that seems to deny them. A more recent argument has been over whether the patterns are unified or multiple, or whether they are meaningful or meaningless—the ultimate dialectical opposition. *Ulysses*, then, magnifies the contradiction, and the inherent disconnection, between the two sides of a bilaterally symmetrical figure, or two moments in a symmetry operation. The disconnection leads us to question our traditional assumptions about causality and development in narrative, especially one that traces a journey. The contradiction, then, leads us to question our traditional assumptions about meaning in fiction.

Samuel Beckett's *Molloy* begins with the narrator telling us: "I am in my mother's room. It's I who live there now. I don't know how I got there." A man comes once a week, gives him money, and takes away the pages. Molloy tells the story of going to find his mother. He starts off with crutches and a bicycle, but is reduced to his crutches alone. Through a series of treacherous experiences, including one where he meets and beats a charcoal burner, he is further reduced to crawling. "Flat on my belly, using my crutches like grapnels, I plunged them ahead of me into the undergrowth, and when I felt they had hold, I pulled myself forward, with an effort of the wrists. . . . And from time to time I said, Mother, to encourage me I suppose. I kept losing my hat, the lace had broken long ago, until in a fit of temper I banged it down on my skull with such violence that I couldn't get it off again. And if I had met any lady friends, if I had had any lady friends, I would have been powerless to salute them correctly."[9]

One of the novel's mirror symmetries is that the more Molloy is physically reduced, the more vital he becomes. Grappling through the undergrowth with his crutches, he is still capable of imagining greeting a lady and treating her with formal politeness. He is even capable of comically describing the symmetry of his degeneration—as his short stiff leg gets stiffer and his good leg gets shorter—for three pages. And of going on for six pages about a symmetry problem: how to circulate sixteen sucking stones throughout the four pockets of his greatcoat, so that he could suck each one, "turn and turn about," without throwing himself off balance.

Another of the story's symmetries is like that of Kekulé's serpent swallowing its tail, for as the story comes around to the end, to his arrival at his mother's room—where he is writing the story—it is being transformed into itself. The only problem is that the circle is not quite complete; there is a gap between the ditch where he finally lands and his mother's bed. "I am in my mother's room. . . . I don't know how I got there." Which leads us to the major, mirror symmetry: between the two parts of the novel.

Part 2 begins with Moran writing a story, or beginning his report: "It is midnight. The rain is beating on the windows" (p. 92). Moran, a complacent bourgeois, is the reverse reflection of Molloy. Like Molloy he is disturbed by a messenger. Gaber arouses him from his sunny garden and sends him in search of Molloy. Well dressed, fully equipped, leading his son, he sets out on his journey. After a "fulgurating pain" in his leg, his son leads him, carries him on the rear of a bicycle, and finally leaves him. Poor, alone, and crippled, he meets and beats a "dim man" who looks like him and reminds us of Molloy's charcoal burner. After an order from Gaber, he returns home looking and acting like Molloy. The story that began conventionally ends sounding like Molloy's with its non sequiturs and self-contradictions: "It is midnight. The rain is beating on the windows. It was not midnight. It was not raining" (p. 176).

That is, Moran, who began as Molloy's reverse reflection, has gone through a complete rotation and has become Molloy. In fact, one way to read the novel is to see part 2 as coming chronologically first. The novel, then, is about Moran becoming Molloy, or about the pompous, middle-class man being reduced to his essentials, discovering a language that is true to the human situation, becoming an artist who can look at his condition honestly and laugh.

But the final laugh is to negate all he has told us—which leads to yet another set of symmetries. "It is midnight. The rain is beating on the windows," he tells us, repeating his opening lines. "It was not midnight. It was not raining." First, there is the negation, the mirror symmetry (with the ellipsis of one phrase) within the ending. Even the tense is reversed, as "is" becomes "was." But this reversal also refers us back in time, to the opening lines, thereby negating Moran's whole story. And if the entire novel is Moran's, with his section chronologically first and Molloy being one of his characters, then Molloy's story is negated as well—as is Molloy, who seemed to be Moran's ideal goal and ultimate manifestation.

To take stock now: There are two symmetrically opposite characters, one of whom goes through a complete rotation and, therefore, becomes the other. And there are two symmetrical stories, which may become one, thereby turning the mirror into a circle. The ending provides yet another reverse reflection or inverse rotation. Nor is this the end, for in the next novel of the trilogy Malone tells stories while waiting to die and recalls Molloy and Moran—they become characters in his stories. And in the final novel they all become characters in a story told by the Unnameable, who is anguished over the fact that he can never speak in his own voice. One of his characters "told me stories about me . . . his voice continued to testify for me, as though woven into mine, preventing me from saying who I was" (p. 303). Through his rotations and reversals—or bilateral symmetries that magnify the contradiction and open the gap between opposite sides—Beckett takes us even farther than Joyce in questioning our traditional notions of character and plot. If Joyce's symmetrical patterns lead us to questions of meaning, Beckett's lead us to problems of knowing. He presses Descartes' doubter to the farthest extreme.

The symmetry of John Barth's *Lost in the Funhouse* takes us in another direction. I will deal only with the first, no, actually the first and second stories. The first story listed in the table of contents is "Frame-Tale." But when we turn to the first page, under the title we encounter a set of directions: "Cut on dotted line. Twist end once and fasten *AB* to *ab*, *CD* to *cd*."[10] What we are told to cut and fasten is a vertical strip along the edge of the page that says: "ONCE UPON A TIME THERE" on one side, and "WAS A STORY THAT BEGAN" on the other. I know few stories that require greater reader participation, or that generate more joy in the breaking of taboos instilled in us by parents, teachers, and librarians. Or that generate more amazement! For once we cut the page and destroy the book we begin an unbelievable symmetry operation. The twist brings the two sides of the page together into a Moebius strip. That is, it turns the two sides into one. We read: "THERE ONCE WAS A STORY THAT BEGAN THERE ONCE WAS A STORY THAT BEGAN THERE . . ." and so on, forever. There is no longer a reverse side, and if we don't believe our eyes, we can run our finger along the surface and find that we never leave the top. More important, when we return to where we started, our finger is upside down. We experience symmetry, then, in the rotation, the inversion that occurs as we travel from the beginning of the strip to the end. And when we discover that the story has turned itself into itself.

In the second story, "Night-Sea Journey," the narrator is a swimmer. He is swimming at night across a great sea, along with thousands of others, millions, all flailing through the waves. He is stronger than most of his companions, many of whom drown in the course of the journey. "I have seen the best swimmers of my generation go under. Numberless the number of the dead" (p. 4). And floating from time to time he wonders, "Is the journey my invention? Do the night, the sea, exist at all . . . apart from my experience of them? Do I myself exist, or is this a dream?" Or, "Who engendered us in some mysterious wise and launched us forth toward some end known but to Him?" What is the reason, the purpose, the justification for his swimming? He doesn't enjoy it. Some "claim to love swimming for its own sake, or sincerely believe that 'reaching the Shore,' 'transmitting the Heritage' . . . is worth the staggering cost. . . . Oh, to be sure, 'Love!' one heard on every side: 'Love it is that drives and sustains us!' " (pp. 3–5).

Gradually we realize that the narrator, with his long tail and streamlined head apparently designed for swimming, is a spermatazoon. He is a tail bearer. But he also is a tale bearer. Just before he buries himself into Her side to be "transfigured," with the last twitch of his old self he bares his tale: *"I am he who abjures and rejects the night-sea journey!"* (p. 11).

The narrator's real self dies: "This fellow transported by passion is not I" (p. 11). It was not Love that sustained him through the journey, but the need to bare the tale that would bear his tail or preserve the old, the real self. He can preserve his old self, however, only by passing the message on to his offspring, that is, by losing himself in Her, by transforming himself into a new self. His message is:

Whoever echoes these reflections: be more courageous than their author! An end to the night-sea journeys! Make no more! And foreswear me when I shall foreswear myself, deny myself, plunge into Her who summons me, singing . . . "Love! Love! Love!" (p. 12)

The Moebius strip is completed as we become recipients of the narrator's message. And, as new tale bearers, *we* have become transformations of the old tail bearer. The two sides of the story have become one: the story of the narrator's night-sea journey has become the story of the story. The narrator has achieved his purpose of preserving his old, real self, but only by losing it and becoming transformed. So the narrator returns to the beginning point inverted. And so does the reader, who, being addressed by the narrator in the second person, becomes a character in his story. The final symmetry is bilateral. On the one hand the rejection of love is necessary to resist the loss of self; on the other hand the affirmation of love is necessary to transmit the tale—which is all there really is of the teller. John Barth explores the symmetries of printed fiction and living "reality." He exploits the symmetries of the Moebius strip to engage us immediately in the ambiguities and contradictions of storytelling, language, and human thought. He engages us in the gap between the operations of language and "reality."

Now let us see what can be done with symmetry on the stage. In Samuel Beckett's *Waiting for Godot* the stage is empty except for a single tree. On stage Vladimir and Estragon are waiting for Godot. Godot is offstage. He never appears, but he is nonetheless a dramatic force throughout the play. The play, then, depends upon a powerful symmetry of opposites: the world offstage and the world onstage. Offstage is the realm of promise and threat. Godot promises some kind of meaning, salvation, or at least an end to the waiting. But offstage is also where "they" beat Gogo at night, between the acts—the intermission being a temporal offstage. Nor is Godot all promise. He beats the messenger's younger brother for no reason we can understand. More important, he fails to keep his appointment, which may be an act of ill will, necessity, indifference, or malicious play. Offstage is what we can never see and never know. Onstage, to the contrary, is all we can see and all we can know. It is the world of Didi and Gogo, where they wait. And into their world from the world offstage come the menacing Pozzo with his slave Lucky, as well as the messenger from Godot. Nor can we be certain that he is delivering the message to the right person, since he calls Didi Mr. Albert.

I have begun with the physical stage because this is what most clearly distinguishes the medium of drama from that of the novel, and because Beckett exploits the limits of his medium in a way that is singularly powerful. We should also look at the symmetries of character and action. Pozzo and Lucky are diametrically opposed to Didi and Gogo. Didi and Gogo choose to remain in each other's company, despite the way they annoy and disappoint one another. They find ways to relate in a world that denies human relationship. They create momentary meanings through their mutual play. And they remain onstage—each act ends with "Let's go," followed by the stage direction *"They do not move."* Pozzo and Lucky, on the contrary, are always on the move. They do not choose relationships but are literally tied together with the rope around Lucky's neck that Pozzo, to maintain his power, is compelled to hold. They are tied, that is, as a master is to his slave, and their dialogue affirms neither mutuality nor meaning.

Finally, there is a symmetry of action, if it can be called action, for, as Vivian Mercier says, in *Godot* "nothing happens, *twice.*"[11] In act 1 Didi and Gogo argue and play while waiting for Godot; Lucky and Pozzo come and go; a boy arrives to say that Mr. Godot won't be coming today; they decide to leave but do not move. In between the acts the tree grows four or five leaves. The second act begins like the first, Pozzo and Lucky come and go, though now Pozzo is blind and Lucky dumb as well as deaf. Again the boy comes to say that Mr. Godot won't keep his appointment, though this time Didi responds with despair. They decide to leave but do not move.

There have been innumerable arguments about the meaning of the play (though the inmates of San Quentin had no trouble understanding what it meant to wait) and about who Godot is. He has been identified with the God of the Old and New Testaments, with a French racing cyclist named Godeau, with the spoken Irish for God, with the French for a hobnailed boot. Beckett says that if he knew who Godot was he would have said so in the play. But Alain Robbe-Grillet puts it best by eschewing causal explanation: "Godot is that character for whom two tramps are waiting at the edge of a road, and who does not come."[12]

Perhaps an even more useful definition, or model, is Beckett's: "I take no sides. I am interested in the shape of ideas. There is a wonderful sentence in Augustine: 'Do not despair; one of the thieves was saved. Do not presume; one of the thieves was damned.' That sentence has a wonderful shape. It is the shape that matters."[13]

Beckett's statement is useful because the "wonderful sentence" is not a sentence. It is two sentences, balanced symmetrically, and separated by a period that defines the grammatical, logical, physical, and metaphysical disconnections between its bilaterally opposed parts.

The Impulse toward Symmetry

Beckett's sentence also derives from and helps clarify the same impulse and discourse that led to the discoveries of the benzene ring, the double helix—and field theory, where a model can be found to explain the fundamental characteristics of modern science and literature. In 1919, after a long night's guard duty in a telephone exchange, Werner Heisenberg was reading Plato's *Timaeus* on a sunny roof of the Training College in Munich. In the beginning, claimed Plato—before God, or the Principle of Order—there were four basic elements: fire, air, water, and earth. But they were unrecognizable, for without God there was no reason or measure. God fashioned these elements by form and number. What this means, as Plato explains, is that fire, air, earth, and water are bodies. And all bodies are solid. And every solid must necessarily contain planes. Every plane rectangular figure is composed of triangles. All triangles are originally of two kinds, each made up of one right and two acute angles: rectangular isosceles and rectangular scalene. When these triangles are combined and rotated they form the symmetrical solids that Plato designated as the basic elements. Fire is a pyramid, composed of four equilateral triangles. Air is an octahedron, composed of eight equilateral triangles. Water is an icosahedron, made up of twenty equilateral triangles. And earth is a cube, where each surface is made up of four rectangular isosceles triangles.

Heisenberg found it hard to translate Plato's Greek. But he found it even harder to believe that "a philosopher of Plato's acumen" could actually believe that the smallest particles of matter were right-angled triangles. Nonetheless, he was "enthralled by the idea" that elementary particles "might reduce to some mathematical form." Almost forty years later, having established the basis of quantum mechanics and begun work on the unified field theory, he came to understand his attraction to Plato. Up to now science had been implicitly following Democritus, for whom the basic elements were material particles. But Heisenberg insisted that in the beginning was not the particle: "In the beginning was symmetry."[14]

Field theory is based on just this shift of allegiance from matter to form. In the classical mechanical view of the universe, reality consisted of material bodies moving through space, imparting force, and causing the movement of other bodies. The pattern of their movement was only an abstraction. In field theory the pattern is not abstract: the pattern is the reality. The field of a bar magnet may be described by lines curving from the positive to the negative pole, the closer the lines the stronger the force. And we can see the pattern when we sprinkle iron filings into the field. But the field exists whether or not the iron filings are there to exhibit its pattern. The electromagnetic field also exists whether or not there is a wire to test its existence. Moreover, the fields of a bar magnet and an electromagnet look exactly the same—even though the sources are entirely different. Differences in source are irrelevant to the effect. Phenomena need not be explained causally. The pattern, the structure of the field alone, is necessary for a complete and accurate account of an event.[15] And essential to the pattern, which identifies both fields and their material manifestation, is symmetry.

OK, classical mechanics could not account for magnets or light, and field theory could. And symmetry is considered prior to—or more fundamentally "real" than—material objects or even fields themselves. How does all this relate to literature? Well, if for material objects moving through space we substitute characters, and if for force we substitute action, we discover that the discourses of physics and literature evolved in parallel ways. In the traditional realistic novel or play (and it is important that "realism" comes from "*res*," meaning "thing"), we watch the way characters affect other characters, or how the action of one character changes another character's course of action. Conversely, we might turn the paradigm of classical physics into a realistic storyline. In both we describe the pattern of action in terms of cause and effect, though we know the pattern itself is an abstraction. We are led to ask questions like what is the first cause or who is Godot? We are disturbed if there is no course of action, or if nothing happens, *twice*. But suppose we consider the pattern as the reality? "I am interested in the shape of ideas. . . . It is the shape that matters." Then we examine the individuating structures, symmetries—and asymmetries.[16]

It is important that asymmetry rather than symmetry characterizes our experience of modern literature. Despite the symmetrical patterns, we are disturbed in *Ulysses* as we shift from present to past, from perspective to perspective, from style to style. Or as we encounter gaps in the storyline. Moreover, despite the symmetries, the Homeric parallel, and the affirmative ending of Joyce's novel, the experience is one of disruption, dislocation, and destabilization. The disruption is not only emotional; it is also epistemological and, as we are discovering, ideological. For we are led to question traditional assumptions about the invariance, or symmetry, between past and present, life and language, the powerful and the powerless. And we are more upset as we encounter the more obvious symmetries of Beckett and Barth—which are not only discontinuous, but continually broken as they give way to new ones.

Breaking Symmetry

This apparent contradiction leads us back to the history of science, which may in turn lead us to understand more about the new fields that modern writers have opened for us. Ironically the search for unification and "perfect symmetry" has led to the discovery of new forces and new fields, and with each new discovery we encounter a disruption—or breaking of symmetry. Indeed, "breaking symmetry" has become a major concept in explaining the evolution of the universe. Nobel Prize winner Abdus Salem explains the concept in terms of a dinner party. A circular table is laid so that a salad plate is set symmetrically between each dinner plate. Unaware of etiquette, the first person to reach for a salad could turn to either the right or the left—thereby breaking the original left-right symmetry. And everyone else would have to follow suit, or someone would be left without a salad. The original symmetry, then, creates a problem. And "the solution to a symmetrical configuration breaks the symmetry" (Pagels, p. 246).

Physicists use the concept of breaking symmetry to explain the creation of the universe—or the big bang theory. When water freezes into a snowflake it loses its original rotational symmetry and becomes a hexagon, which maintains its symmetry only when turned in increments of 60 degrees. As the universe cooled from its original superheated state, it was transformed through a series of broken symmetries. "Our universe today," Heinz Pagels explains, "is the frozen remnant of the big bang" (p. 246).

In the classical, mechanical view of the world—captured by Laplace's ideal intellect and the narrator of the traditional realistic novel—everything can be potentially accounted for. Everything is contained within the kind of rational, closed system that David Bell describes in his discussion of Laplace. There are no empty spaces, uncertainties, or novelties. The modern impulse toward symmetry, which shifted the ground of reality from material things to the structure of fields, opened us to a universe that can be explained by breaking symmetry, a universe of quantum leaps, "catastrophes," uncertainty, real holes, novelty. The literary works I have discussed are characterized by symmetrical—diametrically opposed—patterns of meaning, as well as discontinuities, or gaps, that keep us from resolving the contradictions, that disrupt our equipoise, and that engage us in a temporal, indeed historical, experience of breaking symmetry. We are continually thrust into the moment when a symmetry is breaking and our most basic ontological, epistemological, and ideological assumptions are questioned. For these assumptions have been based on an implicit faith in continuity, balance, poetic compensations, justice, universality. And, without any assurance, we are compelled to choose among meanings and values that, while preserving their original structures, have been radically transvalued.

Notes

1. James D. Watson, *The Double Helix* (New York: New American Library, 1969), p. 126.

2. Heinz Pagels, *Perfect Symmetry: The Search for the Beginning of Time* (New York: Simon and Schuster, 1985).

3. Hermann Weyl, *Symmetry* (Princeton: Princeton University Press, 1952), pp. 3–5.

4. H.S.M. Coxeter, Lecture at Wheaton College, Norton, Mass. Also see his *Regular Polytropes* (New York: Dover Press, 1973), p. 44.

5. Frank Budgen, *James Joyce and the Making of Ulysses* (Bloomington: Indiana Unversity Press, 1960), pp. 67–68.

6. See Joyce's conversations with Frank Budgen, ibid., especially pp. 15 ff.

7. James Joyce, *Ulysses* (New York: Random House, 1961), p. 698.

8. See my "Limits of Realism," *College English* 31 (January 1970): 335–43.

9. Samuel Beckett, *Three Novels by Samuel Beckett* (New York: Grove Press, 1965), pp. 89 ff.

10. John Barth, *Lost in the Funhouse* (Bantam, 1969), p. 1.

11. Vivian Mercier, *Beckett/Beckett* (New York: Oxford University Press, 1977), p. 74.

12. These and other definitions are conveniently listed in Ruth M. Goldstein, ed., *A Discussion Guide for the Play Waiting for Godot* (New York: Grove Press, 1977), pp. 16–17 ff.

13. Quoted by Alan Schneider in "Waiting for Beckett," *Chelsea Review* 2 (September 1958): 3.

14. Werner Heisenberg, *Physics and Beyond: Encounters and Conversations* (New York: Harper & Row, 1971), pp. 7–8 and 240.

15. For a lucid explanation of field theory, see Albert Einstein and Leopold Infeld, *The Evolution of Physics: From Early Concepts to Relativity and Quanta* (New York: Simon & Schuster, 1938), pp. 125–248.

16. This argument was first developed in my paper "Pynchon's Endings," delivered at the 1982 Modern Language Association meeting, subsequently published in *Novel* 18 (Winter 1985): 145–53. For a different application of field theory to modern literature, see N. Katherine Hayles's very useful *The Cosmic Web: Scientific Field Models and Literary Strategies in the Twentieth Century* (Ithaca, N.Y.: Cornell University Press, 1984).

DAVID F. BELL

Balzac with Laplace: Remarks on the Status of Chance in Balzacian Narrative

The word chance thus expresses only our ignorance concerning the causes of phenomena which we observe occurring in succession with no apparent order.
—Laplace

He told himself that Paris was the capital of chance and he actually believed in chance for a moment.
—Balzac

Historians of science have in recent years become more acutely aware of the importance of diverse, even disparate cultural influences upon the formation of scientific theories and have thus been more willing to incorporate broader cultural considerations into their specialized studies. One of the best-known historians of science of the past generation in France, Gaston Bachelard, invented and championed the concept of the *coupure épistémologique*, namely, the theoretical break occurring in the eighteenth century which supposedly established clearly and definitively the difference between scientific and nonscientific thought. However, the present generation of French historians of science, of which Michel Serres is a characteristic representative, has not only criticized the tightly knit scientific community which Bachelard considered essential to the formation of scientific theory, but has radically called into question the neat separation between the scientific and the extrascientific which was the stuff of Bachelardian thought.[1] In a series of provocative readings of scientific, literary, and philosophical texts, Serres has demonstrated that the frontiers between the discursive regions belonging variously to science and to other cultural manifestations are difficult, if not impossible, to trace accurately.

If such an argument is a challenge to historians of science to broaden their approach, it would seem no less a challenge to other cultural critics, literary critics among them, to eschew their own confining, parochial attitude toward science and its history. There might be—and, in fact, I would maintain that Serres has already demonstrated on several occasions that there are—bridges between certain scientific developments and what may be found in the literary texts of a given period. We are perhaps only beginning to realize the potential of such connections, the new light they can bring to readings of literary texts. With the preceding reflections in mind, I would like to turn my attention to a particular confluence of scientific and literary developments during the first part of the nineteenth century in an attempt to illustrate the give-and-take that can exist between science and literature.

In the scientific domain, the early part of the nineteenth century is marked by the triumph of Newtonian doctrine as reformulated and codified by Laplace. An anecdote, doubtless apocryphal, has the Emperor Napoleon asking Laplace why there was no god contained in his cosmology and Laplace responding: "I have no need for such a hypothesis." "The Newtonian agenda . . . had become the official agenda of the most powerful and most prestigious scientific group, the Laplacean school, which dominated the scientific world at a time when the [Napoleonic] Empire dominated Europe."[2] Such preeminence was aided not only by political developments (the military and diplomatic triumphs of Napoleon), but also by very precise cultural factors. The period of the First Empire was one during which the French university system was reorganized, a reform which contributed powerfully to the specialization of scientific personnel. The prominent men of science of the day were converted into teachers and professional researchers who, for the first time in a systematic way, were in charge of the education of their own successors. Conditions were clearly good for the formulation of an official scientific doctrine that could be imposed on the coming generation in a very generalized fashion.[3] Institutional developments, in other words, greatly favored the Laplaceans. At the moment when Laplace was working toward his general codification, his allies and students were obtaining key positions in the newly emerging French university system.

However, the victory of the Laplaceans was in no sense due simply to the play of external forces—it was also a direct result of the perceived success of the Newtonian paradigm itself. The scientific theory that had evolved out of Newton's laws was both convincing and powerful. The world had taken on the appearance of a unified and stable system fully comprehensible by means of the laws Newton had discovered:

> The world is a system, unique, deducible, coherent. But it is a system for a second reason: the apparent exceptions, inequalities, residues are in fact periodic, sometimes secular variations. . . . The world system is closed, finite, comprehensible for the god of the differential equations table, indefinitely predictable because it oscillates, and readable for that very reason all the way back to its origins.[4]

Serres's description of the Laplacean paradigm underscores some important themes. Evident first is the drive toward totalization implied by the Laplacean approach: even if there were still things to be discovered and verifications to be accomplished, that is, even if man's knowledge needed to become more precise, the theoretical framework for understanding the universe now existed and simply needed to be perfected. No further, more-englobing theory was required. Moreover, the universe was closed in the sense that no new, surprising, or unexplained occurrence could be expected. Not only should one theoretically be able to trace the development of the universe back to its origins, but Newtonian theory possessed predictive powers beyond what had been the case prior to its constitution. Although it is true that specific portions of the theory were open to debate and had been very early on (Newtonian optics is a case in point), the fact remains that the Newtonian paradigm, especially as embodied in classical mechanics, provided the only framework for scientific discussion and implied the possibility of an exhaustive knowledge of natural processes through its application.

Perhaps the most characteristic statement of Laplace's own confidence in the progress brought about by classical mechanics can be found in the introduction to his essay on probability. In precisely the context in which Laplace prepares to address the problem of uncertainty and chance, he affirms in the strongest way that they are unfounded and, consequently, that they are progressively disappearing:

> All events, even those which, due to their minuteness, seem to escape the grand laws of nature, are no less the result of those laws than the revolutions of the Sun. Ignoring the forces which link them to the total

system of the universe, we have attributed them to final causes or to chance, depending upon whether they occurred with regularity or without apparent order. But the explanatory strength of these imaginary causes has been successively weakened as the limits of our knowledge have receded. They disappear entirely in the face of true philosophy, which sees in such causes merely the expression of our ignorance as to the real causes of events.[5]

There is absolutely no place for chance in Laplacean theory. The very fact that Laplace chose to deal with the question of chance under the guise of probability is indicative of his attitude. The mathematization of chance, its transformation into a series of calculations applied to large numbers, is a denial of the singular, of events which might break the chain of predictable continuity. Although the universe may be too large and therefore too complex for any mere human intelligence to encompass in its entirety, in theory it would be possible to know everything— the evolution of the universe is absolutely determined and determinable. The position of the ideal observer who would be omniscient is provided for *within the theory itself* and is expressed in terms of a superior intelligence, the famous demon:

> A mind which could, in a given instant, know all the forces which act in nature and the respective positions of the bodies which make it up—if, in addition, it were vast enough to be able to submit these givens to differential analysis—would incorporate in the same formula the movements of the largest bodies in the universe and those of the lightest atom: nothing would be uncertain for it, and the future, as well as the past, would be present before its eyes. (Pp. vi–vii)[6]

The present essay is not the place for a sustained discussion of the questions raised by the image of the demon (discussed briefly, in another context, in Richard Pearce's essay above). Suffice it to say that Laplace participates in the assumption of continuity that Donald Benson treats in his essay in this volume: he posits a continuity between the simplest systems, which we are able to describe fully, and the more complex ones, which are beyond the scope of exact measurement and comprehension. That claim of continuity is what contemporary science criticizes in its attempt to explore the differences between macroscopic and microscopic phenomena, revealing in the process that the postulation of an unproblematic continuity between various levels of phenomena is more a metaphysical gesture than a scientific one. Irrespective of the modern response to Laplace's demon, his image of an ideal observer is a clear expression of the finality and predictive powers claimed for classical mechanics, a discipline in which chance and indeterminism have no place.[7]

What is fascinating for the critic dealing with French literature dating from the period of Laplace's triumph is the fact that at a time when scientists and philosophers of science dreamed of a world fully determined by mechanical laws (an "immense tautology"[8]), the novelist who is often considered to be the inventor of the nineteenth-century French novel, Honoré de Balzac, was formulating a novelistic praxis heavily dependent upon effects created by chance.[9] The unexpected encounters, confusions of identity, plot twists, and surprise confrontations so common in Balzacian narrative are impossible to account for and analyze without addressing the question of the importance and meaning of chance in Balzac's writing.[10] To cite in passing one of many possible examples, when Raphaël de Valentin is drawn inexorably into the gambling house in the first scene of La peau de chagrin and there wagers his whole existence on one hand in a card game, the reader simply cannot ignore the fact that chance has been transformed into a decisive narrative element. What, then, is the relationship between the representation of chance found in Balzac and the scientific attitude toward the same problem? If Balzac does not banish chance from his writing in the manner of his contemporaries in scientific circles—on the contrary, if he seems indeed to relish it—what functional position does he assign to it?

The text which will serve as the focal point in the following discussion is Ferragus, a novella published in 1833. It has been chosen in part because it begins with what could be called an archetypal situation in Balzac's fictional world: a chance meeting between two characters, which creates a situation whose various implications are explored and developed in the course of the narration. Any number of other Balzac stories employ a variation on this structure, which, given its repeatedly prominent position, commands attention. In order to construct a first approach to an understanding of the status of chance in Ferragus, one must therefore reflect carefully upon the structure of the novella's incipit. The narrator begins his story with a series of remarks in which he attempts to create a typology of Parisian streets: "In Paris there are certain streets just as disgraced as a man guilty of some infamous deed, and then there are noble streets, and simply honest streets . . ."[11] This grouping and ordering, well understood by the narrator himself, is unfathomable, in his view, for anyone but a certain type of Parisian, the *flâneur*: "These observations, incomprehensible beyond the confines of Paris, will doubtless be understood by those thoughtful, poetic men of pleasure who, while idly walking [*en flânant*] around the city, know how to harvest the mass of delights floating within its walls at every moment" (4:13).

The *flâneur*, that category of idle observer invented by Balzac, Baudelaire, and their contemporaries, is the very embodiment of the potential for chance encounters. Wandering aimlessly about the city, but always alert to what he sees, the *flâneur* is simultaneously waiting for nothing in particular and waiting for anything and everything. He is expecting nothing, and yet his attitude is one of perfect expectancy. There is no way to predict whether or not the *flâneur* will witness an occurrence that somehow implicates him in a chain of events from which he was previously excluded. Nonetheless, he represents a state of potentiality ripe for transformation through some surprise provocation. This state is not attained without penalty, as the narrator is quick to point out. It is, in fact, a "costly luxury" (4:14). The *flâneur* must spend much time at his occupation (or, rather, nonoccupation) and see many a morning or evening wasted in a pursuit which may ultimately result in nothing tangible. This is the way of the poet. It is not surprising, therefore, to see the narrator place himself in the very category he has just created. The *flâneur*'s path is a vagabond one, just like the narrator's in his opening paragraphs: "Those readers [who have engaged in activities akin to those of the *flâneur*] will excuse this vagabond beginning" (4:14). The narrator himself wanders in search of his own story and encounters it only after an incipit which allows him to speak of other things. We shall have to consider this fact more carefully at a later moment in light of the structure evinced by the conclusion of *Ferragus*.

With the *flâneur* now defined, the narrator actualizes the category he has created by giving it a specific member, a young man who will later be identified as Auguste de Maulincourt:

At eight-thirty in the evening in the Rue Pagevin, at a time when absolutely no wall in that street was bare of disgusting graffiti . . . , a young man, as a result of one of those chance happenings which occur only once in a lifetime, was turning the corner of the Rue Pagevin on foot in order to enter into the Rue des Vieux-Augustins. . . . (4:14)

Because he is there at that very moment—extraordinary *kairos*—Auguste happens to espy a woman who turns out to be none other than the one he has admired and loved at a distance for months: "*She*, in this filth, at this hour!" (4:14). The narrator insists heavily upon the chance nature of the encounter. It is not enough simply to say that it happens fortuitously—it can, he continues, be lived only once in a lifetime. This is a pleonasm, of course, because, by definition, something which occurs by chance can happen only once, cannot, in other words, belong to a series characterized by any regularity attained through repetition. It must be absolutely singular and exceptional. But this is a significant pleonasm which serves to make the unique nature of the encounter stand out even further from the background of everyday events.

The dramatic highlighting of this incident, which provokes the beginning of the plot per se, must be accounted for. The fact that the encounter involves two characters who know each other—the young man has been constantly thinking of nothing but the beautiful young woman in question—tends to lead the reader immediately away from the chance nature of the occurrence. The interweaving of the destinies of Maulincourt and Mme Jules played out after the narrative's opening paragraphs lends an air of inevitability after the fact to their chance encounter. The manner in which the paths of Maulincourt and Mme Jules cross is, nevertheless, the perfect illustration of a definition of chance given by the French mathematician Cournot in his book on probability published in 1843. What Cournot was attempting in the next important work on mathematical probability after Laplace's essay was to stake out a space for chance within the well-ordered Laplacean world. As a recent commentator has written: "For him [Cournot], chance is as real as order, of which it constitutes a kind of opposite, [but] it is nonetheless possible to perceive its laws."[12] Unable to envisage a world in which strict causality does not reign supreme (even chance must have laws) and yet loath to accept the rigidly mechanistic consequences of the Laplacean world view, Cournot tries to steer a middle course.

Balzac with Laplace

He will define chance as the intersection of independent causal sequences: "Events brought about by the combination or conjuncture of phenomena belonging to independent causal series are what we call fortuitous events or the results of chance."[13] The farther removed one causal series is from another, the more their intersection can be considered to belong to the realm of chance. It would be instructive to quote an example provided by Cournot in a later work:

> Suppose a citizen of Paris decides he wants to make a trip into the country and boards a train to take him to his destination. If the train is wrecked, and the traveler is a victim, it will be accidentally so, for the causes leading up to the wreck are independent of the presence of this particular person. These causes would have developed in the same way even though, because of unanticipated changes in his affairs or for other reasons, he had decided to go by another route or to take a different train.[14]

The causal sequence representing the plans and intentions of the traveler has no bearing upon the causal sequence provoking the train wreck. Cournot's attempt to escape the dilemma posed by Laplace's demon is ultimately unsuccessful, because it does not contain a theoretical argument excluding the possibility of a viewpoint from which the two series mentioned in the above example could be linked. The Laplacean demon, in other words, would conceivably be able to trace the two series back to a common origin. Until one destroys the demon, one succumbs to his power. However, Cournot's search for that slightest play in Laplacean theory allowing for the possibility of chance leads him to a type of situation in which the very idea of a search for the common causal origin of two unrelated sequences becomes, at least from a practical point of view, extremely problematic. Moreover, the situation outlined in Cournot's example is quite comparable to the one set forth by Balzac at the beginning of *Ferragus*. The *flâneur* Maulincourt's presence in the Rue Pagevin bears no relation to the appearance of Mme Jules at the same place. The two causal series which lead up to the point of intersection between the two characters' paths are, for any discernible purpose, totally independent. That intersection is indeed, therefore, unique in nature and unpredictable in Cournot's sense. The beginning of Balzac's story is marked by a type of event which, like those of Cournot, probes the limits of Laplacean theory.

It should be remarked that Cournot's effort to redefine a space for chance occurrences is closely related to the Aristotelian definition of chance. Moreover, the example Aristotle uses in the *Physics* to illustrate his point sounds almost like the opening scene of a narrative à la Balzac:

> Example: A man is engaged in collecting subscriptions for a feast. He would have gone to such and such a place for the purpose of getting the money, if he had known. He actually went there for another purpose, and it was only incidentally that he got his money by going there. (2.5, 196b33–34)

This ministory contains two characters (at least) whose paths cross in an unintentional and therefore unpredictable manner. The first character goes somewhere with one purpose in mind and just happens to encounter someone whom he was not expecting to meet, thereby accomplishing unintentionally a second purpose. Maulincourt in the opening scene of *Ferragus* carries this structure one step further, since it could be said that his stroll is in a real sense pointless, without purpose, prompted only by the idleness of a *flâneur*'s empty evening. Moreover, the encounter that eventually takes place is clearly the event which is the farthest from Auguste's mind: "*She*, in this filth, at this hour!" The idealization of Mme Jules by an admiring Maulincourt makes her presence near the Rue Pagevin (a filthy street fit only for poor people and criminals) absolutely inappropriate, the proverbial bolt from the blue.

The incipit of *Ferragus* carves out a space for chance by looking back toward Aristotle and ahead toward Cournot—and in a further development almost to be expected in such a context, immediately associates chance and providence. Auguste's obvious first reaction is to follow Mme Jules once he has seen her in such questionable surroundings. He is able to identify the destination of her foray into the neighborhood of the Rue Pagevin—an old, rundown building in the Rue Soly thoroughly unsuitable for anyone of her social standing. When she disppears into the building, Maulincourt takes up station outside to glean whatever information he can concerning the actions of the woman he secretly adores. At precisely the moment when he perceives the shadow of Mme Jules through a fourth-story window, he receives a blow to the shoulder administered accidentally by a workman carrying a piece of wood: "The young man heard a warning: 'Watch out!' . . . It was a workman's voice.

. . . It was the voice of providence telling his curious spirit: 'What business is this of yours? Take care of your own affairs' " (4:15). Maulincourt's experience on this fateful night combines both chance and providence. Although in principle providence would seem quite different from chance because it implies purpose and final cause, the two are traditionally close to one another. One must remember that the Greek goddess Tyche combines the two functions: as a goddess, she is providential in her actions, but also haphazard in her interventions. Chance and providence share the common characteristic of residing beyond the scope of human intervention. Baffled once by an inexplicable meeting, Maulincourt now receives a providential warning to let well enough alone. Why? The answer, at an abstract level, is that a chance occurrence is irreducible to rational experience, because it is by definition something else entirely—as is the very warning given to Auguste to cease and desist. His efforts to understand can only be in vain and ultimately even fatal.

Despite the warning, Maulincourt throws himself into an attempt to solve the mystery surrounding the dingy apartment that seems to hold some interest for Mme Jules.[15] The chance meeting initiates a series of events which will seem governed by an increasingly inevitable causal logic. In terms of plot, a mystery demands a solution, and the solution will draw an ever-tighter web around the four main characters in the story: Auguste de Maulincourt, Mme Jules, her husband Jules Desmarets, and Ferragus, the father of Mme Jules and the person she was visiting when Auguste glimpsed her in the Rue Pagevin. However, the efforts by Auguste to penetrate the mystery would remain unsuccessful were it not for another fortuitous meeting. Inexperienced in the skills necessary to conduct an investigation into Mme Jules's private life, he is unable to progress despite long efforts: "A novice in this kind of work, he hesitated to question either the doorman or the shoemaker who lived in the building where Mme Jules visited" (4:20).

To move forward in the attempt to solve the mystery of the first chance encounter with Mme Jules, Maulincourt will ultimately need help in the form of a second chance occurrence. While spying to no avail upon the building which has become the center of his attention, he is unexpectedly caught in a rainstorm—the epitome of fortuitous events. He takes shelter in a doorway along with several other passersby. It so happens that Ferragus is among them, a fact that Auguste begins to suspect as a result of what the narrator calls "one of those vagabond reveries which begin with a vulgar question and end in the understanding of a whole world of thoughts" (4:21). A vagabond and *flâneur* at the beginning of the story, just like the narrator himself, Auguste is now served by a wandering attention which again leads him to the heart of the matter. Confirmation of his suspicions is offered when he finds a letter on the ground, apparently fallen from the pocket of the suspicious stranger who disappears quickly after the storm. Chance originates etymologically from the Latin *cadere* meaning to fall: from the falling rain to the fallen letter, Maulincourt is once again guided by an occurrence beyond his own predictive control and becomes definitively caught in a plot unfolding in a manner that will begin rapidly to escape him.

The question of mastery is, of course, a fundamental one here. Chance and mastery are two opposite ends of a spectrum: at one end, a totally unexpected and unpredictable encounter; at the other, the ideal vantage point, Laplace's demon, the observer for whom every causal sequence can be linked to every other. Auguste's attempts to discover the causes at stake in Mme Jules's attachment to a poor, undignified stranger (Ferragus) are the result of his desire to dominate, which means to explain in this context, but also, in a less abstract sense, to master the woman whom he has not succeeded in approaching in any other way. Failing more respectable means to get her attention in the salons they both frequent, he will blackmail her by threatening to reveal her nocturnal visits to the stranger, a weapon he has happened upon by accident. But in his own attempt to assume the position of the demon, Maulincourt will confront someone who is more than his match, always in possession of a better vantage point—a veritable demon in the Laplacean sense. For every move Auguste makes, Ferragus will have a response, a superior, englobing strategy. Moreover, the means used to express Ferragus's position of superiority in this now-deadly game of cause and effect will be a series of apparent chance occurrences, accidents which turn out to be attempts on Maulincourt's life arranged by none other than Ferragus. He who would assume mastery must master even accidental occurrences. A victim of the fascination aroused by two chance encounters which instill in him a false confidence in his own deductive powers, Auguste now becomes the target of a devious criminal.

Without treating these three accidents in detail, suffice it to say that they are all textbook illustrations of Cournot's definition of chance—but this time travestied, mere simulacra of chance occurrences: as Maulincourt drives out of his courtyard, a piece of stone from a scaffolding falls on his carriage, narrowly missing him; in the course of another carriage ride, the axle of his vehicle collapses and nearly crushes him; the Marquis de Ronquerolles, provoked by an apparently harmless remark Maulincourt makes concerning his sister, challenges him to a duel. Although these "accidents" appear superficially haphazard, the weight of repetition ultimately establishes the fact that they are all attributable to Ferragus. At this point, Maulincourt realizes that he has locked horns with a master of causal series. To parry his own amateurish insufficiency, he enlists the help of experts in matters of cause and effect. First, the police: "What one can reasonably expect of them is to look for the causes of an event," says one of his confidants (4:25). In addition, he uses the services of an "old Figaro," a servant who is a skilled detective in his own right, having arranged many a confidential amorous pursuit. All is to no avail—Ferragus always succeeds in remaining one step ahead of his adversary until he finally poisons Auguste: " 'This Ferragus, this Bourignard, or this Monsieur de Funcal is a demon,' cried Maulincourt. . . . 'Into what hideous labyrinth have I stumbled? Where am I headed?' " (4:37).

The critical point made in *Ferragus*, however, is that the complete mastery Ferragus seems at first to enjoy is an illusion. As the threads of his plan to transform himself into a respectable citizen become more numerous and complex, they also begin to escape him, and the fabric of lies he has woven begins to unravel. The proliferation of causal chains reaches a saturation point at which even one who appears originally to possess powers superhuman enough to defy normal deductive limits succumbs to the complexity which is characteristic of worldly phenomena. The murder of Maulincourt only delays the defeat of Ferragus, a defeat which provokes the death of his daughter, the only person he loves, and, consequently, his own slippage into senility. The closing scene in the novella harks back to the incipit and reintroduces the question of the status of chance in what can only be read as a commentary on Ferragus's grand failure, as a reinsertion of the whole tale into a context of the fortuitous which would seem to preclude the mastery Ferragus has struggled so hard to maintain.

The narrator carefully sets the stage for this extraordinary finale. Consumed by grief at the loss of his wife, Jules Desmarets has left Paris for a trip to the provinces after receiving from the hand of Ferragus, in a ferocious gesture of paternal love, the ashes of his dead wife. There is a break in the narrative, whereupon the narrator launches into a discussion of the bizarre characters one can encounter in the streets of Paris. It is worth noting that each of the three moments marked by the appearance of chance events in the novella is framed by this same type of detailed discussion covering some aspect of Paris: Parisian streets in the first instance, the gallery of Parisian pedestrians in the second (i.e., the scene during which Maulincourt retreats into the doorway to escape the rain and finds himself next to Ferragus), and finally, at the novella's conclusion, certain exceptionally bizarre characters one can meet on the boulevards: "While walking along the boulevards of Paris, at the corner of some street or under the arcades of the Palais-Royal, someplace in the world where chance provides the occasion, who has not met a being—man or woman—whose appearance provokes a thousand confused thoughts!" (4:52). Whatever Paris means to Balzac—and much has been said on this subject—one thing is clear in *Ferragus*: Paris is the setting par excellence of chance encounters. To venture out into its streets is to enter into a realm where the unexpected is the rule. Moreover, what one meets there is the necessary material of an artistic creation, sometimes a novel ("this creature becomes embedded in your memory and remains there like the first volume of a novel whose ending escapes you" [4:52]), sometimes a painting ("How is it that none of our painters has yet attempted to reproduce the physiognomies of a swarm of Parisians huddled together under the humid archway of some building during a storm?" [4:21]). It is not surprising that the narrator can view himself only under the guise of the *flâneur*, the person who spends sufficient time in the streets to encounter and collect materials for his creative endeavors.

The discussion of bizarre characters encountered by chance in the streets permits the narrator to cite one such case—a man whom he recently noticed in the area between the Luxembourg Gardens and the Observatory. The topology of this particular part of Paris is perhaps even more intriguing than the character who inhabits it. The text paints a neutral space, one impossible to classify precisely:

> In this area one is no longer in Paris and yet Paris is still there. The place resembles simultaneously a square, a street, a boulevard, a fortification, a garden, an avenue, a road, belonging to the provinces and to the capital. Indeed, it is all that, but it is nothing of that: it is a desert. (4:53)

This "place without a name" (4:53) is in between—not outside, but not quite inside. It is located at a limit, in a region where the order and law of the city begin to weaken, where careful planning and rationality begin to lose their hold. Into this liminal scene rides Jules Desmarets, returning from his country retreat. As he passes by he espies none other than Ferragus, the bizarre creature the narrator has been pursuing since the beginning of his concluding remarks: " 'It's him,' exclaimed Jules upon discovering in this human debris Ferragus XXIII, leader of the Dévorants" (4:53). Jules's exclamation "It's him" echoes Auguste's "*She*, in this filth, at this hour!" Once again the paths of two characters intersect in a totally unpredictable manner. Jules happens to pass through a particular neighborhood while on a trip taking him to an unrelated destination. Ferragus, in his senility, has become a wandering beggar completely cut off from his former life. Their destinies, once so tied together by their mutual love for Mme Jules, now have radically diverged. And yet those paths, those destinies intersect one last time. There is a moral to be extracted here, one that the narrator expresses in Jules's final remarks: " 'How he loved her!' he added after a pause. 'Drive on, cabbie!' he called" (4:53). The fact that Desmarets stops only momentarily and then turns quickly away toward new business is clearly meant to indicate the shallowness of his love for Mme Jules when compared with that of Ferragus, who has been utterly destroyed by his daughter's death. But to remain at that level alone would be to miss some important implications of this final scene.

From the dimly lit, labyrinthine, chaotic streets of a poor section of Paris haunted by a vagabond straggler in the opening scene of *Ferragus*, the narrator leads the reader, in his conclusion, to the vague, disordered, desertlike limits of the city where urban categories weaken and disappear. These two settings are clearly comparable and complementary, both evincing a chaotic topology which defies normal classifications. Moreover, the second region, like the first, is frequented by *flâneurs*, Ferragus among them: "Who are you? Why are you wandering about [Pourquoi flânez-vous]?" (4:52) the narrator wants to ask of the bizarre creatures who are the subject of his concluding reflections. One could easily say that in *Ferragus* a sort of proto-detective story featuring deductive mastery and intricate planning is sandwiched in between two closely related scenes characterized by a curious and troubling disorder. And whereas the beginning of the story is marked by Auguste's transformation, albeit ultimately unsuccessful, from *flâneur* into devious schemer, the end contains the image of a Ferragus who has gone the opposite route, from master of causes to senile vagabond.

The implications of the story's trajectory are far-reaching indeed. In Laplace's theory, chance was viewed as a mere manifestation of the observer's ignorance. The fundamental state of the world conforms to the laws of nature which encompass everything, including that which might at first glance seem to escape them. Even in Cournot's attempt to grant a more independent status to chance occurrences, they remain aberrations, exceptions to the underlying rule, which is that of strict causality. By opening and closing with two scenes of disorder each traversed by an unpredictable encounter, Balzac's *Ferragus* seems to suggest something much more radical. The orderly unfolding of the story is preceded by disorder (an aimless stroll through darkened streets), and that disorder ends only by virtue of a fortuitous event (Auguste's encounter with Mme Jules), which in turn gives rise to an ordered chain of effects. The order attained within the main body of the narrative disintegrates at the end, and the reader finds himself back in a domain where chaos (absence of order) reigns, reestablishing a context in which, once again, the only "law" is that of chance, represented by the brief encounter between Desmarets and Ferragus. What Balzac has done is to invert a traditional hierarchy. Instead of a foundation of order in the form of the laws of nature upon which certain aberrations (chance events) sometimes occur—to be explained away either as examples of our ignorance or as exceptions to the rule—one is presented with a system lacking foundation in the classical sense, because it originates in a disorder transformed into order only by a chance occurrence, one so fortuitous that no law could predict it.

Balzac's structuring choice is, at least in part, a philosophical one. As Cournot himself maintained when writing on probability, mathematical or purely scientific reasoning cannot really get to the heart of the question concerning the status of chance: "One must bring in other notions, other principles of knowledge, in short, one must engage in a philosophical critique" (Cournot, p. 70). The question which the structure of *Ferragus* really poses is that of the hierarchical relationship between order and disorder: "the old problem of knowing whether disorder can only be imagined from the point of view of order (Bergson's thesis), or whether, like Lucretius, one can speak of a primordial disorder or chance."[16] If Balzac had stopped at the idea of introducing Cournot-like occurrences into his narrative, he would already have demonstrated in this manner a tendency, which was to become more and more visible in the scientific domain as the nineteenth century wore on, namely, the attempt to escape from the rigidly mechanistic world view associated with Laplace's version of classical mechanics. But he would have stopped well short of a more radical questioning. The structure of *Ferragus*, however, takes the argument one step further. The framing of the story by two scenes of disorder suggests that disorder is not simply an aberration occasionally added to a fundamental, underlying order, but, rather, that it is primordial.[17] One could safely assert that this is not a position often presented or defended in the history of philosophy—for obvious reasons. Chance and disorder, when taken as primordial elements, are not very firm bases for philosophical reasoning as it is classically understood.

The debate to which Balzac alludes in *Ferragus* was to find its way into scientific theory in the course of the nineteenth century in the form of a new scientific discipline, thermodynamics.[18] However, it would take more than a century for developments in the modern thermodynamic study of open systems to permit a theoretically interesting attempt at including chance as a productive principle of scientific explanation. Certain modern researchers, Ilya Prigogine among them, maintain that chance perturbations, or noise, as information theory proponents would call them, can be incorporated by open systems and used by them to evolve toward increased organization and complexity—an approach that would suggest the precedence of chance over organization (for further discussion of Prigogine, see the Hayles essay). But even this recent hypothesis concerning the status of chance has led to more than one passionate debate.[19] The problem of chance, because it necessarily probes the limits of human knowledge, is a point of intersection between science and philosophy and is perhaps for that reason a problem to which there cannot be an ultimate solution.

But what of the narrator in *Ferragus*? In reading the story's incipit, I suggested that we would have to return to his figure after studying the ending. If none of the other characters in the story succeeds in attaining a position of mastery which would exclude chance, what must we say of the narrator? In many ways, one could maintain that Ferragus is his surrogate. Just as Ferragus seems at one point to control all of Paris, so would the third-person omniscient narrator appear to be a sort of super-Ferragus, maintaining in his firm grasp all the strings of the narrative. In fact, it could be argued that the position of the third-person omniscient narrator corresponds in a striking way to that of Laplace's demon, since, ideally, he is the master of all causal sequences in his story. But this would be to forget what the narrator said of himself in the opening paragraphs of the novella. We must remember that he too wanders in search of his story, unable to begin before holding forth on a subject (the topology of Paris) which has ostensibly little to do with the plot that subsequently develops. Moreover, the ending which we have just analyzed, although it is entitled "Conclusion," appears as something of an afterthought on the narrator's part and is hence much less clear-cut and conclusive than one would expect.

Indeed, the novella could arguably be said to possess three different conclusions—a fact that the narrator himself acknowledges. The first one is the scene at the cemetery where Mme Jules is buried: "Here would seem to end the telling of this story . . ." (4:49). However, the narrator immediately launches into a discussion of the legal implications of death in Paris culminating in the gesture of Ferragus, who restores Mme Jules's ashes to her husband. Still unable to end his tale, the narrator then launches into a third conclusion: the scene of encounter between Ferragus and Desmarets. Just as he wandered in search of his story in the novella's incipit, the narrator now meanders toward a difficult conclusion, becoming once again in the process the *flâneur* he was at the beginning. The edges of what otherwise gives every impression of being a sharply ordered performance by the narrator are slightly frayed, haunted by an air of hesitation, by what would almost seem an inability to get to the point. The reluctance to begin or to end is provoked by the haphazard interests of the narrator, his fascination for the city which struggles against the need to get on with his story. The traditional image of the third-person narrator thus becomes problematic in *Ferragus*. The story seems instead to be bent upon exposing the fundamentally vagabond nature of beginnings and endings in general. Not only do the beginning and the ending of *Ferragus* illustrate the effects of chance encounters that resemble one another to a striking degree, but the narrator himself is ultimately infected by the very structure he attempts to describe.

Written shortly after the resounding triumph of Laplacean physics, Balzac's *Ferragus* fits only uncomfortably within the mechanistic outlook of that theory. In fact, as has now become clear, the story looks resolutely in the direction of modern scientific theories in which chance is given a much more creative and productive role, perhaps even the predominant role. The product of an era marked by a specific scientific context, Balzac nevertheless succeeds in creatively formulating his own view on certain questions through his fictional text. One might well say that this type of relationship between science and literature is regularly the case. The writer does not simply reflect the scientific views which surround him. He, along with thinkers from other cultural sectors, calls attention to phenomena which run contrary to what can be incorporated into the scientific paradigm of his period. In this sense, literature is regularly "experimental," out of step with, and sometimes ahead of, the science which surrounds it.

Notes

1. For a sampling of Michel Serres's writings in English translation, the reader may consult *Hermes: Literature, Science, Philosophy*, ed. Josué V. Harari and David F. Bell (Baltimore: Johns Hopkins University Press, 1982), and Michel Serres, *The Parasite*, trans. Lawrence R. Schehr (Baltimore: Johns Hopkins University Press, 1982).

2. Ilya Prigogine and Isabelle Stengers, *La nouvelle alliance: Métamorphose de la science* (Paris: Gallimard, 1979), pp. 76–77. The translation is mine. All translations of French texts will be my own unless otherwise indicated.

3. Prigogine and Stengers (*Nouvelle alliance*) have argued persuasively that the new science of the nineteenth century, the science of heat (thermodynamics), got its start in technological circles rather than in scientific circles as a result of the stultifying officialization of the French scientific establishment.

4. Michel Serres, *Hermes III: La traduction* (Paris: Minuit, 1974), p. 163.

5. Pierre Simon de Laplace, *Théorie analytique des probabilités* (Paris: Courcier, 1820), p. vi.

6. In his reference to the atomic level here, Laplace indirectly recalls the sustained quarrel between the Newtonians and the French atomists of the eighteenth century. Only when atomistic theories were effectively repressed was Newtonian theory able to triumph in France. For the atomists, unlike the Newtonians, chance was a fundamental element, as it had been ever since the invention of atomistic theories in ancient philosophy. The defeat of the atomists was another expression of the denial of the place and importance of chance within scientific theory.

7. Ever since its invention, the Laplacean demon has had a fundamental impact upon the way in which the question of causality has been framed in physics, as Ernst Cassirer has pointed out: "The defenders as well as the attackers of the causality principle of classical physics seem to be agreed at least in this respect, that this picture may be taken as an adequate expression of the problem." *Determinism and Indeterminism in Modern Physics: Historical and Systematic Studies of the Problem of Causality* (New Haven: Yale University Press, 1956), p. 3. Cassirer and other modern philosophers of science would argue that the Laplacean demon promotes a flawed image of causality in complex systems.

8. Prigogine and Stengers, *Nouvelle alliance*, p. 90.

9. This development, moreover, was not confined only to France. The analysis set forth in my discussion below finds resonances in the work of Dickens in England, for example.

10. Two recent Balzac critics have insisted upon the connection between Balzac's work and the development of melodrama, a literary mode which also depends heavily upon chance. Both, although for quite different reasons, have considered melodrama as the characteristic literary mode of the early nineteenth century. See Peter Brooks, *The Melodramatic Imagination: Balzac, Henry James, Melodrama, and the Mode of Excess* (New Haven: Yale University Press, 1976), and Christopher Prendergast, *Balzac: Fiction and Melodrama* (New York: Holmes and Meier, 1978).

11. Balzac, *Ferragus, La comédie humaine*, ed. Pierre Citron (Paris: Seuil, 1966), 4:13.

12. Jacques Brosse, "Le hasard et les traditions extrême-orientales," in *Traverses* 23 (November 1981): 46.

13. A. A. Cournot, *Exposition de la théorie des chances et des probabilités* (Paris: Librairie de L. Hachette, 1843), p. 73.

14. Antoine Augustin Cournot, *An Essay on the Foundations of Our Knowledge*, trans. Merritt H. Moore (New York: Liberal Arts Press, 1956), p. 41. The work actually dates from 1851.

15. For the reader unfamiliar with *Ferragus*, that mystery consists of several elements. Ferragus (alias Bourignard, alias Funcal) is an escaped criminal who is the father of Mme Jules (and, one might add, a prototype of Balzac's famous Vautrin). Mme Jules's husband, Jules Desmarets, knows nothing of this paternity nor does anyone else in his wife's entourage, and Mme Jules is attempting to conceal her relationship to her father until he can assume a false identity which will hide his criminal background. Hence the danger created by Maulincourt's glimpse of her on a visit to her father.

16. Clément Rosset, *Logique du pire* (Paris: P.U.F., 1971), p. 72.

17. The stochastic vision presented by Balzac here is one which obviously fascinated him. It becomes the central concern of another novella, *Le chez-d'oeuvre inconnu*, of which the subject is a work of art, a painting perched on the limit between order and disorder.

18. It would be possible, although there is no space in the present study, to analyze *Ferragus* in terms of thermodynamics. In such an analysis, disorder would once again play a prominent role, as would the urn of ashes which occupies such a central position in the final pages of the story. It is worthwhile recalling that Sadi Carnot, the first in a line of theoreticians who would formulate the thermodynamic theory which was to supplant classical mechanics, was Balzac's contemporary.

19. Prigogine's position on the question of chance has been roundly criticized by René Thom, the inventor of the mathematical theory of disasters. Moreover, Jacques Monod's popularized explanation of molecular biology, entitled *Chance and Necessity*, in which he gave a prominent position to chance in biological processes, was not well received by many scientists.

Part IV

History and Biography

ROBERT M. YOUNG

Darwin and the Genre
of Biography

The subject of most of the essays in this volume has been the work of artists and scientists. Such work tells us about mutual influence and about ways in which science and fiction are embedded in culture. But I want to turn here away from what is often called "primary" work, to a literary form that is concerned with the creators of that work. Biography is, after all, a literary genre. Looking at the way this genre chooses to see great artists and scientists reveals perhaps more clearly than the original works themselves how implicated in the culture of its time each work is. Biography historicizes. Its language can make no pretense to the timelessness too often attributed to both art and science. Watching how biography actually approaches a writer can tell us a great deal not only about how science reflects its own historical moment, its own personal sources, but about how much our understanding of and our esteem for science are determined by the culture of the moment. In particular, I want here to consider how biography has treated Charles Darwin, and the significance of its omissions and emphases. Equally important, I want to suggest that biography does not merely fill in the "background" of the scientist's life, but also provides the materials that take us to the center of the scientific enterprise itself and cast an unexpected light on its scientificity. The literary form is not to be isolated from the scientific content: both are irresistably cultural.

First, some reflections on the genre. Biography—whatever else it is —is about contingencies and is predicated on the historicity of its

This is the first of what I hope will be a series of studies of the genre of biography. In embarking on this project I have been aided by the generosity of Gillian Beer, Ralph Colp, Jr., John Durant, Elaine Jordan, Ludi Jordanova, Jim Moore, and Jean Radford.

subject matter. It concedes, as part of the basic characteristics of the genre, issues which are in some quarters very controversial indeed. Philosophy and science make claims toward dealing in ahistorical necessities and, if not in all versions of the philosophy of science, in universal truths.

Biography is also about an individual; that is its only relatively uncontroversial defining characteristic. To say more is to plunge into a murky and rapidly expanding debate. What can we know? Are we confined to her or his own memoirs? Are we to trust self-perception? How do we evaluate the judgment of loved ones, friends, enemies? In these matters critical acumen is all. Do we have access to the subject's inner life? What counts as evidence? Can/should we attempt to analyze motivations deeper than conscious, attested intentions?

People who become the subject of biography are usually famous or notorious—as statesmen, warriors, writers, inventors, scientists, captains of industry, artists, campaigners, criminals. The biographer normally attempts to shed light on the publicly known—the claims to fame—of the subject. The most characteristic connections, then, are between the public and the private—the origins, inspirations, costs, lapses, vicissitudes of fame or notoriety. I do not write in ignorance of other kinds of biographies—those of "ordinary" people, those which exploit oral and social history which do not conform to the above, for example, the works of Studs Terkel and Ronald Fraser's *Blood of Spain*. But my comments are aimed at classical biography and make no pretense of canvassing all biography. My interest here is in the biographies of scientists, especially Darwin.

We have, then, the private, perhaps intimate, account of the great or notorious man or woman and his/her achievements/crimes. What of the times? Here I arrive at my own reason for embarking on the study of biography. My model is a humanistic Marxist one of human action and the production of knowledge. It asserts that what happens in history is rather like a "resolution of forces" diagram in physics. Where we find a given object is a net result of the direction and magnitude of the forces acting upon it. This model is not rich enough, of course, since human action includes many poorly understood levels of motivation, so we must include latent forces and reaction formations based on forgotten, repressed, or dimly remembered values and beliefs. I make my task even more daunting by embracing a psychoanalytic view of human motivation, whereby the subject has very little access to the sources of her or his thoughts and actions. So—the model of resolution of forces has to be seen as part of a multilayered process which is not really amenable to simple representation.

To complete my sketch of the bank of interrelated problems which I want to crank up to the genre of biography and then to the case of Darwin, I must turn to the question which vexes the historian of ideas and, most acutely, the historian of scientific ideas. It is the question of *determinations*. It is argued in many quarters and assumed in many others that if we can explain an idea purely in terms of its connection to other ideas, we have no need for additional explanatory factors, whether these be intimately personal forces or large-scale historical ones or both, i.e., historical forces acting on and mediated through the personal.

Historians—and of them especially historians of science—of my acquaintance are very leery of psychohistorical explanations of individual or epochal phenomena. I do not accept their embargo, though I do share many of their doubts. I find it no more congenial to "read off" Newton's discoveries and theories from Frank Manuel's speculations about his unconscious in *A Portrait of Isaac Newton* than to read them off from Boris Hessen's vulgar Marxist "The Social and Economic Roots of Newton's 'Principia.'" But instead of wishing a plague on both their houses, I want to find a way of making both of their enterprises more sophisticated and then integrating them into a single account. A tall order, I know, but the only one that conforms to my own experience of life, including my life as a historian of science.

How then can we pose the problem of biography? Leon Edel says that the central aim of biography "is to relate the life lived to the particular achievement—to tell the life story of a man or woman whose uniqueness makes him or her a valid biographical subject." I'd say this draws the circle too narrowly and disarticulates the subject from wider historical determinations, which are just as important for a writer, be it Henry James or George Eliot, as for a thinker, e.g., William James, or a scientist. My own short version is: how does the individual bear, mediate, and integrate the individual, intellectual, cultural, ideological, and socioeconomic forces which constitute the labor process of her or his production of what interests us about that person, be it knowledge, art, policy, heroism, great good or evil? To include the concept of the labor process is to invoke another model which overlaps the Marxist and psychoanalytic ones. Or rather it is a matrix for them, since the terms of reference of labor process theory offer a very accommodating framework for laying bare the elements and connections or articulations of any product having a use value, whether theory, therapy, thing, act, fact, artifact, policy, treatise, essay, or scientific paper.

There is nothing very grand about a labor process perspective, except that it gives one pause to consider in a fairly orderly way what is being made—what use value—and by what process of purposive human labor, employing what raw materials and with what tools. Raw materials, means of production, purposive activity to produce a use value: these are the terms of reference for thinking about what a biographical subject does and to what end(s). Each element of the analysis should have bearing upon it the direct, indirect, and epochal connections or articulations which influence it and give it the significance it has in the work of the subject. In my experience, drawing diagrams with arrows of different thickness, and with lots of questions and puzzles, helps a lot. So I make lists and jot things down on lots and lots of pieces of paper which can be shuffled until one can hope to see the repetitions and intuit the patterns.

One more preliminary. It relates to our attempts to bring together the sort of determinations to which I have so far only alluded. Purists in the historiography of scientific figures seek to cut their heroes off from any more determinations than are absolutely necessary. Their goal is to celebrate genius, to praise the essence of greatness embodied in an extraordinary individual. "More influences" is thought somehow to mean "less greatness." My own approach is less faithful to the heroine or hero, more promiscuous, if you will, certainly more fully *historical*.

I'd argue that the more plausible candidates for influences contributing to the behavior that we seek to illuminate, the better. I argue, that is, for multiple causation and overdetermination. By this I do not mean that the biographer should shovel influences into the text and reach for, e.g., biorhythms and astrology. Rather, I mean that all plausible candidates for being influential should be mentioned, critically evaluated, weighed and given their due in the light of the biographer's conclusions. I find Peter Gay quite judicious on this subject: "As discoverers and documentors of over-determination, psychoanalysts and historians, each in their own manner, are allies in the struggle against reductionism, against naive and crude monocausal explanations."[1]

> Over-determination is in fact nothing more than the sensible recognition that a variety of causes—a variety, not infinity—enters into the making of all historical events, and that each ingredient in historical experience can be counted on to have a variety—not infinity—of functions. . . . Seek complexity, the historian and the psychoanalyst can say in unison, seek complexity and tame it. (p. 187)

I'd add that it helps to let others know (in notes, if not in the text) about the roads not taken.

Charles Darwin is a very unpromising case study for my attempt to address the problems raised above. True, he was a great man who wrote a lot of books and a lot of letters. Many people wrote about him and to him. There are nearly 14,000 items and 1,800 correspondents involved in the collection which is now in process of publication. His ideas were also greatly noticed in a rich, multifaceted, and multilayered periodical press. He also had recurring, debilitating disorders for decades, suggesting medical and/or psychoanalytic interrelations with his work. He wrote an autobiography (until recently, bowdlerized), and great efforts have been made to preserve and make accessible his notebooks, letters, drafts, and other memorabilia which are of use to biographers.

Why, then, unpromising? First, he was a reticent man. While he spoke of personal matters, he was discreet about intimate ones, e.g., his views on his most private life and on religion. Second, his theory was a very basic and a very general one. By that I mean that historical conjunctions are not as likely to be on the surface as they are, for example, with respect to a theory in social science, the articulations of which are easier to trace to movements of thought and socioeconomic factors in the period.

Third, although he was educated at Edinburgh and Cambridge, spent fifty-five months on a 37,000-mile voyage around the world, and lived in Shrewsbury and London until September 1842, he then took himself to Down in Kent and hardly stirred until he died forty years later. Even Marat, though in his tub, was in the thick of the French revolutionary events in Paris. Proust also comes to mind: mobility and getting out and about are not essential to being a man of one's time, or interesting, as the *Inman Diary* shows, nor do they preclude being a "great man."

Against these seriously discouraging factors we must place the attractiveness of the prize. The theory of evolution by natural selection— what we mean by "Darwinism"—is *the* theory which links humanity to the rest of living nature and living nature to the rest of the conditions of existence on earth. It provides the quintessence of historicity. It is the fundament. If we can link the most basic theory of historicity to the historicity of science and these to the historicity of Darwin, we will, in a way, have found the mother lode.

It would not be inaccurate to say that Darwin has been ill served by his biographers, but it would be unilluminating. My experience is that there is no good biography of any of the figures I would most like to understand "in the round" or as a totality—Newton, Darwin, Marx, George Eliot, Freud, Edison, Willie Nelson. The subjects, of course, are daunting, as are the problems of exposition and interpretation of their leading ideas. There are also many specialists on various aspects of the work of each, waiting to pounce, making one cautious. Howls at various reductionisms come readily to their throats. Better, easier to be subtle on a smaller canvas.

The usual way of dealing with this problem is to be prudent. Tell the life; avoid excurses into motivation. Also tell the ideas and the well-attested influences and reception and reaction to reception and current evaluations. Sketch the times, as setting. Do not try to integrate. The result is unadventurous but reliable, accurate but, I think, desiccated. Gordon Haight's *George Eliot* is my own model of this genre: sound, reliable, useful, the standard source. Other biographies are at the extreme of being frankly gossip, while still others are avowedly expositions of ideas, set in a life. *Home Life with Herbert Spencer*, by his housekeepers, is my favorite at one extreme—quaint gossip—while Ronald Clark's *The Survival of Charles Darwin: A Biography of a Man and an Idea* is an extreme case of the latter. Indeed, half of the book is about the fate of his ideas after Darwin died. A recent reviewer of Clark's book rightly concludes: "There is still no good biography of him."[2]

Whatever other silences there are in Darwin's biography, there are two or three "nonscientific" conceptions which unequivocally connect him to leading philosophical, socioeconomic, and racial (we'd now call them "Social Darwinist") ideas of his time. I am referring to the profound influence of the natural theology of William Paley on Darwin's ideas of adaptation, of Thomas Robert Malthus' principle of population and the survival of the fittest on the rank ordering of peoples—the "races" of the earth. As Marx and Engels rightly observed in more than one place, he was deeply a man of his time.

Engels wrote in 1862, "It is remarkable how Darwin recognises among beasts and plants his English society with its division of labour, competition, opening up of new markets, 'inventions' and the Malthusian 'struggle for existence.'"[3] He later said, "Darwin did not know what a bitter satire he wrote on mankind, and especially on his countrymen, when he showed that free competition, the struggle for existence, which the economists celebrate as the highest historical achievement, is the normal state of the *animal kingdom*."[4]

Fortunately, there is a study of Darwin's biographers which is helpful—at least in showing what has not been done: Frederick Churchill's "Darwin and the Historians."[5] There is also, I am glad to say, one study which lays out the desiderata of a full-fledged biography: James Moore's meticulous analysis "Darwin of Down: The Evolutionist as Squarson-Naturalist,"[6] to which I shall revert.

Darwin's creative process has been subjected to the most searching scrutiny from three related perspectives. Howard Gruber has devoted a highly regarded and meticulously detailed study to his creative process *per se*. Sydney Smith, Peter Vorzimmer, Sandra Herbert, Silvan Schweber, David Kohn, and I, among others, have pondered and minutely reconstructed the texture of his theory building. The third aspect of his creative process is the wider intellectual and ideological resonances of his basic concept—natural selection—which made Darwin's theory the one which converted evolutionism from a widely held form of speculation to the foundation of modern biological science. This topic is closely related to the analogy between the artificial selection of breeders and what happens in nature. The articulations of his thinking have been considered in greatest detail with respect to Malthus' theory of population and Paley's theory of adaptation within natural theology. This domain has been passionately fought over by Sir Gavin de Beer, Vorzimmer, Herbert, Le Mahieu, Bowler, Ospovat, Mayr, and numerous commentators.

Of course, none of the above is a strictly empirical matter, since there are powerful historiographic and ideological reasons for Darwin—or any other scientific thinker—to be articulated with or disarticulated from such blatantly "nonscientific" affiliations. The two most eminent working scientists in this debate, Sir Gavin de Beer and Ernst Mayr, have (I think it is fair to say) expressed righteous indignation to the point of fulmination on this point, while Michael Ghiselin can be said to have bitten one or two people. However powerfully the eminent biologist-historians have pressed their claim to separate Darwin from these key influences, the consensus among scholars who have worked through the manuscript and notebook materials has supported those who would link up Darwin with the ideological currents of his time rather than those who would split him off from them.

Until one grasps just how much hangs on these connections, it could be argued that a surprising amount of printers' ink has been spilled in coupling, uncoupling, recoupling Darwin with and from the urgent debates in theology, political economy, and the philosophy of humanity and society of the late eighteenth and early nineteenth centuries. Putting it another way, Darwin has been washed again and again by those who would cleanse him of ideological pollutants.

Since I have been accused of being one of the most persistent polluters (one critic wrote of my writings, "as a dog returns to his vomit, Young . . ."), I am particularly relieved that the writings of the most meticulous students of the Darwin manuscripts and the most fair-minded of the reviewers of the literature have finally supported the position I share with those who would see Darwin as enmeshed in a tight web of social, cultural, and ideological determinations. I am thinking, in particular, of the conclusions of David Kohn in his "Theories to Work By: Rejected Theories, Reproduction and Darwin's Path to Natural Selection," a most persuasive study which concludes that my argument linking Darwin closely at the crucial point of his discovery of the mechanism of natural selection to Malthus' work on human population and misery is "nearly definitive."[7] The most recent overview of the whole question, "How Did Darwin Arrive at His Theory?" by David Oldroyd[8] is equally clear about the close connection between Darwin's thinking and the wider debate on nature's niggardliness which centered on Malthusianism.

Darwin and the Genre of Biography

Finally, once it was established that Darwin's concept of natural selection was fundamentally Malthusian, the remaining issue over which scholars were in doubt was the extent to which Darwin relied on the analogy between that humanocentric concept of nature and actual human selection in the work of breeders, pigeon fanciers, and others. Vigorous attempts have been made to uncouple Darwin's mechanism of evolution from this analogy, but another careful study, L. T. Evans' "Darwin's Use of the Analogy between Artificial and Natural Selection," convincingly answers the critics on that score.[9]

These issues are of considerable interest. When Darwin says that he always thought his ideas came half out of Sir Charles Lyell's brain and that he hasn't sufficiently stressed this, no one is troubled. This is because the entire surface of Lyell's geological writings is strictly scientific (which is not to say that his assumptions were any less culturally constituted than those of other thinkers). Lyell claimed that only causes now in operation, and in their present intensities, could be invoked to explain the historical changes in the earth and, by extension, plant and animal life. This geological uniformitarianism set the pace and scale for Darwin's theorizing. But we find advocates of a restricted range of influences on a great scientist seeking to explain away Darwin's statement that Paley's *Evidences of Christianity* and his *Natural Theology* were profoundly influential on him as an undergraduate, and the following quotations at the beginning of *On the Origin of Species*:

> But with regard to the material world, we can at least go so far as this—we can perceive that events are brought about not by insulated interpositions of Divine power, exerted in each particular case, but by the establishment of general laws. (Whewell: *Bridgewater Treatise*)

> The only distinct meaning of the word "natural" is *stated, fixed,* or *settled*; since what is natural as much requires and presupposes an intelligent agent to render it so, *i.e.,* to effect it continually or at stated times, as what is supernatural or miraculous does to effect it for once. (Butler: *Analogy of Revealed Religion* [added to 2d ed.])

> To conclude, therefore, let no man out of a weak conceit of sobriety, or an ill-applied moderation, think or maintain, that a man can search too far or be too well studied in the book of God's word, or in the book of God's works; divinity or philosophy; but rather let men endeavour an endless progress or proficience in both. (Bacon: *Advancement of Learning*)

These theological connections threaten their vision of a neat science/ theology break and undermine their attempt to divorce a great scientist (Mayr says "the greatest,") from metaphysical assumptions. This is the sort of evidence which can begin to make sense of otherwise self-contradictory statements like Churchill's: "We have found at the roots of his atheism the remnants of a natural theology which nourished his scientific inventions . . ." (p. 68).

Similarly, the same positivists seek to explain away Malthus' role in Darwin's eureka moment. I say positivists advisedly, since it is a definition of positivism that its advocates attempt to separate scientific facts and theories from the matrix of values, meanings, and historical determinations in which they are embedded and from and by which they are constituted.

The Darwin-Malthus connection is now firmly established and acknowledged by all reputable scholars. It is possible to trace the connection throughout his writings.[10] He is quite straightforward in his autobiography:

> In October 1838, that is, fifteen months after I had begun my systematic enquiry, I happened to read for amusement Malthus on *Population*, and, being well prepared to appreciate the struggle for existence which everywhere goes on from long-continued observation of the habits of animals and plants, it had once struck me that under these circumstances favourable variations would tend to be preserved, and unfavourable ones to be destroyed. The result of this would be the formation of a new species. Here, then, I had at last got a theory by which to work; but I was so anxious to avoid prejudice that I determined not for some time to write even the briefest sketch of it.[11]

In his working notebooks for September and October of 1838, we can find the moment of discovery laid out before our eyes, complete with phrases, dashes, the enthusiasm imprinted on the page.

> [Sept] 28th. We ought to be far from wondering of changes in numbers of species, from small changes in nature of locality. Even the energetic language of Decandolle does not convey the warring of the species as inference from Malthus—increase of brutes must be prevented solely by positive checks, excepting that famine may stop desire.—in nature production does not increase, whilst no check prevail, but the positive check of famine and consequently death. I do not doubt every one till he thinks

deeply has assumed that increase of animals exactly proportionate to the number that can live.— . . .

Population is increase at geometrical ratio in FAR SHORTER time than 25 years—yet until the one sentence of Malthus no one clearly perceived the great check amongst men.—there is spring, like food used for other purposes as wheat for making brandy—Even a *few* years plenty, makes population in man increase & an *ordinary* crop causes a dearth. take Europe on an average every species must have some number killed year with year by hawks by cold &c.—even one species of hawk decreasing in number must affect instantaneously all the rest.—The final cause of all this wedging, must be to sort out proper structure, and adapt it to change.—to do that for form, which Malthus shows is the final effect (by means however of volition) of this populousness on the energy of man. One may say there is a force like a hundred thousand wedges trying [to] force every kind of adapted structure into the gaps in the oeconomy of nature, or rather forming gaps by thrusting out weaker ones.

In another passage he quotes Malthus at some length and concludes, "this applies to one species—I would apply it not only to population & depopulation, but extermination and production of new forms."[12]

Lest this be thought an esoteric dispute, it is worth spelling out the wider issues it bears upon. As I have said, hero-worshiping biographies of scientists set out to celebrate genius and to confine influences to inspiration and to ideas and discoveries inside the scientific community. A decontextualized approach to science is relaxed only to include personal history plus the influence of scientific discoveries and ideas. To show that a scientist's most basic ideas were centrally influenced by the very sorts of conceptions that are abrogated by those who would treat science as above contending social forces, and who claim that scientific developments are neutral, is to bring biography into the growing body of studies which place science inside culture, inside society, inside the ideological and socioeconomic forces which shape the rest of the social world.

Science has, of course, always been inside society, but the way it has been written about has systematically obscured the determinations which constitute its presuppositions, priorities, patronage, and its privileged position. Biographies of scientists have followed suit. Victorian lives and letters were discreet and hagiographic. When, in 1918, Lytton Strachey set out to replace iconology with iconoclastic exposé, the nearest he got to science was that grand hysteric, the lady of the lamp and handmaiden to medicine, Florence Nightingale. The "warts and all" school of biography has yet to penetrate to the scientific hero or heroine, although Phyllis Grosskurth's fine biography *Melanie Klein* is a notable pioneering work in this respect.[13]

There is also a literary and historiographic reason for being interested in the Darwin/Malthus/Paley question. It bears on a vexing biographical question: how do epochal causes act through individuals? It appears to me that they do so in three ways. First, through influences—Paley, Lyell, and Malthus, in the case of Darwin—which can be located more or less clearly. The history of ideas becomes, thereby, a clear, direct, and relatively indisputable helpmate to the biographer. Second, through the social and class location of the subject. Third, through historically specific factors which influence the subject's inner life. I shall dwell here on the role of social and class location and return below to psycho-history. James Moore's study, noted above, is, in my view, a superb achievement in locating Darwin. His position as something akin to a "squire/parson," his patronage, his role in good works, were consistent with his more general ideas, which were finally unsubversive, though troubling. Thanks to Moore, we really do know Darwin's social location and how ideology acted as a material force in the way he lived his beliefs.

By the most meticulous research in local archives and in other areas which historians of science would be likely to ignore or pass by, Moore has greatly illuminated who Darwin was. That is, he has shown how Darwin actually conducted his domestic and local life with respect to matters which are greatly controverted by historians of ideas. This is particularly true of his deep respect for the role of the established church in the community, an institution to which he contributed time, energy, and funds—all of which were greatly valued by the community at Down.

Darwin's secure place inside the Victorian bourgeoisie is given further support by the fact that he is buried in Westminster Abbey. When Darwin died on 19 April 1882, having had several heart attacks in the first few weeks of the year, his family intended to bury him at Down. However, three days later, twenty members of Parliament, including Sir John Lubbock, later Lord Avebury, and Henry C. Bannerman, a future prime minister, wrote to the dean of Westminster, "We hope that you will not think we are taking a liberty if we venture to suggest that it would be acceptable to a very large number of our fellow-countrymen of all classes and opinions that our illustrious countryman, Mr. Darwin, should be buried in Westminster Abbey." And so it came to pass, five days later, that Darwin was buried a few feet from the grave of Newton. His pallbearers included the past, present, and future presidents of the Royal Society, two dukes and an earl. An anthem had been especially composed for the occasion by the Abbey organist and included the words: "Happy is the man who finds wisdom and getteth understanding."[14]

In case it be thought that Darwin's burial betokens only greatness, not acceptability (as with Byron), here are some excerpts from the *Times* of 26 April. Of the body, they said, "the Abbey needed it more than it needed the Abbey." Looking at the matter more broadly, the *Times* said,

> By every title which can claim a corner in that sacred earth, the body of Charles Darwin should be there. Conquerors lie there, who have added rich and vast territories to their native empire. Charles Darwin has, perhaps, borne the fiat of science farther, certainly he has planted its standard more deeply, than any Englishman since Newton. He has done more than extend the boundaries of science; he has established new centres where annexations of fresh and fruitful truths are continually to be made. The Abbey has its orators and Ministers who have convinced reluctant senates and swayed nations. Not one of them all has wielded a power over men and their intelligences more complete than that which for the last twenty three years has emanated from a simple country house in Kent.[15]

It is also worth recalling that Frederick Temple, one of the supporters of scientific naturalism in the wider debate which embraced both *Essays and Reviews* and *On the Origin of Species*, went on to become archbishop of Canterbury. He saw no conflict between evolutionism and Christianity. Darwin was no iconoclast.

We have most to go on in Darwin's case with respect to the influences on and articulations of his ideas, because he was so scrupulous in recording his labor process, his enthusiasms, his reading (including voracious consumption of biographies), and the very passages in the writings of others which struck him—passages conveniently excised from his notebooks for inclusion in his great work, *Natural Selection*, of which *On the Origin of Species* was a précis, and repeatedly recalled in his correspondence. But in order to see we must look, and not rule out important areas of influence because of a narrowly positivist conception of how scientific ideas get conceived. Approaching such ideas via the genre of biography helps us to keep our noses to the right ground. Other epochal causes are much less easy to take into account. Another way hagiographers and positivists try to keep Darwin pure is by attempting to make a sharp separation between Darwin the scientist, on the one hand, and the racist and ideological extrapolations of the so-called Social Darwinists, on the other. There are even those who would argue (not *altogether* unconvincingly) that the Social Darwinists weren't Social Darwinists at all in the popular sense of "the devil take the hindmost."[16] But the most cursory reading of Darwin's works, early, middle and late, shows just how much he was a man of his time in seeing races in competitive and hierarchical relations and in connecting such generalizations to justifications for a wealthy leisured class in the Victorian world.

If we define Social Darwinism as the application of the concepts of "struggle for existence" and "survival of the fittest" to humanity—that is, if we explain social phenomena in terms of competition and conflict and consider these to have a progressive tendency—then Darwin was a Social Darwinist root and branch.[17] Here are some representative passages from the book in which he applied evolutionism to humanity, *The Descent of Man*:

> But the inheritance of property by itself is very far from an evil; for without the accumulation of capital the arts could not progress; and it is chiefly through their power that the civilised races have extended and are now everywhere extending their range, so as to take the place of the lower races.[18]

> There is apparently much truth in the belief that the wonderful progress of the United States, as well as the character of the people, are the results of natural selection; for the more energetic, restless, and courageous men from all parts of Europe have emigrated during the last ten or twelve generations to that great country, and have there succeeded best. (p. 142)

Darwin and the Genre of Biography

Man, like every other animal, has no doubt advanced to his present high condition through a struggle for existence consequent upon his rapid multiplication; and if he is to advance still higher, it is to be feared that he must remain subject to a severe struggle. Otherwise he would sink into indolence, and the more gifted men would not be more successful in the battle of life than the less gifted. Hence our natural rate of increase, though leading to many and obvious evils, must not be greatly diminished by any means. There should be open competition for all men; and the most able should not be prevented by laws or customs from succeeding the best and rearing the largest number of offspring. (p. 618)

I do not quote these passages to pillory Darwin, ahistorically. How odd it would be if Darwin completely transcended his time and place in the world and in society. He was kind and compassionate toward Indians in South America and toward peasants in his own village. He abhorred human bondage. But this did not elevate him above a contemporary British sense of how races and nations rise and fall in history, or from extolling the benefits of the class system in his own time and place. It would not be necessary to stress this if his admirers had not set out to disarticulate and dehistoricize him in this area, as in others.

I have said there were three ways in which epochal causes act through individuals and have discussed two of them. The third way is illuminated by psychohistorical studies done by someone who knows what he or she is doing—a Ralph Colp on Darwin or a Frank Manuel on Newton, though not a Sudhir Kakar on F. W. Taylor, Anne Jardim on Henry Ford, or Freud on Michelangelo. I would expect greater illumination of psychopathology than I would of achievements, but this is often a false distinction, for example, in the interesting psychobiographies of Van Gogh, Luther, and Malcolm X. I am persuaded by Colp's argument that the price Darwin paid for his profoundly unsettling ideas was not a social one but a series of psychosomatic disorders.[19]

We are, then, able to discern much of the social location of Darwin by patient research into parish and family records, correspondence, and knowledge of ambient social and cultural history. We are least well off with respect to the unconscious processes, partly for the obvious reasons that we do not have the subject on the couch as a patient and no amount of research will provide the requisite free associations. In some cases, of course, we do have a lot to go on from people's writings, e.g.,

Proust, Kafka, and Emily Dickinson. We can still try. As Ellmann says (paraphrasing Freud), "where obscurity was hypothesis shall be."[20] But in Darwin's case, though remarkable and admirable efforts have been made, we are still faced with his reticence, celebrated in Geoffrey West's conclusion: "The Darwin the world knows is the whole Darwin."[21] Mind you, there are all those letters being catalogued and printed, and much more will be discernible on all these fronts in the coming years.

If we reflect on the particular disputed influences and settings, the results add up to a reevaluation of one of the most influential figures in the history of thought. Everyone will have her or his own list, e.g., Copernicus, Galileo, Newton, Marx, Freud, Einstein, Gödel, Wiener, Turing. Each brought science to bear on human pretension. Each removed a reason for being humanocentric because of some law or laws that constrain humankind.

But if we look closely—biographically closely—at the man who brought all of life, including humanity, within the domain of natural law, decisively shattering (so the story goes) a theological account of species change, of human origins, human nature, and human destiny, what do we find? We find political economy, ideology, natural theology, anthropomorphism at the heart of the concept of natural selection—his explanatory mechanism—and a deep accommodation with theism in his theory and in his own social location and practice. We find, to put it most polemically, theism and humanism at the heart of the *science* of life, humanity, and mind. I cannot claim to be a close student of many of the figures in the pantheon listed above. In the cases of Marx and Freud, however, I can make some claim of having made comparable careful studies. In those cases I would argue just as strongly for anthropomorphism and humanism at the basis of their views of the world and the place of humanity in it. From the little I know of recent Newtonian studies, I think that there a similar claim could be made. Once again, such studies depend on a fully textured and fully articulated set of biographical inquiries.

As I now see things, biography is not an adjunct to the serious business of understanding nature, human nature, and history. Rather, if we believe that labor is neither nature nor culture but their matrix and that the concept of a person is ontologically prior to those of mind and body, then, by analogy, biography is neither finally personal nor historical but the crucible in which we can forge the best understanding of those forces.

Notes

1. Peter Gay, *Freud for Historians* (Oxford: Oxford University Press, 1985), pp. 75–76.
2. Ralph H. Colp, Jr., "The Survival of Charles Darwin," *American Journal of Psychiatry* 142 (1985): 1507.
3. Karl Marx and Frederick Engels, *Selected Correspondence* (Moscow: Progress, 1965), p. 128.
4. Frederick Engels, *The Dialectics of Nature* (1873–86), 3d ed. (Moscow: Progress, 1964), pp. 35–36.
5. Frederick B. Churchill, "Darwin and the Historians," in R. J. Berry, ed., *Charles Darwin: A Commemoration, 1882–1982* (London: Academic Press, 1982), pp. 45–68.
6. James Moore, "Darwin of Down: The Evolutionist as Squarson-Naturalist," in David Kohn, ed., *The Darwinian Heritage* (Princeton: Princeton University Press, 1985), pp. 435–81.
7. David Kohn, "Theories to Work By: Rejected Theories, Reproduction and Darwin's Path to Natural Selection," *Studies in the History of Biology* 4 (1980): 142.
8. David R. Oldroyd, "How Did Darwin Arrive at His Theory? The Secondary Literature to 1982," *History of Science* 22 (1984):325–74.
9. L. T. Evans, "Darwin's Use of the Analogy between Artificial and Natural Selection," *Journal of the History of Biology* 17 (1984): 113–40.
10. See Robert M. Young, *Darwin's Metaphor: Nature's Place in Victorian Culture* (Cambridge: Cambridge University Press, 1985), pp. 39–44.
11. Charles Darwin, *The Autobiography of Charles Darwin, 1809–1882, with original omissions restored*, ed. Nora Barlow (London: Collins, 1958), p. 120.
12. Sir Gavin de Beer et al., eds., "Darwin's Notebooks on Transmutation of Species," *Bulletin of the British Museum (Natural History) Historical Series* 3, no. 5 (1967): 162–63.
13. Phyllis Grosskurth, *Melanie Klein: Her World and Her Work* (London: Hodder and Stoughton, 1986).
14. Ronald W. Clark, *The Survival of Charles Darwin: A Biography of a Man and an Idea* (London: Weidenfeld and Nicolson, 1984), pp. 196–97.
15. Quoted in James R. Moore, "Charles Darwin Lies in Westminster Abbey," *Biological Journal of the Linnaean Society* 17 (1982): 110–11.
16. Robert C. Bannister, *Social Darwinism: Science and Myth in Anglo-American Social Thought* (Philadelphia: Temple University Press, 1979).
17. See John C. Greene, "Darwin as a Social Evolutionist," *Journal of the History of Biology* 10 (1977): 1–27; and Robert M. Young, "Darwinism *Is* Social," in *Darwinian Heritage*, especially pp. 618–21.
18. Charles Darwin, *The Descent of Man and Selection in Relation to Sex* (1871), 2d ed. (London: Murray, 1874), p. 135.

19. Ralph H. Colp, Jr., *To Be an Invalid: The Illness of Charles Darwin* (Chicago: University of Chicago Press, 1977).

20. Richard Ellmann, "Freud and Literary Biography," in Peregrine Horden, ed., *Freud and the Humanities* (London: Duckworth, 1985), p. 69.

21. Geoffrey West, *Charles Darwin: A Portrait* (New Haven: Yale University Press, 1938), p. x.

Bibliography

Aaron, Daniel, ed. *The Inman Diary: A Public and Private Confession.* Cambridge, Mass.: Harvard University Press, 1985.

Bannister, Robert C. *Social Darwinism: Science and Myth in Anglo-American Social Thought.* Philadelphia: Temple University Press, 1979.

Baron, Samuel H., and Pletsch, Carl, eds. *Introspection in Biography: The Biographer's Quest for Self-Awareness.* London: Analytic Press, 1985.

Bowler, Peter J. "Malthus, Darwin and the Concept of Struggle." *Journal of the History of Ideas* 37 (1976): 631–50.

Brent, Peter. *Charles Darwin: "A Man of Enlarged Curiosity."* London: Heinemann, 1981.

Burkhardt, Frederick, et al., eds. *The Correspondence of Charles Darwin.* Vol. 1: *1821–1836.* Cambridge: Cambridge University Press, 1985.

Caro, Robert A. *The Years of Lyndon Johnson: The Path to Power.* New York: Alfred A. Knopf, 1983.

Churchill, Frederick B. "Darwin and the Historian." In R. J. Berry, ed., *Charles Darwin: A Commemoration, 1882–1982*, pp. 45–68. London: Academic Press, 1982.

Clark, Ronald W. *The Survival of Charles Darwin: A Biography of a Man and an Idea.* London: Weidenfeld and Nicolson, 1984.

Collier, Peter, and Horowitz, David. *The Kennedys.* London: Secker & Warburg, 1984.

Colp, Ralph H., Jr. "Notes on Charles Darwin's *Autobiography.*" *Journal of the History of Biology* 18 (1985): 357–401.

Colp, Ralph H., Jr. "The Survival of Charles Darwin." *American Journal of Psychiatry* 142 (1985): 1507.

Colp, Ralph H., Jr. *To Be an Invalid: The Illness of Charles Darwin.* Chicago: University of Chicago Press, 1977.

Darwin, Charles. *The Autobiography of Charles Darwin, 1809–1882, with original omissions restored.* Ed. Nora Barlow. London: Collins, 1958.

Darwin, Charles. *The Descent of Man and Selection in Relation to Sex* (1871). 2d ed. London: Murray, 1874.

Darwin, Charles. *On the Origin of Species by Means of Natural Selection, or the Preservation of Favoured Species in the Struggle for Life* (1859). Facsimile reprint. New York: Atheneum, 1967; 6th ed. London: Murray, 1872.

Darwin, Francis, ed. *The Life and Letters of Charles Darwin.* 3d ed. 3 vols. London: Murray, 1887.

Darwin and the Genre of Biography

Darwin, Francis, and Seward, A. C., eds. *More Letters of Charles Darwin*. 2 vols. London: Murray, 1903.

de Beer, Sir Gavin. *Charles Darwin*. London: Nelson, 1963.

de Beer, Sir Gavin. "The Evolution of Charles Darwin." *New York Review of Books*, 17 December 1970, pp. 31–35.

de Beer, Sir Gavin, et al., eds. "Darwin's Notebooks on Transmutation of Species." *Bulletin of the British Museum (Natural History) Historical Series* 2, nos. 2–6 (1960–61); and 3, no. 5 (1967).

Drosnin, Michael. *Citizen Hughes*. London: Hutchinson, 1985.

Edel, Leon. "Biography and the Sexual Revolution—Why Curiosity Is No Longer Vulgar." *New York Times Book Review*, 24 November 1985, pp. 13–14.

Ellegard, A. *Darwin and the General Reader: The Reception of Darwin's Theory of Evolution in the British Periodical Press, 1859–1872*. Göteborg: Universitets Arsskrift, 1958.

Ellmann, Richard. "Freud and Literary Biography." In Peregrine Horden, ed., *Freud and the Humanities*, pp, 58–74. London: Duckworth, 1985.

Engels, Frederick. *The Dialectics of Nature* (1873–86). 3d ed. Moscow: Progress, 1964.

Erikson, Eric. *Young Man Luther*. London: Faber, 1972.

Evans, L. T. "Darwin's Use of the Analogy between Artificial and Natural Selection." *Journal of the History of Biology* 17 (1984): 113–40.

Finney, Brian. *The Inner I: British Literary Autobiography of the Twentieth Century*. London: Faber and Faber, 1985.

Fraser, Ronald. *Blood of Spain: The Experience of Civil War, 1936–39.* London: Allen Lane, 1979.

Gay, Peter. *Freud for Historians*. Oxford: Oxford University Press, 1985.

Ghiselin, M. T. *The Economy of Nature and the Evolution of Sex*. Berkeley: University of California Press, 1974.

Ghiselin, M. T. *The Triumph of Darwinian Method*. Berkeley: University of California Press, 1969.

Greene, John C. "Darwin as a Social Evolutionist." *Journal of the History of Biology* 10 (1977): 1–27.

Grosskurth, Phyllis. *Melanie Klein: Her World and Her Work*. London: Hodder & Stoughton, 1986.

Gruber, Howard E. *Darwin on Man: A Psychological Study of Scientific Creativity*. 2d ed. Chicago: University of Chicago Press, 1981.

Gruber, Howard E. "Going the Limit: Toward the Construction of Darwin's Theory." In *The Darwinian Heritage*, pp. 9–34.

Gruber, Howard E. "History and Creative Work: From the Most Ordinary to the Most Exalted." *Journal of the History of the Behavioral Sciences* 19 (1983): 4–14.

Haight, G. S. *George Eliot: A Biography*. Oxford: Oxford University Press, 1968.

Herbert, Sandra. "The Place of Man in the Development of Darwin's Theory of Transmutation." Parts 1 and 2. *Journal of the History of Biology* 7 (1974): 217–58; 10 (1977): 155–227.

Hessen, Boris. "The Social and Economic Roots of Newton's 'Principia.'" In N.

I. Bukharin et al., eds., *Science at the Crossroads*, pp. 147–212. 1931; rpt. London: Cass, 1971.

Hodges, Andrew. *Alan Turing: The Enigma*. London: Burnett Books, 1983.

Holmes, Richard. *Footsteps: Adventures of a Romantic Biographer*. London: Hodder & Stoughton, 1985.

Jardim, Anne. *The First Henry Ford: A Study in Personality and Business Leadership*. Cambridge, Mass.: MIT Press, 1970.

Josephson, Matthew. *Edison: A Biography*. London: Eyre and Spottiswoode, 1961.

Kakar, Sudhir. *Frederick Taylor: A Study in Personality and Innovation*. Cambridge, Mass.: MIT Press, 1970.

Kapp, Yvonne. *Eleanor Marx*. 2 vols. London: Lawrence and Wishart, 1972, 1976.

Keegan, Robert T., and Gruber, Howard E. "Love, Death, and Continuity in Darwin's Thinking." *Journal of the History of the Behavioral Sciences* 19 (1983): 15–30.

Kohn, David. "Theories to Work By: Rejected Theories, Reproduction and Darwin's Path to Natural Selection." *Studies in the History of Biology* 4 (1980): 67–170.

Kohn, David, ed. *The Darwinian Heritage*. Princeton: Princeton University Press, 1985.

Lahr, John. *Notes on a Cowardly Lion: The Biography of Bert Lahr* (1969). New York: Limelight Editions, 1984.

LeMahieu, D. L. "Malthus and the Theology of Scarcity." *Journal of the History of Ideas* 40 (1979): 467–74.

Loewenberg, Peter. *Decoding the Past: The Psychohistorical Approach*. Berkeley: University of California Press, 1985.

Lyell, Charles. *Principles of Geology, being an Attempt to Explain the Former Changes of the Earth's Surface by Reference to Causes Now in Operation*. 3 vols. London: Murray, 1830–33.

Mack, John E. "Psychoanalysis and Historical Biography." *Journal of the American Psychoanalytic Association* 19 (1971): 143–79.

McLellan, David. *Karl Marx: His Life and Thought*. London: Macmillan, 1973.

Malthus, Thomas. *An Essay on the Principle of Population*. London: J. Johnson, 1798; 6th ed. 2 vols. London: Murray, 1826.

Manuel, Frank E. *A Portrait of Isaac Newton*. Cambridge, Mass.: Harvard University Press, 1968.

Marx, Karl, and Engels, Frederick. *Selected Correspondence*. Moscow: Progress, 1965.

Masters, Brian. *Killing for Company: The Case of Dennis Nilsen*. London: Cape, 1985.

Mayhew, Henry. *Mayhew's Characters*. Selected from *London Labour and the London Poor* and edited by Peter Quennell. London: Spring Books, n.d.

Mayr, Ernst. *The Growth of Biological Thought*. Cambridge, Mass.: Harvard University Press, 1982.

Darwin and the Genre of Biography

Moore, James R. "Charles Darwin Lies in Westminster Abbey." *Biological Journal of the Linnaean Society* 17 (1982): 97–113.

Moore, James R. "Darwin of Down: The Evolutionist as Squarson-Naturalist." In *The Darwinian Heritage*, pp. 435–81.

Moore, James R. "Darwin's Genesis and Revelations." *Isis* 76 (1985): 570–80 [essay review on Darwin's correspondence].

Moore, James R. "1859 and All That: Remaking the Story of Evolution-and-Religion." In R. G. Chapman and C. T. Duval, eds., *Charles Darwin, 1809–1882: A Centennial Commemorative*, pp. 167–94, 361–63. Wellington, New Zealand: Nova Pacifica, 1982.

Oldroyd, David R. "How Did Darwin Arrive at His Theory? The Secondary Literature to 1982." *History of Science* 22 (1984): 325–74.

Ospovat, Dov. "Darwin after Malthus." *Journal of the History of Biology* 12 (1979): 211–30.

Ospovat, Dov. *The Development of Darwin's Theory: Natural History, Natural Theology, and Natural Selection, 1838–1859*. Cambridge: Cambridge University Press, 1981.

Pachter, Marc., ed. *Telling Lives: The Biographer's Art*. Washington, D.C.: New Republic Books/National Portrait Gallery, 1979.

Paley, William. *Natural Theology; or, Evidences of the Existence and Attributes of the Deity. Collected from the Appearances of Nature* (1802). London: Baynes, 1816.

Paley, William. *The Works of William Paley*. New ed. 7 vols. Rivington, etc., 1825.

Peterson, Linda H. *Victorian Autobiography: The Tradition of Self-Interpretation*. New Haven: Yale University Press, 1986.

Rogers, James A. "Darwinism and Social Darwinism." *Journal of the History of Ideas* 33 (1972): 265–80.

Schweber, Sylvan. "The Origin of *The Origin* Revisited." *Journal of the History of Biology* 10 (1977): 229–316.

Sewall, Richard B. *The Life of Emily Dickinson* (1974). New York: Farrar, Straus and Giroux, 1980.

Smith, Sydney. "The Origin of 'The Origin' as Discerned from Charles Darwin's Notebooks and His Annotations in the Books He Read between 1837 and 1842." *Advancement of Science*, no. 64 (1960), pp. 391–401.

Stone, Irving. *Lust for Life*. London: Bodley Head, 1975.

Stone, Irving. *The Origin: A Biographical Novel of Charles Darwin*. London: Cassell, 1980.

Strachey, Lytton. *Eminent Victorians* (1918). London: Collins, 1959.

Sulloway, Frank J. *Freud: Biologist of the Mind*. London: Burnett Books, 1979.

Terkel, Studs. *Working* (1974). New York: Avon Books, 1975.

Troyat, Henri. *Tolstoy* (1965). Harmondsworth: Penguin, 1970.

"Two" [Anon]. *Home Life with Herbert Spencer*. Bristol: Arrowsmith, 1906.

Vorzimmer, Peter. "Darwin, Malthus and the Theory of Natural Selection." *Journal of the History of Ideas* 30 (1969): 527–42.

Wachhorst, Wyn. *Thomas Alva Edison: An American Myth*. Cambridge, Mass.: MIT Press, 1981.

West, Geoffrey. *Charles Darwin: A Portrait*. New Haven: Yale University Press, 1938.

Wolfenstein, Eugene V. *The Victims of Democracy: Malcolm X and the Black Revolution*. Berkeley: University of California Press, 1981.

Young, Robert M. "Darwinism *Is* Social." In *The Darwinian Heritage*, pp. 609–38.

Young, Robert M. *Darwin's Metaphor: Nature's Place in Victorian Culture*. Cambridge: Cambridge University Press, 1985.

Young, Robert M. "Freud: Scientist or Humanist?" Delivered to University of Durham, Research Group for the History of the Humanities, 1985.

Young, Robert M. "How Societies Constitute Their Knowledge: Prolegomena to a Labour Process Perspective." Typescript, 1982.

Young, Robert M. "Is Nature a Labour Process?" In Les Levidow and R. M. Young, eds., *Science, Technology and the Labour Process*. 2: 206–32. London: Free Association Books, 1985.

Young, Robert M. "Life among the Mediations: Labour, Groups, Breasts." Paper delivered to Department of History and Philosophy of Science, University of Cambridge, 1986.

Young, Robert M. "Science Is a Labour Process." *Science for People*, no. 43 (1979), pp. 31–37.

Young, Robert M. "Science *Is* Social Relations." *Radical Science Journal*, no. 5 (1977), pp. 65–129.

J A M E S R. M O O R E

The Erotics of Evolution: Constance Naden and Hylo-Idealism

Time was when the mad poet was heeded; when women novelists used alternative science to contest the masculine appropriation of a feminized nature and the male medical concept of the female psyche; when the language of literature and the language of science held shameless creative intercourse. Time was—and now is—when biography served best to explain how individual and epochal forces have led to new perspectives in science. Such are the insights of several essays in this volume. The present chapter seeks to augment and qualify these insights by posing a series of paradoxical contrasts in a narrative of the life of a forgotten feminist philosopher and poet, Constance C. W. Naden (1858–89). Like other so-called mad poets, Naden died young, but for strictly medical reasons. Her "madness" fed on a sense of oneness with a feminized nature rather than on alienation; it was not stultified by medical materialism, but made eloquent. Her poetic creativity, fired by scientific language, subserved her long-term ambition to articulate a grand synthesis in the manner of nineteenth-century philosophers of science. And her chief inspiration in this endeavor, tragically terminated by death, was a retired army surgeon and founder of a philosophical system which together they called "Hylo-idealism."

Whether Hylo-idealism or, for that matter, Naden's poetry should appeal to contemporary feminists is not in question here. The more limited aim of this essay is to exemplify the use of biography as a means of pointing up the deep and dimly understood personal and epochal motive forces behind literary creations that are nominally influenced by science.[1]

Her Mother, Her Self

Women poets of the nineteenth century have too often been remembered for devotional self-effacement in lachrymose verse. In the more eminent writers, at least, it now seems clear that this manner of expression is to be interpreted as a response to the disintegrating tensions in their lives. Dorothy Wordsworth, Emily Brontë, Emily Dickinson, Elizabeth Barrett Browning, and Christina Rossetti—each struggled with the contradictory expectations of women in a male-dominated culture; each agonized over specific dualities bequeathed by a masculine poetic tradition. Chief among the latter was the relationship of man with Mother Nature, the tamer with the tamed. Nature was not available for intimate relations with women. Nature destroyed as well as created; the duality was overcome only through masculine appropriation. Emily Dickinson transposes this romantic dualism into the divided self that structures her poems. Ultimately the conscious self faces death, where alone the meanings that nature cannot give may be obtained. Rossetti also, whose poems are riven with cosmic dualism, find oneness and therefore personal integration in another world, through ecstatic union with Christ. Integration, however, may never be achieved. The "confessional 'I' of poetry" may not exorcise the anxieties and hostilities of life. "Even if the poet's 'I' . . . is a 'supposed person,' the intensity of her dangerous impersonation of this creature may cause her to take her own metaphors literally, enact her themes herself."[2] Madness results: Dickinson's "Nobody" trembling in her room, Amy Stewart gassing herself, Charlotte Mew taking poison. Either wholeness is sought in an autistic world or the poet faces extinction.

Constance Naden was never clinically deranged, although her adamant sense of self owed much to an unpromising childhood. The evidence is sparse and mostly second-hand, but the outlines of her young personality may still be traced in the light of the forces that gave it shape. Both her parents derived their middling prosperity from the commercial expansion of Birmingham at mid-century. Thomas Naden (1824–1916) became a building surveyor like his father and supervised the erection of many of the villa residences in suburban Edgbaston. Latterly he became president of the Birmingham Architectural Association. In Edgbaston lived a retired manufacturer, Josiah Cox Woodhill

(1801–81), who had owned one of the largest wholesale goldsmith and jewelry businesses in the city. He passed his leisure days at Pakenham House as a member of the committee of the Old Library and an elder of Baptist churches. How this bookish Nonconformist became acquainted with the local builder is not difficult to imagine, and their relationship was promptly cemented by recalling a common grief. Naden and Woodhill had each lost a young wife, the latter only nine days after the birth of his first child. While this daughter was still small Woodhill remarried, and in 1830 another daughter was born, Caroline Ann. Naden now proposed to take her as his own second wife. Woodhill gave them his special blessing. The marriage followed, and in January 1858 Caroline produced their first child, Constance Caroline Woodhill Naden. Twelve days later, on 5 February, Caroline was dead. Like a curse, Naden's second loss was a reenactment of Woodhill's first. The child remained to comfort him, but he could scarcely assume responsibility for her himself. Caroline's dying request was that her own mother should have the baby. Both grandparents agreed—their other daughter would soon marry, leaving them alone. And so Constance went as an infant with the grieving couple to inhabit the solemn vastness of Pakenham House. Her father also lived there for a time, then acquired a comfortable villa a short distance away, remarried, and had children. But life and love enough had been arranged for the little one to begin developing an extraordinary sense of her self.

Josiah and Caroline Woodhill reached their sixties before Constance was in her teens. They were old-fashioned churchgoers of the Calvinist persuasion. In their "Puritan house" no lively entertainments took place and "worldly" amusements were banned. Constance therefore grew up a "quaint, retiring, meditative, and silent child." She spoke when spoken to; she obeyed her elders; she reverenced masculine authority. What prospects of variety there were lay in the luxuriant garden, which she came to love, and in her grandfather's large miscellaneous library. Her grandmother, a woman of "refined culture," soon taught her to read, and Constance was later reputed to have devoured the entire collection. This early stimulus served her well when, for the first time at the age of eight, she began to have regular contact with other children at a private day school. Her progress there was undisrupted by examinations, prizes, or other incentives for competition.

The Misses Martin seem to have regarded the attendant stresses as unsuitable for girls. For ten years Constance survived this nonregime, the flower painting and the like, because under the guidance of her grandparents she had become educationally self-reliant. At the same time, however, in forming her first close friendships, she learned that a competitive spirit need not intrude. Accustomed as she was, a precocious child, to exclusive attention, Constance emerged from her schooling as first among equals. She did not lord it over the younger girls but would play Queen Scheherazade, beguiling them with fantastic fables, grotesque impossibilities, and beautiful imaginations. Like George Eliot, with whom she would often be compared, the unmothered daughter had it within her persona, as well as her poetry, to become the mother herself.

Constance loved her grandparents dearly, and they her, but soon it came her turn to grieve the mother she had lost. No doubt she often heard stories of her mother's childhood; when older she learned of the tragic circumstances of her death. The melancholy thought seemed at times perhaps to overshadow life in Pakenham House, for there her mother had once lived, in the very rooms and corridors and in the wonderful garden where Constance played out her vivid fantasies. Thus in the pathetic "Dedication" to her grandparents of *Songs and Sonnets of Springtime* (1881), her first collection of poems, she speaks "Of one whose fond embrace I never knew / Your child, my mother, dear for evermore," and of herself as "One little life, to tend when hers was o'er."[3] The same sentiment appears in the selections Constance translated from German romantic poets: "Comfort in Tears" from Goethe ("My grief is not that I have lost / But that I long in vain"), "The Maiden's Lament" from Schiller ("Let my plaining be powerless / To waken the dead"), "My Only One" from Fischer ("I feel that thou wilt soon depart, / And leave in loneliness this mournful heart"), "Farewell" from Geibel, where a "little maid" is told good night "for evermore," and, finally, from Siebel:

> Bury the dead thou lovest,
> Deep, deep within thy heart;
> So shall they live and love thee
> Till life and thou shall part.
> (*Complete Poetical Works*, p. 160)

The Erotics of Evolution

These translations may well contain authentic traces of childhood grief, although they probably were made in or after Constance's twentieth year. In none does the sentiment derive unambiguously from romantic love. The one poem in *Songs and Sonnets* known to be autobiographical is "Six Years Old." It is set in a garden like the one at Pakenham House, where, Constance sighs, "they've left me alone." She talks to the birds, admires the wall that was "built before I was a baby," and complains about how other children mistreat her, though she wishes for "more of us" at home. She consoles herself with the thought, "when I am mopish and lonely / I always can talk to the trees." Trees, she has been told, are "companions for life," and Constance fancies herself marrying the "great lime-tree" whose small twigs she peels for her games:

> If he died, oh, how much I should miss him!
> (It's only his *dry* sticks I peel)
> I put my arms round him and kiss him,
> And sometimes I think he can feel.
>   (*CPW*, p. 104).

The girlish verses conclude with Constance lying awake in bed and "thinking for hours" about a dream world where she would go with her grandparents "when I'm twenty," write a "grand poem," learn "French, and Italian, and German," and then "marry a prince."

The next poem in the collection begins a cycle of sonnets on nature arranged in calendar order. The title, "January 1879," recalls Constance's majority, the twenty-first anniversary of her birth. She hastens in the poem through a snowy landscape—perhaps her enchanted garden—counting "sad Winter as my foe," yet knowing, "Within my heart I can create the Spring." "These homely scenes, whence first my childish eye / Its own ideal form of beauty chose, / I love forever," she declares; ". . . if I grieved, I could but grieve for those / Who know not Spring, or having known forget." The second sonnet, "To a Hyacinth in January," likens the newborn flower to "some delicate and hidden hope," kept "safe from the New Year's wind, whose touch were death." Then February comes. Constance remembers that fatal touch in "To the First Snowdrop":

Fair, sunny-hearted child of many tears!
Thou, while thy mother Earth forsaken slept,
Didst gather to thyself pure hopes, that crept
Through stormy dreams; and now the sun appears,
White buds reflect each rare faint smile, that cheers
The home where thine unshapen germ was kept,
Safe in deep midnight, while the heavens wept,
Or hung the shuddering trees with frosty spears.

Now springs to life and light each buried joy,
With broken music and with tearful glow,
With drooping blossoms, winter-pale and coy;
For Love shall soon fulfil her long desire—
Her face and breast are memories of snow,
Her Heart, like thine, is lit with vestal fire.

(CPW, p. 111)

Constance may not be original but she is transparent. The "broken music" and "tearful glow" of the newborn baby are unmistakable. It is even possible to glimpse the course of her mother's pregnancy, although this cannot be confirmed. Most striking is how the biblical "life and light" of immortality "springs" from the "vestal fire" of female "Love." This is a dual allusion to the Roman goddess Vesta, and to the virgins who kept her temple flame, rekindled annually in March. The goddess-mother may be a "buried joy," but in Constance come-of-age the "vestal fire" is lit by "all fair creatures of the earth." From them, she adds in the sonnet entitled "March 1879," "I do but gain the beauty that I give; / Your form, your music, in my soul have birth, / And in my life your colours live" (CPW, p. 113).

Here mother, self, and nature become so entwined that one is led to suspect a problem. Has the poet made her peace with life's anxieties by total self-absorption? The dead mother, the solitude, the patriarchal religion—surely this was a recipe for madness. If Constance could not find wholeness in her haunted world, was she not compelled with other women poets to seek it elsewhere, even insanely, through identification with the buried mother in mortal nature? Once the child fancied a tree; finally she fancies herself giving "birth" to the creatures. Does the autistic mind not have its ways?

Yes, indeed, but Constance was not quite deranged; she had only discovered philosophy. Her tutor was a man.

The Erotics of Evolution

Oedipus Wrecks

When nineteenth-century women jettisoned traditional religion for a philosophical creed, they usually set their sights beyond the stars. For every George Eliot or Harriet Martineau, who focused on the material world of science, a hundred others sought fulfillment in cosmic visions, spiritualist entities, and transcendental abstractions. Like their sisters who wrote poetry, they sought selfhood and wholeness in ideal worlds. In 1875, on leaving school, Constance seemed poised to follow suit. The whole tenor of her life so far had been inward and contemplative. The official religion of her household was external, mechanical, even cruel. In her seventeen-year-old sensibility this discrepancy would not have been unfelt or disregarded. Her grandfather was still her spiritual adviser, and Constance got herself to the library in search of fresh inspiration. She discovered Robert Vaughan's *Hours with the Mystics* and the writings of James Hinton. Constance read them both, a clergyman and a physician respectively, but did not enroll as their disciple. She went on annual holiday to the seaside, to the midland resort of Southport, and there in 1876 met a doctor of her own. Mary Shelley had learned an alternative cosmology from Dr. Erasmus Darwin; Eliot and Martineau had abandoned their first faith with the assistance of brother intellectuals. Constance would now become a philosophical materialist under the aegis of Dr. Robert Lewins.

What sort of man was he? How did he appeal to her mind? Unfortunately, even less is known about this aberrant genius than about his impressionable student.[4] Born in 1817, Lewins was approximately the age of Josiah Woodhill when Constance came to Pakenham House, and seven years older than her father. He had been reared in the ways of Highland Calvinism and educated by the Moravian Brotherhood at Neuwied on the Rhine. After obtaining the M.D. from the University of Heidelberg in 1840, he returned to Edinburgh and joined his father's medical practice at Leith. In 1841 he published the Harveian Prize essay and the next year he was licensed by the Royal College of Surgeons of Edinburgh. His career seemed destined to rise. Educated at a prestigious German university and fluent in its tongue, trained at hospitals in Paris and Vienna, he might have acquired an academic post, or at least inherited his father's practice. But in December 1842 came a crisis:

Lewins upped stakes and joined the army. Conflict with his father seems the likely cause. A year later he was serving as an assistant surgeon at the Cape of Good Hope; over the next twenty-five years he became staff surgeon, then surgeon-major, winning a clutch of medals in defense of Christian civilization. In the Crimea he saw two-thirds of the casualties die of disease. Charged with a hospital ship in north China he saw the carnage of British gunboats sunk at Taku forts. In 1868 he retired on a pension and, lacking wife or family, devoted himself obsessively to nurturing irreligion.

Dr. Lewins was one of those exasperating characters who, cursed with the inability to forget, persist in mistaking eclecticism for originality. From Calvinist apologetics he acquired a facility for systematic disputation, from Moravian pietism a mystical impulse, and from both a deep aversion for Christianity. His years in Germany preceded the ascendancy of Feuerbach and the rise of the "medical materialists," so he cut his philosophical teeth, it seems, on pessimism and physiology. With Schopenhauer, he never deferred to academic specialists or doubted the subjectivism of the brain. With a clinician's sense of rectitude, he never tired of making metaphysics from Wöhler's synthesis of the chemical basis of urine. In 1848, while serving in south India, Lewins excogitated a philosophy to save the British Empire from catastrophe. News of revolution in Europe had upset him. Like Schopenhauer, he may have read the Upanishads as well. The immediate sources of his innovation are uncertain, but it seems clear that in subsequent years he confirmed his beliefs on the battlefield. Shell shock, brain lesions, and the like tended to disprove the duality of mind and body. In a charnel house what mattered was flesh and blood. Lewins first called his philosophy "hylo-zoism," then, after 1880, "Hylo-idealism." After returning to England he expounded it in privately printed pamphlets, accompanied by turgid letters, which he sent out unsolicited.[5] While waiting expectantly for converts, he laid siege to the correspondence columns of periodicals.

Constance met Dr. Lewins with his crusade approaching full tilt. By all accounts he was gallant, worldly-wise, and well connected. Accustomed to giving orders, he knew how to browbeat the perplexed. To disciples he seemed omniscient; to others he was just an eccentric Scot. Constance did not make up her mind precipitately. She was callow but no fool. Eventually the doctor did make shipwreck of her inherited beliefs, but not without offering her something both personally and metaphysically more attractive. Animism, dualism, supernaturalism, vitalism—all these had been superseded, according to Lewins, by the hylozoic view that "matter has its own proper life, or energy." In a series of letters between 1878 and 1880, later published in *Humanism versus Theism*, he convinced Constance with two lines of argument to this effect. The first was a rehash of developments in the physical and medical sciences from the standpoint of materialist apologetics. The second, a "common sense" shortcut, was the real basis of his appeal, and he commended it to her as to "a truly independent and self-poised mind."

One need simply think oneself into Bishop Berkeley's position in the *Principles of Human Knowledge*, then draw the opposite conclusion. Put the mind into the brain, put the bishop's feet back on terra firma, and—presto—microcosm and macrocosm are united, all things are ideal and material ("Hylo-ideal") simultaneously, and "the kingdom of heaven is within you."

> Poets have entered this region as rare visitants, but with this clue you may mount on eagle pinions, and dwell as an Autochthone, where they have only fitfully ventured as birds of passage. "Are not the mountains, seas, and skies a part of me and of my soul, as I of them?" asked Byron; but you can answer in the affirmative on data sure and stable as Nature (self-identity) herself as soon as you realise that vital and cosmical force are one and the same. As soon as we grasp the fact that thought and its objects are one, we find that we are Gods; for everything is for us ideal, and ideas are but creations of a certain segment of our own being—of that organ whose function it is to manifest ideation, itself only a special mode of general corporeal sensation. So that all things are for us but modes of our own perception.[6]

Science on this view is but "an autopsy," poetry the cognition of "ideals." Worship becomes "merely *self*-idolatry." Lewins referred to a sense of "indwelling divinity" without which, Constance had told him, she "could not live." He assured her that he also had experienced the feeling, "chiefly in the spring and summer seasons, and especially in places like Kew gardens and Natural History museums." "I feel everything, including my own breath and motion, to be quasi-divine." This divinity, however, could be none other than material nature "herself," for, he declared, "with 'her' thought has alone to deal. In transcending 'her' we . . . fall back upon the lower level of 'lawless and uncertain' fancy" (*HVT*, pp. 13, 15, 24, 25).

So far Lewins' feminization of nature was unremarkable, although its loftiness might have appealed to a serious young woman. But he expatiated further in a manner that suggested how, to one who grieved her mother, nature might restore a special sense of identity. According to the Hylo-idealist doctrine, since "man cannot think anything higher than himself, so far as he *thinks* God he *is* God." Common language bears this out:

> The words *herr, vir, hero*, etc., are all one, and signify the ideal man in thought and deed—the man distinguished from the ordinary animal man (in German *mensch*, in Latin *homo*) by having a divine ideal, the realising of which is his life of life. Even the most vulgar act of the mere animal man—the function of self-reproduction—is termed procreation, as if he were vice-creator. (*HVT*, p. 23)

Here was a delicate subject on which even a doctor would address a young woman with reticence. Lewins immediately changed gear. If masculine language points to God as the masculine ideal, then, equally on Hylo-idealist principles, the primal reality in relation to which all men live is to be identified through language that signifies the primordial human relationship. He went on:

> The term matter—in Latin *materia* = mother, and in itself is a whole system of philosophy. From matter we come, and as from its womb we emerge into special or personal existence, so when this specialised being is no more we return to that Alma Mater whence as embryos we came. . . . The glorious garniture of earth, sea, and heavens around us *may* be "the flowing garments of Deity," but it is something still closer, as it is *certainly* the investing membrane, the pia mater or matrix, which supplies us with force, life, and all things. (*HVT*, pp. 23, 29)

This primal mother had been closest to "primeval man." Materialism, Lewins asserted, was "evidently" his creed. But then the mother had been lost. "Agriological 'medicine men' "—primitive male physicians— with their animistic beliefs became "the great corruptors and sophisticators" of later ages, just as even now "scientists" and "braying" professors propagate a "radical delusion" as to the nature of ultimate reality. But "you," Lewins told Constance again and again, "are one with all the objects of sensation and thought." "You are above detraction. You are in the rare and serene air where all things, including, of course, yourself, look to be what they are in Nature." "Does it not make you tremble with awe to feel that in every drop of water—in every tear you shed— there is electricity enough locked up to form a considerable thunderclap and lightning flash?" (*HVT*, pp. 17, 19, 22, 24, 25)

The Teardrop Explodes

Constance heard in the voice of Dr. Lewins, not a cacophony of dying echoes, the last chorus of romanticism run riot, but familiar harmonies from her enchanted garden. For this he appeared to her as a seer and a saint. She answered him in her poems. *Songs and Sonnets of Springtime* begins with a series of character sketches in verse. Lewins may be glimpsed there as the eponymous "Astronomer" who, lacking brother, friend, or spouse, pursues his lofty truths, inspired by Urania, "awful in her virgin grace"; the "Roman Philosopher" who contests the conversion of his daughter with Christian priests; the "Last Druid" whose ancient shrines are sadly overrun by churches; the "Alchemist" who, "spurning all ties of home, all joyance free," gives his life to "conquering" death; and the "Pilgrim" who awakes in a land where all men live in dreams and sets out "To find the ancient innocence again / In some far land unknown of weary men." These sketches culminate in "Das Ideal," with its dedication: "Meinem verehrten Freunde Herrn Dr. Lewins in Dankbarkeit gewidmet" (*CPW*, pp. 3–78).

A new section begins, and the first poem, "The Lady Doctor," sets the tone. It is the counterpart of "The Astronomer," which opens the book. In it Constance portrays a witchlike spinster "living all alone, / In friendless, dreary, sadness," who has thrown over a youthful suitor to devote her life to medicine. "She valued at the lowest price /Men neither patients for advice / Nor subjects for dissection," and she excelled them as a practitioner. At length, grown "grim and stern" and "uninviting," she longs for the "home of love and gladness" that she might have enjoyed had she married (*CPW*, pp. 81–84). Constance does not blame her for irresolution but points the "moral" that a young woman must choose either to keep her first love or to pursue her ambitions single-mindedly.

"The Lady Doctor" was the first poem Constance ever published. It appeared in 1877, the year after she met Dr. Lewins, and it undoubtedly reflects the ambivalence about a career that he provoked in her. The subsequent poems in *Song and Sonnets* indicate her choice in the matter. These speak facetiously of unscrupulous, patronizing, and unrealistic young men. Although a note of self-reproach may be detected, the verses generally reverberate with determination to avoid romantic attachments. In "Lament of the Cork-cell" Constance again, however, alludes very cleverly to her presentiments by personifying a moribund cell, "once . . . young and tender, / Alive with chemic yearnings," but which now is

> drifting from its mother,
> Naked and homeless in the cruel storm,
> Having no aid of sister or of brother
> Nor any cellulose to keep it warm.
> (*CPW*, pp. 99–100)

Finally, then, there is "Six Years Old," so full of loneliness, love of nature, and aspiration. It rounds out the self-portrait of *Songs and Sonnets* just as "Das Ideal" finishes the composite portrait of Dr. Lewins.

But what of the conversion he inspired? Two of the sonnets Constance placed immediately after "Six Years Old"—those, it will be recalled, that commemorate the fusion through birth and death of mother, self, and nature—were composed in the very months, January through March 1879, when Lewins corresponded with her about the divine motherhood of matter. "To the First Snowdrop" might be shown by textual criticism to belong to this period as well. Other indications that Constance assimilated—"asselfed," as she would say—Lewins' philosophy are scattered in various undated poems. The loss of faith is evident in anguished lines throughout. Sometimes the anguish is about lost certitude, sometimes about insecurity. In "Yearning," the "empty night" will not blot out memories of "past delight" amid present "pain" and "sadness." Sleeplessly, Constance must see

in visions wild,
The joys I cannot gain,
And, like a little lonely child,
Stretch out my arms in vain.
(*CPW*, p. 66)

This theme recurs ironically in "The Carmelite Nun," where the young novice in her "lonely cell" yearns for union with God but cannot help thinking of earthly beauties, of spring and summer, and of her "mother's face" when they parted: "Oh, . . . how she wept, and clung / About my neck in agonized embrace" (*CPW*. pp. 22–24).

Constance at last escaped the loneliness of Pakenham House, the inward cloister of her religious past, by merging herself through Lewins' inverted idealism with the divine Mother in nature. In "Semele" she "loves a God" (invoked as Zeus) who "glows in sea and sky"; in "The Agnostic's Psalm" this God becomes the "Eternal Substance" that pervades her being, "mingling with the secret source of tears" and "bestowing peace for grief." Then in her best known and perhaps most perfectly crafted compositon , "The Pantheist's Song of Immortality," Constance comes to terms with death, the first as well as the last remaining source of fragmentation in her life. An unnamed woman lies in state, wreathed in flowers. "Few sorrows did she know— and all are over; / A thousand joys—but they are all forgot." Her calm and peaceful repose dispels the "dread of dying," for is it not well, Constance asks, that "toil" should cease?

Canst thou repine that sentient days are numbered?
Death is unconscious Life, that waits for birth:
So didst thou live, while yet thy embryo slumbered,
Senseless, unbreathing, e'en as heaven and earth.

The "unconscious Life" of things is the "uncreated Source of toil and passion" that "through everlasting change abides the same." Since its "almighty forces . . . meet to form thee," Constance urges,

Be calmly glad, thine own true kindred seeing,
In fire and storm, in flowers with dew impearled;
Rejoice in thine imperishable being,
One with the Essence of the boundless world.
(*CPW*, pp. 43–45)

237

The deceased woman remains "true kindred," even in her dissolution. The living "Essence" of matter is a motherhood of power. In Constance the teardrop has exploded. Mother and self are one.

Hypatia in Birmingham

With the unlikely help of a retired army surgeon obsessed by Teutonic philosophy, Constance skirted the perils of Victorian young womanhood and made straight for a career. Lewins, far from threatening her sense of identity as the materialist Dr. John threatened Lucy in Brontë's *Villette*, had addressed just those aspects of her well-formed consciousness that constrained her further development. Religion, he confirmed, was to be sought within, not in the external dogmas of a tradition they both knew well. The "self" of religious worship, again he confirmed, was to be identified with the natural world, but not, as Constance had experienced, through the autistic fantasies of a lonely child. Self was the epiphenomenon of the brain. The brain was matter and matter was essentially Mother. Self-worship might therefore be regarded as Mother-worship; the way of identity with the divine Mother in nature lay through self-cultivation, the "asselfing" of natural knowledge. This realization, perhaps more than any other, steeled Constance, finally, to avoid the greatest peril she confronted. Her poems show her struggling, not only with religion and the mother she never knew, but with the expectation that as a woman she would be ever the relative, never absolutely herself. One day she must find fulfillment as someone's wife. Lewins taught her to think and act independently by proclaiming the self-centeredness of perception—"You are above detraction," he had insisted. This transformation of residual autistic tendencies into epistemological monism—"solipsism," he called it—was the key to her single-mindedness. His precepts, no less than his example and sponsorship, became the hidden force behind her fledgling career as a philosopher of science.

By 1881, when Constance completed her conversion to Hylo-idealism, Dr. Lewins had achieved a remarkable influence over her life. No doubt he recognized genius when he saw it; no doubt also he was adept at serving his own ends. A man of catholic interests, as well as cosmic vision, he coaxed Constance out of her garden into the wider world where her poetic insights could be enriched and enlarged to take the form of a philosophical synthesis that he had been unable to achieve. He set her to studying German, which he loved to speak, as well as other languages. He persuaded her to publish her poems and poetic translations. He urged her to travel widely and even took her as far as Coventry to meet Sara Hennell and Charles Bray, the latter of whom subjected her to a phrenological examination and concluded that she possessed the genius of George Eliot. Finally, when T. H. Huxley opened the Josiah Mason College at Birmingham in October 1880 with the promise that there students would imbibe the culture demanded by science, it was no doubt Lewins who encouraged Constance to enroll.

From 1881 to 1887 Mason College became the staging ground for her career. Steeped in Lewins' maxim that "the end of all analysis is synthesis," Constance mastered the principles of one science after another—physiology, chemistry, botany, zoology, geology—even as she set about acquiring a reputation among philosophers in London through the sponsorship of Lewins and a spate of publications. To most of her student contemporaries only her enlarging academic prowess would have been apparent. To Constance the wider scope of her interests, a larger synthesis of philosophy, poetry, and feminism, was always in view. She worked silently but intensively to achieve it.

The full extent of her "extremely dangerous" powers, as one gentleman put it, was perhaps best displayed in Union debates. Her "terrible sixth sense" for hidden sophistries and her prompt retorts, ranging easily from scorn to playful satire, won her the reputation of "Hypatia" among the priests. Here the argument turned on the precise meaning of Darwin's words, there on an assumption which, Constance was pleased to point out, had been expressly controverted by Herbert Spencer. She did not omit to criticize women—"a typical young person with a wasp-waist . . . may be called rather a criminal lunatic than a slave, since her tortures are voluntary"[7]—but her standpoint was always sympathetic. On men she could be more severe. In opposing the resolution "That Hero-Worship is beneficial to the Hero and to the Worshipper," Constance objected that the hero, when worshiped, "feels himself to be a kind of god, and acts accordingly, often with an Olympian disregard of virtue." Hero worship had led to despotism, from Caligula to Mahomet, while intellectual slavery had resulted from the undue veneration of Aristotle, Hippocrates, and Galen. "To the Hero-Worshipper," Constance rested her case, "history appears as an array of kings and great men, to the neglect of the secret and silent forces to which progress is really due."[8]

It is difficult to judge how soon or how far her friends at Mason College were aware of the philosophy that informed such statements. Certainly they knew Constance as an admirer of German culture. In 1884 she published an article on Schiller in the *Mason College Magazine*, asserting her settled view that poetry was the emotional representation of scientific and philosophic truth.

> The laws of your ideal world, including all essential truth, must include the laws of the universe. Conform your being to these, by recognizing them as parts of your own nature, and they will no longer appear as restraints upon free-will, but as its natural expression.[9]

Other articles in the same magazine made clear that these high-flown precepts were anchored securely, if somewhat inelegantly, to the bedrock of mechanistic materialism. Indeed, in November 1884 the magazine reported that Constance had read a paper on "Hylo-idealism" to one of the college societies, arguing that materialism and idealism were two sides of a single truth; but further than this, it seems, she did not reveal the precise nature and affinities of her views. Even in a highly technical account of "Volition," given to the Physiological Society at the college in February 1887, her authorities for believing in neurophysical determinism were Wilhelm Wundt, Henry Maudsley, and G. H. Lewes. No propaganda points were scored; neither here nor elsewhere did she refer to Dr. Lewins.

Constance published her paper on volition in the *Midland Naturalist*, the organ of the Birmingham Natural History and Microscopical Society. Huxley, in his address at the opening of Mason College, had regretted the absence of any provision for teaching sociology in the college curriculum. The society, for their part, soon supplied the defect by establishing a sociological section "for the study of Mr. Herbert Spencer's system of 'Synthetic Philosophy'." In 1884 Constance joined the section with a handful of other students and immediately became its "genius loci." She delivered three expositions of Spencer's work, all of which were published by the society. These essays contained her first extended treatment of evolutionary themes and marked an enlargement of her philosophical outlook. Although she had accepted for some years that nature was to be interpreted as a continuous process of evolution, the subject did not appear controversial from the standpoint of Hylo-idealism. Lewins, for whom cosmic development was a synthetic a priori, judged evolutionists by their adherence to his idée fixe. But for this very reason, because none of them did, Constance might have taken Spencer to task in her essays. His systematic agnosticism, with its objective Unknowable Power underlying all phenomena, and Hylo-idealism, with its epistemological monism and materialism, were by no means consistent; and an eagle-eyed debater would not have missed the point. Again, however, she scarcely tipped her hand. Only implicit references to the wider horizon of her philosophizing could be detected. Only the right hand of Constance knew the deeds of the left.

The Unknowable

Whatever Constance's friends in Birmingham may have known about her philosophical outlook, they must have remained virtually ignorant of its significance in a wider polemical context. This was quite perfectly concealed from them in a large number of letters, articles, and pamphlets that Constance published pseudonymously in London. The company they kept was not always respectable. Sometimes it was infamous and extreme.

Lewins, the veteran letter writer and small-time controversialist was her entrée into this new world through the medium of lowbrow science periodicals. In 1881 he first sponsored Constance as his defender by communicating her essays and letters to the *Journal of Science*. Later they conducted their proselytizing separately in *Knowledge*. Constance contributed a six-part essay and nine letters in early 1885. Lewins managed seven epistles during the same period before the editor slammed his letterbox in their faces. "All this appears to me the veriest logomachy,"[10] he declared. What no one, possibly not even the editors, realized was that only two contributors had been involved. Constance occasionally published over her initials in the *Mason College Magazine*. These she gave invariably as "C. C. W. N." In the *Journal of Science*, however, her early pieces were signed "C. N."; subsequently, when Lewins no longer interceded for her, she began to use "Constance Arden," "C. Arden," and "C. A." By 1885 the motive for her dissimulation would have been obvious to anyone with eyes to see. Three times within a month she appeared in a single issue of *Knowledge* both as herself and as C. N. Constance C. W. Naden dilated on "The Evolution of the Sense of Beauty" and commented on Darwin's idea of variation and the reputation of George Eliot. C. N. argued insistently for Hylo-idealism—in one case on the same page with a letter by her alter ego. Since the contributions under her own name were billed as having been read "at a meeting of the Mason College Union," it would appear that Constance intended to dissociate C. N. from the person she was reputed to be in Birmingham: the exemplary student philosopher and poet, a discreet leader among young women, the offspring of bourgeois Nonconformity.

It is not hard to understand why. The years in which Constance came to intellectual maturity saw the last and greatest efflorescence of organized free thought in Britain. Between 1877 and 1883 leading members of the National Secular Society, which was based in London, brought the movement new supporters as well as fresh opprobrium. Charles Bradlaugh, the president, and Annie Besant, an ardent feminist, published a birth control pamphlet under the auspices of their Freethought Publishing Company; they were tried for obscenity and convicted. G. W. Foote, who later edited *The Freethinker* for the same press, published a series of "comic sketches" mocking the Bible; he was convicted of blasphemy and sentenced as a common criminal. Meanwhile Bradlaugh, a militant atheist like the rest, had begun his long and bitter campaign to be sworn in as a duly elected member of Parliament. He was ultimately successful, but the style and substance of his leadership led to a split in the movement. The "patrician-purists" of the British Secular Union assailed Bradlaugh's bombast, his failures at expediency, his truckling to the masses. None was more lofty or vociferous than W. Stewart Ross, editor of the union's paper, the *Secular Review*, which he dubbed "a journal of agnosticism." [11] He also made agnosticism the specialty of his press, "W. Stewart & Co." of 41 Farringdon Street, thereby incurring snide references to the "Farringdon school of Freethought" from members of the National Secular Society.

The agnostics of the British Secular Union quarreled not just with the atheists of the National Secular Society, but among themselves. Religious agnostics could even be liberal Christians and advertise their faith accordingly. "Absolute" or "pure" agnostics had little attraction for religion; they commended their views on a "scientific" basis, namely the naturalistic realism of Huxley and Spencer. Spencer, however, went so far as to call ultimate reality "The Unknowable," and to some this gave agnosticism a pantheistic appeal. Antireligious agnostics differed from the rest. They resembled plebian atheists for the practical tendency of their doctrines, but, ironically, these doctrines could sometimes distinguish them as the loftiest agnostics of all. Hylo-idealists were the prime example. Under the inspiration of Dr. Lewins they decked a populist appeal to common sense in a coat of many colors, a tissue of English empiricism, German idealism, and mechanistic reductionism. Theirs was a lurid piece of irreligion, ill adapted for the masses; and Ross made it a feature of his press.

Constance published her first pamphlet, *What is Religion?* with W. Stewart & Co. in 1883. She used the nom de plume "C. N." because she wished to conceal from the general public, or at least from the good people of Birmingham, her membership in London's most exclusive agnostic sect. Hylo-idealism, the pamphlet argued, was "the true creed of the scientific secularist."[12] Like other disciples of Dr. Lewins, who plied their doctrines in the Secularist press and periodicals, Constance seems to have favored establishments under the control of Ross and his associate, C. A. Watts, although the Freethought Publishing Company handled several of their works. Four years after the publication of *What is Religion?* she chose the Freethought Publishing Company to issue her edition of Lewins' letters, *Humanism versus Theism*, also under the initials C. N. The letters were preceded by an essay that Constance had contributed in 1884 to the Secularist family magazine, *Our Corner*, at the request of the editor, Annie Besant, Bradlaugh's partner in crime. When Watts began publishing the *Agnostic Annual* in 1885 the Hylo-idealists emerged in force. Constance published as often as anyone—again as C. N.—and the *Agnostic Annual* for 1890 may now go down in history, not only for containing a piece by the eighteen-year-old Bertrand Russell, but for printing an essay by Constance and advertising both volumes of her poems.

Sappho's Legacy

Untainted by association with organized free thought, Constance continued her triumphal progress at Mason College and walked off with the best prize. For one who lacked a competitive spirit and had not registered for a degree, this achievement was the final vindication of her ability to make a career of her own. In 1887 she was awarded the Heslop Gold Medal for an essay, "Induction and Deduction," that would prove to be her most finished effort in the philosophy of science. In this, a "historical and critical sketch" she sought, in Kantian fashion, to assimilate the distinction between induction and deduction to a complex process of "cognitions" and "recognitions."[13] There was a further triumph, and a tragedy, for Constance in her final months at Mason College. The timing of events must have suited her penchant for generative metaphor and dialectic. In the spring of 1887 she delivered herself of a second collection of poems. But even as the *Mason College Magazine* praised the volume (omitting to "criticise the philosophy" it contained), the life Constance had known at Pakenham House, where she still made her home, came to an end. On 21 June, as Birmingham celebrated the queen's jubilee, her grandmother, Caroline Woodhill, quietly died. Constance spent the summer sorting through her effects and arranging for the house to be sold. Then in September, when the will was proved and she had received her "Associateship" of Mason College, Constance turned her back on the "homely scenes" and poignant yearnings that had shaped her youth. The legacy Constance received from her grandmother would enable her to travel abroad for nine months before establishing a comfortable residence in London. The legacy Constance gave to those she left behind was contained in *A Modern Apostle; The Elixir of Life; The Story of Clarice*.

In this new collection Constance is on surer ground. Her anguish has abated, her unbelief is poised, her feminism has matured. The three poems named in the title make up the greater part of the volume. What they lack in profundity is more than compensated for by the autobiographic insights they yield. The narrative line of "A Modern Apostle" (*CPW*, pp. 175–235) was adumbrated in a short story of the same title that Constance published anonymously in the *Mason College Magazine*. The main difference between the two accounts is that in the poem the mother, not the father, counsels Ella, the personification of mathematical genius, to resist the designs of a local preacher of "Pantheistic Socialism" named Alan. "What's the use of all your Conic Sections / If like a fool you yield to your affections?" Alan, who has read Carlyle and, "guilt of dye intenser! / Dallied with Darwin and with Herbert Spencer," was sent from home by his puritan father, despite the pleas of a Scottish mother in whom the "poet flame" burned bright. Now, fancying himself an "annointed seer," he believes in a "God Unknown"; but Ella, with her mother's encouragement, sees through his agnostic faith. "Her Reason tipped the dart, and strung the bow, / To slay his Passion." Yet she is conscience striken. Her "riven self" implores, "Will not some opiate give her dreamful rest / Till she return to the Great Mother's breast?" The answer, "Nay! rather let her maim her shrinking soul," marks the victory of reason over romantic love. Thereafter Alan's visionary preaching fails to quell a starving mob, and he is brought to Ella, mortally wounded and "raving with strange despair / Because he could not find his mother there." Ella effects a reconciliation with his parents, and Alan, in dying, leaves her to "unshrine / All errors, all illusions—theirs, my own." She replies: "I give what e'er I have of strength and skill; / Trust me in this—what Woman can, I will."

Trite, implausible, melodramatic—"A Modern Apostle" may seem all these, yet there is more of fiber and conviction here than in anything Constance had written even a few years earlier. The same may be said of "The Elixir of Life" (*CPW*, pp. 239–67), the second of the title poems, which is clearly a development of "The Alchemist" in *Songs and Sonnets of Springtime*. Here, "in some strange, waking vision," the narrator discerns the Lewins-like figure of the Alchemist to be a philosopher-king from a "slumbrous German town" who has discovered through hermetic arts the secret of eternal life. Constance herself had discovered the Renaissance physician Paracelsus in the interval between her books. She published an essay in the *Journal of Science* that remarked on his debt to "old women" and "beldames" in developing a mystical natural philosophy around the "germ of truth" contained in the doctrine of the unity of macrocosm and microcosm.[14] In "The Elixir of Life," however, the order of indebtedness is reversed: the philosopher-king traverses time and space to bestow immortality on the perfect woman, whom he chooses as his queen. But when this is done the woman conspires to

Of couching flocks it chanted; of the bird
  Nested in shade; of all things that have breath;
Of human fate; and still entranced they heard,
  And knew the harmonies of Birth and Death:
Till downward flowed the dream, and bore her deep
Into the dark unhaunted caves of Sleep.

(*CPW*, p. 288)

Here a pan-erotic vision is nature's benediction on her contented daughter. The womblike, tomblike depth of sleep contrasts starkly with the tragic death of Alan, the motherless visionary, in "A Modern Apostle." It is just the converse of the traumatic awakening in "The Elixir of Life," where Constance dreamt of an immortal philosopher-king struggling to be delivered from his passions. The Life to which both "heroes," bereft of female love, would devote themselves flows naturally through the impassioned Clarice. Since Constance wrote her "Story" while recovering from a sharp illness, it is impossible not to see in it a parable of her own quest for healing, for sexual fulfillment, for wholeness.

Equally, however, it is impossible to interpret "The Story of Clarice" as the expression of a covert yearning to be married. Constance had long since banished the idea, and the new poems everywhere reflect her single-mindedness. Clarice may wed but Ella flatly refuses. In the fourfold *jeu d'esprit* "Evolutional Erotics," most of the humor is achieved at men's expense. And in "The Pessimist's Vision" (*CPW*, p. 329) Constance dreams again, this time of entering a "modern Hell," full of "complex tortures" fueled by "new forms of madness and despair." A demon bars the way, mocking her "lust for pain" with the assurance that it may find full nourishment on earth, "with poignant spice of passion." "Knowest thou not / Fiends wed for hate as mortals wed for love, / Yet find not much more anguish? Be content." Constance cannot have shared this view entirely—the pessimism is, after all, uttered by a fiend. Her characteristic attitude toward marriage was less hostile than indifferent. What mattered to her more was an experience of wholeness, an erotic union of self and nature, that no man could effect. The infernal imagery could be transformed.

On the facing page, opposite "The Pessimist's Vision," is "The Nebular Theory," Constance's rendering of the first verses of the Book of Genesis (*CPW*, p. 328). In the beginning were lifeless, lonely atoms, each knowing naught but

> its own vibrant pang of dearth;
> Until a cosmic motion breathed and hissed
> And blazed through the black silence; atoms kissed,
> Clinging and clustering, with fierce throbs of birth,
> And raptures of keen torment, such as stings
>> Demons who wed in Tophet; the night swarmed
>> With ringèd fiery clouds, in glowing gyres
> Rotating: aeons passed: the encircling rings
>> Split into satellites; the central fires
> Froze into suns; and thus the world was formed.

Furies are howling here; space seethes with imps and banshees. It is Constance making cosmology—her Mother giving birth. "Every one of us creates Nature herself," she had written elsewhere. Reason sees "in the orderly arrangements of the Cosmos only a supreme glorification of matter, the universal mother, and of man, her child." Hylo-idealism asserts "the being of that matrix whose non-being is unthinkable" (*Induction and Deduction*, pp. 160, 166, 199).

Thus nature held no terrors for Constance when, in September 1887, she set off through Europe to the Levant, and from there to India with letters of introduction by courtesy of Dr. Lewins. No pantheist or agnostic could find in nature an ally so intimate as one who claimed to create nature for herself. To Constance Hylo-idealism effected "the reconciliation of poetry, philosophy, and science" even as it offered something more.[15] It made her science erotic. When Gladstone lent her posthumous prestige by tracing her lineage to Sappho, he wrote perhaps better than he knew. But Sappho—little did he realize—had given way to *sophia* before her death. In leaving Birmingham for her oriental tour, Constance also quit poetry to become a feminist philosopher. She returned to London in 1888 with eighteen months to live.

Her Sisters, Her Self

The last poem Constance published before her death marked the rising curve of her career. It appeared during her absence abroad in *The*

Woman's World, a bright new monthly edited in London by Oscar Wilde. Whatever may be concluded about Wilde's reasons for soliciting the piece—in 1889 his first short story, "The Canterville Ghost," was subtitled, "A Hylo-idealistic Romance"—one thing is certain: like Olive Schreiner, Mathilde Blind, Millicent Garrett Fawcett, and other contributors, Constance represented a type of reader to whom he hoped *Woman's World* would appeal. The "culture and courage" of *A Modern Apostle*, at least, had made that clear to him. This "New Woman" prided herself on being a freethinker, resisted marriage but remained intensely moral, struggled against traditional sex roles while retaining "feminine" graces, and above all gave up the cultural norm of self-renunciation for the ideal of self-fulfillment. Constance fitted this description exactly, and a coming decadent such as Wilde, it has been argued, would have shared many of her interests and sympathies. The New Woman was not, however, necessarily a feminist. She need not have believed that self-fulfillment should be sought in promoting the self-fulfillment of her sisters. She need not have supported them in their struggle for equal rights. Personal individualism was not irreconcilable with her ambitions in an era when political individualism was rife, but it is evident that Constance belonged to a different breed.

As a modest *rentier* and a committed Liberal in politics, Constance fulfilled her obligations to society in the usual ways when she had finally settled in London. She joined the Denison Club, whose members wrung their hands (defeatedly in her view) over the condition of the poor. She canvassed on behalf of the Liberal candidate for Marylebone during a parliamentary by-election. But at the same time her charitable and political interests had special regard for women. Besides dispensing numerous "private charities" to worthy individuals, Constance held a large meeting in her drawing room with Dr. Elizabeth Garrett Anderson to raise money in aid of the new "women's hospital" in the Marylebone Road. She became an associate of the Working Ladies' Guild and, just before her death, began arranging to take charge of a block of houses for women of "limited means." Sick and poor women, like their better-placed sisters, also seemed to her politically vulnerable. Constance enrolled as a lecturer for the Central National Committee for Women's Suffrage and for the Women's Liberal Association. Her last public engagement was a lecture on behalf of the association in support of the extended franchise. In all these activities she received the continual aid and encouragement of women friends, just as in Birmingham. Constance was an active member of the Norwood Ladies Debating Society. She belonged to the Somerville Club, which admitted women only. By no means least important, she enjoyed the affection and companionship of Madeline Daniell, who accompanied her to India, shared her home and social interests, and stood by her until the end.

Philosophy, as well as feminism, was an interest the companions shared. For Constance it had become her true vocation, the fulfillment of her quest through poetry and science for erotic union of self and nature. On 17 December 1888 the pair became the seventh and eighth women to be elected to the Aristotelian Society. The membership then numbered over fifty. Constance, who did not suffer ignorance gladly, wasted little time at her first session in getting a "distinguished evolutionist"—probably Darwin's intellectual heir apparent, George Romanes—to admit that he was not thoroughly acquainted with Spencer's *Data of Ethics*.[16] Spencer now played an important role in her quest for a philosophical synthesis, although she questioned his social organicism and could not countenance the doctrine of "The Unknowable." Some eight years had passed since Lewins, at her suggestion, resolved "hylo-zoism" into "Hylo-idealism," thereby emphasizing that "the somatic Self is centre, radius, and periphery" of all things. During this interval she had discovered in Spencer's *Synthetic Philosophy* an evolutionary reconciliation of egoism and altruism in ethics. Now, using Lewins to improve on Spencer, Constance made an original contribution to Hylo-idealism. She began writing a major work on the ethics of evolution. Her aim was to illuminate the "dark side" of the *Synthetic Philosophy* by qualifying its "wholly empirical moral etiology." The evolution of altruism from egoism depends in part, according to Spencer, on the growth of "sympathy" with others. But according to Hylo-idealism, these others are part of one's self already; one's "inner life, emotive and ideal, constitutes all he knows of humanity, individual and collective." The "potentiality of sympathy" therefore does not evolve, but is itself the antecedent condition of moral development. It is "an essential constituent of human nature," a primitive feeling which, when shaped and enlarged by religious, political, and social circumstances, becomes the basis of moral ideals. The precept to "love thy neighbour as thy self," for example, arises not merely—as in Spencer's *Data of Ethics*—from the physical necessity that society must cohere, but also from rational necessity. Self-love is truly love of one's neighbor when one's sympathies are duly enlarged. "Egoism and altruism are not merely conciliated, but identical" (*ID*, pp. 127–128, 131, 132, 135).

A philosophy better suited to a New Woman and a feminist can hardly be imagined. Constance, having found her mother in the Nature she created for herself, now identified other women with her personal quest for self-fulfillment. Always fond of generative metaphor, she made use of Spencer's recapitulation theory:

> It is doubtless true that in youth, and in the earlier stages of society, family ties favour the cultivation of sympathetic feelings. But in later life, and at a later period of social development, such ties frequently help to narrow and specialise the sympathies, setting bounds beyond which they cannot easily pass. This, while valuable in preventing shallow natures from frittering uselessly away what little feeling they possess, is often injurious to deep natures, causing them to pour into some narrow channel an intensity of emotion, which might have fertilised broad regions of life. (*ID*, pp. 125–126)

Constance speaks here as one who had left the pathetic scenes of her childhood to find new and wider channels for the intense emotions her upbringing had instilled. Putting self above family life and marriage had meant, for her, being free for others. Now she commended this enlargement of sympathy to her sisters; she expected it on their behalf from society. "We can never serve humanity in the best way, or completely realise its unity, or our unity with it, unless we have cultivated our own nature to the full, with all its varied powers and sympathies," she urged one of her women friends in Birmingham. This "widening of the sphere of the Golden Rule," first "to barbarians, then slaves, and at last women!" she informed the male-dominated Aristotelian Society in London, also marks the development of morality. "Even animals" would be brought within the pale of ethical progress. "The religion of the future," as Constance wrote elsewhere, "will be a more vivid feeling of life—not of one's own life, but of life in general—a sort of extended sympathy." In predicting the realization of this ideal, "philosophy and poetry meet and clasp hands." (*ID* p. 112).

Constance Redivivus

The feeling of life was never more vivid in Constance, her sympathies never more extended, when slowly but inexorably her body succumbed to the forces of an unideal world. When she last visited Birmingham in October 1889 all her old friends, including "many ladies," gathered to hear her address the Sociological Section with wonted power. But a few days afterward Constance looked pale and drawn. She said nothing about the abdominal pain and inflammation, the fetid discharges, the shivering fits and sweating, all of which increased alarmingly in subsequent weeks when she had returned to London. Convinced that mental hygiene was the better part of physical well-being, she bravely kept up her round of disciplines—the writing, the lecturing, the charities— without neglect of daily exercise. Finally, when the discomfort became unbearable, she sought expert medical advice, probably with help from Dr. Lewins. On 21 November Constance completed a consultation under Dr. Thomas Spencer Wells, a former naval surgeon who had served with Lewins in the Crimea and afterward practically founded modern gynecological surgery. She was told that her only hope lay in submitting to a major operation. Four days later she was confined to bed by her attending physician, W. Chapman Grigg, a future president of the British Gynaecological Society. On 5 December the surgical team arrived at her residence, headed by the redoubtable Robert Lawson Tait.

Lawson Tait came up for the operation from Birmingham, where he had chaired a meeting of the Midland Medical Society the day before. Short and stout with a meaty face and goggle eyes, his potent figure had become a fixture of Birmingham intellectual life in the years when Constance achieved her emancipation. It is questionable whether the two had met previously, but Lawson Tait had in fact presided over the Natural History and Microscopical Society and remained a member of its Sociological Section; he also now served as bailiff and president of council at Mason College. Having shadowed each other socially, at least, he and Constance were also ideologically attuned. In religion Lawson Tait was a freethinker, in politics a Gladstonian Liberal, and in science, if not a partisan of Spencer's, at least a fervid Darwinian and antivivisectionist. It was in the field of medicine that his liberal individualism diverged utterly from hers. Remembered by the profession as "a man rugged and brusque, of great self-reliance, indomitable will and dauntless courage," Lawson Tait acquired his reputation—and, not incidentally, a considerable fortune—through a highly competitive practice. In a series of daring operations interspersed with sharp professional disputes, he relentlessly displaced Spencer Wells as master of the female abdomen. He became a founder and the first president of the British Gynaecological Society in 1885; by the end of 1889, when he prepared Constance for surgery, he was the veteran of some eight thousand major operations. His specialty was the removal of ovaries; his technique was consummate and bold. In a two-year period Lawson Tait once performed 139 consecutive ovariotomies without a single fatality.

Constance would be one of his exceptions through no lapse of clinical judgment or surgical skill. The diagnosis in her case had been correct; the treatment was appropriate and, under the circumstances, the only hope of averting a slow and painful death. Ovarian cysts were then seen as a kind of pathological "pregnancy" resulting from disturbed ovulation. Surgical intervention was indicated on the grounds that in a real pregnancy with complications an operation to save mother or child had become standard practice. In Constance's case the cysts that Lawson Tait removed gave striking support to this analogy, for they were among those "mysterious productions," as his textbook, *Diseases of Women*, called them, which contained embryologic structures such as hair, teeth, and bone. Spencer Wells could find "no rational explanation" for the phenomenon of "dermoid" cysts. Lawson Tait, not untypically, thought he knew better. Citing Darwin's doctrine of "pangenesis," he proposed that the ovum "has in it the power of formative origin of all these structures" quite apart from "fusion with the male germ." Studies of lower animals had shown that this power "originated in the early phases of our ancestry"; thus, by the law of recapitulation, it reactivates "in foetal or infantile life," when the ovum first forms a cyst. "The logical conclusion of this view is," wrote Lawson Tait, "that if such an ovum could get into the uterus after its escape, it would develop into a perfect instance of parthenogenesis."[17]

Within Constance, however, life was not logical, whatever her skill as a Hylo-idealist philosopher. The gestation she had undergone "since birth," on Lawson Tait's view, was not creative but the reverse. Her cysts had enlarged and become infected, the infection had spread, and gangrene had set in. Believing the world to be her brain's creation, she had neglected her other organs, and the operation had been delayed almost beyond hope of recovery. The microcosm in her turned against the macrocosm. The mother's legacy became the daughter's doom. Constance received her death wound, ironically, in a parody of abnormal birth. "The nature of the harvest," she had told the Sociological Section in October, "is predetermined by the nature of the seed that is sown. If we really knew the crop, we could both predict the harvest and could trace its past history from the formation of the ovule to the liberation of the seed when mature."

Poetic and tragic at once, her final liberation came quickly. Constance rejoined the Great Matrix, the "unconscious Life, that waits for birth," as soon as her postoperative equilibrium was disturbed. To cheer her at Christmastide the nurses moved her into the drawing room, where Elizabeth Garrett Anderson had pleaded the cause of sick women. Constance fainted, then revived, then hovered uncertainly for many hours, "Till downward flowed the dream, and bore her deep / Into the dark unhaunted caves of Sleep." Her father had been summoned urgently from Birmingham and was at her side with Madeline Daniell. He had been there, it seemed, twice before. Word of the death returned with him the next day, Christmas eve, and blighted the season for the many friends who had "never ceased to regret that London should have swallowed up in its insatiable gulf the intellect which Birmingham nurtured and honoured." A handful of them gathered on the twenty-eighth in a bitter northeast wind to lay the body beside her mother's at the Old Cemetery in Warstone Lane.

Dr. Lewins did not attend. He alone had known the totality of Constance's life since 1876; he alone perhaps understood the full extent of her quest for personal wholeness. Her life had become "so much bound up with his own," wrote one who knew them both, "that her untimely death affected him as deeply as if she had been his only daughter." His grief expressed the sense of loss in the idolatry of a diminished self: "This world for me, now, has its *Gethsemane*, and its *Golgotha!*" Whereupon he purposed, without saying so, that there should also be a Resurrection.[18] Posterity, according to Hylo-idealism, might recreate the deceased, even in her dissolution, if the memory of her words and person were perpetuated. Immediately Lewins arranged for Constance's writings to be assembled in four volumes and published at his own expense, the philosophy first, then the poetry. In the spring he sent the first volume to Spencer, although he disputed the great agnostic's acclaimed influence on his student. Spencer acknowledged the gift by paying tribute to her "receptivity and originality": "I can think of no woman, save 'George Eliot,' in whom there has been this union of high philosophical capacity with extensive acquisition."[19] The letter went on, however, to remark callously on the "physiological cost" to the "feminine organization" entailed by the development of such powers. Lewins, who had spurred her attainments, could justly feel aggrieved. He did not take up Spencer's magnanimous offer to have his tribute inserted in the second volume of her collected works. The doctor had planned a more enduring memorial than Spencer's reputation could possibly sustain.

On 6 January 1890, a fortnight after the death, Lewins wrote to the chairman of council at Mason College. The medal Constance had received in 1887 for her dissertation, "Induction and Deduction," was established by the college's earliest benefactor, Thomas Pretious Heslop, an eminent local physician. Since the college had seen fit subsequently to commemorate Heslop with a life-sized marble bust, Lewins now proposed that another like it should be created at his own expense, in memory of the woman who, more than any other student, had enriched the academic life of the college in the early period of its existence. The bust was to be made from photographs and a "cast of Miss Naden's face . . . taken after death." On 5 February the proposal came before council under the presidency of Dr. Lawson Tait, and was approved. For many years the memorial bust stood at one side of a great doorway in the German department of the library at Mason College, placed symmetrically with the bust of Heslop opposite. After the removal of the college to Edgbaston—not a mile from Pakenham House—where it became part of Birmingham University, the sculptures were separated. Heslop now inhabits the room named after him in the university library, which holds the rare books and archives. Constance Naden stands forlornly on the staircase in the Shakespeare Institute, "so calm, so child-like, so marble-cold." She is best remembered today by those who adorn her and, in search of passing luck, unselfconsciously rub her nose.

But as a hat rack or a talisman, the graven goddess ill serves her donor's purpose. Dr. Lewins intended that Constance should live on in her hard-won wholeness. Posterity should clasp the sculptured form, Pygmalion-like, until the "pale, cold cheeks of marble" flush with "emotion bright and warm" (*CPW*, p. 340), and her career be recreated. To that end he arranged for the titles by which Birmingham knew her, *Songs and Sonnets of Springtime* and *A Modern Apostle*, to be inscribed for all to see on the spines of two of the stony volumes that form the base of the sculpture. By the same token he determined that the third volume should hide its theme, the spine being reversed, just as the young philosopher concealed from local people the wider significance of her creed. Without that theme, without her creed, however, the goddess remains marble-cold: the matter does not live, the mother is unknown, the daughter abides without her sisters. Lewins would have it thus. Only those can recreate Constance Naden who know the secret of her self. Only those can know the secret who clasp her figure and search diligently for the clue. "Hylo-idealism," darkly inscribed on the spine behind her, is still the touchstone.

Notes

1. This essay is a shortened version of a study to be published with full documentation and a calendar of the works of Constance C. W. Naden.

2. Sandra Gilbert and Susan Gubar, *The Madwoman in the Attic* (New Haven: Yale University Press, 1979), pp. 548–49.

3. *The Complete Poetical Works of Constance Naden* (London: Bickers & Son, 1894), p. xxiii.

4. Information about Lewins has been ferreted out of *The Army List*, the *Times*, the *Lancet*, Boase's *Modern English Biography*, the *Edinburgh Medical and Surgical Journal*, and other sources available in the library of the Wellcome Institute for the History of Medicine, London.

5. *On the Identity of the Vital and Cosmical Principle* (Lewes, Sussex: Printed by Geo. Bacon, 1869); *Life and Mind: Their Unity and Materiality* (Lewes, Sussex: Printed by Geo. Bacon, 1873).

6. Robert Lewins, *Humanism versus Theism; or, Solipsism (Egoism) Equals Atheism in a Series of Letters . . .*, ed. C[onstance] N[aden] (London: Freethought Publishing Co., 1887), pp. 20–21.

7. *Mason College Magazine* 1 (December 1883): 219.

8. "The Union," *Mason College Magazine* 3 (May 1885): 71.

9. Constance Naden, "Schiller as a Philosophic Poet," *Mason College Magazine* 2 (1884): 8.

10. The editor, R. A. Proctor, appended this comment to Naden's letter "Are Tripe and Onions Objective or Subjective?" *Knowledge* 7 (24 April 1885): 355.

11. See Edward Royle, *Radicals, Secularists, and Republicans: Popular Freethought in Britain, 1866–1915* (Manchester: Manchester University Press, 1980), pp. 101–2, 161.

12. *Further Reliques of Constance Naden: Being Essays and Tracts for Our Times,* ed. G. M. McCrie (London: Bickers & Son, 1891), p. 126.

13. Constance Naden, *Induction and Deduction: A Historical and Critical Sketch of Successive Philosophical Conceptions respecting the Relations of Inductive and Deductive Thought, and Other Essays,* ed. R. Lewins (London: Bickers and Son, 1890), pp. 1–100.

14. *Further Reliques of Constance Naden,* pp. 201, 207.

15. Ibid., p. 126.

16. See *Proceedings of the Aristotelian Society* 1/2 (1893): 142–43; and William R. Hughes, *Constance Naden: A Memoir* (London: Bickers & Son, 1890), p. 44.

17. Lawson Tait, *Diseases of Women* (New York: William Wood, 1879), pp. 139–44.

18. George M. McCrie, "In Memoriam—Robert Lewins, M.D.," *Open Court* 9 (22 August 1895): 4607–4608.

19. Spencer to Lewins, 10 June 1890, in Hughes, *Constance Naden,* pp. 89–90.

Bedlam and Parnassus: Mad People's Writing in Georgian England

Using hindsight and consulting convenience, historians divide the past up into categories, and, once trapped by these, we readily talk as if the minds and voices of the past operated within sealed worlds. Here there is literature, there science and its appendages, medicine and psychiatry. Up there are writers and poets, down here ordinary people. Or there is the world of the sane divided from the world of the mad. We picture these bodies of consciousness as distinct, but as "influencing" each other in various ways, in particular (because it is convenient to label them as polar opposites) as "in conflict." There is some truth in these pictures of bodies of thought colliding with each other like ice floes in a sea; but they can also badly distort the way we understand the contours of consciousness in time past.

It has been a consistent theme of this volume that the discourse of science draws on, participates in, reflects the wider discourse of the general culture. It is not exempt from metaphor, nor from narrative impulses. Gillian Beer identifies its distinction from literature in its creation of an inevitable in ordinary discourse. Katherine Hayles, similarly, talks of the way scientists work to exclude all semiotic "noise"— and only partially succeed, of course. On close inspection, the boundaries blur, and historians of science, perhaps even more than scientists themselves, need to work with an awareness of the arbitrariness of the distinctions they often need to use. Science, as David Bell tries to show (drawing himself on the work of Michel Serres), participates in the culture's dominant myths and can sometimes be anticipated by literature itself.

In this essay I shall be talking about the relations between science and literature in a different, although related, way. I will be looking at how cultural conceptions of madness and poetry directly, literally impinge on the "scientific" conception of them—on who is institutionalized and who is regarded as genius, on how the "English malady" is perceived and defined. I shall be considering the consequence of recognizing the historical and cultural contingency of some of our categories, and dealing, particularly, with the thought systems historians customarily call madness and rationality, poetry and common speech, literature and medicine. But for the moment I wish to dissolve away, or at least suspend, our preoccupation with the boundaries between them. I want to assume that they shared at any one time at least as much as divided them, that the minds of poets and doctors, and the mad and the sane, were informed by common thought patterns, and that shifts which occurred in poetics or the treatment of the mad were occasioned not necessarily by the "influence" of, or by "conflict" with, external disciplines, but rather by complex, internal processes of the formation and reformation of rationalities and representations. And within that general framework, I want to trace some shifts in consciousness happening during "the long eighteenth century" in respect to two main questions. First the larger question: how was speech interpreted as an index of insanity or a token of rationality? Second the more specific question: what happened to the long-standing tradition which saw "madness" as a key attribute of the poet? Important shifts of viewpoint occurred during this period, but they are of a kind too subtle to be rendered by formulae such as "psychiatry versus poetry" or "from poetic inspiration to medical madness."

When Ezra Pound wrote accusingly,

> It has been your habit for long to do away
>   with good writers,
> You either drive them mad, or else blink at
>   their suicides,
> Or else you condone their drugs, and talk of
>   insanity and genius,
> But I will not go mad to please you[1]

he was of course repudiating the yokings of madness and genius, melancholy and poetry, reiterated ever since Plato and Aristotle and encapsulated in Dryden's couplet in *Absolom and Achitophel* (1680):

Great wits are sure to madness near allied,
And thin partitions do their bounds divide.

A prime irony of the human condition, moralists had long noted, was that though speech raised man above the brutes (in the beginning, after all, was the word; Adam named the animals, Orpheus charmed them), language itself readily became perverted, turned source or symptom of mental disorder. Talking nonsense, or talking nonstop, betrayed *homo sapiens*. Lycanthropy—baying at the moon—catcalling, chattering like monkeys, all plunged man once more down into animality.

In aiming to explore the dialogue between speech (especially poetry) and madness in the Georgian century, I shall triangulate from several viewpoints, including psychiatry and literature, but I shall also listen to the sufferers themselves. This last is important because, as Pound complained, the voice of the mad is so easily drowned by the din of stereotypes and psychobabble. Particularly in the case of mad writers, today's facile pop Freudianism links neurosis, creativity, and art while, slightly earlier, fin-de-siècle psychiatry held that madness was art's double, the two merging in the doomed, diseased degenerate—witness for instance J. F. Nisbet's *Insanity of Genius*:

> examples of men of letters lapsing into or approaching insanity—Swift, Johnson, Cowper, Southey, Shelley, Byron, Campbell, Goldsmith, Charles Lamb, Walter Savage Landor, Rousseau, Chatterton, Pascal, Chateaubriand, George Sand, Tasso, Alfieri, Edgar Allen Poe, etc.[2]

Resurrecting the voice of the mad is difficult. There were few Boswells to take down their table talk, and so we must rely on snatches, as when Betsy Sheridan reported the delirious George III dictating commentaries on Cervantes.[3] Most records of mad idiom from the past come from playwrights,[4] novelists, and journalists, who may or may not have had firsthand experience, but who routinely turned their experiences into literary clichés, as when Ned Ward, recounting in his *London Spy* a supposed visit to Bedlam, reported such

> drumming of doors, ranting, holloaing, singing and rattling, that I could think of nothing but Don Quevedo's vision, where the damn'd broke loose, and put Hell in an uproar.[5]

If this be Bedlam, it is Bedlam filtered through the vision of Pandemonium drawn by a Spanish satirist. Maybe the ranting was real; but do we believe Ward when he depicts one of the Bedlamites

> holding forth with much vehemence against Kingly government. I told him he deserv'd to be hang'd for talking of treason. "Now," says he, "you're a fool, for we madmen have as much privilege of speaking our minds as an ignorant dictator when he spews out his nonsense to a whole parish . . . you may talk what you will, and nobody will call you in question for it. Truth is persecuted everywhere abroad, and flies hither for sanctuary, where she sits as safe as a knave in a church, or a whore in a nunnery. I can use her as I please and that's more than you dare to."
> (p. 50)

This witty fool is surely just Ward's mouthpiece for the upside-down-world jibe that in a crazy nation only lunatics are sane, and under oppression, only madness is true liberty.[6]

Or take, half a century later, the sentimental novelist Henry Mackenzie, in his *Man of Feeling* (1771), showing his hero, Harley, encountering a female Bedlamite:

> "My Billy is no more!" said she, "do you weep for my Billy? Blessings on your tears! I would weep too, but my brain is dry: and it burns, it burns, it burns!" She drew nearer to Harley.—"Be comforted, young Lady," said he, "your Billy is in heaven." "Is he, indeed? and shall we meet again? . . . when I can, I pray; and sometimes I sing; when I am saddest, I sing:—You shall hear me, hush!
>
> > Light be the earth on Billy's breast,
> > And green the sod that wraps his grave!"[7]

Here Ophelia is surely far more vivid to Mackenzie than is Bedlam. Sander Gilman has warned us not to misread paintings of the mad.[8] They were meant not as snapshots or clinical records but as coded warnings or satires. Similarly *ut pictura, poesis*: when encountering madmen in plays or novels, it would be foolish to take fiction for fact.

Luckily historians do have a window onto the minds of certain mad people through what the mad themselves wrote down. Even in asylums, the mad in Georgian England rarely seem to have been denied pen and paper (that therapy was perhaps reserved for a later age, as

Virginia Woolf was to find out),[9] and the writings of a handful survive, in print or manuscript. Some—such as the poet William Cowper's memoirs—were composed after recovery from a bout of insanity, serving by way of spiritual autobiography or *apologia pro vita sua*. Caution is clearly needed before we interpret such retrospective rationalizations as authentic "tapes" of the mind at the end of its tether. Yet others were penned during what we, but not necessarily their authors, would see as episodes of disturbance, and offer rich and hitherto essentially untapped sources for recovering the mental states of the mad.

With all such writings, the historian's job is not to go in for retrospective diagnosis, to decide which poets were really mad (any more than to judge which madmen were truly poetical), but to understand how the cultural and medical boundaries of rationality, responsibility, and art were drawn and redrawn over the centuries. One currently fashionable approach to this—a vulgarized amalgam of "labeling theory" and the writings of Michel Foucault—suggests that insanity has simply been a label imposed from the social heights as a device to disqualify deviants. But that is simplistic. How the boundary lines that demarcate the mad have actually been fixed has been a far more complex process than that, in both the general and the more specific case, subject to the negotiating powers of several distinct parties, including psychiatrists, public opinion, and the sufferers themselves, all operating within particular frames of knowledge and power, values and role options. In the rest of this essay, I shall explore one instance of this shaping of mental disorder, examining how the participants—doctors, men of letters, and the sufferers— tussled to draw and redraw the geography of Bedlam and Parnassus, insanity and poetry.

Like poets, madmen stand out because of their strange speech. Thus, in the mid-seventeenth century, Nicholas Culpeper reassured his readers that they could easily tell the mad, as they were "sometimes laughing, sighing . . . doting, crying out, threatening," and so forth; and, as Michael MacDonald has shown, common Stuart descriptions of lunatics included terms such as "babbling," which pointed to their jabbering, dislocated speech, their wordplay, riddling, or possession by voices from beyond, like the woman who cried out, "Christ Jesus have mercy on me," day and night for a whole year.[10]

Poets too speak in distinctive tongues. They too were assumed to be possessed by what Plato called "divine fury," a view endorsed in Shakespeare's sentiment that "the lunatick, the lover and the poet are of imagination all compact," and his description of the poet's act of creation:

> The poet's eye in a fine phrensy rolling
> Doth glance from heav'n to earth, from earth to heav'n
> And, as imagination bodies forth
> The forms of things unknown, the poet's pen
> Turns them to shape, and gives to aiery nothing
> A local habitation and a name.

For his part, Aristotle had drawn the character of the melancholy genius, and this triad of madness, melancholy, and poetic inspiration had been synthesized by Renaissance humanism and crystallized in the mad poet Tasso.[11] To dub a poet mad was to pay him a compliment. As Michael Drayton praised Kit Marlowe:

> For that fine madness still he did retain,
> Which rightly should possess a poet's brain.

These stereotypes echoed certain realities of Tudor and Stuart England. Like Shakespeare's motley fools, actual court jesters such as Will Somers and Richard Tarlton were marked out by their zany behaviour (real or impersonated), and feted for their improvisations, ditties, riddles, and sayings.[12] As put on stage by Jacobean playwrights, Bedlam always had its complement of poetasters and wits who'd lost their wits. And herein life mimicked art. Visiting what was commonly dubbed the Academy of Bedlam, John Evelyn found one inmate "mad with making verses,"[13] and if he'd come a few years later he'd have met the eminent poet and dramatist Nathaniel Lee, crazed by writing, drink, and poverty.[14] Ex-Bedlamites tramped the highways, licensed to beg, and their numbers it seems were swelled by opportunistic sane beggars ("Abraham men") who, like Edgar in *King Lear*, posed as Bedlamites. They commonly sang for their supper, and a corpus of what purported to be their songs was printed as "Bedlamite ballads,"with verses like this:

> I'll bark against the Dog-Star
> I'll crow away the morning,
> I'll chase the moon till it be noon
> And I'll make her leave her horning,

> But I'll find merry mad maudline,
> I'll seek whate'er betides her,
> And I will love beneath or above
> The dirty earth that hides her.[15]

Thus in the public ear and in literary circles, the gift of tongues established a certain kinship between poetry and lunacy. Montaigne was perhaps somewhat unusual in the late sixteenth century for chiding Tasso and his idolators for self-indulgently wallowing in madness.[16] But certain mad poets themselves grew far more equivocal than Tasso about playing out that role. Take James Carkesse. Carkesse had been a clerk at the navy office under Samuel Pepys in Restoration England. A casualty of office politics, he felt himself being plotted against, and was locked up in a private madhouse in Finsbury and later in Bedlam under the physician Dr. Allen.

Under confinement, he wrote a collection of verse, published on his release in 1679 under the title *Lucida intervalla*.[17] The fascination of Carkesse's poems is that they draw upon the conceits of mad poetry (following the great tradition of praisers of folly from Erasmus to Burton, Carkesse used the prerogative of lunacy to flay a crazy world),[18] and yet paradoxically and rather self-defeatingly, they also seek to deny the poet's own identity as a mad poet.

The sheer ambivalence of this project appears in contradictory poem titles (one is headed "Poets are Mad," another, "Poet no Lunatick"); in the name of the collection (doesn't "lucid intervals" imply the author is still basically insane?); and in the Burtonian epigraph *semel insanivimus omnes* (we're all mad).[19]

The world's irrational, argues Carkesse. Physicians are lunatics, and Bedlamites sane, or at least would be but for the physician's treatment:

> Says He, who more wit than the Doctor had,
> Oppression will make a wise man Mad;
> . . . .
> Therefore, Religio Medici (do you mind?)
> This is not Lunacy in any kind:
> But naturally flow hence (as I do think)
> Poetick Rage, sharp Pen, and Gall in Ink.
> A Sober Man, pray, what can more oppress,
> Than force by Mad-mens usage to confess
> Himself for Mad? (p. 39)

Carkesse's complaint is that he is sane. What is mistaken for lunacy is not lunacy at all, but poetic inspiration:

> Doctor, this pusling Riddle pray explain:
> Others your Physick cures, but I complain
> It works with me the clean contrary way,
> And makes me poet, who are Mad they say.
> The truth on't is, my Brain's well fixt condition
> Apollo better knows, than his Physitian:
> 'Tis Quacks disease, not mine, my poetry
> By the blind Moon-Calf, took for Lunacy.
>
> (p. 32)

It is crucial, Carkesse insists, to tell the poet apart from the madman and explode the evil doctrine of *"nullum magnum ingenium (absit verbo invidia) sine mixtura dementiae"*:

> It goes for current truth, that ever some madness
> Attends much Wit, 'tis strange in sober sadness:
> . . . .
> Hence they are call'd, by Plot of poor and rich,
> Madmen, whose wit's above the standard pitch:
> . . . .
> But sure, when Friends and you me Mad concluded,
> 'Twas you your senses lost, by th'Moon deluded.
>
> (p. 24)

Carkesse alleged that Dr. Allen (whom he dubs "Mad-quack") informed him "that till he left off making Verses, he was not fit to be discharg'd" (p. 51). But this only proved Mad-quack's folly. For poetry was neither source nor symptom of madness, but was medicinal: after all, wasn't Apollo god both of poetry and healing?

Carkesse is pivotal yet hard to evaluate. We would need to know more about why he was locked up: he claimed merely to have been feigning madness, and that the foolish physician had mistaken his "madness in the masquerade" for a "sensless condition" (p. 10), but why he should have been feigning madness in the first place he doesn't explain. And other elements in his story—his claims to have been visited in Bedlam by royalty and nobility—alert our suspicions (p. 25). Above all, he comes across as Janus-faced. He is steeped in the tradition of learned wit epitomized a generation earlier by Robert Burton, who had joyously embraced his mission as a melancholy misanthrope ("I am as foolish, as mad as anyone").[20] Yet he also repudiated it, no doubt in part because, unlike Burton, he was shut up not in Christ Church but in Bedlam College.

Carkesse's self-disinheritance from the office of mad poet, however ambiguous, was then echoed and elaborated through the succeeding century.[21] Certain schools of literary historians might point to Swift, Collins, Smart, Cowper, and others and say: here indeed are the mad poets of Georgian England, driven to despair by the impossibility of poetry in the age of reason and asinine politeness. But this would be to miss the point. With few exceptions, these writers did not write, and certainly did not wish to be seen, in the traditional guise of the mad poet or the moody melancholy genius. It is this cultural shift, mediated through the thoughts of psychologists, poets, doctors, and sufferers alike, which I now wish to explore. The individual threads of the story are well known; the interconnections between them deserve attention.

The myth of the mad poet suffered its most sustained degradation from the Augustan, largely Tory, satirists who aimed to discredit the flood of "dunce" verse and other New Learning rubbish of the moderns by dubbing it the vomit of lunatics and depicting the madman as a dangerous egoist void of humanity.[22] This conflation of madness, animality, and nonsense appears most cacophonously in the sports-day episode in Pope's *Dunciad*.

> Now turn to diff'rent sports (the Goddess cries)
> And learn, my sons, the wond'rous pow'r of Noise.
> With Shakespear's nature, or with Johnson's art,
> Let others aim: 'Tis yours to snake the soul
> With Thunder rumbling from the mustard bowl,
> With horns and trumpets now to madness swell,
> Now sink in sorrows with a tolling bell:
> Such happy arts attention can command,
> When fancy flags, and sense is at a stand.
> Improve we these. Three Cat-calls be the bribe
> Of him, whose chatt'ring shames the Monkey tribe:
> And his this Drum, whose hoarse heroic base
> Drowns the loud clarion of the braying Ass.
> Now thousand tongues are heard in one loud din:
> The Monkey-mimics rush discordant in;
> 'Twas chatt'ring, grinning, mouthing, jabb'ring all,

Bedlam and Parnassus

And Noise and Norton, Brangling and Breval,
Dennis and Dissonance, and captious Art,
And Snip-snap short, and Interruption smart,
And Demonstration thin, and Theses thick,
And Major, Minor, and conclusion quick.
"Hold (cry'd the Queen) a Cat-call each shall win:
Equal your merits! equal is your din!
But that this well-disputed game may end,
Sound forth my Brayers, and the welkin rend."[23]

But Swift equally explores the phenomenon of *vox et praeterea nihil* via the first-person narrators of *Gulliver's Travels* and *A Tale of a Tub*, garrulous windbags, compulsively digressing, and lacking any glimmer of true self-awareness, culminating in the hope expressed by the *Tale's* hero that he will eventually be able "to write upon nothing."[24] Scriblerian satire plays heavily on the geographical proximity of Bedlam to Grub Street, a device paralleled in Defoe's *The Consolidator*, which includes in its lunar-cum-lunatic geography "a map of *Parnassus* with an exact Delineation of all the Cells, Apartments, Palaces and Dungeons, of that most famous Mountain, with a Description of its Heighth, and a learned Dissertation, proving it to be the properest place, next to the P[arliament] House, to take a Rise at, for a flight to the World in the Moon."[25]

Dunce poetry has no divine madness about it, precisely because it is not a gift from on high, but rather wells up from below. Dunce afflatus is mere flatulence, oozing out from diseased guts and issuing in what Pope called "a morbid secretion from the brain." In Swift's apothegm: "the corruption of the senses is the creation of the spirit."[26] True poetry by contrast flowed from healthy minds and healthy bodies. Pope claimed: "I was never hippish in my life," just as Swift prided himself on being "a perfect stranger to the spleen."

Thus Dunce verse was as antithetical to true poetry as madness to sanity, sickness to health. When

The dog star rages! Nay, 'tis past a doubt
All Bedlam or Parnassus is let out.

A cordon sanitaire to protect the healthy was the only answer:

Shut, shut the door, good John.[27]

267

Other critical movements also helped erode the validity of the idea of the mad poet. Important here was the critique of religious enthusiasm gathering momentum from the Restoration.[28] For one characteristic of the sects thus stigmatized was their pentecostalism. The Saints of the eighteenth and nineteenth centuries still believed God used His prophets as mouthpieces for His Word, frequently uttered in esoteric tongues, and sometimes even in verse, unintelligible except to the chosen. Thus John Perceval became a convert to the Glasgow Row sect (the Irvingites) in the early 1830s, for whom the mark of the elect was fluency in gibberish, "resembling the Greek language," as Perceval put it. Attracted to the sect because it fulfilled the key text of St. John, "the Word was with God and the Word was God," Perceval found that when God spoke to him, "I was usually addressed in verse." Once confined in an asylum, he found one of its advantages was that "I might hollo or sing as my spirits commanded me."[29] For most people, however, the prophetic pretensions of the religious lunatic fringe were crazy, and these in turn through a process of guilt by association helped to undermine poetic frenzy.

Another contributing factor was the post-Restoration development of philosophical nominalism. Powerful currents in English ideas from Bacon to the Enlightenment came to prize fact over fiction, number over rhetoric, things and actions over words.[30] Poetry per se rarely came under attack. But a poetics in which (as Pope put it) "the sound must seem an echo to the sense" jeopardized those strands of poetry which celebrated the magical, mystical, or numinous powers of words, and revered language as the key to wisdom. The mad poet lost his license to conjure with words.

One further philosophical shift seriously eroded the type of the mad poet. That was a changing view of the function of the imagination. Literary history has often argued that the Georgian age was poetically sterile to the extent that it denied the imagination. That isn't true. Certainly, from Hobbes to Johnson, the "dangerous prevalence of imagination" was indeed attacked.[31] But mainstream epistemology and aesthetics from Locke onward, as popularized by Addison and Akenside, saw the imagination as indispensable in generating ideas, and hence as a healthy, integral operation of the mind.[32] It is too often forgotten how positively psychological and psychiatric opinions re-

garded the imaginative faculty. As Dr. John Gregory put it, "the pleasures of the imagination [are] peculiar to the human species,"[33] or
(taking the view from across the Atlantic) in Dr. Benjamin Rush's
words,

> The Imagination is a Source of immense delight. Its pleasures have been
> celebrated in verse by Dr. Akenside, and in prose by Mr. Addison.
> Creation is the business of this faculty.[34]

Regarded another way, it was deficit of imagination that was a form of
disease: that was idiotism.[35]

The point is not that the psychology of the Georgians devalued the
creative imagination and therefore distrusted the mad poet (it didn't);
but that by viewing imagination as a universal faculty, vital to all
cognition, it made the poet seem normal. Or, put another way, the
Georgians denied that the mark of the poet lay in imaginative fire alone.
As the psychiatric physician John Conolly expressed it at the very end of
the Georgian age:

> No error can be more unjust towards the whole race of poets, than to
> suppose them to be persons merely distinguished by imagination. It was
> either Steele or Addison, who, in reply to a correspondent who desired
> to know what was necessary to a man in order to become a great poet,
> replied, "that he should be a very accomplished gentleman;" and the
> answer, if properly understood, is no less true than it is witty and brief.
> With the active imagination indispensable to the poet, is conjoined a
> most vigilant attention, great readiness of comparison, chiefly of re-
> semblances,—a memory most retentive; and a judgement highly correct,
> and even fastidious.[36]

If, however, in the eyes of post-Lockian psychology, the poet was
normal, the madman wasn't. This could be because the madman lacked
"judgment" (that faculty vital both to Locke's theory of cognition and to
Augustan poetics); indeed Dr. John Monro, physician to Bedlam,
deemed "vitiated judgement" the stigma of the insane.[37] Alternatively,
it could be because the lunatic suffered from "deluded imagination,"
which Monro's rival, William Battie, physician to St. Luke's Asylum,
deemed "not only an indisputable but essential character of madness."[38] The notion of deluded imagination flowed of course from
Locke's doctrine of the (mis)association of ideas. The distempered

imagination characteristically suffered from hyperactivity. As Thomas Arnold, Lockian psychiatrist and madhouse keeper, put it:

> The imagination is too active when it is for ever busily employed; is led by the slightest associations to pass with facility from one object to another; is disposed to arrange and connect, by such slight associations, the most dissimilar, and incongruous; and to ramble with rapidity through an endless variety: or dwells incessantly upon the lively, and indelible impression, of some one object of passion.[39]

Galloping imagination was, viewed another way, the mark of the failure of the powers of attention or control. For Dr. Alexander Crichton, the influential psychiatric theorist writing at the close of the eighteenth century, imagination might be either voluntary or involuntary.[40] Voluntary imagination (i.e., restrained by will) begets ideas and art: involuntary imagination collapses into madness. Similarly, John Conolly a generation later described how imagination generated associations of ideas:

> But so long as the association of ideas is not beyond our power of suspension and revision, we are not mad: . . . When the association of ideas is so involuntary, so imperative and uncontrollable, that we cannot command it, cannot revise and correct it, . . . then we have lost our reason; then the faculty of imagination is in morbid excess, the power of attention is impaired, and comparison being no longer exercised, we are mad concerning that particular association of ideas. (pp. 154–55)[41]

Such views were of course no mere esoteric psychiatric speculations, but were the common coin of educated opinion. Thus, alarmed by his own "vain imaginations" and fearing a descent into insanity, Dr. Johnson confided to his journal in 1772:

> I had formerly great command of my attention, and what I did not like could forbear to think. But of this power which is the highest importance to the tranquillity of life, I have for some time past so much exhausted.[42]

And, revealingly, Swift himself had seen the divide between the voluntary and involuntary activity of the imagination as the acid test both of poetry and sanity. He endorsed the view that

> the difference betwixt a mad-man and one in his wits, in what related to speech, consisted in this: That the former spoke out whatever came into

his mind, and just in the confused manner as his imagination presented the ideas. The latter only expressed such thoughts as his judgment directed him to chuse, leaving the rest to die away in his memory. And that if the wisest man would at any time utter his thoughts, in the crude indigested manner as they came into his head, he would be looked upon as raving mad.

This notion that madness lies in exercising no mental censorship at all was then applied by Swift as a touchstone for distinguishing good from bad verse. "I waked at two this morning," he wrote playfully,

> with the two above lines in my head, which I had made in my sleep, and I wrote them down in the dark lest I should forget them. But as the original words being writ in the dark, may possibly be mistaken by a careless or unskilful transcriber, I shall give a fairer copy, that two such precious lines may not be lost to posterity.

What are these lines?

> I walk before no man, a hawk in his fist,
> Nor am I a brilliant, whenever I list.[43]

Swift's point of course was that the couplet was utterly meaningless.

My argument—necessarily highly schematized—has been that amongst Georgian philosophers, psychiatrists, poets, and men of letters, opinion converged to disengage true poetry from madness. Their characterizations of the essence of genius bear this out. Renaissance humanism had often endorsed the Aristotelian notion of melancholy genius: and, mutatis mutandis, the fin-de-siècle decadent and degenerationist movements were much later to diagnose the genius as insane. But Enlightenment outlooks argued otherwise, stressing the healthiness of genius. Admittedly, such proponents of the "English malady" as Dr. George Cheyne saw the bright and brilliant as suffering worst from the diseases of civilization;[44] but Cheyne wasn't talking about insanity, or even about Aristotelian melancholy, and he stressed the essential healthiness of geniuses such as Isaac Newton.

What is crucial about eighteenth-century discussions is their refusal to identify genius with mere force of imagination. As Thomas Arnold put it, "too great imagination is entirely distinct from genius," for "genius cannot exist in any eminent degree without judgement; and judgement is the power of regulating the activity of imagination" (pp.

265–66). Hence, concluded Arnold, it would be foolish to equate genius and madness; for it was "men of little genius and weak judgement" who were "peculiarly liable to every species of notional insanity" (p. 83), a view later endorsed by John Conolly in contending that "there is much popular error entertained concerning the connexion of talent with madness" (p. 129).

Georgian medical psychology thus held genius in esteem, but believed the hallmark of true genius was to be balanced and sane. Poetics and aesthetics took a similar line. William Sharpe's *A Dissertation upon Genius* (1755), Edward Young's *Conjectures on Original Composition* (1759), and Alexander Gerard's *An Essay upon Genius* (1774) all stressed the value of originality, but viewed literary creation essentially as an outpouring of the original healthy psyche, by analogy with the natural generative growth of the vegetable kingdom.[45] Thus the claims of the mind to possess a plastic power of creation could be advanced while shunning the demonic, the dangerous, or the morbid. Gerard for instance explicitly protected the vegetative genius capable of true "soul" and sublimity from allegations of mere irrationality:

> A perfect judgement is seldom bestowed by Nature, even on her most favoured sons; but a very considerable degree of it always belongs to real genius . . . Pindar is judicious even in his irregularities. The boldness of his fancy, if it had been under no control from reason, would have produced, not wild sublimity, but madness and frenzy.[46]

And it is worth remembering that the Georgian formulation of genius as healthy was largely adopted by the romantics. Romanticism doubtless had its morbid tendencies—Byron and his satanism, Keats being half in love with easeful death. But, anticipating Lionel Trilling, it trenchantly staked a claim for the artist not as psychologically flawed but as a whole—as creator, legislator, hero, god. For Blake, "art is the tree of life," a far cry from the fin-de-siècle decadent vision of art and life as mortal enemies. When Charles Lamb proclaimed "the sanity of true genius," he was swimming with the romantic tide.[47]

If, then, key strands in Georgian poetics, psychology, and psychiatry converged to worship the trinity of a healthy mind, a healthy body, and healthy writing, and thus dissolved the divine madness of poetic genius, what were the effects in practice? First, the mad poet or the melancholy scholar became a less conspicuous presence. Early in the seventeenth century Robert Burton had donned the mantle of the melancholy genius and produced in his *Anatomy of Melancholy* a vast self-consuming artifact acting out the paradox of the melancholy of genius.[48] No Georgian psychiatric writer played *Burton Junior* (*Tristram Shandy*, perhaps the closest equivalent, had little of Burton's morbidity, and was expressly written "against the spleen").[49] Those eighteenth-century psychiatric texts that dwell on the diseases of civilization are very different, having little to say in fact about the crazy wit who'd lost his wits. This is confirmed by a glance at the real lives of the kind of Grub Street hacks pilloried as madmen in the *Dunciad*. Many perished of neglect, poverty and drink; but the real dunces didn't sink into insanity and get locked up in asylums. Kit Smart was confined not because he was a zany poet but because of his religious zeal, his ceaseless urge to pray in public.

The fading presence of the mad poet is confirmed by the portrait of the madhouse in Georgian novels. From Smollett's *Sir Launcelot Greaves* to Mary Wollstonecraft's *Maria, or the Wrongs of Woman*, Thomas Holcroft's *Anna St. Ives*, and the Gothic craze, the madhouse bears a weighty symbolic load; yet with the exception of Smollett's Dick Distich, the mad wit, poet, or scholar is absent from their pages. Indeed, largely because madhouse scenes usually focus upon a *sane* hero or heroine wrongfully confined, these novelists made little attempt to capture the idiom of the insane or probe their minds. Where is the English equivalent of Gogol's *Diary of a Madman*? Moreover, there arose no cult of the mad novelist stepping into the shoes of the mad poet.

If that was the image of fictional asylums, what was true of the real ones? Faulty records prevent us from knowing how many mad poets the asylums housed or how many of the insane broke into verse. But those madhouse keepers who published case studies give us a clue. Works such as William Perfect's *Select Cases* or John Haslam's *Observations on Insanity* show that mad versifiers were not totally absent from the asylums. Perfect reported a "woman of great vivacity of imagination [who] would very often express herself in well adapted metre," blessed with a "wonderful facility at finding out rhymes";[50] and one of the Bedlamites Haslam portrayed was a schoolmaster who thought himself Anacreon.[51] But these were the only instances of the type in two lengthy books of case notes; the madman turned poet had become a rare species compared with mad saviors, politicians, lovers, bishops, monarchs, and so forth.

What then of the famous mad poets themselves?[52] I have suggested that the role of the mad poet or wit, railer or jester was once, within a humanist tradition, highly eligible. James Carkesse enacted, even while repudiating, the part of the mad poet. Similarly, his contemporary George Trosse positively embraced the role of the madman possessed by the Devil. In his spiritual autobiography Trosse described how the Devil had made him mad, yet his madness had proved a constructive experience, purging him, and through tribulation leading him to God. Thus madness had proved valuable in and integral to his religious awakening.[53] By contrast, later authors more commonly presented their experiences of madness in negative tones. For William Cowper madness was pure terror; its recurrences, actual and anticipated, were omens of the eternal perdition facing him, a doom not a dawn.[54] Samuel Johnson dreaded the prospect of impending mental collapse in the same light.[55]

It should also be stressed that several confined lunatics, such as Alexander Cruden and Samuel Bruckshaw, did not aim in their auto-biographical writings to capitalize on the license the conceit of madness might have offered them, but vociferously denied their derangement point-blank.[56] Analysis of Cruden's and Bruckshaw's strident self-vindications might well convince today's psychiatrists that they did protest their sanity too much. My point, however, is that such men did not see the mask of insanity to be in any way eligible. Desperate defense of sanity was preferable to the license of lunacy.

The same applies to the clutch of eminent Georgian mad poets themselves. Few wrote verse *in persona poetae*, or drew on a link between divine madness and poetic flame. William Collins probably declined into chronic depression precisely because of anxiety that his poetic flow had dried up.[57] For him, mental disturbance generated not poetic expression but silence. Similarly, William Cowper took to verse not as an outpouring of divine madness but to distract himself from morbid introspection (in G. K. Chesterton's apt phrase, for Cowper poetry was medicine not disease: damned by John Calvin, he was almost saved by

John Gilpin). It is thus savagely ironic that Blake should have cast Cowper in the role of the mad poet, recording a vision in which

Cowper came to me and said: "O that I were insane always. I will never rest. Can you not make me truly insane? . . . You retain health and yet are as mad as any of us all—over us all—mad as a refuge from unbelief—from Bacon, Newton and Locke."[58]

Surely that is the last thing that the tormented Cowper would ever have wished.

I do not wish to overstate my point. There were exceptions. Kit Smart did indeed write his greatest poem, *Jubilate agno*, while in an asylum, and it is clear that for Smart, mental eccentricity—an impulsion to praise God ceaselessly—provided the inspiration, form, and content for his verse, and "mad verse" provided the right medium within which he —like Blake later—could express his distance from such fashionable gods of his age as polite society and popular Newtonianism.[59]

Many features of *Jubilate agno* have long been identified as symptomatic of a peculiar mind—its fascination with puns, word play, alphabetic letters, sheer sound, and its remorselessly reiterative form. What has been understood only more recently is the immense poetic craft Smart exercised over his work (no mere mad effusion) and how far its form, such as the antiphonal structure of the answering "Let" and "For" verses, sought to recapture the poetics of the Old Testament as recently analyzed by Robert Lowth.[60]

Smart and Blake aside, it remains true that few mad poets saw their mental condition as a source of poetic strength or status. The verse John Clare wrote while in High Beech Asylum expressed the deepest loss, both personal and poetic.[61] Or take the little-known volume of verse written by the Bedlamite Arthur Pearce, and published by John Perceval in 1851. Pearce's poems don't directly address the dilemma of his own mental alienation, and certainly don't claim that madness has filled him with inspiration. Quite the reverse. He explicitly apologized that he could offer only "humble jangling verse," because the "hubbub and dingdong" of Bedlam served to "scare away all the Muses of Parnassus."[62]

For Georgians such as Cowper and Johnson, writing was prophylactic against madness rather than the refined expression of it, and the poetic effusions of the mad came to be seen not as art but as nonsense. In part these attitudes spelt out a commonsense precautionary fear of inflaming fevered brains. Thus Samuel Johnson insisted that the melancholic must "divert distressing thoughts":

> Let him take a course of chymistry, or a course in rope-dancing, or a course of anything to which he is inclined at the time. Let him contrive to have as many retreats for his mind as he can, as many things to which it can fly from itself.

As he lectured Boswell, who certainly toyed with the siren of melancholy:

> make it an invariable and obligatory law to yourself, never to mention your own mental diseases; if you are never to speak of them you will think on them little, and if you think little of them, they will molest you rarely.[63]

In part such attitudes reflected the deep-seated psychiatric dictum that psychic disorder was fundamentally somatic in source. From this it would follow that the voices of the mad were not relations of authentic higher levels of consciousness but expressions of pain. In this vein, the early-eighteenth-century Newtonian physician Dr. Nicholas Robinson claimed that the Huguenot exiles, the French prophets, were not divinely inspired but merely subject to "strong convulsive fits," and that the spoutings of Quakers and sectaries such as James Nayler, George Fox, and Lodowick Muggleton were "nothing but the effect of mere madness, and arose from the stronger impulses of a warm brain."[64]

This in turn left Georgian psychiatry extraordinarily—one might say willfully—deaf to the messages coded in the stories of the mad. Take Dr. Robinson again. Discussing cases of the spleen, he reported:

> It is not long ago since a very learned and ingenious Gentleman, so far started from his Reason, as to believe, that his Body was metamorphos'd into a Hobby-Horse, and nothing would serve his Turn, but that his Friend, who came to see him, must mount his Back and ride. I must confess, that all the philosophy I was Master of, could not dispossess him of this Conceit; 'till by application of generous Medicines, I restor'd the disconcerted nerves to their regular Motions, and, by that Means, gave him a Sight of his Error. (p. 191)

Thus the answer was medicine not meanings. This failure of hermeneutics marks a turning point in the transactions between the disturbed and their physicians. Michael MacDonald has shown that the spoken word, and in particular, dialogue, had been important in the therapeutics of the early-seventeenth-century doctor Richard Napier, extending even to formal means such as exorcism.[65] Such communicative practices certainly lasted into the eighteenth century. As Dr. George Baglivi stressed:

> I can scarce express what influence the Physician's Words have upon the patient's Life, and how much they sway the Fancy; for a Physician that has his Tongue well hung, and is master of the Art of Persuading, fastens, by the mere Force of Words, such a Vertue upon his Remedies, and raises the Faith and Hopes of the patient to that pitch, that sometimes he masters difficult Diseases with the silliest Remedies.[66]

His contemporary, Timothy Rogers, thought the best remedies for melancholy lay in soothing talk,[67] and the physician Bernard Mandeville offered a practical demonstration in his *Treatise of the Hypochondriack and Hysterick Passions*, through his literary use of the dialogue form, of how the doctor, by arousing interest and creating distractions, could heal the hypochondriac without medicine.[68]

Yet these techniques fell into disfavor or disuse. And particularly with the rise of the asylum, traditional modes of the talking cure gave way to cure by silence or therapeutic noncommunication.[69] At his private asylum William Perfect, for example, claimed his favored technique was to keep patients in individual cells, far from the madding crowd of relatives, friends, and other lunatics. Through depleting medicines, he would exhaust the babel of their thoughts. Of one patient he wrote: "I never suffered him to be spoken with"; as a result, he recovered so as to speak "rationally and just" (p. 45).

Silence and suppression were not the marks of cruel, benighted asylum practice but prized features of the enlightened, progressive, and apparently successful strand of "moral therapy." At the York Retreat (an asylum unique to the ears of visitors for its peace and quiet), it was policy to refuse to enter into dialogue with the delusions of the patients, but instead to distract the distracted. As its spokesman, Samuel Tuke, put it:

In regard to melancholics, conversation on the subject of their despondency, is found to be highly injudicious. The very opposite method is pursued. Every means is taken to seduce the mind from its favourite but unhappy musings, by bodily exercise, walks, conversation, reading and other innocent recreations.[70]

Earlier traditions had viewed the voices of the mad as important, often dangerous (as with demonic possession), perhaps revelatory (as with the mad prophet or poet). But those traditions were undercut and outmoded as a result of a concert of various pressures and preferences, as I have argued specifically in the case of the mad poet. The resulting decline of dialogue between society and psychiatrist on the one hand, and the disturbed on the other (increasingly "shut up" in both senses), could however, have deeply distressing, even disastrous, consequences for the sufferers. John Perceval was a patient in the 1830s in liberal asylums such as Brislington and Ticehurst under the enlightened moral therapy regimes of physicians such as Edward Long Fox. Nevertheless he felt himself silenced into annihilation, treated "as if I were a piece of furniture, an image of wood, incapable of desire or will as well as judgement."

It was not likely, therefore, that I should confide the difficulties of my mind to men who, by slighting the origin of them, betrayed their presumption, whilst affecting excellent acuteness.

Thus a kind of folie à deux was generated, in which, as Perceval saw it, physician and patient mutually refused to communicate with each other. As Perceval put it:

I was not, however, once addressed by argument, expostulation, or persuasion. The persons round me consulted, directed, chose, ordered, and force was the unica and ultima ratio applied to me. If I were insane, in my resolution to be silent, because I was sure that neither of the doctors, or of my friends, would understand my motives, or give credit to facts they had not themselves experienced; they were surely no less insane, who because of my silence, forgot the use of their own tongues.[71]

Thus by the Early Victorian age the psychiatric environment had sealed the alienation of language and lunacy.

To draw the threads together, I have been arguing that Christian prophecy, Platonic divine fury, and Aristotelian melancholy genius could traditionally interweave to give the voice of madness great potency. To play the mad poet was a prerogative, if it also proved a cage. This tradition underwent transformation during the eighteenth century. Voices from beyond became too disturbing, too subversive. As insanity increasingly became stigmatized, poets themselves severed their connection with madness, and psychiatry came to deny that the words of the mad had any meaning. To understand these shifts we will need to cast our gaze outward, to a wider social history, which will explore the impact of the demystification of the world and the rise of a hegemonic rational culture of the propertied and the polite.

Notes

1. Quoted in T. Szasz, *The Therapeutic State* (New York, 1984), p. 158.
2. J. F. Nisbet, *The Insanity of Genius* (London, 1900), chap. 4. For "degenerationist" psychiatry and art see Max Nordau, *Degeneration* (New York, 1895); C. Lombroso, *The Man of Genius* (London, 1891); E. Kretschmer, *The Psychology of Men of Genius* (College Park, Md., 1970); W. R. Bett, *The Infirmities of Genius* (London, 1952); T. B. Hyslop, *The Great Abnormals* (London, 1925).
3. *Betsy Sheridan's Journal*, ed. W. Lefanu (London, 1960), pp. 130 ff.
4. See above all R. R. Reed, *Bedlam on the Jacobean Stage* (Cambridge, Mass., 1952).
5. Ned Ward, *The London Spy* (London, 1955), p. 48.
6. See S. Billington, *A Social History of the Fool* (Brighton, 1984), chaps. 3 and 4.
7. H. Mackenzie, *The Man of Feeling* (Oxford, 1970), p. 34.
8. S. Gilman, *Seeing the Insane* (Chichester, 1982).
9. S. Trombley, *"All That Summer She Was Mad": Virginia Woolf and her Doctors* (London, 1981). For autobiographical constructs see P. M. Spacks, *Imagining a Self* (Cambridge, Mass., 1972).
10. For these seventeenth-century perceptions see M. MacDonald, *Mystical Bedlam* (Cambridge, 1981), esp. pp. 116–18 and 279.
11. For Renaissance concepts of genius and melancholy see R. Klibansky, E. Panofsky, and F. Saxl, *Saturn and Melancholy* (London, 1964); G. Tonelli, "Genius: From the Renaissance to 1770," in P. Wiener, ed., *Dictionary of the History of Ideas* (New York, 1973), 2:293–97; M. A. Screech, *Ecstasy and the Praise of Folly* (London, 1980); R. S. Kinsman, "Folly, Melancholy, and Madness: A Study in Shifting Styles of Medical Analysis and Treatment, 1450–1675," in Kinsman, ed., *The Darker Vision of the Renaissance* (Berkeley and London, 1974), pp. 273–320; R. Wittkower and M. Wittkower, *Born under Saturn* (London, 1963); B. G. Lyons, *Voices of Melancholy* (London, 1971).
12. See Billington, *Social History of the Fool*, and E. Welsford, *The Fool* (London, 1935).

13. Quoted in Reed, *Bedlam on the Jacobean Stage*, p. 23. See also Max Byrd, *Visits to Bedlam: Madness and Literature in the Eighteenth Century* (Columbia, S.C., 1974); E. G. O'Donoghue, *The Story of Bethlehem Hospital* (London, 1914); A. Masters, *Bedlam* (London, 1977).

14. R. C. Ham, *Otway and Lee* (New Haven, 1931).

15. J. Lindsay, *Loving Mad Tom: Bedlamite Verses of the Sixteenth and Seventeenth Centuries* (1927; rpt. New York, 1970).

16. M. Screech, *Montaigne and Melancholy* (London, 1983), pp. 37 ff.

17. J. Carkesse, *Lucida Intervalla* (London, 1679); reprinted with an introduction by M. V. De Porte by the Augustan Reprint Society (Los Angeles, 1979).

18. W. Kaiser, *Praisers of Folly* (London, 1964).

19. For recent discussions of the ambivalence of Burton, see Roy Porter, "Anglicanism and Psychiatry: Robert Burton and Sir Thomas Browne," to appear in S. Narasimhan, *Essays for Enid Welsford* (Cambridge, Eng., 1987).

20. R. Burton, *The Anatomy of Melancholy*, ed. F. Dell and P. Jordan Smith (New York, 1927), p. 101.

21. Of course, the "world-turned-upside-down" genre of Bedlamite literature continued in the eighteenth century. See, for example, *The enthusiastic infidel detected, being the trial of a moral philosopher before the Grand Senate of Bedlam on a statute of lunacy . . . by a brother lunatic* (London, 1743). There was also a genre of verse about lunatics written by the sane poets. See, for example, Hildebrand Jacob, "Bedlam," *Works* (London, 1735), pp. 11–25.

22. For a taste of the analyses of this topic, see M. V. De Porte, "Digressions and Madness in *A Tale of a Tub* and *Tristram Shandy*," *Huntingdon Library Quarterly* 34 (1970): 43–57; R. Paulson, *Theme and Structure in Swift's "Tale of a Tub"* (New Haven, 1960); J. R. Clark, *Form and Frenzy in Swift's "Tale of a Tub"* (Ithaca, 1970); D. B. Morris, "The Kinship of Madness in Pope's *Dunciad*," *Philological Quarterly* 51 (1972): 813–31; G. Rosen, "Forms of Irrationality in the Eighteenth Century," in H. E. Pagliaro, ed., *Studies in Eighteenth Century Culture* (Cleveland, 1972), pp. 255–88.

23. *The Poems of Alexander Pope*, ed. J. Butt (London, 1963), p. 744.

24. Jonathan Swift, *A Tale of a Tub and Other Satires*, ed. K. Williams (London, 1975), p. 133. For the art of writing nonsense, see R. Steele, *Periodical Journalism* (Oxford, 1959), pp. 152 ff.

25. [D. Defoe], *The Consolidator; or, Means of Sundry Transactions from the World in the Moon* (London, 1705). I owe this point to Simon Schaffer. See P. Rogers, *Grub Street* (London, 1972).

26. J. Swift, "The Mechanical Operation of the Spirit," *Tale of a Tub and Other Satires*, p. 176. See also Morris, "Kinship of Madness in Pope's *Dunciad*" pp. 813–31; Paulson, *Theme and Structure in Swift's "Tale of a Tub"*; J. F. Sena, "Swift, the Yahoos, and the English Malady," *Papers in Language and Literature* 7 (1971): 300–303.

27. Alexander Pope, "Epistle to Dr. Arbuthnot," *Poems of Alexander Pope*, p. 597.

28. See, for example, B. R. Kreisler, *Miracles, Convulsions and Ecclesiastical*

Politics in Early Eighteenth Century Paris (Princeton, 1978); R. Knox, *Enthusiasm* (London, 1950); G. Rosen "Enthusiasm: 'A Dark Lanthorn of the Spirit,' " *Bulletin of the History of Medicine* 42 (1958): 393–421; G. Williamson, "The Restoration Revolt against Enthusiasm," *Studies in Philology* 30 (1933): 571–603; S. I. Tucker, *Enthusiasm: A Study in Semantic Change* (Cambridge, Eng., 1972); H. Schwartz, *Knaves, Fools, Madmen and That "Subtile Effluvium"* (Gainesville, Fla., 1978).

29. *Perceval's Narrative: A Patient's Account of his Psychosis, 1830–1832*, ed. G. Bateson (Stanford, 1961) pp. 46, 271.

30. For a discussion of this point bringing in the medical dimension, see Roy Porter, "The Doctor and the Word," *Medical Sociology News* 9 (1983): 21–28. There is a stimulating discussion in I. Couliano, *Eros et magie* (Paris, 1984).

31. On fear of imagination, see M. V. De Porte, *Nightmares and Hobbyhorses* (San Marino, Cal., 1974), p. 17, quoting Zachary Mayne: "*Imagination* is almost continually, in some Degree or other, hurtful and prejudicial to the Understanding. For let the Mind think never so closely and intently, and with the greatest Heed and Circumspection, it will frequently, unawares, bring before its View Ideas that have little or no Relation to the Subject Matter of its Thoughts and Meditations"; D. F. Bond, " 'Distrust' of Imagination in English Neoclassicism," *Philological Quarterly* 14 (1935): 54–69; idem, "The Neo-Classical Psychology of the Imagination," *ELH* 4 (1937): 245–64; S. Cunningham, "Bedlam and Parnassus: Eighteenth Century Reflections," in B. Harris, ed., *Eighteenth Century Studies* 24 (London, 1971): 36–55.

32. E. L. Tuveson, *Imagination as a Means of Grace* (Berkeley, 1960); J. Engell, *The Creative Imagination: Enlightenment to Romanticism* (Cambridge, Mass. 1981); B. Hepworth, *The Rise of Romanticism* (Manchester, 1978). For specific literary examples, see J. Addison and R. Steele, *The Spectator*, nos. 411–21, and M. Akenside, *The Pleasures of the Imagination* (London, 1741).

33. John Gregory, *A Comparative View of the State and Faculties of Man with Those of the Animal World* (Edinburgh, 1788), p. 7.

34. E. T. Carlson, J. L. Wollcock, and P. S. Noel, eds., *Benjamin Rush's Lectures on the Mind* (Philadelphia, 1981), P. 603.

35. G. Cheyne, *The English Malady* (London, 1733), p. 52. Similarly, Locke distinguished idiots from the mad: "In fine, the defect in naturals seems to proceed from want of quickness, activity, and motion in the intellectual faculties, whereby they are deprived of reason; whereas *madmen*, on the other side, seem to suffer by the other extreme. For they do not appear to me to have lost the faculty of reasoning, but having joined together some ideas very wrongly, they mistake them for truths; and they err as men do that argue right from wrong principles. For, by the violence of their imaginations, having taken their fancies for realities, they make right deductions from them. Thus you shall find a distracted man fancying himself a king, with a right inference require suitable attendance, respect, and obedience: others who have thought themselves made of glass, have used the caution necessary to preserve such brittle bodies. Hence it comes to pass that a man who is very sober, and of a right understanding in all

other things, may in one particular be as frantic as any in *Bedlam*. . . . In short, herein seems to lie the difference between idiots and madmen: that madmen put wrong ideas together, and so make wrong propositions, but argue and reason right from them; but idiots make very few or no propositions, and reason scarce at all." *An Essay concerning Human Understanding*, ed. J. Yolton (London, 1961), book 2, chap. 101, p. 127.

36. J. Conolly, *Indications of Insanity* (London, 1830), pp. 148–49.

37. R. Hunter and I. Macalpine, eds., *A Treatise on Madness by William Battie and Remarks on Dr. Battie's Treatise by John Monro* (London, 1962), p. 4.

38. Ibid., pp. 61–62.

39. T. Arnold, *Observation on the Nature, Kinds, Causes and Prevention of Insanity*, 2 vols. (London, 1806), 2:83.

40. A. Crichton, *An Inquiry into the Nature and Origin of Mental Derangement*, 2 vols. (London, 1778), 1:5 ff.

41. See also R. Hoeldtke, "The History of Associationism and British Medical Psychology," *Medical History* 11 (1967): 46–65; M. H. Abrams, *The Mirror and the Lamp* (New York, 1953); idem, *Natural Supernaturalism* (London, 1971); G. S. Rousseau, "Science and the Discovery of the Imagination in Enlightened England," *Eighteenth Century Studies* 3 (1960–70): 108–35; P. M. Spacks, *The Insistence of Horror* (Cambridge, Mass., 1962); N. Powell, *Fuseli: The Nightmare* (London, 1973); G. S. Rousseau, "Science," in P. Rogers, ed., *The Context of English Literature: The Eighteenth Century* (London, 1978), pp. 153–207; M. Kallich, *The Association of Ideas and Critical Theory in Eighteenth Century England* (The Hague, 1970).

42. For extensive discussion, see Roy Porter, "The Hunger of Imagination: Approaching Samuel Johnson's Melancholy," in W. F. Bynum, R. Porter, and M. Shepherd, eds. *The Anatomy of Madness*, 2 vols. (London, 1985), 1:63–88.

43. Quoted in M. V. De Porte, *Nightmares and Hobbyhorses*, p. 67.

44. For the literature, see Roy Porter, "The Rage of Party: A Glorious Revolution in English Psychiatry?" *Medical History* 37 (1983): 35–50.

45. For discussions of genius and creativity, see G. Becker, *The Mad Genius Controversy* (Beverly Hills, 1978); N. Willard, *Le génie et la folie* (Paris, 1963); M. Butler, *Romantics, Rebels and Reactionaries* (London, 1981); H. M. Jones, *Revolution and Romanticism* (Cambridge, Mass, 1974). For a contemporary adumbration, see "On Genius and Common Sense" in W. Hazlitt, *Table Talk* (London, 1936), pp. 31–50. See also P. E. Vernon, ed., *Creativity* (Harmondsworth, 1970); A. Rothenberg, *The Emergent Goddess* (Chicago and London, 1979); M. A. Coles, ed., *Essays on Creativity in the Sciences* (New York, 1963); B. Ghiselin, ed., *The Creative Process* (Berkeley, 1954).

46. Quoted in Becker, *Mad Genius Controversy*, p. 26.

47. See C. Lamb, "The Sanity of True Genius," *The Last Essays of Elia*, ed. G. E. Hollingsworth (London, n.d.), p. 46: "So far from the position holding true, that great wit (or genius, in our modern way of speaking) has a necessary alliance with insanity, the greatest wits, on the contrary, will ever be found to be the sanest writers. It is impossible for the mind to conceive a mad Shakespeare. The

greatness of wit, by which the poetic talent is here chiefly to be understood, manifests itself in the admirable balance of all the faculties." Lamb's view is echoed by the romantic physician Thomas Beddoes, who asked, "Why have so few great poets run mad?" *Hygeia*, 3 vols. (Bristol, 1802–3), 3: 85. See p. 51: "The imagination of the poets is content with personifying inanimate objects. That of lunatics frequently goes a great deal further, and strips them of their own personality. It would not be believed, were it not so perpetually experienced, that a human being could come to conceive himself made of butter; or that his legs were of straw; or that he was a barley-corn. The fact proves the force of imagination; and perhaps may be in some measure explained. An invalid of great brilliancy of parts once said to me, that but for a particular expectation, 'he would as soon be a nettle in a country church-yard.'" For French decadents see R. Williams, *The Horror of Life* (London, 1980); J. Pierrot, *The Decadent Imagination* (Chicago, 1982).

48. Burton, *Anatomy of Melancholy*; S. Fish, *Self-Consuming Artifacts* (Berkeley, 1972).

49. See Roy Porter, "Against the Spleen," in V. Grosvenor Myer, ed., *Laurence Sterne: Riddles and Mysteries* (London, 1984), pp. 84–98.

50. William Perfect, *Select Cases in the Different Species of Insanity* (Rochester, 1787), p. 63.

51. J. Haslam, *Observations on Insanity* (London, 1808), p. 145.

52. For some introduction to the writings of mad people in general and mad poets in particular in eighteenth-century England see D. Peterson, ed., *A Mad People's History of Madness* (Pittsburgh, 1982); M. MacDonald, "Insanity and the Realities of History in Early Modern England," *Psychological Medicine* (1981): 11–25; Roy Porter, "Being Mad in Georgian England," *History Today* (December 1981), pp. 42–48; A. Cruden, *The London Citizen Exceedingly Injured* (London, 1739); idem, *The Adventures of Alexander the Corrector* (London, 1754); E. Oliver, *The Eccentric Life of Alexander Cruden* (London, 1934); A. Sherbo, *Christopher Smart* (Ann Arbor, 1967); William Cowper, *Memoir of the Early Life of William Cowper* (London, 1816); M. J. Quinlan, *William Cowper* (Minneapolis, 1953); M. Golden, *In Search of Stability: The Poetry of William Cowper* (New Haven, 1969); C. Ryskamp, *William Cowper of the Inner Temple, Esq.* (Cambridge, Eng., 1959); *Perceval's Narrative*. For some related suggestive analysis see H. M. Feinstein, "The Prepared Heart: A Comparative Study of Puritan Theology and Psychoanalysis," *American Quarterly* 22 (1970): 166–76; F. Baker, " 'Mad Grimshaw' and His Covenants with God: A Study in Eighteenth Century Psychology," *London Quarterly and Holborn Review* 82 (1958): 211–15, 271–78.

53. G. Trosse, *The Life of the Reverend Mr. George Trosse* (London, 1714), discussed in Peterson, *Mad People's History of Madness*, pp 26–27.

54. Cowper, *Memoir of the Early Life of William Cowper, Esq., written by himself, and never before published, with an appendix, containing some of Cowper's religious letters, and other documents, illustrative of the memoir* (London, 1816). See also Quinlan, *William Cowper*; Golden, *In Search of Stability*; and Ryskamp, *William Cowper of the Inner Temple*.

55. See Porter, "Hunger of Imagination."

56. See the discussions in Peterson, *Mad People's History of Madness*, pp. 39–64, and Samuel Bruckshaw, *One More Proof of the Iniquitous Abuse of Private madhouses* (London: The author, 1774). See also William Belcher, *Address to Humanity: Containing a Letter to Dr. Thomas Monro; a receipt to make a lunatic, and seize his estate; and a sketch of a true smiling hyena* (London, 1796).

57. W. Ober, "Madness and Poetry: A Note to Collins, Cowper and Smart," *Boswell's Clap and Other Essays* (Carbondale, Ill., 1979), pp. 137–92.

58. *Complete Writings of William Blake*, ed. G. Keynes (Oxford, 1972), p. 772.

59. Sherbo, *Christopher Smart*.

60. See the discussion in L. Feder, *Madness in Literature* (Princeton, 1980), pp. 192 ff., and K. Williamson, Introduction, *The Poetical Works of Christopher Smart*, Vol. 1 (Oxford, 1980), pp. xv–xxx.

61. See *John Clare's Autobiographical Writings*, ed. E. Robinson (Oxford, 1983); M. Storey, *The Poetry of John Clare: A Critical Introduction* (London, 1974).

62. *Poems by a Prisoner in Bethlehem*, ed. John Perceval (London, 1851), pp. 7, 42.

63. See the discussion in A. Ingram, *Boswell's Creative Gloom* (London, 1982), pp. 144 ff.

64. N. Robinson, *A New System of the Spleen* (London, 1729), pp. 247, 250. Cf. Cheyne, *English Malady*, pp. 123–24: "There is a kind of melancholy, which is called religious, because it is conversant about matters of religion, although often the persons so distempered have little solid piety. And this is merely a bodily disease, produced by an ill habit or constitution."

65. MacDonald, *Mystical Bedlam*, 9–10.

66. G. Baglivi, *The Practice of Physick* (London, 1723), p. 47.

67. Timothy Rogers, *A Discourse Concerning Trouble of Mind* (London, 1691).

68. B. Mandeville, *A Treatise of the Hypochondriack and Hysterick Diseases* (London, 1730). For patient/doctor contact see Roy Porter, ed., *Patients and Practitioners: Lay Perceptions of Medicine in Preindustrial Society* (Cambridge, Eng., 1985).

69. See Roy Porter, "In the Eighteenth Century, Were English Lunatic Asylums Total Institutions?" *Ego: Bulletin of the Department of Psychiatry, Guy's Hospital* (Spring 1983), pp. 12–34.

70. S. Tuke, *A Description of the Retreat at York* (York, 1813), p. 151.

71. *Perceval's Narrative*, pp. 122, 121.

Part V

Feminist Critiques of Science

ANNE K. MELLOR

Frankenstein:
A Feminist Critique of Science

From a feminist perspective, the most significant dimension of the relationship between literature and science is the degree to which both enterprises are grounded on the use of metaphor and image. The explanatory models of science, like the plots of literary works, depend on linguistic structures which are shaped by metaphor and metonymy. The feminist reader is perhaps most sensitized to those symbolic structures which employ gender as a major variable or value. When Francis Bacon announced, "I am come in very truth leading to you Nature with all her children to bind her to your service and make her your slave,"[1] he identified the pursuit of modern science with a form of sexual politics: the aggressive, virile male scientist legitimately captures and enslaves a passive, fertile female nature. Mary Shelley was one of the first to comprehend and illustrate the dangers inherent in the use of sexist metaphors in the seventeenth-century scientific revolution.

Mary Shelley grounded her fiction of the scientist who creates a monster he can't control upon an extensive understanding of the most recent scientific developments of her day. More important, she used this knowledge both to analyze and to criticize the more dangerous implications of both the scientific method and its practical results. Implicitly, she contrasted what she considered "good" science—the detailed and reverent description of the workings of nature—to "bad" science, the hubristic manipulation of the forces of nature to serve man's private ends. In *Frankenstein, or the Modern Prometheus,* she illustrated the potential evils of scientific hubris and at the same time challenged any conception of science and the scientific method that rested on a gendered definition of nature as female. Fully to appreciate the significance of Mary Shelley's feminist critique of modern science, we must look first at the particular scientific research upon which her novel is based.

I

The works of three of the most famous scientists of the late eighteenth and early nineteenth century—Humphry Davy, Erasmus Darwin, and Luigi Galvani—together with the teachings of two of their ardent disciples, Adam Walker and Percy Shelley, were crucial to Mary Shelley's understanding of science and the scientific enterprise. While no scientist herself (her description of Victor Frankenstein's laboratory is both vague and naive; apparently Victor does all his experiments in a small attic room by the light of a single candle), Mary Shelley nonetheless had a sound grasp of the concepts and implications of some of the most important scientific work of her day. In her novel, she distinguishes between those scientific researches which attempt to describe accurately the functionings of the physical universe and those which attempt to *control* or *change* that universe through human intervention. Implicitly, she celebrates the former, which she associates most closely with the work of Erasmus Darwin, while she calls attention to the dangers inherent in the latter, found in the work of Davy, Galvani, and Walker.

Victor Frankenstein chooses to work within the newly established field of chemical physiology; thus, he must be familiar with recent experiments in the disparate fields of biology, chemistry, mechanics, physics, and medicine. M. Waldman, Victor's chemistry professor at the University of Ingolstadt, observes that "a man would make but a very sorry chemist, if he attended to that department of human knowledge alone," and therefore advises Victor "to apply to every branch of natural philosophy, including mathematics."[2]

Victor and Professor Waldman's concept of the nature and utility of chemistry is based upon Humphry Davy's famous introductory lecture to a course in chemistry given at the newly founded Royal Institution on 21 January 1802.[3] Immediately published as *A Discourse, Introductory to a Course of Lectures on Chemistry*, this pamphlet is probably the work that Mary Shelley read on Monday, 28 October 1816, just before working on her story of Frankenstein.[4] Waldman's enthusiasm for and description of the benefits to be derived from the study of chemistry seem to be derived from Davy's remarks, as does Victor Frankenstein's belief that chemistry might discover the secret of life itself.

Davy probably also supplied Mary Shelley's description of the first parts of Professor Waldman's introductory lecture on chemistry—the opening "recapitulation of the history of chemistry and the various improvements made by different men of learning," followed by "a cursory view of the present state of the sciences," an explanation of several key terms and a few preparatory experiments (*F,* p. 42)—which come not so much from Davy's *Discourse* as from his later textbook, *Elements of Chemical Philosophy* (London, 1812), which Percy Shelley ordered from Thomas Hookham on 29 July 1812.[5] This may be the book listed in Mary's *Journal* on 29, 30 October, 2 and 4 November 1816, where Mary notes that she "read Davy's 'Chemistry' with Shelley" and then alone. A glance at the table of contents of this book would have given Mary Shelley the outline she attributes to Waldman: a brief history, followed by a discussion of several specific elements and compounds, with descriptions of experiments performed. The contents probably also provided her with the description of the lectures on natural philosophy that Victor Frankenstein attended in Geneva:

> Some accident prevented my attending these lectures until the course was nearly finished. The lecture being therefore one of the last was entirely incomprehensible to me. The professor discoursed with the greatest fluency of potassium and boron, of sulphates and oxyds, terms to which I could affix no idea. (*F,* p. 36)

Davy's *Discourse,* written to attract and keep a large audience, provided Mary Shelley with both the content and the rhetoric of Waldman's final panegyric on modern chemistry, which directly inspired Victor Frankenstein's subsequent research. Waldman concludes,

> The ancient teachers of this science . . . promised impossibilities, and performed nothing. The modern masters promise very little; they know that metals cannot be transmuted, and that the elixir of life is a chimera. But these philosophers, whose hands seem only made to dabble in dirt, and their eyes to pore over the microscope or crucible, have indeed performed miracles. They penetrate into the recesses of nature, and shew how she works in her hiding places. They ascend into the heavens;

they have discovered how the blood circulates, and the nature of the air we breathe. They have acquired new and almost unlimited powers; they can command the thunders of heaven, mimic the earthquake, and even mock the invisible world with its own shadows. (*F*, p. 42)

Davy, in his celebration of the powers of chemistry, asserted that "the phenomena of combustion, of the solution of different substances in water, of the agencies of fire, the production of rain, hail, and snow, and the conversion of dead matter into living matter by vegetable organs, all belong to chemistry."[6] Arguing that chemistry is the basis of many other sciences, including mechanics, natural history, mineralogy, astronomy, medicine, physiology, pharmacy, botany, and zoology, Davy insists,

> How dependent, in fact, upon chemical processes are the nourishment and growth of organized beings; their various alterations of form, their constant production of new substances; and, finally, their death and decomposition, in which nature seems to take unto herself those elements and constitutent principles which, for a while, she had lent to a superior agent as the organs and instruments of the spirit of life! (*Discourse*, no. 8)

After detailing the necessity of chemical knowledge to all the operations of common life, including agriculture, metalworking, bleaching, dyeing, leather tanning, and glass and porcelain making, Davy paints an idealistic portrait of the contemporary chemist, who is informed by a science that

> has given to him an acquaintance with the different relations of the parts of the external world; and more than that, it has bestowed upon him powers which may be almost called creative; which have enabled him to modify and change the beings surrounding him, and by his experiments to interrogate nature with power, not simply as a scholar, passive and seeking only to understand her operations, but rather as a master, active with his own instruments. (*Discourse* no. 16)

Davy then sketches an even more visionary picture of the scientist of the future, who will discover the still unknown general laws of chemistry,

> for who would not be ambitious of becoming acquainted with the most profound secrets of nature; of ascertaining her hidden operations; and of exhibiting to men that system of knowledge which relates so intimately to their own physical and moral constitution? (*Discourse*, no. 17)

These are Waldman's chemists, who "penetrate into the recesses of nature, and shew how she works in her hiding places."

The result of such activity, Davy confidently predicts, will be a more harmonious, cooperative and healthy society. True, he cautions, "We do not look to distant ages, or amuse ourselves with brilliant, though delusive dreams, concerning the infinite improveability of man, the annihilation of labour, disease, and even death" (*Discourse*, no. 22). But even as Davy apparently disavows the very dream that would inspire Victor Frankenstein, he claims for his own project something very similar: "we reason by analogy from simple facts. We consider only a state of human progression arising out of its present condition. We look for a time that we may reasonably expect, for a bright day of which we already behold the dawn" (*Discourse*, no. 22). Having boldly stated the social benefits to be derived from the pursuit of chemistry, Davy concludes by insisting on the personal gratifications to be gained: "it may destroy diseases of the imagination, owing to too deep a sensibility; and it may attach the affections to objects, permanent, important, and intimately related to the interests of the human species," even as it militates against the "influence of terms connected only with feeling" and encourages instead a rational contemplation of the universal order of things (*Discourse*, no. 26).

In fairness to Davy, he was very skeptical about Victor Frankenstein's chosen field, the new field of chemical physiology. Commenting on just the kind of enterprise Frankenstein pursues, the search for the principle of life itself, Davy warns:

> if the connexion of chemistry with physiology has given rise to some visionary and seductive theories; yet even this circumstance has been useful to the public mind in exciting it by doubt, and in leading it to new investigations. A reproach, to a certain degree just, has been thrown upon those doctrines known by the name of the chemical physiology; for in the applications of them speculative philosophers have been guided rather by the analogies of words than of facts. Instead of slowly endeavouring to lift up the veil concealing the wonderful phenomena of living nature; full of ardent imaginations, they have vainly and presumptuously attempted to tear it asunder. (*Discourse*, no. 9)

Mary Shelley clearly heeded Davy's words, for she presents Victor Frankenstein as the embodiment of hubris, of that satanic or Faustian presumption which blasphemously attempts to penetrate the sacred mysteries of the universe.

But in contrast to Davy, Mary Shelley doubted whether chemistry itself—insofar as it involved a "mastery" of nature—produced only good. She substituted for Davy's complacent image of the happy scientist living in harmony with both his community and himself the frightening image of the alienated scientist working in feverish isolation, cut off both physically and emotionally from his family, friends, and society. Victor Frankenstein's scientific researches not only bring him no satisfaction; they also leave him, as Laura Crouch has observed, disgusted with the entire scientific enterprise.[7] Detached from a respect for nature and from a strong sense of personal responsibility for the products of one's research, scientific experimentation and purely objective thought can and do produce monsters. Mary Shelley might have found trenchant support for her view in Humphrey Davy's praise for one of chemistry's most notable achievements: "in leading to the discovery of gunpowder, [chemistry] has changed the institutions of society, and rendered war more independent of brutal strength, less personal, and less barbarous."[8]

In contrast to Davy, Erasmus Darwin provided Mary Shelley with a powerful image of what she considered "good" science, a careful observation and celebration of the operations of nature with no attempt radically to alter either the way nature works or the institutions of society. Percy Shelley acknowledged the impact of Erasmus Darwin's work on his wife's novel when he began the Preface to the 1818 edition of *Frankenstein* with the assertion that "the event on which this fiction is founded has been supposed, by Dr. Darwin, and some of the physiological writers of Germany, as not of impossible occurrence" (*F*, p. 1). To what specific suppositions, theories, and experiments, by Erasmus Darwin and others, did Percy Shelley allude? Mary Shelley, in her Preface to the 1831 edition, referred to an admittedly apocryphal account of one of Dr. Darwin's experiments. During one of Byron and Shelley's many long conversations to which she was "a devout but nearly silent listener," Mary Shelley recalled,

> various philosophical doctrines were discussed, and among others the nature of the principle of life, and whether there was any probability of its ever being discovered and communicated. They talked of the experi-

ments of Dr. Darwin (I speak not of what the doctor really did or said that he did, but, as more to my purpose, of what was then spoken of as having been done by him), who preserved a piece of vermicelli in a glass case till by some extraordinary means it began to move with voluntary motion. (*F*, p. 227)

Even though Mary Shelley acknowledges that the animated piece of vermicelli is probably a fiction, Erasmus Darwin's theories have significant bearing on her purposes in *Frankenstein*.

Erasmus Darwin was most famous for his work on evolution and the growth of plants, and it is this work that Mary Shelley affirmed. Victor Frankenstein is portrayed as a direct opponent of Darwin's teachings, as an anti-evolutionist and a parodic perpetrator of an erroneous "Creation Theory." To perceive this dimension of Victor Frankenstein's project, we must first review the basic tenets of Erasmus Darwin's theories as they appear in his major works, *The Botanic Garden* (1789, 1791), *Zoonomia; or, The Laws of Organic Life* (1794), *Phytologia* (1800), and *The Temple of Nature* (1803).

Eighteenth-century scientists generally conceived of the universe as a perfect, static world created by divine fiat at a single moment in time. This universe, metaphorically represented as a "great chain of being," manifested myriad and minute gradations between the species, but these relationships were regarded as fixed and permanent. As Linnaeus, the great eighteenth-century classifier of all known plant life, insisted in his *Systema Naturae* (1735), "Nullae species novae"—no new species can come into existence in a divinely ordered, perfect world. But by the end of the eighteenth century, under pressure from Herschel's new discoveries in astronomy, Cuvier's paleontological researches, William Smith's studies of fossil stratification, Sprengel's work on botanical crossbreeding and fertilization, and observations made with an increasingly powerful microscope, together with a more diffuse Leibnizian "natural theology" that emphasized the study of nature and her interactions with human populations, the orthodox Linnaean concept of an immutable physical universe had begun to weaken.[9]

Erasmus Darwin was inspired by the researches of the Comte du Buffon, the "father of evolution," who in his huge *Histoire naturelle* (44 volumes, 1749–1804) had described myriads of flora and fauna and interspersed comments on the progressive "degeneration" of life forms from earlier and more uniform species, often caused by environmental or climatic changes. Although he adhered to the concept of the *scala naturae* and the immutability of species, Buffon was the first to discuss seriously such central evolutionary problems as the origin of the earth, the extinction of species, the theory of "common descent," and in particular the reproductive isolation between two incipient species.[10] Significantly, it was to Buffon that Victor Frankenstein also turned after his early disillusionment with the alchemists, and Buffon whom he "still read . . . with delight" (*F*, p. 36).[11] But it was Erasmus Darwin who for English readers first synthesized and popularized the concept of the evolution of species through natural selection over millions of years.

By 1803, Erasmus Darwin had accepted, on the basis of shell and fossil remains in the highest geological strata, that the earth must once have been covered by water and hence that all life began in the sea. As Darwin concisely summed up this theory of evolution in his notes to *The Temple of Nature*,

> After islands or continents were raised above the primeval ocean, great numbers of the most simple animals would attempt to seek food at the edges or shores of the new land, and might thence gradually become amphibious; as is now seen in the frog, who changes from an aquatic animal to an amphibious one, and in the gnat, which changes from a natant to a volant one.
>
> At the same time new microscopic animacules would immediately commence wherever there was warmth and moisture, and some organic matter, that might induce putridity. Those situated on dry land, and immersed in dry air, may gradually acquire new powers to preserve their existence; and by innumerable successive reproductions for some thousands, or perhaps millions of ages, may at length have produced many of the vegetable and animal inhabitants which now people the earth.
>
> As innumerable shell-fish must have existed a long time beneath the ocean, before the calcareous mountains were produced and elevated; it is also probable, that many of the insect tribes, or less complicate animals, existed long before the quadrupeds or more complicate ones.[12]

Meditating on the suggestion that mankind descended from "one family of monkeys on the banks of the Mediterranean" that learned to use and strengthen the thumb muscle and "by this improved use of the sense of touch . . . acquired clear ideas, and gradually became men," Darwin speculated,

Perhaps all the productions of nature are in their progress to greater perfection! an idea countenanced by modern discoveries and deductions concerning the progressive formation of the solid parts of the terraqueous globe, and consonant to the dignity of the Creator of all things. (*Temple of Nature*, p. 54)

Darwin further suggested that such evolutionary improvement is the direct result of sexual selection:

A great want of one part of the animal world has consisted in the desire of the exclusive possession of the females; and these have acquired weapons to bombard each other for this purpose, as the very thick, shield-like, horny skin on the shoulder of the boar is a defense only against animals of his own species, who strike obliquely upwards, nor are his tusk for other purposes, except to defend himself, as he is not naturally a carnivorous animal. So the horns of the stag are not sharp to offend his adversary, but are branched for the purpose of parrying or receiving the thrusts of horns similar to his own, and have therefore been formed for the purpose of combating other stags for the exclusive possession of the females; who are observed, like the ladies in the times of chivalry, to attend the car of the victor.[13]

Erasmus Darwin anticipated the modern discovery of mutations, noting in his discussion of monstrous births that monstrosities, or mutations, may be inherited: "Many of these enormities of shape are propagated, and continued as a variety at least, if not as a new species of animal. I have seen a breed of cats with an additional claw on every foot" (*Zoonomia*, 1794, 1: 501).

In relation to *Frankenstein*, Erasmus Darwin's most significant evolutionary concept was that of the hierarchy of reproduction. Again and again, in *Zoonomia*, in *The Botanic Garden*, in *Phytologia*, and in *The Temple of Nature*, Darwin insisted that sexual reproduction is at a higher evolutionary level than hermaphroditic or solitary paternal propagation. As Darwin commented in his note "Reproduction" in *The Temple of Nature*,

The microscopic productions of spontaneous vitality, and the next most inferior kinds of vegetables and animals, propagate by solitary generation only; as the buds and bulbs raised immediately from seeds, the lycoperdon tuber, with probably many other fungi, and the polypus, volvox, and taenia. Those of the next order propagate both by solitary and sexual reproduction, as those buds and bulbs which produce flowers as well as other buds or bulbs; and the aphis and probably many other insects. Whence it appears, that many of those vegetables and animals, which are produced by solitary generation, gradually become more perfect, and at length produce a sexual progeny.

A third order of organic nature consists of hermaphrodite vegetables and animals, as in those flowers which have anthers and stigmas in the same corol; and in many insects, as leeches, snails, and worms; and perhaps all those reptiles which have no bones. . . .

And, lastly, the most perfect orders of animals are propagated by sexual intercourse only. (*Temple of Nature*, Additional Notes, pp. 36–37)

This concept of the superiority of sexual reproduction over paternal propagation was so important to Erasmus Darwin that it forced him radically to revise his concept of reproduction in his third, "corrected" edition of *Zoonomia*. In 1794, Darwin had argued, following Aristotle, that male plants produce the seed or embryo, while female plants provide only nourishment to this seed, and by analogy, had contended "that the mother does not contribute to the formation of the living ens in normal generation, but is necessary only for supplying its nutriment and oxigenation" (*Zoonomia*, 1794, 1: 487). He then attributed all monstrous births to the female, saying that deformities result from either excessive or insufficient nourishment in the egg or uterus (p. 497). But by 1801, Darwin's observations of both animal and vegetable mules had convinced him that both male and female seeds contribute to the innate characteristics of the species (see *Zoonomia*, 1801, 2: 296–97. Interestingly, while Darwin no longer attributed monstrous births to uterine deficiencies or excesses, he continued to hold the *male imagination* at the moment of conception responsible for determining both the sex of the child and its outstanding traits:

I conclude, that the act of generation cannot exist without being accompanied with ideas, and that a man must have at this time either a general idea of his own male form, or of the forms of his male organs; or an idea of the female form, or of her organs, and that this marks the sex, and the peculiar resemblances of the child to either parent. (*Zoonomia*, 1794, p. 524; 1801, 2: 270)

The impact of the female imagination on the seed in utero is less intense, argued Darwin, because it lasts for a longer period of time and is therefore more diffuse. It follows that Darwin, in 1801, attributed the bulk of monstrous births to the *male* imagination, a point of obvious relevance to *Frankenstein*.

Erasmus Darwin's work on what he called "the economy of vegeta-tion" has equally significant implications for *Frankenstein*. Darwin's comments on plant nutrition, photosynthesis, and the use of fertilizers and manures in *Phytologia* for the first time put gardening and agricul-ture on a sound scientific basis.[14] Again and again in this lengthy work, Darwin emphasized the necessity to recycle all organic matter. His discussion of manures runs to over 25,000 words and is by far the largest section in this book on plant agriculture. The best manures, Darwin reports, are:

> organic matters, which . . . will by their slow solution in or near the surface of the earth supply the nutritive sap-juice to vegetables. Hence all kinds of animal and vegetable substances, which will undergo a digestive process, or spontaneous solution, as the flesh, fat, skin and bones of animals; with their secretions of bile, saliva, mucus; and their excretions of urine and ordure; and also the fruit, meal, oil, leaves, wood of vegetables, when properly decomposed on or beneath the soil, supply the most nutritive food to plants.[15]

He urges every gardener and farmer to save all organic matter for manure, "even the parings of his nails and the clippings of his hair" (p. 241), and further urges the heretical notion that the soil nourished by the decomposition of human bodies ought to be available for growing plants. Mourning the waste of rich soil in churchyards and cemeteries, he argues that

> proper burial grounds should be consecrated out of towns, and divided into two compartments, the earth from one of which, saturated with animal decomposition, should be taken away once in ten or twenty years, for the purposes of agriculture; and sand or clay, or less fertile soil, brought into its place. (p. 243)

Throughout his writings, Darwin described a universe that is con-stantly evolving in abundant creativity. Donald Hassler tellingly de-fines Darwin's vision of "material forces moving inexorably over vast distances of time and space, with no supernatural or anthropological agency, to produce nearly infinite configurations of organic and inorga-nic matter" as Darwin's "comic materialism."[16] The phrase neatly com-bines Darwin's comic acceptance of limitations with his sense for the infinitely expansive potential of the universe. I myself would classify Darwin's celebration of a universe that generates itself out of "one central chaos" and returns to that chaos in a catastrophe that "may again by explosions produce a new world" (*Temple of Nature*, pp. 166–67) as yet another example of English romantic irony, of that revolutionary conception of a universe that is not created by divine fiat but is rather in constant process, merrily multiplying itself out of an abundant chaos or what Friedrich Schlegel called the *Fülle*.[17]

Mary Shelley was introduced to Darwin's thought both by her father and later by her husband, who had been heavily influenced by Darwin's evolutionary theories while writing "Queen Mab." Percy Shelley first read *The Botanic Garden* in July 1811, and in December 1812 he ordered Darwin's *Zoonomia* and *The Temple of Nature* from the booksellers Hookham and Rickman.[18] The extensive impact of Darwin's evolutionary and agricultural theories, as well as of his poetic language, on Percy Shelley's Notes to "Queen Mab" and on such poems as "The Cloud," "The Sensitive Plant," and *Prometheus Unbound* has been well documented.[19] It is clear that Darwin's work remained vivid in Percy Shelley's mind throughout the period in which Mary Shelley was writing *Frankenstein*, as his prefatory comment to the novel testifies.

II

Reading *Frankenstein* against the background of Darwin's work, we can see that Mary Shelley directly pitted Victor Frankenstein, that modern Prometheus, against those gradual evolutionary processes of nature described by Darwin. Victor Frankenstein wants to originate a new life form quickly, by chemical means. In his Faustian thirst for knowledge and power, he dreams:

> Life and death appeared to me ideal bounds, which I should first break through, and pour a torrent of light into our dark world. A new species would bless me as its creator and source; many happy and excellent natures would owe their being to me. (*F*, p. 49)

Significantly, in his attempt to create a new species, Victor Frankenstein substitutes solitary paternal propagation for sexual reproduction. He thus reverses the evolutionary ladder described by Darwin. And he engages in a notion of science that Mary Shelley deplores, the idea that science should manipulate and control rather than describe and understand nature.

Moreover, his imagination at the moment of conception is fevered and unhealthy; as he tells Walton,

> Every night I was oppressed by a slow fever, and I became nervous to a most painful degree; . . . my voice became broken, my trembling hands almost refused to accomplish their task; I became as timid as a love-sick girl, and alternate tremor and passionate ardour took the place of wholesome sensation and regulated ambition. (*F*, p. 51)

Under such mental circumstances, according to Darwin, the resultant creation could only be a monster. Frankenstein has further increased the monstrousness of his creation by making a form that is both larger and more simple than a normal human being. As he acknowledges to Walton, "As the minuteness of the parts formed a great hindrance to my speed, I resolved, contrary to my first intention, to make the being of a gigantic stature; that is to say, about eight feet in height, and proportionably large" (*F*, p. 49). Darwin had observed that nature moves "from simpler things to more compound" (*Phytologia*, p. 118); in defying nature's law, Victor Frankenstein has created not a more perfect species but a degenerative one.

In his attempt to override natural evolutionary development and to create a new species sui generis, Victor Frankenstein enacts a parody of the orthodox creationist theory. While he denies the unique power of God to create organic life, he confirms the capacity of a single creator to originate a new species. Thus he simultaneously upholds the creationist theory and parodies it by creating only a monster. In both ways, he blasphemes against the natural order of things. He moves down rather than up the evolutionary ladder; he reverses human progress and perverts the law of the survival of the fittest. And he denies the natural mode of human reproduction through sexual procreation.

Victor Frankenstein perverts natural evolutionary progress in yet another way. Despite Darwin's insistence that all dead organic matter—including decomposing human flesh and bones found in cemeteries—ought to be saved for compost heaps and manure, Victor Frankenstein removes human flesh and bones from graveyards. And he does so not in order to generate life organically through what Darwin described as "spontaneous animal vitality in microscopic cells"[20] but to create a new life form through chemical engineering. Frankenstein has thus disrupted the natural life cycle. His attempt to control and speed up the transformation of decomposing organic material into new life forms by artificial means violates the rhythms of nature.

Mary Shelley's novel implicitly invokes Darwin's theory of gradual evolutionary progress to suggest both the error and the evil of Victor Frankenstein's bad science. The genuine improvement of the species can result only from the fusing of both male and female sexuality. In trying to have a baby without a woman, Frankenstein denies to his child the maternal love and nurturance it requires, the very nourishment that Darwin explicitly equated with the female sex. Frankenstein's failure to embrace his smiling creature with maternal love, his horrified rejection of his own creation, spells out the narrative consequences of solitary paternal propagation. But even if Frankenstein had been able to provide his child with a mother's care, he could not have prevented its social ostracism and misery.

It is therefore a triple failure of imagination that curses Victor Frankenstein. First, by not imaginatively identifying with his creation, Frankenstein fails to give his child the parental support he owes to it. He thereby condemns his creature to become what others behold, a monster. Second, by imagining that the male can produce a higher form of evolutionary species by lateral propagation than by sexual procreation, Frankenstein defines his own imagination as profoundly antievolutionary and thus antiprogressive. Third, in assuming that he can create a perfect species by chemical means, Frankenstein defies a central tenet of romantic poetic ideology: that the creative imagination must work spontaneously, unconsciously, and above all organically, creating forms that are themselves organic heterocosms.

Moreover, in trying to create a human being as God created Adam, out of earth and water, all at once, Victor Frankenstein robs nature of something more than fertilizer. "On a dreary night in November, . . . with an anxiety that almost amounted to agony," Victor Frankenstein infused "a spark of being into the lifeless thing that lay" at his feet (*F*, p. 52). At that moment Victor Frankenstein became the modern Prometheus, stealing fire from the gods to give to mankind and thus overthrowing the established, sacred order of both earth and heaven. At that moment he transgressed against nature.

To understand the full implications of Frankenstein's transgression, we must recognize that his stolen "spark of life" is not merely fire; it is also that recently discovered caloric fluid called electricity. Victor's interest in legitimate science is first aroused by the sight of lightning destroying an old oak tree; it is then that he learns of the existence of electricity and replicates Benjamin Franklin's experiment with kite and key and draws down "that fluid from the clouds" (*F*, p. 35). In the late eighteenth century, there was widespread interest in Franklin's and Father Beccaria's discoveries of atmospheric electricity, in static electricity, and in artificial or mechanical electricity generated through such machines as the Leyden jar. Many scientists explored the possibility, derived from Newton's concept of the ether as an elastic medium capable of transmitting the pulsations of light, heat, gravitation, magnetism, and electricity, that the atmosphere was filled with a thin fluid that was positively and negatively charged and that could be identified as a single animating principle appearing under multiple guises (as light, heat, magnetism, etc.). Erasmus Darwin speculated that the perpetual necessity of air to the human organism suggests that "the spirit of animation itself is thus acquired from the atmosphere, which if it be supposed to be finer or more subtle than the electric matter, could not long be retained in our bodies and must therefore require perpetual renovation."[21] And Humphry Davy, founder of the field of electrochemistry, first gave authoritative voice to a theory of matter as electrically charged atoms. In his *Elements of Chemical Philosophy*, Davy argued:

> Whether matter consists of indivisible corpuscles, or physical points endowed with attraction and repulsion, still the same conclusions may be formed concerning the powers by which they act, and the quantities in which they combine; and the powers seem capable of being measured by their electrical relations, and the quantities on which they act of being expressed by numbers. (p. 57)

He further concluded that

> it is evident that the particles of matter must have space between them; and . . . it is a probable inference that [each body's] own particles are possessed of motion; but . . . the motion, if it exist, must be a vibratory or undulatory motion, or a motion of the particles round their axes, or a motion of particles round each other. (p. 95)

Reading Darwin and Davy encouraged Percy Shelley in scientific speculations that he had embarked upon much earlier, as a schoolboy at Dr. Greenlaw's Syon House Academy in 1802. Inspired by the famous lectures of Dr. Adam Walker, Percy Shelley had early learned to think of electricity and the processes of chemical attraction and repulsion as modes of a single polarized force. Walker even identified electricity as the spark of life itself. At the conclusion of his discussion of electricity in his *A System of Familiar Philosophy*, Walker enthused,

> Its power of exciting muscular motion in apparently dead animals, as well as of increasing the growth, invigorating the stamina, and reviving diseased vegetation, prove its relationship or affinity to the *living principle*. Though, Proteus-like, it eludes our grasp; plays with our curiosity; tempts enquiry by fallacious appearances and attacks our weakness under so many perplexing subtilties; yet it is impossible not to believe it the soul of the material world, and the paragon of elements![22]

Percy Shelley's basic scientific concepts had long been familiar to Mary Shelley, ever since the early days of their relationship when he ritually celebrated his birthday by launching fire balloons.[23] That Percy Shelley endorsed Adam Walker's identification of life with electricity is everywhere apparent in his poetry. The imagery of *Prometheus Unbound* explicitly associates electricity with love, light, and life itself, as in the final act where the Spirit of the Earth, earlier imaged as a Cupid figure, becomes a radiant orb—or "ten thousand orbs involving and involved"—of pure energy. And on the forehead of the spirit sleeping within this "sphere within sphere" is a "star" (or negative electrode) that shoots "swords of azure fire" (the blue flames of electrical discharges) or

> Vast beams like spokes of some invisible wheel
> Which whirl as the orb whirls, swifter than thought,
> Filling the abyss with sun-like lightnings,
> And perpendicular now, and now transverse,
> Pierce the dark soil, and as they pierce and pass,
> Make bare the secrets of the Earth's deep heart.[24]

When Victor Frankenstein steals the spark of being, then, he is literally stealing Jupiter's lightning bolt, as Benjamin Franklin had proved. But in Percy Shelley's terms, he is also stealing the very life of nature, the source of both love and electricity.

Fully to appreciate the science that lies behind Victor Frankenstein's endeavors, however, we must remember that in the 1831 Preface to *Frankenstein*, Mary Shelley specifically associated electricity with galvanism. In 1831, Victor Frankenstein is disabused of his belief in the alchemists by a "man of great research in natural philosophy" who teaches him the "theory which he had formed on the subject of electricity and galvanism" (*F*, p. 238); and in her Preface, Mary Shelley directly linked the attempt to give life to dead matter with galvanism. After referring to Dr. Darwin's vermicelli experiment, she writes: "Not thus, after all, would life be given. Perhaps a corpse would be reanimated; galvanism had given token of such things: perhaps the component parts of a creature might be manufactured, brought together, and endued with vital warmth" (*F*, p. 227).

In 1791 the Bolognese physiologist Luigi Galvani published his *De Viribus Electricitatis in Motui Musculari* (or *Commentary on the Effects of Electricity on Muscular Motion*),[25] in which he came to the conclusion that animal tissue contained a heretofore neglected innate vital force, which he called "animal electricity" but which was subsequently widely known as "galvanism"; this force activated both nerves and muscles when spanned by an arc of metal wires connected to a pile of copper and zinc plates. Galvani believed that his new vital force was a form of electricity different from both the "natural" form of electricity produced by lightning or by the torpedo and electric eel and the "artificial" form produced by friction (i.e., static electricity). Galvani argued that the brain is the most important source of the production of this "electric fluid" and that the nerves acted as conductors of this fluid to other nerves and muscles, the tissues of which act much like the outer and inner surfaces of the widely used Leyden jar. Thus the flow of animal electric fluid provided a stimulus which produced contractions of convulsions in the irritable muscle fibers.

Galvani's theories made the British headlines in December 1802 when, in the presence of their Royal Highnesses the Prince of Wales and the dukes of York, Clarence, and Cumberland, Galvani's nephew, disciple, and ardent defender, Professor Luigi Aldini of Bologna University, applied a voltaic pile connected by metallic wires to the ear and nostrils of a recently killed ox head. At that moment, "the eyes were seen to open, the ears to shake, the tongue to be agitated, and the nostrils to swell, in the same manner as those of the living animal, when irritated and desirous of combating another of the same species."[26] But Professor Aldini's most notorious demonstration of galvanic electricity took place on 17 January 1803. On that day he applied galvanic electricity to the corpse of the murderer Thomas Forster. The body of the recently hanged criminal was collected from Newgate, where it had lain in the prison yard at a temperature of 30 degrees Fahrenheit for one hour, by the president of the College of Surgeons, Mr. Keate, and brought immediately to Mr. Wilson's anatomical theater where the following experiments were performed. When wires attached to a pile composed of 120 plates of zinc and 120 plates of copper were connected to the ear and mouth of the dead criminal, Aldini later reported, "the jaw began to quiver, the adjoining muscles were horribly contorted, and the left eye actually opened" (p. 193). When the wires were applied to the dissected thumb muscles, they "induced a forcible effort to clench the hand"; when applied to the ear and rectum, they "excited in the muscles contractions much stronger. . . . The action even of those muscles furthest distant from the points of contact with the arc was so much increased as almost to give an appearance of re-animation." And when volatile alkili was smeared on the nostrils and mouth before the galvanic stimulus was applied, "the convulsions appeared to be much increased . . . and extended from the muscles of the head, face, and neck, as far as the deltoid. The effect in this case surpassed our most sanguine expectations," Aldini exults, and remarkably concludes that "vitality might, perhaps, have been restored, if many circumstances had not rendered it impossible" (pp. 194–95). Here is the scientific prototype of Victor Frankenstein, restoring life to dead bodies.

An event so notorious and so widely reported in the popular press must have been discussed in both the Shelley and Godwin households at the time and would have been recalled, however inaccurately, during the conversations between Shelley and Byron in which the possibility of reanimating a corpse was discussed. Indeed, the popular interest in galvanic electricity reached such a pitch in Germany that an edict forbidding the use of decapitated criminals' heads for galvanic experiments was passed in Prussia in 1804. It is probably to these events, as well as to experiments in Germany by F. H. A. Humboldt, C. J. C. Grapengiesser, and Johann Caspar Creve and reports of them published by J. A. Heidmann and Lorenz Oken, that Percy Shelley referred in his Preface to *Frankenstein* when he insisted that "the event on which this fiction is founded has been supposed, by Dr. Darwin and some of the physiological writers of Germany, as not of impossible occurrence" (*F*, p. 6). Even though Erasmus Darwin never fully endorsed the revolutionary theory of Galvani and Volta that electricity is the cause of muscular motion, he was convinced that electricity stimulated plant growth (*Botanic Garden*, 1: 463).

Mary Shelley's familiarity with these galvanic experiments came not only from Shelley and Byron, but also from Byron's physician, Dr. William Polidori. As a medical student at the University of Edinburgh, Polidori had been exposed to the latest galvanic theories and experiments by the famous Edinburgh physician Dr. Charles Henry Wilkinson, whose review of the literature, *Elements of Galvanism in Theory and Practice*, was published in 1804. Dr.Wilkinson continued research on galvanism and developed his own galvanic treatments for intermittent fevers, amaurosis, and quinsy, and he reported several successes.

III

Mary Shelley based Victor Frankenstein's attempt to create a new species from dead organic matter through the use of chemistry and electricity on the most advanced scientific research of the early nineteenth century. But *Frankenstein* reflects much more than merely an intelligent use of the latest scientific knowledge. Perhaps because she was a woman, Mary Shelley understood that much of the scientific research of her day incorporated an attempt to dominate the female.

Francis Bacon heralded the seventeenth-century scientific revolution as a calculated attempt to control and exploit female Nature: "I am come in very truth leading to you Nature with all her children to bind her to your service and make her your slave." Bacon's metaphor of a passive, possessable female nature radically transformed the traditional image of female nature as Dame Kind, the "all creating" and bounteous mother earth who single-handedly bore and nourished her children. But it was Bacon's metaphor that structured much of the new scientific writing in England in the eighteenth century. Isaac Barrow, Newton's teacher, declared that the aim of the new philosophy was to "search

Nature out of her Concealments, and unfold her dark Mysteries,"[27] while Robert Boyle noted contemptuously that "some men care only to know Nature, others desire to command her."[28] Henry Oldenburg, a future secretary of the Royal Society, invoked Bacon to support his assertion that the "true sons of learning" are those men who do not remain satisfied with the well-known truths but rather "penetrate from Nature's antechamber to her inner closet."[29] As Brian Easlea concludes, many seventeenth-century natural philosophers and their successors viewed the scientific quest as a virile masculine penetration into a passive and by herself uncreative female nature, a penetration that would, in Bacon's words, not merely exert a "gentle guidance over nature's course" but rather "conquer and subdue her" and even "shake her to her foundations."[30]

A product of the scientific revolution of the seventeenth century, Frankenstein had been taught to see nature the way Bacon did, as female but inert. He sees nature "objectively," as something separate from himself, a passive and even dead "object of my affection"[31] that can and should be penetrated, analyzed, and controlled. He thus accords nature no living soul or "personhood" that requires recognition or respect.

Wordsworth had articulated the danger inherent in thinking of nature as something distinct from human consciousness. A reader of Wordsworth, Mary Shelley understood nature in his terms, as a sacred all-creating mother, a living organism or ecological community with which human beings interact in mutual dependence; to defy this filial bond, as Frankenstein does, is to break one's ties with the source of life and health. Hence Frankenstein becomes ill in the process of carrying out his experiment: "every night I was oppressed by a slow fever, and I became nervous to a most painful degree"; and at its completion, he collapses in "a nervous fever" that confines him to his sickbed for several months.

But Mary Shelley's critique of objective, rationalistic thought goes beyond Wordsworth's romantic organicist notion that "we murder to dissect." As Gillian Beer has suggested elsewhere in this volume, scientific discourse often depends upon metaphors that reflect the dominant concerns of the culture. Mary Shelley perceived a potentially dangerous metaphor inherent in the scientific thought of her day.

Nature is female, Dame Kind, Mother Earth (see Sally Shuttleworth's essay in this volume). As "all creating nature," she can be seen as the abundantly providing, ever nurturing mother, the blessed source of life itself. But this sacramental view of female nature has been foresworn by Waldman, Frankenstein, and many of the leading scientists of Mary Shelley's day. As Professor Waldman proclaims, scientists "penetrate into the recesses of nature, and shew how *she* works in *her* hiding places" (*F*, p. 42, my emphasis). Nature has become the passive female whose sole function is to satisfy male desires. Carolyn Merchant, Evelyn Fox Keller, and Brian Easlea have drawn our attention to the negative consequences of this identification of nature as the passive female. Construing nature as the "other" has led, as Merchant shows, to the increasing destruction of the environment and the disruption of the delicate ecological balance between man and nature. Moreover, as Keller has suggested in her studies of how the making of men and women has affected the making of science, the professional scientific demand for "objectivity" and detachment often masks a prior psychological alienation from the mother and an aggressive desire to dominate the female sex object. The result can be a dangerous division between what C. P. Snow called the "two cultures," between the power-seeking practices of science and the concerns of humanists with moral responsibility, emotional communion, and spiritual values. The scientist who analyzes, manipulates, and attempts to control nature unconsciously engages in a form of oppressive sexual politics. Construing nature as the female other, he attempts to make nature serve his own ends, to gratify his own desires for power, wealth, reputation.

Frankenstein's scientific project is clearly an attempt to gain power. He is inspired by Waldman's description of scientists who "have acquired new and almost unlimited powers; they can command the thunders of the heaven, mimic the earthquake, and even mock the invisible world with its own shadows" (*F*, p. 42). He has sought the power of a father over his children, of God over his creation. "A new species would bless me as its creator and source; many happy and excellent natures would owe their being to me. No father could claim the gratitude of his child so completely as I should deserve theirs," he exults (*F*, p. 49). More subtly yet more pervasively, Frankenstein has sought power over the female. He has "pursued nature to her hiding places" (*F*, p. 49) in an attempt not only to penetrate nature and show how her hidden womb works but actually to steal or appropriate that womb. In effect, Frankenstein has tried to usurp the function of the female in the reproductive cycle and thus eliminate the necessity, at least for the purposes of the biological survival of mankind, of female sexuality.

A fear of female sexuality is implicit in a patriarchal construction of gender.[32] Uninhibited female sexual experience threatens the foundation of patriarchal power: the establishment of patrilineal kinship networks together with the conveyancing of both property and prestige by inheritance entailed upon a male line. Significantly, in the patriarchal world of Geneva pictured in the novel, female sexuality is strikingly repressed. All the women are presented as sexless: Caroline Beaufort is a devoted daughter and chaste wife; Elizabeth Lavenza's relationship with Victor is that of a sister; even Safie merely holds hands with her beloved Felix.

In this context, the murder of Elizabeth Lavenza on her wedding night becomes doubly significant. As several critics have noted, the scene of her death is based on a painting Mary Shelley knew well, Henry Fuseli's *The Nightmare*. The corpse of Elizabeth lies in the attitude in which Fuseli placed his nightmare ridden woman: "She was there, lifeless and inanimate, thrown across the bed, her head hanging down, and her pale and distorted features half covered by her hair" (*F*, p. 193). Fuseli's woman is an image of female erotic desire, both lusting for and terrified of the succubus that crouches upon her breasts. Invoking this image, Mary Shelley alerts us to what Victor fears: his bride's sexuality.[33] For Elizabeth might never have been killed had Victor not sent her into their nuptial bedroom alone. Returning to the body of the murdered Elizabeth, Victor "embraced her with ardour; but the deathly languor and coldness of the limbs told me, that what I now held in my arms had ceased to be the Elizabeth whom I had loved and cherished" (*F*, p. 193). Victor most passionately desires his bride when he knows she is dead. The allusion to his earlier dream, when he thought to embrace the living Elizabeth but instead held in his arms the corpse of his mother, reveals Victor's most powerful erotic desire, a desire to possess the dead mother.

Afraid of female sexuality and the power of human reproduction it enables, both Frankenstein and the patriarchal society he represents use the technologies of science and the laws of the polis to control and repress women. But Mary Shelley portrays Frankenstein's desire to penetrate and usurp the female as monstrous, unattainable, and finally self-destructive. For nature is not the passive, inert, or "dead" matter that Frankenstein imagines;[34] she resists and revenges his attempts. During his research, nature denies to Victor Frankenstein both mental and physical health: "my enthusiasm was checked by my anxiety, and I appeared rather like one doomed by slavery to toil in the mines, or any other unwholesome trade, than an artist occupied by his favourite employment. Every night I was opppressed by a slow fever, and I became nervous to a most painful degree" (*F*, p. 51). Victor continues to be tormented by anxiety attacks, bouts of delirium, periods of distraction and madness. As soon as he determines to blaspheme against nature a second time, by creating a female human being, nature torments him with a return of his mental illness: "Every thought that was devoted to it was an extreme anguish, and every word that I spoke in allusion to it caused my lips to quiver and my heart to palpitate" (*F*, p. 156); "my spirits became unequal; I grew restless and nervous" (*F*, p. 162). In the end, Frankenstein's obsession with destroying his creature exposes him to such mental and physical distress that he dies before his twenty-fifth birthday.

Moreover, nature pursues Victor Frankenstein with the very electricity he has stolen: lightning, thunder, and rain rage around him. On the November night on which he steals the "spark of being" from nature, "the rain . . . poured from a black and comfortless sky" (*F*, p. 54). He glimpses his creature during a flash of lightning at Plainpalais (*F*, p. 71) and first speaks with him as "rain poured down in torrents, and thick mists hid the summits of the mountains" (*F*, p. 91). Setting sail from the Orkney island after he has destroyed his female creature, Frankenstein is pursued by a fierce wind and high waves that threaten his own life (*F*, p. 169). Frankenstein ends his life and his pursuit of his monster surrounded by the aurora borealis, the electromagnetic field of the north pole. The atmospheric effects of the novel, which most readers have dismissed as little more than the traditional trappings of Gothic fiction, in fact manifest the power of nature to revenge herself upon those who transgress her sacred boundaries. The elemental forces that

Victor has released pursue him to his hiding places, hounding him like avenging Furies, denying him the capacity for natural procreation.

The novel thus calls into question the gendered metaphor on which much Western scientific theory and practice is founded. The attempt of science to penetrate, possess, and control Mother Nature entails both a violation of the sacred rights of nature and a false belief in the "objectivity" or "rationality" of scientific research. When it construes nature as a passive and possessable female, Western science encodes a sexist metaphor that has profoundly troubling implications, not only for women but for human survival. As Frankenstein's monster tells him, "Remember that I have power; . . . I can make you so wretched that the light of day will be hateful to you" (F, p. 165). Like Victor Frankenstein, modern scientists have too often treated nature as the "other," to be exploited rather than understood and served through detailed, loving, and noninterventionist description. In their search for the truth about the workings of the physical universe, they have ignored the possibility that their manipulations of nature might harm her. Too often, they have failed to take responsibility for the predictable consequences of their research, failed to care for their own technological progeny. As Mary Shelley first perceived, a scientific method founded on the gendered construction of nature as the female other, as the passive object of desire, hence possessable and exploitable, can produce monsters, even monsters of biological, chemical, and nuclear warfare capable of destroying civilization as we know it.

Notes

1. Quoted in Benjamin Farrington, "Temporis Partus Masculus: An Untranslated Writing of Francis Bacon," *Centaurus* 1 (1951), p. 197.

2. Mary Wollstonecraft Shelley, *Frankenstein; or, The Modern Prometheus* (1818 Text), ed. James Rieger (New York: Bobbs-Merrill, 1974; rpt. Chicago: University of Chicago Press, 1982), p. 43.

3. Sir Harold Hartley discusses the importance to Davy's career of this introductory lecture in *Humphry Davy* (London: Nelson, 1966).

4. *Mary Shelley's Journal*, ed. Frederick L. Jones (Norman: University of Oklahoma Press, 1947), p. 67. Laura Crouch argued that the *Discourse* is the book listed by Mary Shelley in her Journal under Books Read in 1816 as "Introduction to Davy's Chemistry." See "Davy's *A Discourse, Introductory to a Course of Lectures on Chemistry*: A Possible Scientific Source of *Frankenstein*," *Keats-Shelley Journal* 27 (1978): 35–37. Mary Shelley would have known of Humphry Davy's

work since childhood; she may even have been introduced to him when Davy dined with Godwin on 16 February 1801.

5. Percy Bysshe Shelley, *The Letters of Percy Bysshe Shelley,* ed. Frederick Jones (Oxford: Clarendon, 1964), 1: 319.

6. Humphry Davy, *A Discourse, Introductory to a Course of Lectures on Chemistry* (London: J. Johnson, 1802), 5–6.

7. Crouch, "Davy's *A Discourse,*" p. 43.

8. Humphry Davy, *Elements of Chemical Philosophy* (London, 1812), p. 58.

9. See chapters 1 and 2 of Loren Eiseley's *Darwin's Century: Evolution and the Men Who Discovered It* (Garden City, N.Y.: Doubleday, 1958) and Ernst Mayr's *The Growth of Biological Thought: Diversity, Evolution, and Inheritance* (Cambridge, Mass.: Belknap Press, 1982), pp. 301–41.

10. Mayr, *Growth of Biological Thought,* pp. 329–37.

11. Percy Shelley also read Buffon attentively. In his journal letter to Peacock of 23 July 1816, Shelley alludes to the first volume of Buffon's work *La théorie de la terre,* in the course of describing the glaciers of Mont Blanc: "I will not pursue Buffon's sublime but gloomy theory, that this earth which we inhabit will at some future period be changed into a mass of frost" (*Letters,* 1: 499).

12. Erasmus Darwin, *The Temple of Nature* (London: John Johnson, 1803), pp. 29–30.

13. Erasmus Darwin, *Zoonomia; or, The Laws of Organic Life* (London: John Johnson, 1794; 3d "corrected" ed., 1801), Vol. 1 (1794), p. 503.

14. Desmond King-Hele, *Erasmus Darwin* (London: Macmillan, 1963), p. 3.

15. Erasmus Darwin, *Phytologia; or, The Philosophy of Agriculture and Gardening* (London: John Johnson, 1800), p. 254.

16. Donald M. Hassler, *Erasmus Darwin,* (New York: Twayne, 1973), p. 17.

17. Anne K. Mellor, *English Romantic Irony* (Cambridge, Mass.: Harvard University Press, 1980), chap. 1.

18. P. B. Shelley, *Letters,* 1: 129.

19. For the influence of Erasmus Darwin on Percy Shelley's thought and poetry see Carl Grabo, *A Newton among Poets: Shelley's Use of Science in "Prometheus Unbound"* (Chapel Hill: University of North Carolina Press, 1930), pp. 22–74; Desmond King-Hele's *Shelley: His Thought and Work* (London: Macmillan, 1960), pp. 162–64, as well as his *Erasmus Darwin,* pp. 144–51; Kenneth Neill Cameron, *The Young Shelley: Genesis of a Radical* (London: Victor Gollancz, 1951), pp. 121, 240; Robert M. Maniquis, "The Puzzling *Mimosa:* Sensitivity and Plant Symbols in Romanticism," *Studies in Romanticism* 8 (1969): 129–55.

20. Erasmus Darwin discusses this process in *The Temple of Nature,* Additional Note 1: "Spontaneous Vitality of Microscopic Animals," pp. 1–11.

21. Erasmus Darwin, *The Botanic Garden* (London: John Johnson, part. 1: "The Economy of Vegetation," 1791; pt. 2: "The Loves of the Plants," 1789), Canto I, note to line 401.

22. Adam Walker, *A System of Familiar Philosophy* (London, 1799), p. 391.

23. Richard Holmes, *Shelley: The Pursuit* (New York: E. P. Dutton, 1975), pp. 149, 344.

24. Percy Bysshe Shelley, *"Prometheus Unbound,"* *The Complete Poetical Works of Percy Bysshe Shelley,* ed. Thomas Hutchinson (Oxford: Oxford University Press, 1905), 4. 274–79.

25. Luigi Galvani, *De Viribus Electricitatis in Motui Musculari. Commentarius* (Bologna, 1791); *Commentary on the Effects of Electricity on Muscular Motion,* trans. M. G. Foley, with notes and introduction by I. Bernard Cohen (Norwalk, Conn.: Burndy Library, 1953).

26. John Aldini. *An Account of the Late Improvements in Galvanism, with a series of Curious and Interesting Experiments performed before the Commissioners of the French National Institute and repeated lately in the Anatomical Theatres of London; to which is added, An Appendix, containing the author's Experiments on the Body of a Malefactor executed at New Gate* (London: Cuthell and Martin, 1803), p. 54. (This book is an English translation of the original French text, *Essai théorique et expérimentale sur le galvanisme* published in Paris in 1802 and translated into German by F. H. Martens and published at Leipzig in 1804.)

27. Isaac Barrow, *The Usefulness of Mathematical Learning Explained and Demonstrated* (1734; London: Frank Cass, 1770), p. xxx.

28. Robert Boyle, *The Works of Robert Boyle,* ed. Thomas Birch, 6 vols. (London, 1772), 1: 310.

29. *Correspondence of Henry Oldenburg,* ed. Rupert Hall and Marie Hall (Madison: University of Wisconsin Press, 1965), 1: 113.

30. Brian Easlea, *Science and Sexual Oppression, Patriarchy's Confrontation with Woman and Nature* (London: Weidenfeld and Nicolson, 1981), pp. 83–86.

31. This phrase was deleted by Percy Shelley from Mary Shelley's manuscript of *Frankenstein* (now in the Bodleian Library, Abinger Dep. c. 477/1). Her original version of the passage at *F,* 50, lines 31–33 reads thus: "I wished, as it were, to procrastinate my feelings of affection, until the great object of my affection was compleated."

32. One of the first and still most insightful analyses of the psychological and cultural dimensions of male hostility to female sexuality appears in Karen Horney's essays, collected in *Feminine Psychology,* ed. Harold Kelman (London: Routledge and Kegan Paul, 1967), especially "The Flight from Womanhood" (1926), pp. 54–70; "The Distrust between the Sexes" (1930), pp. 108–18; and "The Dread of Woman" (1932), pp. 133–46.

33. Paul Cantor has discussed Victor Frankenstein's rejection of normal sexuality in *Creature and Creator: Myth-making and English Romanticism* (New York: Cambridge University Press, 1984), pp. 109–15.

34. While I am in large agreement with Mary Poovey's analysis of Frankenstein's egoistic desire (in *The Proper Lady and the Woman Writer* [Chicago: University of Chicago Press, 1984], pp. 123–33), I do not share her view that the nature we see in *Frankenstein* is "fatal to human beings and human relationships" (p. 126). Poovey fails to distinguish between Frankenstein's perception of nature as "dead" matter and Mary Shelley's own vision of nature as a sacred ecological system in which human beings ought to participate in conscious harmony.

SALLY SHUTTLEWORTH

"The Surveillance of a Sleepless Eye": The Constitution of Neurosis in *Villette*

The fame of the "mad wife" in *Jane Eyre* has ensured that the writings of Charlotte Brontë are firmly associated in the public mind with a preoccupation with madness. Brontë's interest in the demarcation of insanity is not restricted to this one text but is pursued in her final novel, *Villette*, where the narrator is subject, seemingly, to hallucinations, undergoes a nervous collapse, and discusses her symptoms at great length with a doctor. Despite this foregrounding of medical expertise, no one has, as yet, placed *Villette* in the context of the intense psychological debates conducted in the scientific writings and popular press of the mid-Victorian era.

Insanity and nervous disease were the subject of acute public concern at this time. The mid-century witnessed the founding of public asylums and the professionalization of the medical treatment of insanity, developments which were accompanied by detailed discussions in the periodical press concerning the functions and processes of the mind. The aim of this essay is to place *Villette* within this social and scientific discourse on psychology, and to analyze the ways in which the novel both absorbs and resists the definitions and codifications of female experience offered by the male medical establishment.

Charlotte Brontë takes as her subject in *Villette* the inner processes of mind of a subject who defines herself, at one stage in her narrative, as "constitutionally nervous."[1] When writing *Jane Eyre*, Brontë had deliberately created a split between Jane and her "dark double"[2]—the concealed and imprisoned "mad" wife of Rochester—offering, through a process of analogy and contrast, an analysis of the social construction of insanity. In *Villette* she confronts the issue of psychological instability more directly through the figure of her narrator, Lucy Snowe, focusing now, not on the flamboyant extreme of "mania," but on the more subtle area of the constitution of neurosis. Through the autobiographical account of "calm," "shadow-like" Lucy, the archetypal unreliable narrator, Brontë both explores and interrogates contemporary theories of mental alienation.

The text of *Villette* is dominated by the practice of surveillance. The constant self-surveillance and concealment which marks Lucy's own narrative account is figured socially in the institutional practices of those who surround her. All characters spy on others, attempting, covertly, to read and interpret the external signs of faces, minds, and actions. Madame Beck runs her school according to the watchwords "'surveillance,' 'espionage'" (p. 99); M. Paul reads Lucy's countenance on her arrival in Villette, and later studies her through his "magic lattice"; and Père Silas focuses on her "the surveillance of a sleepless eye"—the Roman Catholic confessional (p. 592). Lucy is subjected to educational, professional, and religious surveillance. Each observer tries to read her inner self through the interpretation of outer signs. This practice takes its most authoritative form in the narrative in the medical judgments of Dr. John.

After Lucy's first encounter with the nun, as she is attempting to read Dr. John's letter, he in turn tries to "read" her: "I look on you now from a professional point of view, and I read, perhaps, all you would conceal—in your eye, which is curiously vivid and restless: in your cheek, which the blood has forsaken; in your hand, which you cannot steady" (p. 355). Dr. John directs onto Lucy the gaze of medical authority, calmly confident of his ability to define inner experience from outer signs. His verdict is distinguished by his insistence on his professional status, and by his unshakable belief that, no matter how hard Lucy might try to hide from his gaze, he would penetrate through to her innermost secrets. The rhetoric of unveiling and penetrating the truth, so prevalent in nineteenth-century science, is here located as a discourse of power: male science unveils female nature.[3]

All those who subject Lucy to surveillance present her with interpretations of her mind and character, but only Dr. John claims the authority of science for his interpretation (though M. Paul, to a lesser extent, also assumes this power when he offers a phrenological reading of her skull). Against the descriptive labels offered by Madame Beck and Père Silas, Dr. John presents a whole language of analysis and a theory of psychological functioning. His diagnosis on this occasion is that it is "a matter of the nerves," a "case of spectral illusion . . . following on and resulting from long-continued mental conflict" (pp. 357, 358). The terms of his analysis are drawn directly from contemporary medical science where the subject of "spectral illusion" proved a constant source of debate.[4] Against more visionary explanations of the nun, who functions as a site of crucial interpretative conflict in the text, he offers a materialist explanation based on the functioning of the nervous system. On one level, the text falsifies Dr. John's materialist explanation by presenting an even more material cause—the physical presence of the Count de Hamal masquerading as a nun. The authority of science is not, however, thereby erased from the text. The very inadequacy of the "literal" explanation, indeed, feeds further speculation into the question of the relationship between body and mind which functions as a subtext in the novel. As readers interpreting the signs of Lucy's discourse, we are constantly tempted by the text into reenacting the role of Dr. John, as we attempt to pierce through the external linguistic signs of the narrative to a concealed unity lying below. The text, however, frustrates all such quests for a hidden unitary meaning, deliberately undermining the social and psychological presuppositions which underlie such a quest.

In focusing interpretative attention in the novel on Lucy's "sightings" of the nun, Brontë is deliberately raising the issue of Lucy's psychological stability. Hallucinations, as Brontë was clearly aware, were classically regarded as signs of madness.[5] Lucy herself invokes this mode of explanation on her first glimpse of the nun, challenging the reader to say, "I was nervous, or mad" (p. 351). Despite Lucy's stated resistance to Dr. John's system of analysis, she constantly employs contemporary scientific language to describe her own psychological functioning. The term "nervous system," which she finds alien and technical when used by Dr. John, has already figured largely in her narrative (p. 261). Other terms from contemporary scientific discourse, such as "monomania," "hypochondria," and "hysteria" are also employed with precision in her analysis. Scientific language in the novel is not confined to Dr. John's specific diagnoses—the imposition of "male reason" on a largely Gothic text—it frames Lucy's narrative construction of her self.

In order to understand Brontë's explorations of the psyche in *Villette* it is essential to place the novel in the context of mid-nineteenth-century medical and social debate. Unlike her contemporaries George Eliot and Wilkie Collins, for instance, who explicitly recorded their indebtedness to psychological theory, Brontë has not generally been noted for her interest in this area.[6] Evidence from her novels and letters, however, which are permeated with contemporary psychological vocabulary, suggests a rather different picture. The following analysis will draw on the diverse sources through which psychological debate penetrated into the Haworth household: local newspapers, periodicals, texts in the Keighley Mechanics' Institute Library, and, perhaps most significantly, the Reverend Brontë's secular bible: Thomas John Graham's *Domestic Medicine*.[7] This text, which clearly stands behind the authority of Dr. John Graham Bretton, has been annotated throughout by Patrick Brontë, revealing a wealth of reading in psychological medicine and a personal interest in nervous diseases (Patrick records his fears concerning his own psychological health, and the symptoms of Branwell).

The preoccupation with nervous disorder in *Villette* reflects contemporary social concern. The mid-Victorian press was full of alarmist reports concerning supposed dramatic increases in the numbers of the insane, while the borders between sanity and insanity also seemed to be called into question. As a writer observed in the *Times*, July 1853, "Nothing can be more slightly defined than the line of demarcation between sanity and insanity. . . . Make the definition too narrow, it becomes meaningless; make it too wide, the whole human race are involved in the drag-net."[8] The observation reflects the radical shift in social attitudes toward insanity in the nineteenth century which culminated in the passing of the two Lunatic Acts in 1845 and the setting up of public asylums. For the first time the insane were sharply distinguished from the criminal or pauper. This development was directly related, however, to the rise of theories of "moral management" for the treatment of the insane, which stressed the recuperability of the mentally ill, thus breaking down any absolute barrier between sanity and insanity.[9] While earlier theorists had tended to stress the animal nature of the insane, the moral managers stressed their membership in a common humanity. Thus at the same time that insanity was being constructed as a distinct social category, the borders separating it from sanity were also being eroded.

The social and institutional change signaled by the founding of the public asylums was underpinned by the growing professionalization of medical practice, and by the growth of a new specialty—alienism, or psychological medicine. Doctors henceforth claimed the exclusive right to define and treat insanity. Their claims to authority were supported by developments in physiological research which designated the brain and nervous system as the site of mental life.[10] The social and philosophical debate concerning the constitution of the self is crystallized in each era in the discussion of insanity, as Roy Porter clearly demonstrates in his analysis of the eighteenth century in this volume. The crucial term in pre-1860s debate was control. At the same time that the popular and scientific press offered increasing numbers of articles on dreams, apparitions, and the operations of the unconscious mind, the dominant ideology remained that of self-control, as exemplified in John Barlow's work entitled *Man's Power over Himself to Prevent or Control Insanity* (1843). Popular response to mesmerism underlined this duality. Thus one critic could account for the attraction of mesmerism in terms only of an "imbecility of the nervous system, a ready abandonment of the will, a facility in relinquishing every endowment which makes man *human*."[11] Fear of the loss of control, of public exposure, underlies this attack. Emphasis on an individual's necessary responsibility for action is coupled with an overwhelming sense that control is at every moment liable to be overthrown.

The nineteenth-century preoccupation with control has been linked, by Andrew Scull, to the economic nexus. The shift in the treatment of the insane, as the external mechanisms of restraint of whips and chains were replaced by an emphasis on internal control and the inner discipline of the mind, was directly related, he argues, to the rise of laissez-faire economics: lunatics, like the industrial work force, had to be taught the principles of " 'rational' self-interest" which governed the marketplace.[12] The individualist philosophy encapsulated in Samuel Smiles's notion of "self-help" governed the treatment of the insane. The asylum formed a microcosm of Victorian society: social and psychological ordering was achieved through constant surveillance, or "careful watching," and its psychological reflex, the internalization of social controls.[13]

Women held a different relationship to this system than men: the medical construction of categories of insanity reinforced the sexual stereotypes of social discourse[14] The debates concerning self-control were underpinned by the traditional nature-culture polarity; women were assimilated to the side of nature. The metaphorical construction of nature as female, discussed by Anne Mellor in her essay on *Frankenstein*, is given practical force here. As the preeminent theorist of insanity, Esquirol, observed: "Physical causes act more frequently upon women than men."[15] Menstruation, childbirth, lactation, all contributed to the myth of "feminine vulnerability": women were seen to possess a biological predisposition to insanity. The social construction of women, which endowed them with feeling, but little reason, also thereby reduced their capacity to resist the onslaughts of the body. Thus at the same time that the Victorian social code ruthlessly enforced ideas of "modesty" and "decorum" in female behavior, it also presented women with an image of their own powerlessness actively to achieve these qualities. In the mid-century criminal trial, where insanity had come to be a recognized plea, women, like children and idiots, were held to be not "responsible" for their actions.[16]

The success of this medicosocial constitution of the feminine can be judged, as Showalter has observed, by the evident collusion of middle-class women in this process: "how eagerly they embraced insanity as an explanation of their unfeminine impulses, and welcomed the cures that would extinguish the forbidden throb of sexuality or ambition."[17] In analysis of *Villette*, I will be concerned to examine how far Lucy Snowe, in constructing her narrative, resists such collusion, and how far she recapitulates the definitions and codifications of female experience offered by the male medical establishment.

Brontë's depiction of Lucy's life shows clearly how institutional practices of surveillance are inscribed within the self. Medical surveillance is matched by Madame Beck's professional control, which Lucy relates directly to the practices of industry, referring to her "system of managing and regulating this mass of machinery" (p. 99). Madame Beck's machine seems to function independently of any personal intervention, operating rather on the participants' internalization of the mechanisms of control. As Foucault observes of the principles of Bentham's Panopticon (which he takes as paradigmatic of nineteenth-century modes of social control), "He who is subjected to a field of visibility, and who knows it, assumes responsibility for the constraints of power; he makes them play spontaneously upon himself; he inscribes in himself the power relation in which he simultaneously plays both roles; he becomes the principle of his own subjection."[18] Lucy clearly demonstrates this psychological pattern, allowing all her actions to be dictated by the sense that she might be overlooked. Thus at one stage she even invests inanimate nature with the qualities of spy: "the eyes of the flowers had gained vision, and the knots in the tree-boles listened like secret ears" (p. 161).

The third form of surveillance to which Lucy is subject is that of the Roman Catholic church. Her impulse to confession—the voluntary revelation of the secrets of the inner self—represents for Lucy the nadir of her mental state. Worn out by suffering consequent on her internalization of the social contradictions of the female role, she sacrifices the last vestiges of her autonomy, thus opening herself up to the continued intervention of both medical and religious authorities in her life (and precipitating her entry into the "very safe asylum" offered by the Brettons) (p. 244). Père Silas proves even more assiduous in his "treatment" than Dr. John. From that moment on, as he later informs her, he had not "for a day lost sight of you, nor for an hour failed to take in you a rooted interest" (p. 571). He envisages her "passed under the discipline of Rome, moulded by her high training, inoculated with her salutary doctrines" (the manuscript originally read "sane" doctrines). With its aim of total dominion over the mind through the discipline of its sane/salutary doctrines, Lucy's Roman Catholic church replicates precisely the alientists' system of moral management of the insane.

The perceived threat of the church to Lucy does not end with her confession. As her relationship with Dr. John is subject always to the scrutiny of Madame Beck "glid[ing] ghost-like through the house, watching and spying everywhere" (p. 100), so her relationship with M. Paul is attended by that "ghostly troubler" (p. 600), Père Silas, and the threat of the confessional: "We were under the surveillance of a sleepless eye: Rome watched jealously her son through that mystic lattice at which I had knelt once, and to which M. Emmanuel drew nigh month by month—the sliding panel of the confessional" (p. 592). Lucy's use of the term "magic lattice" echoes, significantly, M. Paul's description of his "post of observation," his window overlooking the garden, where he sits and "reads" "female human nature": "Ah, magic lattice! what miracles of discovery hast thou wrought" (p. 528). The "magic lattice" forms another medium for the male gaze to penetrate through to the recesses of the female psyche, furnishing information which is then appropriated to judge and censor, in accordance with male definitions of female decorum (M. Paul rejects Zelie St. Pierre on the basis of his observations). Lucy herself, M. Paul observes, wants "checking, regulating, and keeping down." She needs "watching, and watching over" (p. 526). Lucy vehemently repudiates M. Paul's methods: "To study the human heart thus, is to banquet secretly and sacrilegiously on Eve's apples. I wish you were a Protestant" (p. 530). The phrase "Eve's apples," used in connection with the voyeuristic practice of spying on women, takes on a decisive sexual charge. The implicit connection, made throughout the book, between Roman Catholicism and the threatened exposure, and suppression, of female sexuality is here brought to the surface.

The school legend of the nun "buried alive, for some sin against her vow" (p. 148) establishes a chain of association between nuns, ghosts, and sexuality which reverberates throughout the novel. Lucy, burying her precious letters from Dr. John above the nun's grave, is associating the unspecified "sin" with sexual transgression. Her "sightings" of the nun occur, significantly, at moments of heightened sexual tension, while the ghostly pursuit to which she is subject seems to embody externally her own activities of self-suppression. Lucy's violent antagonism to Roman Catholicism, treated so often by critics as an intrusion of Brontë's personal prejudice, stems from this sexual nexus. The intensity of her response is signaled initially by her seemingly excessive reactions to the nightly "lecture pieuse": "it made me so burning hot, and my temples and my heart and my wrist throbbed so fast, and my sleep afterwards was so broken with excitement, that I could sit no longer" (p. 163). The description of the content of the tales helps explain Lucy's extreme response: they contain "the dread boasts of confessors, who had wickedly abused their office, trampling to deep degradation high-born ladies, making of countesses and princesses the most tormented slaves under the sun." It is this "abuse of office" which Lucy most fears: the subjection of the self to a male authority consequent on the revelation of the inner self. The explicit sexual nature of this subjection is suggested by the only named tale, that of Elizabeth of Hungary, whose source for Brontë was Charles Kingsley's virulently anti-Catholic poem *The Saint's Tragedy*.[19] The poem chronicles the effects, in Kingsley's view, of the "Manichean contempt" for sexuality of the Roman Catholic church: Elizabeth's guilt concerning sexual desire leads to her total subjection to her priest, whose motives are seen to be an unsavory mixture of sexual lust, worldly ambition, and crude love of power.

In constructing Lucy's self-contradictory narrative, with its displacements, evasions, and ghostly sightings, which clearly signal to the modern reader the presence of sexual repression, Brontë was not unconsciously articulating patterns in the human psyche which were to remain unrecognized, or even untheorized, until the advent of Freud. Sexuality, and specifically female sexuality, was frequently cited as a primary cause of nervous disorder and insanity in nineteenth-century discussions of mental illness. Ideas of women's sexual neurasthenia, as exemplified in Acton's writings, were directly counterpointed by theories of female psychology which stressed women's "vulnerability": the mysterious processes of menstruation (whose causes remained, for the mid-Victorians, threateningly inexplicable), childbirth, and lactation, which linked them to the natural world, also predisposed them, physiologically, to passion.[20] In the seventeenth century, William Harvey had drawn a comparision between women and animals in heat, observing that "in like manner women occasionally become insane through ungratified desire." They are saved only through "good nurture," and innate modesty.[21] Virtually the same sentiments were repeated in the nineteenth century by the progressive alienist John Bucknill: "Religious and moral principles alone give strength to the female mind," he observed. "When these are weakened or removed by disease, the subterranean fires become active, and the crater gives forth smoke and flame"[22] (a process which is literally embodied by Brontë in the burning of Thornfield by the demonic Mrs. Rochester, and in the outbreak of fire in the theater as the "fallen angel" Vashti is acting).

The idea of a specific sexual cause of mental disorder reappeared with renewed force in the nineteenth century following the work of Pinel (acknowledged founder of the new "humanitarian" treatment of the insane), who suggested that mental alienation might proceed, not from an organic disease of the brain, but rather from a "moral" (or functional) disorder.[23] His influential study of mental alienation stressed sexuality as a major factor in hysteria (a disorder which, although no longer attributed to the wanderings of the womb, was still recognized as a primarily female province). Medical texts of the nineteenth century emphasized repeatedly that hysteria occurred mainly in young, unmarried women.[24]

By the mid-century, commentators, eschewing earlier coyness, directly addressed the possible destructive consequences of continence. Thus Feuchtersleben argued, for example, in *The Principles of Medical Psychology* (1845, Eng. trans. 1847), that hysteria arose most frequently in women from "the want of exercise in those sexual functions intended by nature for use and disappointed desire or hope."[25] The equation of women's "natural" state and sexual activity figures even more decisively in Robert Carter's study *On the Pathology and Treatment of Hysteria* (1853), which outlines the first systematic theory of repression. Carter argues that the suppression of sexual passion is one of the primary causes of hysteria, and women, both by nature and social convention, are rendered more susceptible than men. Although woman is "much under [the] dominion" of sexual desire, "if unmarried and chaste, [she] is compelled to restrain every manifestation of its sway."[26] While Harvey extolled the "good nurture" and "innate modesty" of women which enabled them to "tranquilize the inordinate passions of the mind," Carter turns this formulation on its head, to show how social conventions of female passivity actually produce insanity.

Brontë's endorsement of Carter's position is clearly revealed in *Shirley*, where the disappointed Caroline, denied the social right to address her lover, reflects on the life of the old maid, comparing it directly to the life-denying existence of nuns, "with their close cell, their iron lamp, their robe strait as a shroud, their bed narrow as a coffin. . . . these having violated nature, their natural likings and antipathies are reversed: they grow altogether morbid."[27] Denial of sexuality is explicitly associated with the violation of nature. As in Carter's theory of repression, natural energies, if thwarted, turn back on themselves to create perverted forms. The attractive Caroline is not permitted to become "morbid." She is subjected instead to the physical ailment of brain fever which allows her mental faculties and personality to remain fundamentally intact.[28] In *Villette*, by contrast, Brontë actively explores the mental effects of repression, exposing, through the twists and turns of her narrative, the morbid processes of mind of her designedly uncongenial "Miss Frost."[29]

The question of Lucy's actual instability must remain unanswered if we, as readers, are to avoid falling into the error of Dr. John in assuming unproblematic access to a realm of hidden "truth." It is possible, however, to trace the degree to which Lucy, in analysis of her own history, draws on the constructions of appropriate and "insane" feminine behavior to be found in mid-nineteenth-century psychological science. In her explicit use of contemporary scientific terms, Lucy draws attention to the explanatory complexes which underpin the often unconscious associations that direct her interpretation of behavior. Her first noticeable use of scientific terminology occurs in her judgment on what she perceives to be the emotional excesses of the child Polly's behavior with regard to her father: "This, I perceived, was a one-idead nature; betraying that monomaniac tendency I have ever thought the most unfortunate with which man or woman can be cursed" (p. 16). The idea of monomania, displaced here onto Polly, is later appropriated by Lucy for herself to describe her distress at losing Dr. John's letter: " 'Oh! they have taken my letter!' cried the grovelling, groping, monomaniac" (p. 353).[30] The "curse" of monomania to which Lucy here refers was first defined by Esquirol as an "anormal condition of the physical or moral sensibility, with a circumscribed and fixed delirium" (p. 200). In the more developed definition of James Prichard, the chief popularizer of Esquirol's theories in England, monomania was seen as a form of "partial insanity, in which the understanding is partially disordered or under the influence of some particular illusion, referring to one subject, and involving one train of ideas, while the intellectual powers appear, when exercised on other subjects, to be in a great measure unimpaired."[31] Monomania was thus a form of insanity, unmarked by mania, which could exist within the compass of normal life. Esquirol's categories of insanity were founded on assumptions of "feminine vulnerability." Women, he believed, were more susceptible, both physiologically and psychologically, to religious and erotic melancholy, and hence to the "hallucinations the most strange and frequent" (p. 109) of religious and erotic monomania (a conjunction of religion and sexuality which clearly lies behind the figure of the nun).

Lucy's monomania follows the course of Esquirol's erotic monomania, which he defines as a literal disease, a "chronic cerebral affection . . . characterized by an excessive passion" (p. 335). Reflecting the cultural attitudes of his era, Esquirol divides sexual afflictions into chaste erotomania, whose origins lie in the imagination, and "obscene," "shameful and humiliating" nymphomania and satyriasis, which originate in the organs of reproduction. Erotomaniacs' affections are "chaste and honourable"; they "never pass the limits of propriety." Instead, they tend to "forget themselves; vow a pure, and often secret devotion to the object of their love; make themselves slaves to it; execute its orders with a fidelity often puerile; and obey also the caprices that are connected with it" (p. 336). The description offers an outline of Lucy's "chaste," obsessional behavior; her devotion to Dr. John, like that of the erotomaniac, is secret.

Esquirol's formulation of erotomania, like his other categories of insanity, dresses recognized social stereotypes in the authority of science. In his hands, the disease becomes socially respectable. Erotomaniacs, he insists, do not, even in fantasy, seek fulfillment of their desires: "The erotomaniac neither desires, nor dreams even, of the favors to which he might aspire from the object of his insane tenderness" (p. 336). The social repression, so evident in Lucy's narrative, which forbade women the articulation, or even conscious acknowledgment, of their desires, is encoded in his very definition of the disease. Esquirol's theory of erotomania, however, does not merely reinforce accepted social wisdom: chaste, hopeless passion is transformed into a cerebral disease, and must henceforth be treated as a possible symptom of insanity. The fear of mental illness signaled by Lucy's references to monomania underpins all her narrative: insanity is no longer limited to the recognizably disruptive forces of sexual desire, which may be locked away in the attic, but lurks as an incipient threat even in the "chaste" repressed imaginings of the "respectable" woman.

The structure of *Jane Eyre* had seemed to vindicate the mid-Victorian ideological position that successful regulation of the mental economy would lead to material social success. Bertha is sent to her death so that Jane can achieve the bourgeois dream. *Villette*, a more radical work than *Jane Eyre*, refuses this compromise. The novel calls into question the doctrine of control, thus implicitly challenging the economic model of healthy regulation which underpinned mid-Victorian theories of social, psychological, and physiological functioning. The mind, like the body, or the social economy, was to be treated as a system to be guided, regulated, and controlled. As John Elliotson observed, "the laws of the mind are precisely those of the functions of all other organs,—a certain degree of excitement strengthens it; too much exhausts it."[32] In the mental as in the social economy, the aim must be to obtain maximum efficiency, neither overstretching nor underdeploying the natural resources. Theories of insanity drew on this model. Whether the cause were seen to be physical or moral, menstrual irregularities or the exclusive direction of the efforts of the mind into one channel, the net effect was that of unbalancing the body's natural economy which was founded on the free flow of "secretions" and a hierarchical regulation of the mental forces.[33] Such theories of the bodily economy were based, however, on normative, gender-specific, codes of social behavior. The social construction of insanity went hand in hand with that of femininity.

Lucy, in her vocabulary, seems initially to endorse enthusiastically the world view propounded by contemporary alienists and phrenologists, that cultivation of the correct faculties and suppression of the troublesome lower propensities would lead directly to social advancement. Launched in her teaching career she feels satisfied "I was getting on; not lying the stagnant prey of mould and rust, but polishing my faculties and and whetting them to a keen edge with constant use" (p. 113).[34] Such confidence soon dissolves, however, to be replaced by a rather different theory of social and psychological life. Brontë still uses the vocabulary of regulation and control, but to rather different effect. Lucy's efforts at regulation are no longer seen to be healthful. She strives for a literal form of live burial, recapitulating the experience of the nun: "in catalepsy and a dead trance, I studiously held the quick of my nature" (p. 152). In a world where inner energies, when duly regulated, can find no external outlet, it is better, Lucy argues, that they be suppressed, if they are not to become self-consuming. Alternatively, they should be allowed to range in the world of fantasy. Thus she deliberately rejects Hag Reason, for the saving spirit of the imagination (p. 327), while the "Real"—that realm to which the moral managers sought so assiduously to return their patients—is figured for her in the iconography of the fallen women: "Presently the rude Real burst coarsely in—all evil, grovelling, and repellent as she too often is" (p. 153). The description, which prefigures the emergence of that "grovelling, groping, monomaniac" Lucy herself, suggests the consequences for women of living according to male-defined reality (the "Real" here is the casket containing the love letter which simultaneously dismisses Lucy as a sexual possibility and condemns her as a monster). Lucy's narrative, which dissolves the real into the imaginary, challenges male constructions of the social and psychological world.

This is not to suggest, however, that Lucy thereby steps entirely outside the formulations of psychological experience to be found in contemporary science. Her descriptions of her sufferings during the long vacation follow medical wisdom in assigning both physical and moral causes for this "strange fever of the nerves and blood" (p. 222). Her sexual fantasies and nightmares of rejection are underpinned by the responsiveness of her physical frame to the storms and tempests outside, held by contemporary alienists to occasion and exacerbate insanity (see Graham, p. 392; Esquirol, p. 31). In thus projecting herself as a physical system, at the mercy of external physical changes, Lucy is able to deny her responsibility for her mental disorder: it is her "nervous system" which cannot stand the strain; the controlling rational ego is dissolved into the body. The figure of the cretin, however, with its "propensity . . . to evil" (p. 220), stands as a warning projection of a model of mind where the physical is dominant, and the passions and propensities are not subject to any mental restraint.

Lucy seems to shift in and out of physiological explanation of the self at her convenience. In opposition to Dr. John, she denies understanding his diagnosis: "I am not quite sure what my nervous system is, but I was dreadfully low-spirited" (p. 261). Her attempt to define why she went to confession is marked by a similar resistance: "I suppose you will think me mad for taking such a step, but I could not help it: I suppose it was all the fault of what you call my 'nervous system' "(p. 264). Lucy's resistance to Dr. John seems to stem less from the actual content of his medical verdicts than from his reduction of her to a bundle of symptoms, open to his professional definition and control.

Her battle for control over self-definition and interpretation of the processes of her own mind is not conducted solely with Dr. John; the fiery M. Paul also enters the lists. On encountering Lucy in the art gallery after her illness, M. Paul berates her for her unfeminine behavior in not being able to look after the cretin: "Women who are worthy the name," he proclaims, "ought infinitely to surpass our coarse, fallible, self-indulgent sex, in the power to perform such duties" (p. 290). The covert subject of this conversation is clearly the model of the female mind which suggested that women are more "naturally" able than men to suppress their "evil propensities." Lucy, in self-defense, resorts to another male model of the female mind, asserting a physical illness: "I had a nervous fever: my mind was ill" (p. 290). Diminished responsibility, which figured so largely in mid-Victorian trials of female criminals, becomes the basis of her excuse for "unwomanly" conduct. Unlike Dr. John, M. Paul refuses to accept this model of the mind and so draws attention back again to his own image of the constitution of the feminine. Dismissing the idea of nervous fever, he points instead to Lucy's "temerity" in gazing at the picture of Cleopatra. The portrait of the fleshy Cleopatra, and the four pictures of "La vie d'une femme," "cold and vapid as ghosts," which M. Paul prefers for Lucy's instruction in the arts of femininity, take on iconographic significance in the narrative, representing the two alternative models for womanhood created by men.[35] Lucy's challenge to these models, implicit throughout her narrative, takes decisive form in the Vashti section.

The narrative sequence which culminates in the performance of Vashti actually starts, not in the theater, but with Lucy's apparent sighting, that evening, of the nun. Dr. John, refusing to respect her reticence, invokes once more his professional authority to diagnose the symptoms of her "raised look," thus provoking Lucy's angry dismissal of his explanation: "Of course with him, it was held to be another effect of the same cause: it was all optical illusion—nervous malady, and so on. Not one bit did I believe him; but I dared not contradict: doctors are so self-opinionated, so immovable in their dry, materialist views" (p. 368). Lucy rejects the "doctor's" opinion on principle, although his physiological explanation appears perhaps surprisingly close to views she herself has expressed elsewhere. The grounds of her objection to Dr. John's "dry" materialism are made explicit, however, in her analysis of their mutual responses to the performance of Vashti.

For Lucy, Vashti on stage transcends socially imposed sex roles; she is neither woman nor man, but a devil, a literal embodiment of inner passion: "Hate and Murder and Madness incarnate, she stood" (p. 369). Lucy's response is to invoke the male author of a rather different image of womanhood: "Where was the artist of the Cleopatra? Let him come and sit down and study this different version. Let him seek here the mighty brawn, the muscle, the abounding blood, the full-fed flesh he worshipped: let all materialists draw nigh and look on" (p. 370). In a significant elision, Lucy has drawn together the materialism of doctors who seek to explain the processes of the mind with reference only to the physiological behavior of the nerves, and the materialism of men who construct their images of women with reference only to the physical attributes of the flesh. The creation of the feminine in male-executed art is directly allied to the medical construction of women.

Lucy perceives, in Vashti, a force which could reenact the miracle of the Red Sea, drowning Paul Peter Rubens (sic) and "all the army of his fat women," but Dr. John remains unresponsive to her challenge. He replicates, in the "intense curiosity" with which he watches her performance, the professional gaze he has recently imposed on Lucy. His verdict underscores, for Lucy, his indifference to the inner movements of female experience: "he judged her as a woman, not an artist: it was a branding judgment" (p. 373). Dr. John's response is determined entirely by predefined categories of suitable female behavior. As in his medical practice, he is insulated from any attempt to understand the causes or experiential detail of the cases he is examining through his possession of a socially validated system of classification which allows him to speak with unreflecting authority. Like his counterparts in the Book of Esther (from where the name Vashti is drawn), he trusts to the codification of male power to protect him from the "demonic" challenge of female energy. (Queen Vashti's refusal to show her beauty to the people at the king's command had provoked, from a worried male oligarchy, a proclamation "into every province according to the writing thereof, and to every people after their language, that every man should bear rule in his own house" [Esther, 1:22]).

In choosing to equate medical and artistic constructions of the female identity through the notion of "materialism," Brontë was drawing on the terms of contemporary debate. As an artistic term, implying the "tendency to lay stress on the material aspects of the objects represented," the word materialism seems to date only from the 1850s (*O.E.D.*). Although the philosophical usage of materialism dates back to the eighteenth century, it had, at the time of Brontë's writing, become the focus of a virulent social and theological debate concerning the development of psychological theories which stressed that the brain was the organ of mind. Phrenology and mesmerism were located, in the popular press, at the center of this controversy, as evidenced by the 1851 *Blackwood's* article which inveighed against the phreno-mesmerism of authors who believed that "upon the materialism of life rest the great phenomena of what we were wont to call mind."[36] Lucy's objections to materialism are not based on the religious grounds of contemporary debate; nor, as her own use of physiological vocabulary demonstrates, are they founded on an opposition to physiological explanation of the mind per se. Her rejection of medical and artistic materialism stems rather from the rigid and incomplete nature of their conception; she objects less to the idea of an interrelationship between body and mind than to their rather partial vision of this union. Under the medical and artistic gaze, woman is *reduced* to flesh and the material functioning of nerves.

In describing the impact of Vashti, Lucy herself employs the vocabulary of contemporary physiological psychology; Vashti's acting, "instead of merely irritating imagination with the thought of what *might* be done, at the same time fevering the nerves because it was *not* done, disclosed power like a deep, swollen, winter river, thundering in cataract, and bearing the soul, like a leaf, on the steep and steely sweep of its descent" (p. 371). The term "irritating" here is a technical one as used, for example, in Graham's observation that "the nervous headache generally occurs in persons with a peculiar irritability of the nervous system" (p. 332). Coupled with the idea of "fevering the nerves," it suggests two different levels of response within the nervous system, while the concluding imagery of the thundering river draws on physiological ideas of channeled energy within the brain. The power disclosed is both internal and external: it describes the force of Vashti's own inner energy, and the impact on the observer, Lucy. In this metaphorical usage of contemporary physiological theory, Brontë dramatizes an even closer integration of body and mind than physiology envisaged, while simultaneously breaking down traditional boundaries of the self. Mind is not reduced to body, it becomes literally "embodied," as Lucy earlier observed: "To her, what hurts becomes immediately embodied: she looks on it as a thing that can be attacked, worried down, torn in shreds. Scarcely a substance herself, she grapples to conflict with abstractions. Before calamity she is a tigress; she rends her woes, shivers them in convulsed abhorrence" (p. 370). While the artist reduces woman to a material expanse of flesh, and the doctor to a mere encasement of nerves, Vashti reveals a true union between the worlds of mind and body: abstractions, the experiential details of mental life which physiology cannot describe, are given material form. In her treatment of Vashti, as throughout the novel, Brontë actually employs contemporary physiological theory to break through the narrow definition of the self it proposes.

The description of Vashti tearing hurt into shreds anticipates Lucy's later destruction of the figure of the nun:

All the movement was mine, so was all the life, the reality, the substance, the force; as my instinct felt. I tore her up—the incubus! I held her on high—the goblin! I shook her loose—the mystery! And down she fell—down all round me—down in shreds and fragments—and I trode upon her. (p. 681)

Like Vashti, Lucy undertakes a material destruction of an inner hurt: the force and *substance* are Lucy's own.[37] The term "incubus," with its associations of sexuality and mental disturbance, draws together the arenas of physical and mental life. In nineteenth-century psychological usage, incubus had become synonymous with nightmare. In a passage noted by Patrick Brontë in his *Domestic Medicine*, Robert Macnish observed, in *The Philosophy of Sleep*, that it was possible to suffer nightmare while awake and in "perfect possession of [the] faculties." Macnish records that he had "undergone the greatest tortures, being haunted by spectres, hags, and every sort of phantom—having, at the same time, a full consciousness that I was labouring under incubus, and that all the terrifying objects around me were the creations of my own brain.[38] Brontë takes this idea of waking nightmare, or incubus, one stage further, giving it a literal embodiment in her fiction which defies attempts to demarcate the boundaries between "creations of the brain" and external forms.

Brontë offers, in *Villette*, a thorough materialization of the self. The construct "Lucy" is not a unified mental entity, located within a physiological frame, but rather a continuous process which extends beyond the confines of the flesh. Lucy's entire mode of self-articulation breaks down the hierarchy of outer and inner life upon which definitions of the "Real" (and sanity) depend. Her description of the death of Hope, for instance, parallels that of the literal burial of the letters: "In the end I closed the eyes of my dead, covered its face, and composed its limbs with great calm" (p. 421.). The burial itself is figured as the wrapping of grief in a "winding-sheet." Later, as Lucy pauses beside the grave, she recalls "the passage of feeling therein buried" (p. 524). Metaphor has become inoperable: it functions, as Lucy's text makes clear, only if the speaker endorses normative social demarcations between different states. Thus the classrooms which initially only "seem" to Lucy to be like jails quickly become "filled with spectral and intolerable memories, laid miserable amongst their straw and their manacles" (p. 652). The controlling distance of "seems" is collapsed, as "memories," normally restricted to the realm of the mind, take on vivid physical form.

Lucy's intricate dramatizations of her feelings undermine traditional divisions between external social process and inner mental life, revealing their fictional status.[39] Her tale of Jael, Sisera, and Heber, for example, simultaneously portrays physiological pain, psychological conflict, and the social drama of repression. Speaking of her desire to be drawn out of her present existence, Lucy observes:

> This longing, and all of a similar kind, it was necessary to knock on the head; which I did, figuratively, after the manner of Jael to Sisera, driving a nail through their temples. Unlike Sisera, they did not die: they were but transiently stunned, and at intervals would turn on the nail with a rebellious wrench; then did the temples bleed, and the brain thrill to its core. (p. 152)

The distinction between figural and literal quickly fades, as the inner psychic drama develops, the the rebellious desires themselves perpetuate their torture, in a description which captures the physiological and psychological experience of socially inflicted repression (the term "thrill" carried the medically precise meaning, in the mid-nineteenth century, of "vibratory movement, resonance, or murmur").

The famous account of Lucy's opiate-induced wanderings into the night landscape of Villette also dissolves the divisions between inner and outer realms, as social experience now takes on the qualities of mental life, defying the normal boundaries of time and space. Amidst the physical forms of Cleopatra's Egypt, Lucy witnesses the figures of her inner thoughts parade before her eyes. Even here, however, where she seems most free from external social controls, she is still subject to fears of surveillance: she feels Dr. John's gaze "oppressing" her, seeming ready to grasp "my identity . . . between his never tyrannous, but always powerful hands" (p. 661). As dominant male, and doctor, empowered by society to diagnose the inner movements of mind, and legislate on mental disease, Dr. John threatens Lucy's carefully nurtured sense of self. Identity, as Brontë has shown throughout Villette, is not a given, but rather a tenuous process of negotiation between the subject and surrounding social forces.

The opposition to male materialism, voiced by Lucy in her confrontation with medical authority, gives dramatic expression to the interrogation of male constructions of the female psyche which underpins the narrative form of Villette. In seeking to avoid the surveillance of religious, educational and medical figures, trying to render herself illegible, Lucy attempts to assume control over the processes of her own self-definition. Yet her narrative, as I have argued, reveals a clear internalization of the categories and terms of contemporary medical psychology. Lucy employs physiological explanations of mental life and appropriates to herself theories of a female predisposition to neurosis and monomania. In creating the autobiography of her troubled heroine, whose commitment to evasion and displacement is articulated in the very title of her book, Brontë explores both the social implications of contemporary psychological theory and its inner consequences. The form of her account, with its dissolution of divisions between inner psychological life and the material social world, suggests an alternative vision—one that challenges the normative psychological vision implicit in male definitions of the "Real."

Notes

1. Charlotte Brontë, *Villette*, ed. H. Rosengarten and M. Smith (Oxford: Oxford University Press, 1984), p. 531.

2. S. Gilbert and S. Gubar, *The Madwoman in the Attic: The Woman Writer and the Nineteenth-Century Literary Imagination* (New Haven: Yale University Press, 1979), p. 360.

3. See Michel Foucault, *The Birth of the Clinic* (London: Tavistock, 1973), chaps. 7–9; and L. J. Jordanova, "Natural Facts: A Historical Perspective on Science and Sexuality," in C. P. MacCormack and M. Strathern, eds., *Nature, Culture and Gender* (Cambridge: Cambridge University Press, 1980).

4. Two works in the Keighley Mechanics' Institute, where the Brontës borrowed books, offer, for example, extensive discussions of the relationship between "spectral illusion" and insanity: John Abercrombie, *Inquiries concerning the Intellectual Powers* (Edinburgh: Waugh and Innes, 1832), and Robert Macnish, *The Philosophy of Sleep* (Glasgow: W. R. M'Phun, 1830).

5. See R. Hunter and I. Macalpine, *Three Hundred Years of Psychiatry, 1535–1860* (London: Oxford University Press, 1963), p. 1059.

6. For a discussion of George Eliot's indebtedness, see S. Shuttleworth, *George Eliot and Nineteenth-Century Science: The Make-Believe of a Beginning* (Cambridge: Cambridge University Press, 1984). Wilkie Collins' relationship to contemporary psychology is the subject of a book by Jenny Taylor, forthcoming from Methuen.

7. Thomas John Graham, *Modern Domestic Medicine* (London: Simpkin and Marshall et al., 1826). This work is in the Brontë Parsonage Museum, together with several other of the Reverend Brontë's medical books.

8. Quoted in V. Skultans, *Madness and Morals: Ideas on Insanity in the Nineteenth Century* (London: Routledge and Kegan Paul, 1975), p. 172.

9. For an account of this transition and the development of "moral management" in England see A. T. Scull, *Museums of Madness: The Social Organization of Insanity in Nineteenth-Century England* (London: Allen Lane, 1979); M. Foucault, *Madness and Civilization: A History of Insanity in the Age of Reason*, trans. R. Howard (London: Tavistock, 1971); and R. Smith, *Trial by Medicine: Insanity and Responsibility in Victorian Trials* (Edinburgh: Edinburgh University Press, 1981).

10. Smith, *Trial by Medicine*, p. 35.

11. "What Is Mesmerism?" *Blackwood's* 70 (1851): 84.

12. Scull, *Museums of Madness*, p. 72.

13. See E. Showalter, "Victorian Women and Insanity," *Victorian Studies* 23 (1980): 166.

14. See Jordanova, "Natural Facts," and Smith, *Trial by Medicine*, chap. 7.

15. J. E. D. Esquirol, *Mental Maladies: A Treatise on Insanity*, trans. E. K. Hunt (1845; rpt. New York: Hafner, 1965), p. 48.

16. See Smith, *Trial by Medicine*, chap. 7.

17. Showalter, "Victorian Women and Insanity," p. 175.

18. M. Foucault, *Discipline and Punish: The Birth of the Prison*, trans. A. Sheridan (Harmondsworth: Penguin, 1979), pp. 202–3.

19. J. Carlisle, "A Prelude to *Villette*: Charlotte Brontë's Reading, 1850–52," *Bulletin of Research in the Humanities* 82 (1979): 409. For Brontë's response to the poem see T. J. Wise and J. A. Symington, *The Brontës: Their Lives, Friendships and Correspondence*, 4 vols. (Oxford: Basil Blackwell, 1933), 3: 268–69.

20. John Elliotson, whose work the Reverend Brontë commends in his copy of Graham, observes in *Human Physiology*, 5th ed. (London: Longmans, 1840), that the source of the menstrua is entirely unclear.

21. Quoted in Hunter and Macalpine, *Three Hundred Years of Psychiatry*, p. 131.

22. Quoted in Showalter, "Victorian Women and Insanity," p. 167.

23. See I. Veith, *Hysteria: The History of a Disease* (Chicago: University of Chicago Press, 1965), pp. 175–84.

24. See Macnish, *Philosophy of Sleep*, pp. 139, 143, and George Man Burrows, *Commentaries on Insanity* (1828), quoted in Skultans, *Madness and Morals*, p. 226.

25. Quoted in Veith, *Hysteria*, p. 191.

26. Quoted in ibid., p. 201.

27. Charlotte Brontë, *Shirley*, ed. H. Rosengarten and M. Smith (Oxford: Oxford University Press, 1979), 2: 440–41.

28. Although Caroline's illness is never specifically defined as "brain fever," it carries all the usual symptoms. See A. C. Peterson, "Brain Fever in Nineteenth-Century Literature: Fact and Fiction," *Victorian Studies* 19 (1976): 439–64.

29. Brontë's original name for Lucy was "Frost." As she observes in a letter to W. S. Williams (6 November 1852): "A *cold* name she must have . . . for she has about her an external coldness." Wise and Symington, *Brontës*, 4:18.

30. The edition here actually reads "monamaniac." I presume, however, that this is a printing error.

31. J. C. Prichard, *A Treatise on Insanity and Other Disorders Affecting the Mind* (Philadelphia: Haswell, Barrington and Haswell, 1837; rpt. New York: Arno Press, 1973), p. 16.

32. Elliotson, *Human Physiology*, p. 37.

33. These were two of the causes cited by Graham, *Modern Domestic Medicine*, p. 392.

34. Her vocabulary is precisely that employed in the annual report of the Keighley Mechanics' Institute in 1832: "The faculties of the mind can only be preserved in a sound and healthful state by constant exercise. . . . as the metallic instrument corrodes and wastes with indolence and sloth, so with continued use, an edge is produced capable of cutting down every obstacle."

35. For an analysis of the functions of these paintings see Gilbert and Gubar, *Madwoman in the Attic*, p. 420.

36. "What Is Mesmerism?" p. 81.

37. Mary Jacobus, in her excellent article on *Villette*, offers a slightly different reading of this passage: see "The Buried Letter: Feminism and Romanticism in *Villette*," in Jacobus, ed., *Women Writing and Writing about Women* (London: Croom Helm, 1979), p. 54.

38. Macnish, *Philosophy of Sleep*, p. 136.

39. As Inga-Stina Ewbank has observed in *Their Proper Sphere: A Study of the Brontë Sisters as Early Victorian Female Novelists* (London: Edward Arnold, 1966), the personifications, lengthened into allegories of Lucy's emotional crises, "do not arrest the action of *Villette*, for in a sense they *are* the action: even more than in *Jane Eyre* the imagery of *Villette* tends to act out an inner drama which superimposes itself on, or even substitutes for external action" (p. 189).

Epilogue

Epilogue

This volume has ranged in its concerns from the rather abstruse realms of philosophy of science, with its continuing debates about the rationality of scientific argument and development, its battles over paradigms and epistemology, to the life and death of a particular, scientifically oriented woman of the Victorian period. It has concluded with some remarkable demonstrations of the way—historically—science has incorporated into its definitions distinctively male perceptions of female nature and experience. Without entering into the epistemological issues here for one more reprise, one finds the evidence that science is as social as literature, that it is in large part culturally defined. To say this is not to argue that its propositions are consequently invalid; but it is to urge that it be looked at not only from the perspectives of practicing scientists, engaged in the details of some parts of its workings, but from those of critics, artists, philosophers, sociologists of knowledge. A great deal is at stake in such looking. Science is a kind of literature, and it can be read—one would hope sympathetically and knowledgeably—by those who are not scientists, just as great literature can be read valuably by those who are not novelists, poets, dramatists.

If the first and primary "lesson" of this volume is that science and literature are mutually embedded in culture, nourish each other, and can illuminate each other, that doesn't get us very far. Steven Shapin insists on more than such a conclusion in his consideration of a sociology of scientific knowledge: "Work is often thought to be completed when it can be concluded that 'science is not autonomous,' or that 'science is an integral part of culture,' or even that there are interesting parallels or homologies between scientific thought and social structures."[1] Or literary structures, we might add.

Similarly, a second "lesson," derivable from the first, marks only a beginning. As I claimed in my introduction, the essays in this volume have all begun with the assumption that the positivist model of the history of science and of scientific method cannot hold. None of them considers either literature or science as a purely rational, universal construction, whose development is dependent on the rationality and accuracy with which it pursues the truth. As Barry Barnes has put it,

> Science is not a set of universal standards, sustaining true descriptions and valid inferences in different specific cultural contexts; authority and control in science do not operate simply to guarantee an unimpeded interaction between "reason" and experience. Scientific standards themselves are part of a specific form of culture; authority and control are essential to maintain a sense of the reasonableness of that specific form.[2]

The recognition that there is a social dimension to all human activity, science and literature alike, leads almost inevitably to the further recognition that what had appeared to be universally true, "natural," has about it a historically determinate quality. Strict internalist histories of either science or literature become suspect, as both subjects open themselves up to wider cultural investigation, and their assumptions, procedures, conclusions are understood to be connected with phenomena that are anything but universal.

Naden's cosmology, since it didn't become part of the paradigms of contemporary thought, can be placed rather obviously. Similarly, since "ether" is no longer part of contemporary physics, it is relatively easy to read Donald Benson's literary extensions of the ether controversy as further evidence of the all too literary nature of certain aspects of nineteenth-century science. But as Thomas Kuhn would have us recognize, to come to terms with the history of science one needs to ask oneself how it was possible for intelligent people to believe something so obviously "wrong." And of course, at the time, it wasn't "wrong." No more "wrong," at least, than, say, the literary style of "realism," with its implicit faith in the possibilities of representation. Critics nowadays have put the idea of representation under severe pressure, and all too often they read back into history either by evaluating negatively those writers who were committed to the idea of representation, or by demonstrating that they really weren't after all. What is missing here is the cultural constitution of thought.

Epilogue

My hope is that these essays, ranging from the speculative analysis of the possibilities of scientific language to close empirical analyses of how madness and literature were conceived of and demarcated or how an intelligent woman of the nineteenth century wove together in her life both science and poetry, will have done something to get beyond the first implications of the "lessons" I have been describing. They should help, in these particular instances at least, to give evidence of how all thought is culturally constituted.

There are, to be sure, no scientists represented in this volume. The writers are literary critics and scholars, historians, and historians of science. But scientists, for the most part, are less likely to talk about what they are doing than to do it, while part of what it is that critics and historians *do* is talk about what they are doing. This, inevitably, puts a heavier weight on the right side of the copula in "science and literature," but it is a weight for which there is no need to apologize.

The significance of this enterprise is partly that it opens for cultural criticism and analysis a field of knowledge which is both the most authoritative in our culture and the least accessible to criticism and understanding. It is concerned to extend techniques of analysis and interpretation from literature and the social sciences, to science itself. Similarly, it is concerned to demonstrate how the constructions of science permeate the imaginations of our writers and help shape the very way critics can think about them. And finally, this volume attempts to demonstrate from a variety of angles the mutualities in the radically divergent activities of science and literature, their common social and thematic origins, the cognate nature of their assumptions and procedures.

It is important, finally, to recognize that to withdraw both of these activities from the universal and therefore atemporal conditions to which they often aspire is to denigrate neither. Science becomes no less "rational" because its connections with theology, ideology, mythology are exposed. But the idea of rationality itself must be withdrawn from the universal. And for literature, the location of its languages in Humphry Davy or Erasmus Darwin or Helmholtz or contemporary medical treatises intensifies through specification and enriches its metaphorical possibilities. Science and literature speak to each other because they are siblings, with all the conceivable tensions that such a relationship implies. No doubt they need further analysis.

Notes

1. Steven Shapin, "History of Science and Its Sociological Reconstruction," *History of Science* 20 (1982): 176.
2. Barry Barnes, *Thomas Kuhn and Social Science* (New York: Columbia University Press, 1982).

Notes on Contributors

GILLIAN BEER is Reader at the University of Cambridge and a Fellow of Girton College. Her most recent book is *George Eliot* for Harvester Press. *Darwin's Plots* (Routledge) has been reprinted in paperback. She has published widely on Victorian and early modern literature, and her recent work develops her interests in science, feminism, and critical theory.

DAVID F. BELL teaches French literature at Duke University. With Josué Harari he has edited Michel Serres' *Hermes* (Johns Hopkins), a project which was important in directing his interests toward the relations between science and literature. He has completed a book-length study of politics and economics in Zola's *Rougon Marquart* series, and has begun a book on the problem of chance in narrative.

DONALD R. BENSON is Professor of English at Iowa State University. He has published widely on aspects of the relations of science to literature in the nineteenth and twentieth centuries, and most recently on implications of changing assumptions about space for seventeenth-and nineteenth-century literature, art, and science.

PETER ALLAN DALE is Professor of English at the University of California, Davis. His first book was *The Victorian Critic and the Idea of History* (Harvard), and he has published on a broad range of Victorian topics. He is completing a book-length study on the relation between science and literary theory in the nineteenth-century.

N. KATHERINE HAYLES is Associate Professor of English at the University of Iowa. She is author of *The Cosmic Web* (Cornell) and is currently working on a study tracing the connections between information theory and modern fiction.

GEORGE LEVINE, editor of the Wisconsin series on Science and Literature, is Professor of English at Rutgers University. His *Realistic Imagination* (Chicago) initiated a continuing study of the relations between science and literature, and he has completed a book on the way Darwinian thought permeated nineteenth-century narrative.

ANNE K. MELLOR is Professor of English at the University of California, Los Angeles. Her work has focused on Romanticism—most recently, *English Romantic Irony* (Harvard)—and feminism. She has completed a book on the novels of Mary Shelley and is currently at work on a study of English women of letters, 1780–1830.

James R. Moore is lecturer in History of Science and Technology in the Open University. With a continuing interest in both science and religion, he is author of *The Post-Darwinian Controversies* and a forthcoming book on Charles Darwin.

JAMES PARADIS is Associate Professor in the Department of Humanities at MIT. He is author of *T. H. Huxley: Man's Place in Nature*, and co-editor of *Victorian Science and Victorian Values: Literary Perspectives*, which has recently been reissued by Rutgers University Press.

RICHARD PEARCE is Professor of English at Wheaton College. His most recent book is *The Novel in Motion* (Ohio State), and he has published on such subjects as criticism in the novel and Thomas Pynchon. He has edited *Critical Essays on Thomas Pynchon* (G. K. Hall) and is completing a book, *The Politics of Narration: James Joyce, Virginia Woolf, and William Faulkner.*

ROY PORTER is Senior Lecturer in the Social History of Medicine at the Wellcome Institute for the History of Medicine in London. He has worked on the history of geology, and his current work focuses upon quackery, psychiatry, and popular health care. He has coedited the *Dictionary of the History of Science* (Macmillan) and *The Anatomy of Madness* (Tavistock), and is author of *English Society in the Eighteenth Century* (Penguin).

SALLY SHUTTLEWORTH teaches in the English Department at Leeds University. Her interest in the relations between science and literature is manifest in, her book *George Eliot and Nineteenth-Century Science* (Cambridge). More recently, she has written on physiology and phrenology in Charlotte Brontë. She is currently a fellow of Cornell University's Society for the Humanities.

Notes on Contributors

ROBERT M. YOUNG is editor of *Free Associations* and *Science as Culture* and Managing Director of Free Association Books. His works include *Mind, Brain and Adaptation: Darwin's Metaphor; Crucible: Science in Society* (television series); he also co-edited *Changing Perspectives in the History of Science* and *Science, Technology and the Labour Process.*

Index

Index

Bazerman, Charles, 86*n1*
Beccaria, Father, 301
Becker, G. 282*n45*
Beckett, Samuel: *Molloy*, 167; *Molloy*, symmetry in, 169–71, 177; *Waiting for Godot*, 167; *Waiting for Godot*, symmetry in, 173–74
Beckett, Thomas, 46
Bedlam, 263, 264–66, 269
Bedlamite ballads, 263–64
Beer, Gillian, 6, 20, 23, 26, 59, 106, 119, 121, 127, 133, 139, 143, 145, 146, 165, 258, 306
Beer, Sir Gavin de, 209, 210
Belcher, William, 284*n56*
Bell, David F., 27, 29*n19*, 46, 125, 133, 177, 258
Benson, Donald R., 27, 119, 183, 340
Bernard, Claude, distinguishes between art and science, 39
Bernstein, Richard, 17, 31*n26*
Bertrand, Joseph, 52
Besant, Annie, 242, 243
Bhaskar, Roy, 30*n19*
Big bang theory, 177
Biography, 203–24; aim of, 205–6; of C. Darwin, 203, 207, 208–19; as gossip, 208; of Newton, 205; psychobiography, 217; of scientific figures, 27, 206, 208, 213-14; study of, using a Marxist model, 204, 205
Birth control, pamphlet on, published by Freethought, 242
Blake, William, 275
Bloomfield, Leonard, on scientific language, 42, 43, 44
Bohr, Niels: achievements described by Einstein, 38; influence of literature on, 6
Boltzmann, Ludwig, and equation for entropy, 120
Boswell, James, 276
Bowen, Barbara, 86*n1*
Bowler, Peter J., 209
Boyle, Robert, 86*n1*, 305; *A Continuation of New Experiments, Physico-Mechanical*, written as a letter, 81; *Certain Hydrostatical Paradoxes*, 74, 75,

76, 79; discussed by Shapin and Schaffer, 21; and essays as letters, 81; and the experimental essay, 59, 72, 74–79, 80, 85–86; *Experiments and Considerations Touching Colours*, 74, 80; and Galileo, 72; "The History of Fluidity and Firmness," 73; *New Experiments, Physico-Mechanical, Touching the Spring of Air*, 74, 80; *New Experiments and Observations Touching Cold*, 76; Newton follows style of, 85; *The Origin of Forms and Qualities according to the Corpuscular Philosophy*, 76; and *Philosophical Transactions*, 73; *Proemial Essay*, 60, 77; *Sceptical Chymist*, 73–74, 79; and sense experience, 74–75, 77
Bradlaugh, Charles, 242
Bradley, A. C., connects Wordsworth with Hegel, 95
Brannigan, Augustine, on the scientist in literature, 38
Bray, Charles, 239
Brillouin, Leon, signs in equations for information and entropy, 120, 123
British Gynaecological Society, 253
British Secular Union, 242–43
Bromwich, David, 30*n15*
Brontë, Charlotte: anti-Catholic, 321; preoccupation with madness, 313, 316; and psychology, 316; *Villette*, 316–35
Brontë, Emily, 226
Brontë, Patrick, 316
Brooks, Peter, 198*n10*
Browning, Elizabeth Barrett, 226
Bruckshaw, Samuel, 274, 284*n56*
Bryan, William F., 88*n16*
Bucknill, John, 321
Buffon, Georges Louis Leclerc, comte de, 293–94, 311*n11*
Burton, Robert, 265–66; *Anatomy of Melancholy*, 273
Butler, M., 282*n45*
Byron, George, 272, 292, 304

Calvin, John, 274
Cameron, Kenneth Neill, 311*n19*

Index

353

Index

Prendergast, Christopher, 198n10
Prichard, James, 323
Prigogine, Ilya, 129, 195, 198n3
Probability. *See* Chance
Proctor, R. A., 257n10
Proust, Marcel, 207–8, 218
Psychiatry, Georgian, 258–84
Psychobiographies, 217
Psychology: and female experience, 313, 315, 318, 320, 322; and G. Lewes, 104; and positivist theory, 103; practice of, 317; scientific terms used in, 315–16, 323, 326–27, 329
Psychometrics, and Gould, 20
Pynchon, Thomas: *Crying of Lot 49*, 6, 51; *Gravity's Rainbow*, 164
Pyrrhonists, and Montaigne, 64, 66

Quinlan, M. J., 283n52

Radiation, and J. Tyndall, 41
Raphael, "Madonna di San Sisto," 100
Rattansi, P. M., 86n3
Realism, scientific, 14–15, 21
Rich, Adrienne: "Waking in the Dark," 49–50
Richards, I. A., 30n16
Robbe-Grillet, Alain, on anthropomorphism of language, 51
Robinson, Dr. Nicholas, 276, 284n64
Rodin, Auguste, 153
Rogers, Timothy, 277
Roman Catholicism, in Brontë's *Villette*, 319, 320–21
Romanes, George, 250
Rorty, Richard, 17, 31n26, 113, 116n42; *Philosophy and the Mirror of Nature*, 18
Rose, Steven: on language of discovery, 44–45, 46; on scientific language, 49
Ross, W. Stewart, 242, 243
Rossetti, Christina, 226
Rothenberg, A., 282n45
Royal Society, 79; and literature corrupting thought, 11; motto, 60; presidents of, as C. Darwin's pallbearers, 215; publications of, 80, 82, 83

Rubens, Peter Paul, 328
Rush, Dr. Benjamin, 269
Ruskin, John, 22
Russell, Bertrand, 243
Ryan, Michael, 139
Ryskamp, C., 283n52

St. Luke's Asylum, 269
Salem, Abdus, 165, 177
Salisbury, Lord, 149
Saussure, Ferdinand de, 121, 126
Schachterle, Lance, 139n1
Schaffer, Simon, 21, 30n17
Schiller, Johann, 240
Schlegel, Friedrich, 298
Schopenhauer, Arthur, 232
Schweber, Silvan, 209
Scientific language, 3–4, 6–9, 18, 22, 24–27, 35–57; analogy with literature, 5; aphorisms used in, by Bacon, 70; Bacon links to Scripture, 67; definitions of, 44; difference from literary language, 4, 14, 36, 54; hostility towards, 8, 9, 22, 23; impersonality of, 11, 39; influence of literature in, 6; linguistic positivism in, 42–44; and poetic communication, 35–36; readability of, 339; regulation of, and S. Rose, 46; rejects literature, 11; translation of, 52; as used by Darwin, 20; used in psychology, 315–16, 323, 326–27, 329
Scull, Andrew T., 317, 333n9
Secular Review, 242
Semantic noise, 134
Serres, Michel, 29n9, 119, 180–82, 197n1; on relationship of science and literature, 8
Sexist language, 287
Sextus Empiricus, 61, 64
Shakespeare, William, 263
Shannon, Claude E., 123, 141n22; cites N. Wiener's work on cybernetics, 133; diagrams communication system, 125–26; and entropy, 132–33; on equivocation in messages, 130, 131–32; on information theory, 125–

DESIGNED BY DAVID FORD
COMPOSED BY MODERN TYPE & DESIGN, INC., CLEARWATER, FLORIDA
MANUFACTURED BY
EDWARDS BROTHERS, INC., ANN ARBOR, MICHIGAN
TEXT AND DISPLAY LINES ARE SET IN PALATINO

Library of Congress Cataloging-in-Publication Data
One culture.
1. English literature—19th century—History and
criticism.   2. Science in literature.   3. Literature
and science.   4. French literature—History and
criticism.   I. Levine, George, 1931–
II. Rauch, Alan.
PR38.S35054   1987   820'.9'356   87-40143
ISBN 0-299-11300-0
ISBN 0-299-11304-3 (pbk.)